ACCA
STUDY TEXT

Paper 2.3

Business Taxation
(Finance Act 2000)

BPP's NEW STUDY TEXTS FOR ACCA's NEW SYLLABUS

- Targeted to the syllabus and study guide

- Quizzes and questions to check your understanding

- Clear layout and style designed to save you time

- Plenty of exam-style questions

- Chapter Roundups and summaries to help revision

- Mind Maps to integrate the key points

BPP Publishing
February 2001

First edition February 2001

ISBN 07517 0729 5

British Library Cataloguing-in-Publication Data
A catalogue record for this book
is available from the British Library

Published by

BPP Publishing Ltd
Aldine House, Aldine Place
London W12 8AW

www.bpp.com

Printed in England by DACOSTA PRINT,
1A Mildmay Avenue, London
N1 4RS (020 7354 6200)

We are grateful to the Association of Chartered Certified Accountants for permission to reproduce past examination questions and questions from the pilot paper. The suggested solutions to the illustrative questions have been prepared by BPP Publishing Limited.

Contents

THE BPP STUDY TEXT

Aims of this Study Text

To provide you with the knowledge and understanding, skills and application techniques that you need if you are to be successful in your exams

This Study Text has been written around the **Business Taxation** syllabus.

- It is **comprehensive**. It covers the syllabus content. No more, no less.

- It is written at the **right level**. Each chapter is written with the ACCA study guide in mind.

- It is targeted to the **exam**. We have taken account of the pilot paper, questions put to the examiners at the recent ACCA conference, the latest syllabus guidance notes and the assessment methodology.

To allow you to study in the way that best suits your learning style and the time you have available, by following your personal Study Plan (see page (x))

You may be studying at home on your own until the date of the exam, or you may be attending a full-time course. You may like to (and have time to) read every word, or you may prefer to (or only have time to) skim-read and devote the remainder of your time to question practice. Wherever you fall in the spectrum, you will find the BPP Study Text meets your needs in designing and following your personal Study Plan.

To tie in with the other components of the BPP Effective Study Package to ensure you have the best possible chance of passing the exam (see page (vi))

BPP PUBLISHING

Recommended period of use	Elements of the BPP Effective Study Package
Three to twelve months before the exam	**Study Text** Use the Study Text to acquire knowledge, understanding, skills and the ability to use application techniques.
One to six months before the exam	**Practice & Revision Kit** Attempt the tutorial questions and complete the interactive checklists which are provided for each topic area in the Kit. Then try the numerous examination questions, for which there are realistic suggested solutions prepared by BPP's own authors.
From three months before the exam until the last minute	**Passcards** Work through these short, memorable notes which are focused on what is most likely to come up in the exam you will be sitting.
One to six months before the exam	**Success Tapes** These cover the vital elements of your syllabus in less than 90 minutes per subject with these audio cassettes. Each tape also contains exam hints to help you fine tune your strategy.
Three to twelve months before the exam	**Breakthrough Videos** Use a Breakthrough Video to supplement your Study Text. They give you clear tuition on key exam subjects and allow you the luxury of being able to pause or repeat sections until you have fully grasped the topic.

HELP YOURSELF STUDY FOR YOUR ACCA EXAMS

Exams for professional bodies such as ACCA are very different from those you have taken at college or university. You will be under **greater time pressure before** the exam - as you may be combining your study with work as well as in the exam room. There are many different ways of learning and so the BPP Study Text offers you a number of different tools to help you through. Here are some hints and tips: they are not plucked out of the air, but **based on research and experience.** (You don't need to know that long-term memory is in the same part of the brain as emotions and feelings - but it's a fact anyway.)

The right approach

1 The right attitude

Believe in yourself	Yes, there is a lot to learn. Yes, it is a challenge. But thousands have succeeded before and you can too.
Remember why you're doing it	Studying might seem a grind at times, but you are doing it for a reason: to advance your career.

2 The right focus

Read through the Syllabus and learning outcomes	These tell you what you are expected to know and are supplemented by Exam Focus Points in the text.
Study the Pilot Paper	The pilot paper is likely to be a reasonable guide of what you should expect in the exam.

3 The right method

The big picture	You need to grasp the detail - but keeping in mind how everything fits into the big picture will help you understand better. • The **Introduction** of each chapter puts the material in context. • The **Syllabus content, study guide** and **Exam focus points** show you what you need to **grasp.** • **Mind Maps** show the links and key issues in key topics.
In your own words	To absorb the information (and to practise your written communication skills), it helps **put it into your own words.** • **Take notes.** • Answer the **questions** in each chapter. As well as helping you absorb the information you will practise your written communication skills, which become increasingly important as you progress through your ACCA exams. • Draw **mind maps.** We have some examples. • Try 'teaching' to a colleague or friend.

Give yourself cues to jog your memory	The BPP Study Text uses **bold** to **highlight key points** and **icons** to identify key features, such as **Exam focus points** and **Key terms.** • Try **colour coding** with a highlighter pen. • Write **key points** on cards.

4 The right review

Review, review, review	It is a **fact** that regularly reviewing a topic in summary form can **fix it in your memory**. Because **review** is so important, the BPP Study Text helps you to do so in many ways. • **Chapter roundups** summarise the key points in each chapter. Use them to recap each study session. • The **Quick quiz** is another review technique to ensure that you have grasped the essentials. • Go through the **Examples** in each chapter a second or third time.

Suggested study sequence

Tackle the chapters in the order you find them in the Study Text. Taking into account your individual learning style, you could follow this sequence.

Key study steps	Activity
Step 1 **Topic list**	Each numbered topic is a numbered section in the chapter.
Step 2 **Introduction**	This gives you the **big picture** in terms of the **context** of the chapter. The content is referred to the **Study Guide**, and the **Exam Guide** shows how the topic is likely to be examined. In other words, it sets you **objectives for study.**
Step 3 **Knowledge brought forward boxes**	Not applicable for this subject.
Step 4 **Explanations**	Proceed methodically through the chapter, reading each section thoroughly and making sure you understand.
Step 5 **Key terms and Exam focus points**	• **Key terms** can often earn you *easy marks* if you state them clearly and correctly in an appropriate exam answer. • **Exam focus points** give you a good idea of the examiner's focus.
Step 6 **Note taking**	Take brief notes if you wish, avoiding the temptation to copy out too much.
Step 7 **Examples**	Follow each through to its solution very carefully.
Step 8 **Case examples**	Not applicable for this subject.
Step 9 **Questions**	Make a very good attempt at each one.
Step 10 **Answers**	Check yours against ours, and make sure you understand any discrepancies.
Step 11 **Chapter roundup**	Work through it very carefully, to make sure you have grasped the major points it is highlighting.
Step 12 **Quick quiz**	When you are happy that you have covered the chapter, use the **Quick quiz** to check how much you have remembered of the topics covered.

Key study steps	Activity
Step 13 **Question(s) in the Question bank**	Either at this point, or later when you are thinking about revising, make a full attempt at the **Question(s)** suggested at the very end of the chapter. You can find these at the end of the Study Text, along with the **Answers** so you can see how you did. We highlight those that are introductory, and those which are of the standard you would expect to find in an exam.

Developing your personal Study Plan

Preparing a Study Plan (and sticking closely to it) is one of the key elements in learning success.

Step 1. How do you learn?

First you need to be aware of your style of learning. There are four typical learning styles. Consider yourself in the light of the following descriptions and work out which you fit most closely. You can then plan to follow the key study steps in the sequence suggested.

Learning styles	Characteristics	Sequence of key study steps in the BPP Study Text
Theorist	Seeks to understand principles before applying them in practice	1, 2, 3, 4, 7, 8, 5, 9/10, 11, 12, 13 (6 continuous)
Reflector	Seeks to observe phenomena, thinks about them and then chooses to act	
Activist	Prefers to deal with practical, active problems; does not have much patience with theory	1, 2, 9/10 (read through), 7, 8, 5, 11, 3, 4, 9/10 (full attempt), 12, 13 (6 continuous)
Pragmatist	Prefers to study only if a direct link to practical problems can be seen; not interested in theory for its own sake	9/10 (read through), 2, 5, 7, 8, 11, 1, 3, 4, 9/10 (full attempt), 12, 13 (6 continuous)

Step 2. How much time do you have?

Work out the time you have available per week, given the following.

- The standard you have set yourself
- The time you need to set aside later for work on the Practice & Revision Kit and Passcards
- The other exam(s) you are sitting
- Very importantly, practical matters such as work, travel, exercise, sleep and social life

Note your time available in box A.

A [   ] Hours

Step 3. Allocate your time

- Take the time you have available per week for this Study Text shown in box A, multiply it by the number of weeks available and insert the result in box B.

B [   ]

- Divide the figure in Box B by the number of chapters in this text and insert the result in box C.

C [   ]

Step 4. Implement

Set about studying each chapter in the time shown in box C, following the key study steps in the order suggested by your particular learning style.

This is your personal **Study Plan**.

Short of time: *Skim study technique?*

You may find you simply do not have the time available to follow all the key study steps for each chapter, however you adapt them for your particular learning style. If this is the case, follow the **skim study** technique below (the icons in the Study Text will help you to do this).

- Study the chapters in the order you find them in the Study Text.

- For each chapter, follow the key study steps 1-3, and then skim-read through step 4. Jump to step 11, and then go back to step 5. Follow through steps 7 and 8, and prepare outline answers to questions (steps 9/10). Try the Quick quiz (step 12), following up any items you can't answer, then do a plan for the Question (step 13), comparing it against our answers. You should probably still follow step 6 (note-taking), although you may decide simply to rely on the BPP Passcards for this.

Moving on...

However you study, when you are ready to embark on the practice and revision phase of the BPP Effective Study Package, you should still refer back to this Study Text, both as a source of **reference** (you should find the list of key terms and the index particularly helpful for this) and as a **refresher** (the Chapter roundups and Quick quizzes help you here).

And remember to keep careful hold of this Study Text - you will find it invaluable in your work.

SYLLABUS

Aim

To develop knowledge and understanding in the core areas of tax related to business and their employees.

Objectives

On completion of this paper candidates should be able to:

- explain the operation of the UK tax system

- prepare computations of the corporation tax liability for individual companies and groups of companies

- prepare computations of the income tax liability for employees, sole traders and partnerships

- prepare computations of the chargeable gains arising on incorporated and unincorporated businesses

- explain and apply the principles and scope of value added tax

- explain the impact of National Insurance Contributions on employees, employers and the self-employed

- explain the use of exemptions and reliefs in deferring or minimising tax liabilities

- demonstrate the skills expected at Part 2

Position of the paper in the overall syllabus

An understanding of the formats of accounts used for sole traders, partnerships and companies from Paper 1.1 *Preparing Financial Statements* is assumed. There is no substantial integration with other papers in Part 2.

The coverage in Paper 2.3 will provide the grounding for the study of the optional Paper 3.2 *Advanced taxation*.

Paper 3.2 develops the topics by applying the tax knowledge to problems encountered in practice, by giving more emphasis to planning to minimise or defer tax and by examining the interaction of taxes.

SYLLABUS

1 Corporate business

(a) Scope of corporation tax

(b) Residence

(c) Profits chargeable to corporation tax

    (i) Schedule D Case I
    (ii) Capital allowances
    (iii) Relief for trading losses
    (iv) Schedule A
    (v) Schedule D Case III

(d) Charges on income

(e) Chargeable gains

    (i) Principles and scope
    (ii) The basis of calculation
    (iii) The identification and application of relevant exemptions and reliefs

(f) Calculation of the corporation tax liability

(g) Overseas aspects

    (i) Trading overseas via a subsidiary or a branch
    (ii) Double taxation relief
    (iii) Transfer pricing

(h) Groups of companies

(i) Self assessment system

    (i) Payment of the corporation tax liability
    (ii) Form CT61 and quarterly accounting

(j) Value added tax

2 Unincorporated businesses

(a) Basic income tax computation

(b) Self assessment system

(c) Schedule D Case I/II

    (i) Badges of trade
    (ii) Computation of assessable profit
    (iii) Basis of assessment
    (iv) Change of accounting date
    (v) Capital allowances
    (vi) Relief for trading losses
    (vii) Partnerships
    (viii) Personal pensions

(d) Capital gains tax

    (i) Principles and scope (restricted to business assets)
    (ii) The basis of calculation
    (iii) The identification and application of relevant exemptions and reliefs

(e) Value added tax

(f) Class 2 and Class 4 NIC

3 Employees

(a) Schedule E

    (i) Basis of assessment
    (ii) Allowable deductions
    (iii) PAYE system
    (iv) Benefits in kind

(b) Occupational pension schemes

(c) Class 1 and Class 1A NIC

4 Tax planning

(a) Employment v self-employment
(b) Remuneration packages
(c) Choice of business medium
(d) Incorporation of a business
(e) Disposal of a business
(f) Directors and shareholders

Excluded topics

The following topics are specifically excluded from Paper 2.3.

1 **Corporate business**

    (a) Scope of corporation tax

        (i) Investment companies
        (ii) Close companies
        (iii) Companies in receivership and liquidation
        (iv) Anti-avoidance legislation
        (v) Reorganisations
        (vi) Purchase by a company of its own shares
        (vii) Personal service companies

    (c) Profits chargeable to corporation tax

        (i) Research and development expenditure

        (ii) Capital allowances for agricultural buildings, patents, scientific research and know how

        (iii) Furnished holiday lettings

        (iv) Non-trading deficits on loan relationships

        (v)   The corporate venturing scheme

   (e) Chargeable gains

        (i)   Assets held at 31 March 1982

        (ii) Part disposals

        (iii) Leases, chattels and wasting assets

        (iv) A detailed question on the pooling provisions for shares (pre 6 April 1998 acquisitions)

   (g) Overseas aspects

        (i)   Controlled foreign companies
        (ii) Foreign companies trading in the UK

   (h) Groups of companies

        (i)   Consortia

   (i)   Value added tax

        (i)   Group registration

        (ii) Imports, exports and trading within the European Community

        (iii) Partial exemption

        (iv) Second-hand goods scheme

        (v)   The capital goods scheme

        (vi) In respect of property and land: leases and do-it-yourself builders

        (vii) Penalties apart from the default surcharge, serious misdeclarations (but not repeated misdeclarations) and default interest

        (viii)Special schemes for retailers

2   **Unincorporated businesses**

   (a) Basic income tax computation

        (i)   Personal allowances other than the personal allowance for people aged under 65
        (ii) Non-business charges on income
        (iii) Joint property of husbands and wives, maintenance payments and minor children
        (iv) Schedule A
        (v)   Schedules D Cases III and VI
        (vi) Individual savings accounts
        (vii) The enterprise investment scheme and venture capital trusts
        (viii)Foreign income, non-residents and double taxation relief
        (ix) Income from trusts and settlements
        (x)   Anti-avoidance legislation

   (c) Schedule D Case I/II

        (i)   As for corporate businesses
        (ii) Farmers averaging of profits
        (iii) Loss relief for shares in unquoted trading companies
        (iv) Investment income and charges of a partnership
        (v)   The allocation of notational profits and losses for a partnership

(d) Capital gains tax

    (i)   As for corporate businesses

    (ii) Calculation of the indexation allowance

    (iii) Retirement relief

    (iv) Reinvestment relief

    (v)   Principal private residence

    (vi) Partnership capital gains

    (vii) Overseas aspects

    (viii)Losses in the year of death

    (ix) The transfer of assets between a husband and wife

    (x)   The exemption of gilt edged securities and qualifying corporate bonds

    (xi) The payment of CGT by annual instalments

    (xii) Capital sums received in respect of the loss, destruction or damage of an asset

    (xiii)Relief for losses incurred on loans made to traders

(e) Value added tax

    (i)   As for corporate businesses

(f) Class 2 and Class 4 NIC

    (i)   The offset of trading losses against non-trading income (for Class 4 NIC)

3   Employees

(a) Schedule E

    (i)   Share and share option incentive schemes for employees

    (ii) Payments on the termination of employment, and other lump sums received by employees

(b) Occupational pension schemes

    (i)   A detailed knowledge of the conditions that must be met to obtain Inland Revenue approval for an occupational pension scheme

(c) Class 1 and Class 1A NIC

    (i)   The calculation of directors' NIC on a month by month basis

Key areas of the syllabus

The key topic areas, taken directly from the syllabus content list, are as follows.

1   Corporate business

(a) Scope of corporation tax

(c) Profits chargeable to corporation tax

(d) Charges on income

(f) Calculation of the corporation tax liability

(i) Self assessment system

2   Unincorporated business

(a) Basic income tax computation

(b) Self assessment system

(c) Schedule D case I/II

3   Employees

(a) Schedule E

Paper 2.3

Business Taxation FA 2000
(United Kingdom)
Study Guide

1   CORPORATE BUSINESSES

(a)   Scope of corporation tax

- Define the terms 'period of account', 'accounting period' and 'financial year'.
- Explain when an accounting period starts and finishes.

(b)   Residence

- Explain how the residence of a company is determined.

(c)   Profits chargeable to corporation tax

(i)   Schedule D Case I.

- State the expenditure that is allowable in calculating the tax-adjusted profit.
- Explain how relief can be obtained for pre-trading expenditure.

(ii)   Capital allowances.

- Define plant and machinery for capital allowances purposes.
- Calculate writing down allowances and first year allowances.
- Explain the treatment of motor cars.
- Compute balancing allowances and charges.
- Explain the treatment of short life assets and long life assets.

- Define an industrial building for industrial buildings allowance purposes.
- Calculate industrial buildings allowance for new and second-hand buildings.
- Compute the balancing adjustment on the disposal of an industrial building.

(iii)   Relief for trading losses.

- Explain how trading losses can be carried forward.
- Explain how trading losses can be claimed against income of the current or previous accounting periods.
- State the factors that will influence the choice of loss relief claim.

(iv)   Schedule A

- Compute the Schedule A profit.
- Explain the treatment of a premium received for the grant of a short lease.
- Explain how relief for a Schedule A loss is given.

(v)   Schedule D case III

- Explain how profits from loan relationships and interest received are assessed under Schedule D case III.

(d)   Charges in income

- Explain the treatment of charges on income.

(e)   Chargeable gains

(i)   Principles and scope.

- Prepare a basic capital gains computation.
- State the allowable deductions.
- Calculate the indexation allowance.

(ii)   The basis of calculation.

- Explain the treatment of capital losses.
- Explain the identification rules for disposals of shares and securities.
- Apply the pooling provisions for shares and securities.
- Explain the treatment following a bonus issue, rights issue or takeover.

(iii)   The identification and application of relevant exemptions and reliefs.

- Explain and apply rollover relief.

(f)   Calculation of the corporation tax liability

- Prepare a basic corporation tax computation.

- Explain the implications of receiving franked investment income.
- Calculate the corporation tax liability at the starting rate, small company rate and full rate, and apply tapering relief.

(g) Overseas aspects

(i) Trading overseas via a subsidiary or a branch

- Compare the UK tax treatment of an overseas branch to an overseas subsidiary.

(ii) Double taxation relief

- Calculate double taxation relief for withholding tax and underlying tax.

(iii) Transfer pricing

- Explain and apply the transfer pricing rules.

(h) Groups of companies

- Define an associated company.
- Define a 51% group and explain the benefits of making a group election.
- Define a 75% group.
- Explain and apply the reliefs available to members of a 75% group.
- Define a 75% capital gains group.
- Explain and apply the reliefs available to members of a 75% capital gains group.

(I) Self assessment system

(i) Payment of the corporation tax liability.

- Describe the features of self-assessment.
- Explain how the Inland Revenue can enquire into a self-assessment return.
- Calculate interest on overdue tax.
- Explain how large companies are required to account for corporation tax on a quarterly basis.

(ii) Form CT61 and quarterly accounting

- Explain how companies account for income tax on a quarterly basis on form CT61.

(j) Value Added Tax

- Describe the scope of VAT.
- State the circumstances in which a person must register for VAT, and explain the advantages of voluntary VAT registration.
- State the circumstances in which pre-registration input VAT can be recovered.
- Explain how a person can deregister for VAT.
- Explain how VAT is accounted for and administered.

- Explain how the tax point is determined.
- List the information that must be given on a VAT invoice.
- Describe the principles that apply to the valuation of supplies.
- State the circumstances in which input VAT is non-deductible.
- Describe the relief that is available for bad debts.
- List the principal zero-rated and exempt supplies.
- Describe the cash accounting and the annual accounting schemes.
- State the circumstances in which the default surcharge, a serious misdeclaration penalty, and default interest will be applied.

2 UNINCORPORATED BUSINESSES

(a) Basic income tax computation

- Prepare a basic income tax computation.
- Explain the treatment of savings income and dividends.
- Explain the treatment of business charges on income.

(b) Self assessment system

- Describe the features of self-assessment
- Calculate payments on account and balancing payments/repayments
- Calculate interest on overdue tax and state the penalties that can be charged.
- Explain how the Inland Revenue can enquire into a self-assessment return.

(c) Schedule D case VII

(i) Badges of trade

- Describe and apply the badges of trade.

(ii) Computation of assessable profit

- As for corporate business.

(iii) Basis of assessment

- Explain the basis of assessment
- Compute the assessable profits on commencement and cessation.

(iv) Change of accounting date

- State the factors that will influence the choice of accounting date.
- State the conditions that must be met for a change of accounting date to be valid.
- Compute the assessable profits on a change of accounting date.

(v) Capital allowances

- As for corporate businesses.

(vi) Relief for trading losses.

- Explain how trading losses can be carried forward.
- Explain how trading losses can be claimed against total income and chargeable gains.
- Explain the relief for trading losses in the early years of a trade.
- Explain terminal loss relief.

(vii) Partnerships

- Explain how a partnership is assessed to tax.
- Allocate assessable profits between the partners following a change in the profit sharing ratio or a change in the members of the partnership.
- Describe the alternative loss relief claims that are available to partners.

(viii) Personal pensions

- Explain the relief given for contributions to a personal pension scheme.

(d) Capital gains tax

(i) Principles and scope (restricted to business assets).

- As for corporate businesses.
- Define a business asset for the purposes of taper relief.
- Compute taper relief (including non-business assets).

(ii) The basis of calculation

- As for corporate businesses.

(iii) The identification and application of relevant exemptions and reliefs.

- Explain and apply holdover relief for the gift of business assets.
- Explain and apply the relief available when a business is transferred to a limited company.

(e) Value Added Tax

- As for corporate businesses.

(f) Class 2 and Class 4 NIC

- Calculate class 2 NIC.
- Calculate class 4 NIC.

3 EMPLOYEES

(a) Schedule E

(i) Basis of assessment

- State the factors that determine whether an engagement is treated as employment or self-employment.
- Explain the basis of assessment.
- Describe the income assessable.

(ii) Allowable deductions

- List the allowable deductions, including travelling expenses.
- Explain the use of the fixed profit car scheme.

(iii) PAYE system

- Explain the PAYE system

(iv) Benefits in kind

- Identify PIID employees.

- Explain how benefits in kind are assessed.

(b) **Occupational pension schemes**

- State the main features of an occupational pension scheme.

- Explain the significance of an occupational pension scheme being approved by the Inland Revenue.

(c) **Class 1 and Class 1A NIC**

- Calculate class 1 NIC.
- Calculate class 1A NIC.

4   TAX PLANNING

(a) **Employment v self-employment**

- Compare the tax implications of employment as compared to self-employment.

(b) **Remuneration packages**

- Compare alternative remuneration packages.

(c) **Choice of business medium**

- Compare the tax position of a director/shareholder with that of a sole trader.

(d) **Incorporation of a business**

- Explain the factors that must be considered when incorporating a business.

(e) **Disposal of a business**

- Explain the tax implications arising on the disposal of a business.

(f) **Directors and shareholders**

- Compute whether remuneration or a dividend is the most tax effective way to extract profit from a company.

OXFORD BROOKES BSc (Hons) IN APPLIED ACCOUNTING

The standard required of candidates completing Part 2 is that required in the final year of a UK degree. Students completing Parts 1 and 2 will have satisfied the examination requirement for an honours degree in Applied Accounting, awarded by Oxford Brookes University.

To achieve the degree, you must also submit two pieces of work based on a **Research and Analysis Project**

- A 5,000 word **Report** on your chosen topic, which demonstrates that you have acquired the necessary research, analytical and IT skills.

- A 1,500 word **Key Skills Statement**, indicating how you have developed your interpersonal and communication skills.

BPP was selected by the ACCA to produce the official text *Success in your Research and Analysis Project* to support students in this task. The book pays particular attention to key skills not covered in the professional examinations.

> AN ORDER FORM FOR THE NEW SYLLABUS MATERIAL, INCLUDING THE OXFORD BROOKES PROJECT TEXT, CAN BE FOUND AT THE END OF THIS STUDY TEXT.

BPP PUBLISHING

THE EXAM PAPER

Approach to examining the syllabus

The examination is a three hour paper divided into two sections.

The following approach will be adopted in setting the first three papers (December 2001, June 2002 and December 2002) under the new syllabus.

Only core topics will be examined in Section A. A non-core topic may form part of a question (such as a chargeable gain in a corporation tax computation), but this will account for a maximum of ten marks. At least 40 of the 55 available marks in Section A will be of a computational nature.

- Question 1 will be on a corporate business (for approximately 30 marks).

- Question 2 will be on an unincorporated business and/or employees (for approximately 25 marks).

The questions in Section B will be a mix of computational and written, and include the minimisation or deferment of tax liability by the identification and application of relevant exemptions and reliefs.

- Question 3 will be on VAT (either for an incorporated business or an unincorporated business).

- Question 4 will be on capital gains (either for an incorporated business or an unincorporated business).

- Question 5 will be on either groups or companies or overseas aspects.

- Question 6 will be on one of the six listed tax planning topics.

- Question 7 will be on any area of the syllabus, but will typically deal with a core topic that has not been covered in Section A. For example, partnerships, relief for trading losses or self-assessment.

		Number of Marks
Section A:	2 compulsory questions	55
Section B:	Choice of 3 from 5 questions (15 marks each)	45
		100

Tax rates, allowances and benefits will be given in the examination paper.

Additional information

The ACCA applies a six-month rule in that questions requiring an understanding of new legislation will not be set until at least six calendar months after the last day of the month in which the legislation received Royal Assent. The same rule applies to the effective date of the provisions of an Act introduced by Statutory Instruments. It would, however, be considered inappropriate to examine legislation it is proposed to repeal or substantially alter.

Knowledge of section numbers will not be needed to understand questions in this paper, nor will students be expected to use them in their answers. If students wish to refer to section numbers in their answers they may do so and will not be penalised if old, or even incorrect, section numbers are used.

Names of cases or a detailed knowledge of the judgement are not required but knowledge of the principles decided in leading cases is required.

Analysis of pilot paper

Section A

1   Calculation of CT payable. Quarterly payments of CT. (30 marks)
2   IT for employee/sole trader. Payment of IT. (25 marks)

Section B

3   VAT registration. Input tax. Deregistrations
4   Business asset taper relief. Gains on shares
5   Group relief. CT liability
6   Employee/self employed distinction. NICs. IT under Sch D II or Sch E
7   Partnership profit allocation. Losses

TAX RATES AND ALLOWANCES

A INCOME TAX

1 *Rates*

	1999/00		2000/01	
	£	%	£	%
Starting rate	1 - 1,500	10	0 – 1,520	10
Basic rate	1,501 - 28,000	23	1,521 – 28,400	22
Higher rate	28,001 and above	40	28,401 and above	40

In 2000/01 savings (excl. Dividend) income is taxed at 20% if it falls in the basic rate band. Dividend income in both the starting rate and the basic rate bands is taxed at 10%. Dividend income within the higher rate band is taxed at 32.5%.

2 *Allowances*

	1999/00	2000/01
	£	£
Personal allowance	4,335	4,385

3 *Car fuel scale charges*

	2000/01	
	Petrol	Diesel
	£	£
Cars having a cylinder capacity		
1,400 cc or less	1,700	2,170
1,401 cc to 2,000 cc	2,170	2,170
More than 2,000 cc	3,200	3,200
Cars not having a cylinder capacity	3,200	3,200

4 *Fixed profit car scheme - 2000/01 rates*

	On first 4,000 miles	On each mile over 4,000
Size of car engine		
Up to 1,000 cc	28p	17p
1,000 cc - 1,500 cc	35p	20p
1,501 cc - 2,000 cc	45p	25p
Over 2,000 cc	63p	36p

5 *Personal pension contribution limits*

Age	Maximum percentage %
Up to 35	17.5
36 – 45	20.0
46 – 50	25.0
51 – 55	30.0
56 – 60	35.0
61 or more	40.0

Subject to earnings cap of £90,600 for 1999/00 and £91,800 for 2000/01

6   *Capital allowances*

	%
Plant and machinery	
Writing down allowance*	25
First year allowance (acquisitions 2.7.97 - 1.7.98)**	50
First year allowance (acquisitions after 2.7.98)	40
First year allowance (information and communication technology equipment - period 1.4.00 - 31.3.03)	100
Industrial buildings allowance	
Writing down allowance: post 5.11.62	4
pre 6.11.62	2

* 6% reducing balance for certain long life assets.

** 12% for certain long life assets.

B   CORPORATION TAX

1   *Rates*

Financial year	Full rate %	Small companies rate %	Starting rate	Marginal relief Fraction	Lower limit for starting rate £	Upper limit for starting rate £	Upper limit for SCR £	Lower Limit for SCR £
1994	33	25	-	1/50	-	-	1,500,000	300,000
1995	33	25	-	1/50	-	-	1,500,000	300,000
1996	33	24	-	9/400	-	-	1,500,000	300,000
1997	31	21	-	1/40	-	-	1,500,000	300,000
1998	31	21	-	1/40	-	-	1,500,000	300,000
1999	30	20	-	1/40	-	-	1,500,000	300,000
2000	30	20	10	1/40	10,000	50,000	1,500,000	300,000

2   *Marginal relief*

$(M - P) \times I/P \times$ Marginal relief fraction

C   VALUE ADDED TAX

1   *Registration and deregistration limits*

	To 31.3.00	From 1.4.00
Registration limit	£51,000	£52,000
Deregistration limit	£49,000	£50,000

2   *Scale charges for private motoring*

2000/2001 (VAT inclusive)

	Quarterly	
	Petrol	Diesel
Up to 1400 cc	256	232
1401 to 2000 cc	325	232
Over 2000cc	478	295

D   RATES OF INTEREST

Official rate of interest: 10% (assumed)

Rate of interest on unpaid/overpaid tax: 10% (assumed)

E   CAPITAL GAINS TAX

1   *Retail prices index (January 1987 = 100.0)*

	1982	1983	1984	1985	1986	1987	1988	1989	1990
Jan		82.6	86.8	91.2	96.2	100.0	103.3	111.0	119.5
Feb		83.0	87.2	91.9	96.6	100.4	103.7	111.8	120.2
Mar	79.4	83.1	87.5	92.8	96.7	100.6	104.1	112.3	121.4
Apr	81.0	84.3	88.6	94.8	97.7	101.8	105.8	114.3	125.1
May	81.6	84.6	89.0	95.2	97.8	101.9	106.2	115.0	126.2
Jun	81.9	84.8	89.2	95.4	97.8	101.9	106.6	115.4	126.7
Jul	81.9	85.3	89.1	95.2	97.5	101.8	106.7	115.5	126.8
Aug	81.9	85.7	89.9	95.5	97.8	102.1	107.9	115.8	128.1
Sept	81.9	86.1	90.1	95.4	98.3	102.4	108.4	116.6	129.3
Oct	82.3	86.4	90.7	95.6	98.5	102.9	109.5	117.5	130.3
Nov	82.7	86.7	91.0	95.9	99.3	103.4	110.0	118.5	130.0
Dec	82.5	86.9	90.9	96.0	99.6	103.3	110.3	118.8	129.9

	1991	1992	1993	1994	1995	1996	1997	1998	1999	2000★	2001★
Jan	130.2	135.6	137.9	141.3	146.0	150.2	154.4	159.5	163.4	167.5	173.5
Feb	130.9	136.3	138.8	142.1	146.9	150.9	155.0	160.3	163.7	168.0	174.0
Mar	131.4	136.7	139.3	142.5	147.5	151.5	154.4	160.8	164.1	168.5	174.5
Apr	133.1	138.8	140.6	144.2	149.0	152.6	156.3	162.6	165.2	169.0	175.0
May	133.5	139.3	141.1	144.7	149.6	152.9	156.9	163.5	165.6	169.5	175.5
Jun	134.1	139.3	141.0	144.7	149.8	153.0	157.5	163.4	165.6	170.0	176.0
Jul	133.8	138.8	140.7	144.0	149.1	152.4	157.5	163.0	165.1	170.5	176.5
Aug	134.1	138.9	141.3	144.7	149.9	153.1	158.5	163.7	165.5	171.0	177.0
Sept	134.6	139.4	141.9	145.0	150.6	153.8	159.3	164.4	166.2	171.5	177.5
Oct	135.1	139.9	141.8	145.2	149.8	153.8	159.6	164.5	166.5	172.0	178.0
Nov	135.6	139.7	141.6	145.3	149.8	153.9	159.6	164.4	166.7	172.5	178.5
Dec	135.7	139.2	141.9	146.0	150.7	154.4	160.0	164.4	167.3	173.0	179.0

★   Estimated figures.

2   *Annual exemption (individuals)*

	£
1997/98	6,500
1998/99	6,800
1999/00	7,100
2000/01	7,200

3   Taper relief: Disposals after 6 April 2000

Number of complete years after 5.4.98 for which asset held	Business assets % of gain chargeable	Non business assets % of gain chargeable
0	100	100
1	87.5	100
2	75	100
3	50	95
4	25	90
5	25	85
6	25	80
7	25	75
8	25	70
9	25	65
10 or more	25	60

G   NATIONAL INSURANCE 2000/01

Class 1 contributions

	£
Employee	
Primary threshold *earnings.*	3,952 (£76 pw)
Upper earnings limit (UEL)	27,820 (£535 pw)
Employer	
Secondary threshold	4,385 (£84 pw)

Employee contributions	10% on earnings between the primary threshold and the UEL (8.4% if contracted out)
Employer contributions	12.2% on earnings above secondary threshold (Reduced rates on earnings between secondary threshold and UEL if contracted out)

Class 1A contributions

Rate 12.2%

Class 2 contributions

Rate	£2.00 pw
Small earnings exception	£3,825 pa

Class 4 contributions

Rate	7%
Lower earnings limit	£4,385
Upper earnings limit	£27,820

Part A
Corporate businesses

Chapter 1

AN OUTLINE OF CORPORATION TAX

Topic list	Syllabus reference
1 Introduction to the UK tax system	-
2 The scope of corporation tax	1a, 1b
3 Profits chargeable to corporation tax	1a, 1d
4 Accounting periods	1a
5 The charge to corporation tax	1f

Introduction

We start our study of tax with an introduction to the UK tax system.

As the taxation of companies is a vitally important part of the Business Taxation syllabus we then look at corporation tax (CT). This is the tax that a company must pay on its profits.

In this chapter you will learn both how to compute the profits on which a company must pay tax and how to compute the corporation tax liability on those profits.

Study guide

Residence

- Explain how the residence of a company is determined

Scope of corporation tax

- Define the terms 'period of account', 'accounting period', and 'financial year'

- Explain when an accounting period starts and finishes

Calculation of the corporation tax liability

- Prepare a basic corporation tax computation

- Explain the implications of receiving franked investment income

- Calculate the corporation tax liability at the starting rate, small company rate and full rate, and apply tapering relief

Charges on income

- Explain the treatment of charges on income

Exam guide

Sections 1a, 1d and 1f are key topics. They are likely to be examined in Question 1 (approximately 30 marks) in Section A.

Residence is likely to be examined in Question 5 (15 marks) in Section B.

1 INTRODUCTION TO THE UK TAX SYSTEM

1.1 Central government raises revenue through a wide range of taxes. Tax law is made by **statute** and as this can be notoriously ambiguous and difficult to understand, the Revenue are currently involved in a project to rewrite it in simpler more user-friendly language.

Statute is interpreted and amplified by **case law**. The Inland Revenue also issue:

(a) **statements of practice**, setting out how they intend to apply the law;

(b) **extra-statutory concessions**, setting out circumstances in which they will not apply the strict letter of the law;

(c) a wide range of **explanatory leaflets**;

(d) **business economic notes**. These are notes on particular types of business, which are used as background information by the Inland Revenue and are also published;

(e) the **Tax Bulletin**. This is a newsletter giving the Inland Revenue's view on specific points. It is published every two months;

(f) the **Internal Guidance**, a series of manuals used by Inland Revenue staff.

However, none of these Inland Revenue publications has the force of law.

A great deal of information and the Inland Revenue publications can now be found on the Revenue's internet site.

1.2 The main taxes, their incidence and their sources, are set out in the table below.

Tax	*Suffered by*	*Source*
Income tax	**Individuals**	Income and Corporation Taxes Act 1988 (ICTA 1988) and subsequent Finance Acts; Capital Allowances Act 1990 (CAA 1990)
Corporation tax	**Companies**	As above
Capital gains tax	**Individuals** **Companies** (which pay tax on capital gains in the form of corporation tax)	Taxation of Chargeable Gains Act 1992 (TCGA 1992) and subsequent Finance Acts
Value added tax	**Businesses**, both incorporated and unincorporated	Value Added Tax Act 1994 (VATA 1994) and subsequent Finance Acts

1.3 **Finance Acts** are passed each year, incorporating proposals set out in the **Budget**. They make changes which apply mainly to the year ahead. This Study Text includes the provisions of the Finance Act 2000.

1.4 **Income tax, capital gains tax and corporation tax are direct taxes. Value added tax is an indirect tax** because it is imposed on taxpayers through the chain of supply (see later in this text).

1.5 The **Treasury** formally imposes and collects taxation. The management of the Treasury is the responsibility of the Chancellor of the Exchequer. The Treasury appoint the **Board of Inland Revenue** (sometimes referred to, particularly in names of court cases, as the **Commissioners of Inland Revenue (CIR)**), a body of civil servants. The Board administers income tax, corporation tax, capital gains tax and national insurance contributions. Rules on the administration of these taxes are contained in the **Taxes Management Act 1970 (TMA 1970)**.

1.6 The UK is divided into a number of **regions** (each under a regional controller). Each region is subdivided into **districts** (although some specialist offices, such as the Contributions Agency which is an Executive Office of the Revenue that deals with National Insurance, also exist). Each district has a **district inspector** in charge and he is assisted by other inspectors and clerical staff. The official title for an inspector is **HM Inspector of Taxes (HMIT)**. The main work of the districts consists of examining the returns and accounts of individuals, businesses and companies.

1.7 The collection of tax is not the responsibility of inspectors but of **collectors** of taxes. The collector will pursue unpaid tax through the courts. In extreme circumstances, the collector may seize the assets of the taxpayer.

1.8 Although the functions of 'Collectors' and 'Inspectors' are currently kept separate the Treasury is considering combining them and has enacted legislation which enables 'Collectors' and 'Inspectors' to be interchangeable terms in the legislation. The term '**Officer of the Board**' is now generally used in legislation.

1.9 The structure of offices set out above is also being changed. **Taxpayer service offices** are being set up to do routine checking, computation *and* collection work, while **Taxpayer district offices** investigate selected accounts, deal with corporation tax and enforce the payment of tax when it is not paid willingly. **Taxpayer assistance offices** handle enquiries and arrange specialist help for taxpayers.

1.10 The **General Commissioners** (not to be confused with the CIR) are appointed by the Lord Chancellor to hear **appeals** against Revenue decisions. They are part-time and unpaid. They are appointed for a local area (a **division**). They appoint a clerk who is often a lawyer or accountant and who is paid for his services by the Board of Inland Revenue.

1.11 The **Special Commissioners** are also appointed by the Lord Chancellor. They are full-time paid professionals. They generally hear the more complex appeals.

1.12 **Many taxpayers arrange for their accountants to prepare and submit their tax returns. The taxpayer is still the person responsible for submitting the return and for paying whatever tax becomes due: the accountant is only acting as the taxpayer's agent.**

2 THE SCOPE OF CORPORATION TAX

2.1 Companies must pay corporation tax on their **profits chargeable to corporation tax** for each **accounting period**. We look at the meaning of these terms below.

> **KEY TERM**
>
> A '**company**' is any corporate body (limited or unlimited) or unincorporated association.

2.2 The term 'company' includes sports clubs or political associations which are not run as partnerships. Charities and local authorities are not liable to corporation tax.

BPP PUBLISHING

The residence of companies

2.3 **A company incorporated in the UK is resident in the UK. A company incorporated abroad is resident in the UK if its central management and control are exercised here.** Central management and control are usually treated as exercised where the board of directors meet.

3 PROFITS CHARGEABLE TO CORPORATION TAX

3.1 A company may have both income and gains. As a general rule income arises from receipts which are expected to recur regularly (such as the profits from a trade) whereas chargeable gains arise on the sale of capital assets which have been owned for several years (such as the sale of a factory used in the trade).

3.2 A company may receive income from various sources. **Most income is taxed under a set of rules known as a schedule.** Schedule D is divided into cases.

Schedule A	Income from land and buildings (rents and so on) in the UK
Schedules B and C	Abolished
Schedule D	
Case I	Profits of trades
Case III	Interest from non trading loan relationships
Case V	Income from foreign possessions (for example foreign dividends, rents, business profits and pensions)
Case VI	Any annual profits not falling under any other schedule or case (such as casual commissions)

3.3 **The schedules and cases are important because each has its own set of rules.** Once we have decided that income is taxed under, say, Schedule A, the rules of Schedule A determine the amount of income taxed in any period. Each of the types of income that a company might receive is considered in detail later in this text.

3.4 A company receives some income, known as **taxed income**, net of income tax. For example, patent royalties are received net of basic rate income tax (22% since 6.4.00). Interest income (other than bank and building society interest) is normally received net of income tax at 20%.

3.5 **The gross amount of taxed income, ie the amount received plus the income tax withheld at source is included in the computation of a company's profits chargeable to corporation tax** (see below). For example, a patent royalty received of £7,800 is grossed up by multiplying it by 100/100-22. This gives £10,000 gross (£7,800 received plus £2,200 income tax withheld at source by the payer) to include in the computation of profits. We will see how the income tax withheld at source must be dealt with later in this text.

3.6 All taxed income other than interest income is included as a separate item in the corporation tax computation (see the proforma below). Interest income is included either within Schedule D Case I or within Schedule D Case III income. We look at interest income later in this text.

3.7 **A company's profits chargeable to corporation tax are arrived at by aggregating its various sources of income and chargeable gains and then deducting charges on income.** Here is a pro forma computation. All items are explained later in this text.

	£
Schedule D Case I	X
Schedule D Case III	X
Schedule D Case V	X
Schedule D Case VI	X
Schedule A	X
Taxed income (gross)	X
Chargeable gains	X
Total profits	X
Less charges on income (gross)	(X)
Profits chargeable to corporation tax (PCTCT) for an accounting period	X

Exam focus point

It would be of great help in the exam if you could learn the above proforma. Then when answering a corporation tax question you could immediately reproduce the proforma and insert the appropriate numbers as you are given the information in the question.

3.8 **Dividends received from UK resident companies are not included in the profits chargeable to corporation tax.** The one exception to this rule is where shares are held as trading assets, and not as investments, any dividends on those shares will be treated for tax purposes as trading profits.

Charges on income

3.9 Having arrived at a company's total profits, charges on income are deducted to arrive at the profits chargeable to corporation tax (PCTCT).

KEY TERM

A **charge on income** is a payment which tax law allows as a deduction.

3.10 Examples of charges on income include

(a) patent royalties
(b) copyright royalties
(c) charitable donations paid under the gift aid scheme (see below)

3.11 **A company must withhold basic rate income tax from any patent royalties paid.** The income tax withheld must be accounted for to the Inland Revenue. The method used to account for the income tax withheld is covered later in this text. Essentially, any tax withheld must be paid to the Inland Revenue if it cannot be matched with tax suffered on income received net.

3.12 The basic rate of income tax has been 22% since 6.4.00. This means that if a patent royalty of £10,000 gross is to be paid, the company must withhold income tax of £2,200 and make a net payment of £7,800. Prior to 6.4.00 the basic rate of income tax was 23%.

3.13 **The gross amount of the charges paid in an accounting period is deducted in the computation of profits chargeable to corporation tax.**

3.14 **Copyright royalties and payments to charity under the gift aid scheme (see below) are paid gross.**

Donations to charities

3.15 Almost all donations of money to charity can be made under the **gift aid scheme** whether they are one off donations or are regular donations. **Gift aid donations are paid gross.**

3.16 Donations to charities which are incurred wholly and exclusively for the purposes of a trade are deducted in the calculation of Schedule D Case I profits instead of as charges on income. We will look at the calculation of Schedule D Case I profits later in this text.

4 ACCOUNTING PERIODS

4.1 **Corporation tax is chargeable in respect of accounting periods.** It is important to understand the difference between an accounting period and a period of account. A period of account is any period for which a company prepares accounts; usually this will be 12 months in length but it may be longer or shorter than this. An accounting period starts when a company starts to trade, or otherwise becomes liable to corporation tax, or immediately after the previous accounting period finishes. An accounting period finishes on the earliest of:

- 12 months after its start;
- the end of the company's period of account;
- the commencement of the company's winding up;
- the company's ceasing to be resident in the UK;
- the company's ceasing to be liable to corporation tax.

4.2 **If a company has a period of account, exceeding 12 months (a long period), it is split into two accounting periods: the first 12 months and the remainder.** For example, if a company prepares accounts for the sixteen months to 30 April 2000, the two accounting periods for which the company will pay corporation tax will be the twelve months to 31 December 1999 and the four months to 30 April 2000.

4.3 Where a company has a long period of account (as in the above example), profits are **allocated to the relevant periods** as follows:

- **Trading income** before capital allowances is apportioned on a **time basis**. Capital allowances are a form of tax depreciation that will be covered later in this text.
- **Capital allowances are calculated for each accounting period.**
- **Schedule A and Schedule D Case III** income is allocated to the period in which it accrues.
- **Taxed income** is allocated to the period in which it is received.
- **Schedule D Case VI** income is apportioned on a time basis.
- **Schedule D Case V income is allocated to the period to which it relates.**
- **Chargeable gains** are allocated to the **period in which they are realised.**
- **Charges on income** are deducted in the accounting **period in which they are paid.**

Question: Long period of account

M Ltd had the following results for its fifteen month accounting period ended 30 September 2000.

	£
Trading profits	150,000
Chargeable gains	
- realised 4.5.00	5,000
- realised 1.9.00	4,000
Charges paid (gross)	
- 4.10.99	1,000
- 5.8.00	2,000

The company was not entitled to any capital allowances

Compute the profits chargeable to corporation tax for the two accounting periods falling into this period of account.

Answer

	Y/e 30.6.00	3 m/e 30.9.00
	£	£
Trading profits	120,000	30,000
Chargeable gains	5,000	4,000
Less charges paid	(1,000)	(2,000)
Profits chargeable to corporation tax	124,000	32,000

5 THE CHARGE TO CORPORATION TAX

5.1 **The rates of corporation tax are fixed for financial years. A financial year runs from 1 April to the following 31 March and is identified by the calendar year in which it begins.** For example, the year ended 31 March 2001 is the financial year 2000 (FY 2000).

5.2 The full rate of corporation tax is 30% for FY 1999 and FY 2000. Rates for earlier years are given in the rates and allowances tables in this text.

Exam focus point

The examiner has stated that the following standardised terms will be used in the requirements of examination questions on corporation tax:

Tax liability: the total corporation tax liability.
Tax payable: the corporation tax liability after deducting any tax suffered at source.

The small companies rate (SCR)

5.3 The SCR (20% for FY 1999 and FY 2000) applies to the profits chargeable to corporation tax of UK resident companies whose 'profits' are not more than £300,000.

5.4 **'Profits' means profits chargeable to corporation tax plus the grossed-up amount of dividends received from UK companies other than those in the same group.** Since 6.4.99 UK company dividends have been received net of a 10% tax credit. We, therefore, gross dividends received up by multiplying them by 100/90. Prior to 6.4.99 dividends were grossed up by multiplying them by 100/80.

5.5 You may see the grossed up amount of dividends received referred to as **franked investment income.**

9

Question: The small companies rate

B Ltd had the following results for the year ended 31 March 2001.

	£
Schedule D Case I	42,000
Dividend received 1 May 2000	9,000

Compute the corporation tax liability for the year.

Answer

	£
Schedule D Case I	42,000
Dividend plus tax credit £9,000 × 100/90	10,000
'Profits' (below £300,000 limit)	52,000
Corporation tax liability £42,000 × 20%	£8,400

The starting rate

5.6 **A new 10% starting rate of corporation tax was introduced with effect from 1 April 2000 (FY 2000). It applies to companies with 'profits' of up to £10,000.**

Question: The starting rate of corporation tax

Dexter Limited has the following income for the year ended 31 March 2001.

(a) Schedule D, Case I income of £9,500; and
(b) Franked investment income of £300.

Calculate the corporation tax liability for the year.

Answer

	£
Schedule D, Case I	9,500
Franked investment income	300
'Profits'	9,800
Corporation tax liability on PCTCT £9,500 × 10%	£950

Marginal relief

5.7 **Small companies marginal relief (sometimes called tapering relief) applies where the 'profits' of an accounting period of a UK resident company are over £300,000 but under £1,500,000. We first calculate the corporation tax at the full rate and then deduct:**

$(M - P) \times I/P \times$ marginal relief fraction

**where M = upper limit (currently £1,500,000)
P = 'profits' (see above)
I = PCTCT**

The marginal relief fraction is 1/40 for FY 1997 to FY 2000 inclusive.

Question: Small companies marginal relief

Lenox Ltd has the following results for the year ended 31 March 2001.

	£
PCTCT	296,000
Dividend received 1 December 2000	12,600

Calculate the corporation tax liability.

Answer

	£
PCTCT	296,000
Dividend plus tax credit £12,600 × 100/90	14,000
'Profits'	310,000

'Profits' are above £300,000 but below £1,500,000, so small companies' marginal relief applies.

	£
Corporation tax on PCTCT £296,000 × 30%	88,800
Less: small companies' marginal relief	
£(1,500,000 – 310,000) × ⌈296,000/310,000 × 1/40⌋	28,406
	60,394

5.8 **For companies with 'profits' between £10,001 and £50,000 the small companies rate less a starting rate marginal relief applies from 1 April 2000.** The formula for calculating this marginal relief is the same as that given above except that 'M' is the upper limit for starting rate purposes. (£50,000 – FY 2000). The small companies rate only applies in full when 'profits' exceed £50,000.

Question: Starting rate marginal relief

Armstrong Ltd has the following income for its year ended 31 March 2001:

		£
(a)	Schedule D, Case I	29,500
(b)	Franked investment income	3,000

Calculate the corporation tax liability.

Answer

	£
Schedule D Case I	29,500
Franked investment income	3,000
Profits	32,500

	£
Corporation tax at small companies rate:	
£29,500 × 20%	5,900
Less: starting rate marginal relief –	
1/40 × (£50,000 – £32,500) × £29,500/£32,500	(397)
Corporation tax payable	5,503

Changes in the rate - Accounting periods straddling 31 March

5.9 **If there is a change in the corporation tax rate, and a company's accounting period does not fall entirely within one financial year, the profits of the accounting period are apportioned to the two financial years on a time basis.** Note that the profits as a whole are apportioned. We do not look at components of the profit individually, unlike apportionment of profits of a long period of account to two accounting periods.

Question: A change in the rate

Frances Ltd makes up accounts to 31 December each year. For the year ended 31 December 1999 its profit and loss account was as follows.

	£
PCTCT	644,000
Dividends plus tax credits	10,000
'Profits'	654,000

The full rate of corporation tax was 31% in FY 1998.

Calculate the corporation tax liability for the year.

Answer

	FY 1998 3 months to 31 March 1999 £	FY 1999 9 months to 31 December 1999 £
PCTCT (divided 3:9)	161,000	483,000
'Profits' (divided 3:9)	163,500	490,500
Lower limit for SCR		
FY 1998 £300,000 × 3/12	75,000	
FY 1999 £300,000 × 9/12		225,000
Upper limit for SCR		
FY 1998 £1,500,000 × 3/12	375,000	
FY 1999 £1,500,000 × 9/12		1,125,000

	£	£
Tax on PCTCT		
FY 1998: £161,000 × 31%		49,910
Less small companies marginal relief		
£(375,000 − 163,500) × 161,000/163,500 × 1/40		(5,207)
		44,703
FY 1999: £483,000 × 30%	144,900	
Less small companies marginal relief		
£(1,125,000 − 490,500) × 483,000/490,500 × 1/40	(15,620)	
		129,280
Corporation tax liability		173,983

5.10 The 'profits' falling into each financial year determines the rate of corporation tax that applies to the PCTCT of that year. This could be the full rate, the small companies' rate or, for periods falling into FY 2000, the starting rate.

Question: Period straddling 1 April 2000

Hewson Ltd had the following results for its year ended 30 September 2000.

Schedule D Case I	£9,500
Franked investment income	£300

Calculate the corporation tax liability for the year.

Answer

	FY 1999 6 months to 31.3.00 £	FY 2000 6 months to 30.9.00 £
'Profits' (£9,800)	4,900	4,900
Profit chargeable to corporation tax	4,750	4,750
Lower limit for starting rate (– : 6m)	-	5,000
Lower limit for SCR (6m : 6m)	150,000	150,000
Corporation tax payable		
£4,750 × 20%		950
£4,750 × 10%		475
Total corporation tax liability for 12 months APE 30.9.00		1,425

Associated companies and short accounting periods

> **KEY TERM**
>
> The expression 'associated companies' in tax has no connection with financial accounting. For tax purposes a company is associated with another company if either controls the other or if both are under the control of the same person or persons (individuals, partnerships or companies). Whether such a company is UK resident or not is irrelevant (even though non-UK resident companies cannot benefit from the starting rate, small companies rate or from marginal relief). Control is given by holding over 50% of the share capital or the voting power or being entitled to over 50% of the distributable income or of the net assets in a winding up.

5.11 **If a company has one or more 'associated companies', then the profit limits for starting rate and small companies rate purposes are divided by the number of associated companies + 1 (for the company itself).**

5.12 Companies which have only been associated for part of an accounting period are deemed to have been associated for the whole period for the purpose of determining the profit limits.

5.13 An associated company is ignored for these purposes if it has not carried on any trade or business at any time in the accounting period (or the part of the period during which it was associated). **This means that you must ignore dormant companies.** A holding company counts as not carrying on any trade or business so long as:

- its only assets are shares in subsidiaries;

- it is not entitled to deduct any outgoings as charges or management expenses; and

- its only profits are dividends from subsidiaries, which are distributed in full to its shareholders.

Question: Associated companies

J Ltd has two associated companies. In the year ended 31 December 2000, it had profits chargeable to corporation tax of £400,000. Dividends of £45,000 were received on 30 September 2000. What is the corporation tax payable for the year?

Answer

Year ended 31.12.2000 falls 3 months into FY 1999 and 9 months into FY 2000

	FY 1999	FY 2000
	£	£
Profits chargeable to corporation tax	100,000	300,000
Profits for small companies rate purposes (400,000 + 45,000 × 100/90)	112,500	337,500
Lower limit for small companies rate	25,000	75,000
Upper limit for small companies rate	125,000	375,000

As there are two associated companies (plus J Ltd), the upper and lower limits are divided by 3.

Small companies marginal relief applies in both years.

	£
FY 1999	
£100,000 × 30%	30,000
Less	
$£(125,000 - 112,500) \times \dfrac{100,000}{112,500} \times \dfrac{1}{40}$	(278)
FY 2000	
£300,000 × 30%	90,000
Less	
$£(375,000 - 337,500) \times \dfrac{300,000}{337,500} \times \dfrac{1}{40}$	(833)
	118,889

5.14 **The profit limits are reduced proportionately if an accounting period lasts for less than 12 months.**

Question: Short accounting periods

For the nine months to 31 January 2001 a company with no other associated companies had PCTCT of £278,000 and no dividends received. Compute the corporation tax liability.

Answer

(a) Reduction in the lower limit as the accounting period is only nine months long
£300,000 × 9/12 = £225,000

(b) Reduction in the upper limit
£1,500,000 × 9/12 = £1,125,000

(c) 'Profits' = £278,000

(d) Corporation tax

	£
£278,000 × 30%	83,400
Less small companies' marginal relief £(1,125,000 - 278,000) × 1/40	(21,175)
Corporation tax liability	62,225

Chapter roundup

- Profits chargeable to corporation tax are income plus gains minus charges.

- Companies pay corporation tax on their profits chargeable to corporation tax profits of each accounting period.

- Tax rates are set for financial years.

- Companies may be entitled to the starting rate, the small companies rate or to marginal relief, depending on their 'profits' (profits chargeable to corporation tax plus grossed up dividends received).

Quick quiz

1   How is taxed income dealt with in a corporation tax computation? (see para 3.5)

2   Give an example of a charge on income that is paid net of income tax. (3.11)

3   When does an accounting period end? (4.1)

4   How are profits of a long period of account divided between accounting periods? (4.3)

5   Which companies are entitled to the starting rate of corporation tax? (5.6)

6   What is the marginal relief formula? (5.7)

7   How is tax calculated when an accounting period straddles a change in the corporation tax rate? (5.9)

8   What is an associated company? (5.11 and Key term above)

Now try the question below from the Exam Question Bank

Number	Level	Marks	Time
1	Exam	20	36 mins

MINDMAP

PROFITS CHARGEABLE TO CORPORATION TAX **?**

1 SCHEDULE D CASE I • Adjust accounts for disallowables +/- • Depreciation etc Non trade etc • Remove items not taxed under DI • Work out capital allowances and deduct • Plant & machinery • Industrial buildings	**TRADING PROFITS**	**+**
SCHEDULE A Compute Schedule A profit on an accruals basis Deductible vs non deductible expenses	**RENT INCOME**	**+**
SCHEDULE D CASE III Compute net interest from non-trading loans or investments on accruals basis NB interest received/paid for trading purposes is Schedule D Case I	**INTEREST FROM NON-TRADING LOAN**	**+**
SCHEDULE D CASE V Payments ⟶ gross up for withholding / underlying tax	**FOREIGN INCOME**	**+**
TAXED INCOME Gross up patent royalties received	**%**	**+**
CHARGEABLE GAINS Proceeds - cost - indexation allowance ⟶ then consider roll over / hold over	- Sales of assets eg copyrights buildings etc	**+**
CHARGES ON INCOME Trade: patent royalties paid net Non trade: Gift aid paid gross NB Remember difference between trade and non-trade charges	**£**	**-**
PROFITS CHARGEABLE TO CORPORATION TAX		**=**

Chapter 2

SCHEDULE D CASE I

Topic list	Syllabus reference
1 The adjustment of profits	1c(i)
2 Deductible and non-deductible expenditure	1c(i)
3 Income not taxable under Schedule D Case I	1c(i)
4 Deductible expenditure not charged in the accounts	1c(i)
5 The cessation of trades	1c(i)

Introduction

We have seen how to compute a company's total profits. In this chapter we see how to compute one particular type of a company's profits, namely its Schedule D Case I profits.

Schedule D Case I profits are the profits that arise from a company's trade. Your starting point in computing Schedule D Case I profits is always the net profits in a company's accounts but this must be adjusted to arrive at the taxable Schedule D Case I profits. For tax purposes, standard rules on the computation of profits are used instead of individual company accounting policies, so as to ensure fairness.

Study guide

Schedule D Case I

- State the expenditure that is allowable in calculating the tax-adjusted profit

- Explain how relief can be obtained for pre-trading expenditure

Exam guide

Section 1c is a key topic. it is likely to be examined in Question 1 in Section A or Question 7 (15 marks) in Section B.

1   THE ADJUSTMENT OF PROFITS

1.1   Although the net profit before taxation shown in the accounts is the starting point in computing the taxable trading profit, many adjustments may be required to find the profit taxable under Schedule D Case I.

1.2   Here is an illustrative adjustment.

		£	£
Net profit per accounts			140,000
Add:	expenditure charged in the accounts which is not deductible under Schedule D Case I		80,000
			220,000
Less:	profits included in the accounts but which are not taxable under Schedule D Case I	40,000	
	expenditure which is deductible under Schedule D Case I but has not been charged in the accounts	20,000	
			60,000
Profit adjusted for tax purposes			160,000

You may refer to deductible and non-deductible expenditure as allowable and disallowable expenditure respectively. The two sets of terms are interchangeable.

Accounting policies

1.3 **As a rule, accounts drawn up on normal accepted accounting principles are acceptable for tax purposes.** Two special points are worth noting.

- If there is a legal action in progress, the best estimate of the cost should be debited, not the most prudent estimate.

- Under SSAP 9, a loss on a long-term contract is recognised as soon as it is foreseen. Anticipating a loss in this way is not acceptable for tax purposes, so the debit to profit and loss must be added back.

1.4 The taxable profits of a trade, must normally be computed on a basis which gives a true and fair view, subject to adjustments permitted or required by tax law.

Rounding

1.5 Where a single company (not a group of companies) has an annual turnover of at least £5,000,000 and prepares its accounts with figures rounded to at least the nearest £1,000, figures in computations of adjusted profits (including non-trading profits but excluding capital gains) may generally be rounded to the nearest £1,000.

Exam focus point

When adjusting profits as supplied in a profit and loss account confusion can arise as regards to whether the figures are net or gross. Properly drawn up company accounts should normally include all income gross. Charges should also be shown gross. However, some examination questions include items 'net'. Read the question carefully.

2 DEDUCTIBLE AND NON-DEDUCTIBLE EXPENDITURE

Payments contrary to public policy and illegal payments

2.1 **Based on case law, fines and penalties are not deductible.** However, the Revenue usually allow employees' parking fines incurred in parking their employer's cars while on their employer's business. Fines relating to directors however, are never allowed.

2.2   A payment is (by statute) not deductible if making it constitutes an offence by the payer. This covers protection money paid to terrorists, and also bribes. Statute also prevents any deduction for payments made in response to blackmail or extortion.

Capital expenditure

2.3   **Capital expenditure is not deductible. The most contentious items of expenditure will often be repairs** (revenue expenditure) **and improvements** (capital expenditure).

- The cost of restoration of an asset by, for instance, replacing a subsidiary part of the asset is revenue expenditure. Expenditure on a new factory chimney replacement was allowable since the chimney was a subsidiary part of the factory (*Samuel Jones & Co (Devondale) Ltd v CIR 1951*). However, in another case a football club demolished a spectators' stand and replaced it with a modern equivalent. This was held not to be repair, since repair is the restoration by renewal or replacement of subsidiary parts of a larger entity, and the stand formed a distinct and *separate* part of the club (*Brown v Burnley Football and Athletic Co Ltd 1980*).

- The cost of initial repairs to improve an asset recently acquired to make it fit to earn profits is disallowable capital expenditure. In *Law Shipping Co Ltd v CIR 1923* the taxpayer failed to obtain relief for expenditure on making a newly bought ship seaworthy prior to using it.

- The cost of initial repairs to remedy normal wear and tear of recently acquired assets is allowable. *Odeon Associated Theatres Ltd v Jones 1971* can be contrasted with the *Law Shipping* judgement. Odeon were allowed to charge expenditure incurred on improving the state of recently acquired cinemas.

2.4   Other examples to note include:

- A one-off payment made by a hotel owner to terminate an agreement for the management of a hotel was held to be revenue rather than capital expenditure in *Croydon Hotel & Leisure Co v Bowen 1996*. The payment did not affect the whole structure of the taxpayer's business; it merely enabled it to be run more efficiently.

- A one-off payment to remove a threat to the taxpayer's business was also held to be revenue rather than capital expenditure in *Lawson v Johnson Matthey plc 1992*.

- An initial payment for a franchise (as opposed to regular fees) is capital and not deductible.

2.5   The costs of **registering patents and trade marks** are specifically allowed as a deduction.

Appropriations

2.6   **Depreciation, amortisation and general provisions are not deductible.** A specific provision against a particular trade debt is deductible if it is a reasonable estimate of the likely loss.

Where payments are made to or on behalf of employees, the full amounts are deductible but the employees may be taxed on benefits in kind if the payment has a private element.

Charges on income

2.7   **Charges on income, such as patent royalties, are added back in the calculation of Schedule D Case I profit. They are deducted instead from total profits in computing profits chargeable to corporation tax. The amount added back to the accounts profit (on**

BPP PUBLISHING

an accruals basis) and the amount deducted as a charge on income (on a cash basis) may differ.

Entertaining and gifts

2.8 **Entertaining for and gifts to employees are normally deductible.** Where gifts are made, or the entertainment is excessive, a charge to tax may arise on the employee under the benefits in kind legislation.

2.9 **Gifts to customers not costing more than £10 per donee per year are allowed if they carry a conspicuous advertisement for the business and are not food, drink, tobacco or vouchers exchangeable for goods.**

2.10 Gifts to charities may be allowed although many will fall foul of the 'wholly and exclusively' rule below. If a gift aid declaration is made in respect of a gift, tax relief will be given as a charge on income under the gift aid scheme, not as a schedule D Case I deduction.

2.11 **Tax relief is available** for certain donations of trading stock and equipment (see below). **All other expenditure on entertaining and gifts is non-deductible.**

Expenditure not wholly and exclusively for the purposes of the trade

2.12 **Expenditure is not deductible if it is not for trade purposes (the remoteness test), or if it reflects more than one purpose (the duality test).**

2.13 **The remoteness test** is illustrated by the following cases.

- *Strong & Co of Romsey Ltd v Woodifield 1906*
  A customer injured by a falling chimney when sleeping in an inn owned by a brewery claimed compensation from the company. The compensation was not deductible: 'the loss sustained by the appellant was not really incidental to their trade as innkeepers and fell upon them in their character not of innkeepers but of householders'.

- *Bamford v ATA Advertising Ltd 1972*
  A director misappropriated £15,000. The loss was not allowable: 'the loss is not, as in the case of a dishonest shop assistant, an incident of the company's trading activities. It arises altogether outside such activities'.

- Expenditure which is wholly and exclusively to benefit the trades of several companies (for example in a group) but is not wholly and exclusively to benefit the trade of one specific company is not deductible (*Vodafone Cellular Ltd and others v Shaw 1995*).

- *McKnight (HMIT) v Sheppard (1999)* concerned expenses incurred by a stockbroker in defending allegations of infringements of Stock Exchange regulations. It was found that the expenditure was incurred to prevent the destruction of the taxpayer's business and that as the expenditure was incurred for business purposes it was deductible. It was also found that although the expenditure had the effect of preserving the taxpayer's reputation, that was not its purpose, so there was no duality of purpose.

2.14 The **duality test** is illustrated by the following case.

- *Mallalieu v Drummond 1983*
  Expenditure by a lady barrister on black clothing to be worn in court (and on its cleaning and repair) was not deductible. The expenditure was for the dual purpose of enabling the barrister to be warmly and properly clad as well as meeting her professional requirements.

Subscriptions and donations

2.15 **The general 'wholly and exclusively' rule determines the deductibility of expenses. Subscriptions and donations are not deductible unless the expenditure is for the benefit of the trade.** The following are the main types of subscriptions and donations you may meet and their correct treatments.

- Trade subscriptions (such as to a professional or trade association) are generally deductible.

- Charitable donations are deductible only if they are small and to local charities. Tax relief may be available for donations under the gift aid scheme. In the latter case they are not a deductible Schedule D Case I expense.

- Political subscriptions and donations are generally not deductible. However, if it can be shown that political expenditure is incurred for the survival of the trade then it may be deducted. This follows a case in which it was held that expenditure incurred in resisting nationalisation was allowable on the grounds that it affected the survival of the business (*Morgan v Tate and Lyle Ltd 1954*).

- When a company makes a gift of equipment manufactured, sold or used in the course of its trade to an educational establishment or for a charitable purpose, nothing need be brought into account as a trading receipt or (if capital allowances had been obtained on the asset - see the next chapter) as disposal proceeds, so full relief is obtained for the cost. The donor company must claim relief within two years of the end of the accounting period of the gift. The value of any benefit to the donor from the gift is taxable.

- Where a donation represents the most effective commercial way of disposing of stock (for example, where it would not be commercially effective to sell surplus perishable food), the donation can be treated as for the benefit of the trade and the disposal proceeds taken as £Nil. In other cases, the amount credited to the accounts in respect of a donation of stock should be its market value.

Legal and professional charges

2.16 **Legal and professional charges relating to capital or non-trading items are not deductible.** These include charges incurred in acquiring new capital assets or legal rights and in issuing shares.

Charges are deductible if they relate directly to trading. Deductible items include:

- legal and professional charges incurred defending a company's title to fixed assets;
- charges connected with an action for breach of contract;
- expenses of the **renewal** (not the original grant) of a lease for less than 50 years;
- charges for trade debt collection;
- normal charges for preparing accounts/assisting with the self assessment of tax liabilities.

2.17 Accountancy expenses arising out of an enquiry into the accounts information in a particular period's return are not allowed where the enquiry reveals discrepancies and additional liabilities for the period of enquiry, or any earlier period, which arise as a result of negligent or fraudulent conduct.

Where, however, the enquiry results in no addition to profits, or an adjustment to the profits for the period of enquiry only and that assessment does not arise as a result of negligent or fraudulent conduct, the additional accountancy expenses are allowable.

Part A: Corporate businesses

Bad and doubtful debts

2.18 **Only bad debts incurred in the course of a business are deductible for taxation purposes.** Thus loans to employees written off are not deductible unless the business is that of making loans, or it can be shown that the writing-off of the loan was an emolument laid out for the benefit of the trade. If a trade debt is released as part of a voluntary arrangement under the Insolvency Act 1986, or a compromise or arrangement under s 425 Companies Act 1985, the amount released is deductible as a bad debt.

2.19 General doubtful debt provisions are not deductible, but specific provisions and write-offs against individual debts are deductible. The only adjustment needed to the accounts profit is to add back an increase (or deduct a decrease) in the general provision.

Interest

2.20 **Interest paid on a loan taken out for trade purposes (a trading loan relationship) is a deductible Schedule D Case I expense.** Similarly interest received on a trading loan relationship is included within Schedule D Case I profits. This means that no adjustment to the accounts profit is required for such interest.

2.21 Interest paid and received on loans not taken out for trade purposes (non trading loan relationships) is deductible/ taxable under Schedule D Case III. This means that the accounts profit must be adjusted to exclude such interest.

2.22 Loan relationships will be looked at in more detail later in this text.

Pre-trading expenditure

2.23 Expenditure incurred before the commencement of trade (**pre-trading expenditure**) is deductible, if it is incurred within seven years of the start of trade and it is of a type that would have been deductible had the trade already started. It is treated as a trading expense incurred on the first day of trading.

Miscellaneous deductions

2.24 The **costs of seconding employees to charities or educational establishments are deductible.**

2.25 **If emoluments for employees are charged in the accounts but are not paid within nine months of the end of the period of account, the cost is only deductible for the period of account in which the emoluments are paid.** When a tax computation is made within the nine month period, it is initially assumed that unpaid emoluments will not be paid within that period. The computation is adjusted if they are so paid.

Emoluments are treated as paid at the same time as they are treated as received for Schedule E purposes (see later in this text).

2.26 **Redundancy payments made when a trade ends are deductible** on the earlier of the day of payment and the last day of trading. If the trade does not end, they can be deducted as soon as they are provided for, so long as the redundancy was decided on within the period of account, the provision is accurately calculated and the payments are made within nine months of the end of the period of account.

2.27 Here is a list of various other items that you may meet.

Item	Treatment	Comment
Educational courses for staff	Allow	
Removal expenses (to new business premises)	Allow	Only if not an expansionary move
Contribution to expenses of agents under the payroll deduction scheme	Allow	
Redundancy pay in excess of the statutory amount	Allow	If the trade ceases, the limit on allowability is $3 \times$ the statutory amount (in addition to the statutory amount)
Compensation for loss of office and ex gratia payments	Allow	If for benefit of trade: *Mitchell v B W Noble Ltd 1927*
Counselling services for employees leaving employment	Allow	If qualify for exemption from Schedule E charge on employees (see later in this text)
Contributions to any of: local enterprise agencies; training and enterprise councils; local enterprise companies; business link organisations; individual learning accounts (ILA)	Allow	The ILA must qualify for a discount or grant and contributions must be available to all employees generally.
Pension contributions (to schemes for employees and company directors)	Allow	If paid, not if only provided for; special contributions may be spread over the year of payment and future years
Premiums for insurance: against an employee's death or illness to cover locum costs or fixed overheads whilst the policyholder is ill	Allow	Receipts are taxable
Payments to employees for restrictive undertakings	Allow	Taxable on employee
Damages paid	Allow	If not too remote from trade: *Strong and Co v Woodifield 1906*
Preparation and restoration of waste disposal sites	Allow	Spread preparation expenditure over period of use of site. Pre-trading expenditure is treated as incurred on the first day of trading. Allow restoration expenditure in period of expenditure

Exam focus point

In the exam you could be given a profit and loss account and asked to calculate 'taxable profit'. You must look at every expense in the accounts to decide if it is (or isn't) 'tax deductible'. This means that you must become familiar with the many expenses you may see and the correct tax treatment. Look at the above paragraphs again noting what expenses are (and are not) allowable for tax purposes.

3 INCOME NOT TAXABLE UNDER SCHEDULE D CASE I

3.1 **There are three types of receipts which may be found in the accounting profits but which must be excluded from the Schedule D Case I computation.** These are:

(a) **capital receipts;**
(b) **income taxed in another way** (at source or under another case or schedule);
(c) **income specifically exempt from tax.**

Compensation received in one lump sum for the loss of income is likely to be treated as income (*Donald Fisher (Ealing) Ltd v Spencer 1989*).

3.2 Income taxed under another schedule, for example Schedule A income is excluded from the computation of Schedule D Case I profits but it is brought in again further down in the computation of profits chargeable to corporation tax. Similarly capital receipts are excluded from the computation of Schedule D Case I income but they may be included in the computation of chargeable gains.

3.3 In some trades, (eg petrol stations), a wholesaler may pay a lump sum to a retailer in return for the retailer's only supplying that wholesaler's products for several years (an **exclusivity agreement**). If the payment must be used for a specific capital purpose, it is a capital receipt. If that is not the case, it is a revenue receipt. If the sum is repayable to the wholesaler but the requirement to repay is waived in tranches over the term of the agreement, each tranche is a separate revenue receipt when the requirement is waived.

4 DEDUCTIBLE EXPENDITURE NOT CHARGED IN THE ACCOUNTS

4.1 Capital allowances (see the next chapter) **are** an example of **deductible expenditure not charged in the accounts.**

4.2 A second example is **an annual sum** which can be deducted by a company that has paid **a lease premium to a landlord who is taxable on the premium under Schedule A** (see later in this text). Normally, the amortisation of the lease will have been deducted in the accounts and must be added back as an appropriation.

Question: Calculation of Sch D Case I profit

Here is the profit and loss account of Pring Ltd, a trading company.

	£	£
Gross operating profit		30,000
Patent royalties received		860
		30,860
Wages and salaries	7,000	
Rent and rates	2,000	
Depreciation	1,500	
Bad debts written off	150	
Provision against a fall in the price of raw materials	5,000	
Entertainment expenses	750	
Patent royalties	1,200	
Bank interest (paid for trade purposes)	300	
Legal expenses on acquisition of new factory	250	
		(18,150)
Net profit		12,710

(a) No staff were entertained.
(b) The provision of £5,000 is charged because of an anticipated trade recession.
(c) Patent royalties were received and paid net but have been shown gross.

Compute the profit taxable under Schedule D Case I.

Answer

	£	£
Profit per accounts		12,710
Add: Depreciation	1,500	
Provision against a fall in raw material prices	5,000	
Entertainment expenses	750	
Patent royalties paid (to treat as a charge)	1,200	
Legal expenses	250	
		8,700
		21,410
Less patent royalties received (taxed income)		(860)
Adjusted trading profit taxable under Sch D Case I		20,550

5 THE CESSATION OF TRADES

5.1 **Post-cessation receipts** (including any releases of debts incurred by the company) **are taxable under Schedule D Case VI**.

5.2 **Post-cessation expenses can be deducted so long as they would have been deductible had the trade continued,** and they did not arise as a result of the cessation. Capital allowances which the company was entitled to immediately before the discontinuance but which remain unrelieved can also be deducted.

Valuing trading stock on cessation

5.3 **When a trade ceases, the closing stock must be valued**. The higher the value, the higher the profit for the final period of trading will be.

5.4 If the stock is sold to a UK trader who will deduct its cost in computing his taxable profits, it is valued under the following rules.

(a) If the seller and the buyer are unconnected, take the actual price.

(b) If the seller and the buyer are connected, take what would have been the price in an arm's length sale.

(c) However, if the seller and the buyer are connected, the arm's length price exceeds both the original cost of the stock and the actual transfer price, and both the seller and the buyer make an election, then take the greater of the original cost of the stock and the transfer price. The time limit for election is two years after the end of the accounting period of cessation.

5.5 In all cases covered above, the value used for the seller's computation of profit is also used as the buyer's cost.

> **KEY TERM**
>
> Companies are **connected** with anyone controlling them, with other companies under common control and with partnerships under common control.

5.6 If the stock is not transferred to a UK trader who will be able to deduct its cost in computing his profits, then it is valued at its open market value as at the cessation of trade.

Chapter roundup

- Disallowable expenditure must be added back to the accounts profit in the computation of Schedule D Case I income whilst receipts not taxable under Schedule D Case I must be deducted from the accounts profit.

- Expenditure not charged in the accounts that is deductible under Schedule D Case I must be deducted when computing Schedule D Case I income.

Quick quiz

1   What must be added back to the accounts profit in the computation of Schedule D Case I profits. (see para 1.2)

2   What are the remoteness test and the duality test? (2.12)

3   What is the tax treatment of gifts of plant to educational establishments? (2.15)

4   What relief is available for pre-trading expenditure? (2.23)

5   In which period of account are emoluments paid 12 months after the end of the period for which they are charged deductible? (2.25)

6   What relief is available for redundancy pay? (2.26)

Now try the question below from the Exam Question Bank

Number	Level	Marks	Time
2	Exam	12	22 mins

Chapter 3

CAPITAL ALLOWANCES

Topic list	Syllabus reference
1 Capital allowances in general	1c(ii)
2 The definition of plant	1c(ii)
3 Allowances on plant and machinery	1c(ii)
4 Short-life assets	1c(ii)
5 Hire purchase and leasing	1c(ii)
6 Successions	1c(ii)
7 Industrial buildings – types	1c(ii)
8 Allowances on industrial buildings	1c(ii)

Introduction

Depreciation cannot be deducted in computing trading profits. Instead, capital allowances are given. In this chapter, we look at capital allowances on plant and machinery and industrial buildings.

Our study of plant and machinery falls into three parts. Firstly, we look at what qualifies for allowances: many business assets get no allowances at all. Secondly, we see how to compute the allowances and lastly, we look at special rules for assets with short lives, for assets which the taxpayer does not buy outright and for transfers of whole businesses.

We then look at industrial buildings. Again, we start off by looking at what qualifies for the allowances and then how to compute the allowances.

Study guide

Capital allowances

- Define plant and machinery for capital allowances purposes

- Calculate writing down allowances and first year allowances

- Compute balancing allowances and charges

- Explain the treatment of motor cars

- Explain the treatment of short life assets and long life assets

- Define an industrial building for industrial buildings allowance purposes

- Calculate industrial buildings allowance for new and second-hand buildings

- Compute the balancing adjustment on the disposal of an industrial building

Exam guide

This is part of Section 1c and so is a key topic. Again, it is likely to be examined in Question 1 in Section A or Question 7 in Section B.

1 CAPITAL ALLOWANCES IN GENERAL

1.1 Capital expenditure is not in itself an allowable Schedule D Case I deduction, but it *may* attract capital allowances. Capital allowances are treated as a trading expense and are deducted in arriving at Schedule D Case I profits. Balancing charges, effectively negative allowances, are added in arriving at those profits.

1.2 Allowances are available on expenditure falling into the following categories:

- plant and machinery;
- industrial buildings.

1.3 **Capital allowances are calculated for accounting periods.**

1.4 **For capital allowances purposes, expenditure is generally deemed to be incurred when the obligation to pay becomes unconditional.** This will often be the date of a contract, but if for example payment is due a month after delivery of a machine, it would be the date of delivery. However, amounts due more than four months after the obligation becomes unconditional are deemed to be incurred when they fall due.

2 THE DEFINITION OF PLANT

2.1 **There are two sources of the rules on what qualifies as plant and is therefore eligible for capital allowances.** (Machinery is also eligible, but the word 'machinery' may be taken to have its everyday meaning.) **Statute** lists items which do not qualify, but it does not give a comprehensive list of other items which do qualify. There are several **cases** in which certain items have been accepted as plant. A few items such as thermal insulation and computer software are plant by statute.

The statutory exclusions

Buildings

2.2 **Expenditure on a building and on any asset which is incorporated in a building or is of a kind normally incorporated into buildings does not qualify as expenditure on plant unless the asset falls within the list of exceptions given** below. Even if an asset falls within that list, it does not follow that it is plant (although it probably will be, because the list is based on cases in which assets have been held to be plant and on Revenue practice).

2.3 In addition to complete buildings, **the following assets count as 'buildings', and are therefore not plant.**

- Walls, floors, ceilings, doors, gates, shutters, windows and stairs
- Mains services, and systems, of water, electricity and gas
- Waste disposal, sewerage and drainage systems
- Shafts or other structures for lifts etc

2.4 **The following assets** which would normally count as 'buildings' **can still be plant.**

- Electrical (including lighting), cold water, gas and sewerage systems:
  - (i)   provided mainly to meet the particular requirements of the trade; or
  - (ii)   provided mainly to serve particular machinery or plant.
- Space or water heating systems and powered systems of ventilation.
- Manufacturing and display equipment.

- Cookers, washing machines, refrigeration or cooling equipment, sanitary ware and furniture and furnishings.

- Lifts etc.

- Sound insulation provided mainly to meet the particular requirements of the trade.

- Computer, telecommunication and surveillance systems.

- Sprinkler equipment, fire alarm and burglar alarm systems.

- Any machinery.

- Strong rooms in bank or building society premises; safes.

- Partition walls, where movable and intended to be moved.

- Decorative assets in the hotel, restaurant or similar trades; advertising hoardings.

- Glasshouses which have, as an integral part of their structure, devices which control the plant growing environment automatically; swimming pools.

2.5   In addition, the following items may be 'plant'.

- Caravans provided mainly for holiday lettings
- Movable buildings intended to be moved in the course of the trade

2.6   When a building is sold, the vendor and purchaser can make a joint election to determine how the sale proceeds are apportioned between the building and its fixtures. There are anti-avoidance provisions that ensure capital allowances given overall on a fixture do not exceed the original cost of the fixture.

Structures

2.7   **Expenditure on structures** and on works involving the alteration of land **does not qualify as expenditure on plant** unless the asset falls within the list of exceptions given below. Even if an asset falls within that list, it does not follow that it is plant (although it probably will be, because the list is based on cases in which assets have been held to be plant and on Revenue practice).

2.8   A 'structure' is a fixed structure of any kind, other than a building.

2.9   **The following items**, which would normally count as 'structures' **can still be plant**.

- Expenditure on altering land for the purpose only of installing machinery or plant

- Pipelines, and also underground ducts or tunnels with a primary purpose of carrying utility conduits

- Silos provided for temporary storage and storage tanks

- Fish tanks and fish ponds

- A railway or tramway

2.10   In addition, expenditure may qualify as plant despite these rules if the assets bought are items which qualify as plant under the rules in Paragraphs 2.28 and 2.29 below.

Land

2.11 Land or an interest in land does not qualify as plant and machinery. For this purpose 'land' excludes buildings, structures and assets which are installed or fixed to land in such a way as to become part of the land for general legal purposes.

Case law

2.12 The original case law **definition of plant** (applied in this case to a horse) **is 'whatever apparatus is used by a businessman for carrying on his business: not his stock in trade which he buys or makes for sale; but all goods and chattels, fixed or movable, live or dead, which he keeps for permanent employment in the business'** (*Yarmouth v France 1887*).

2.13 Subsequent cases have refined the original definition and have largely been concerned with the **distinction between plant actively used in the business (qualifying) and the setting in which the business is carried on (non-qualifying). This is the 'functional' test.**

2.14 The cost of excavating and concreting a dry dock was allowed as capital expenditure on plant. The dock played an active part in the operation of the company's trade (*CIR v Barclay Curle & Co 1969*).

2.15 The cost of concrete grain silos has been allowed. Although used to store grain they were more than buildings: they were 'specially constructed for the purpose of rendering more efficient the process of unloading and distribution' (*Schofield v R & H Hall 1975*).

2.16 The whole cost of excavating and installing a swimming pool was allowed to the owners of a caravan park. *CIR v Barclay Curle & Co 1969* was followed: the pool performed the function of giving 'buoyancy and enjoyment' to the persons using the pool (*Cooke v Beach Station Caravans Ltd 1974*).

2.17 A barrister succeeded in his claim for his law library: 'Plant includes a man's tools of his trade. It extends to what he uses day by day in the course of his profession. It is not confined to physical things like the dentist's chair or the architect's table' (*Munby v Furlong 1977*).

2.18 Office partitioning was allowed. Because it was movable it was not regarded as part of the setting in which the business was carried on (*Jarrold v John Good and Sons Ltd 1963*).

2.19 A ship used as a floating restaurant was regarded as a 'structure in which the business was carried on rather than apparatus employed ... ' (Buckley LJ). No capital allowances could be obtained (*Benson v Yard Arm Club 1978*). The same decision was made in relation to a football club's spectator stand. The stand performed no function in the actual carrying out of the club's trade (*Brown v Burnley Football and Athletic Co Ltd 1980*).

2.20 At a motorway service station, false ceilings contained conduits, ducts and lighting apparatus. They did not qualify because they did not perform a function in the business. They were merely part of the setting in which the business was conducted (*Hampton v Fortes Autogrill Ltd 1979*).

2.21 Light fittings, decor and murals can be plant. A company carried on business as hoteliers and operators of licensed premises. The function of the items was the creation of an atmosphere conducive to the comfort and well being of its customers (*CIR v Scottish and Newcastle Breweries Ltd 1982*).

2.22 On the other hand, it has been held that when an attractive floor is provided in a restaurant, the fact that the floor performs the function of making the restaurant attractive to customers is not enough to make it plant. It functions as premises, and the cost therefore does not qualify for capital allowances (*Wimpy International Ltd v Warland 1988*).

2.23 General lighting in a department store is not plant, as it is merely setting. Special display lighting, however, can be plant (*Cole Brothers Ltd v Phillips 1982*).

2.24 Free-standing decorative screens installed in the windows of a branch of a building society qualified as plant. Their function was not to act a part of the setting in which the society's business was carried on; it was to attract local custom, and accordingly the screens formed part of the apparatus with which the society carried on its business (*Leeds Permanent Building Society v Proctor 1982*).

2.25 In *Bradley v London Electricity plc 1996* an electricity substation was held not to be plant because it functioned as premises in which London Electricity carried on a trading activity rather than apparatus with which the activity was carried out.

2.26 A building holding car wash equipment is not plant, even if the design of the building is a key element in the car wash system (*Attwood v Anduff Car Wash Ltd 1995*).

2.27 A special greenhouse, constructed with a particular type of glass and with manually operated ventilation panels, is not plant (*Gray v Seymours Garden Centre (Horticulture) 1995*).

Expenditure deemed to be on plant and machinery

2.28 Plant and machinery capital allowances are also available on:

- expenditure incurred by a company in complying with fire regulations for a building which it occupies;

- expenditure by a company on thermal insulation of an industrial building;

- expenditure by a company in meeting statutory safety requirements for sports ground.

On disposal, the sale proceeds for the above are deemed to be zero, so no balancing charge (see below) can arise.

Computer software

2.29 **Capital expenditure on computer software** (both programs and data) **qualifies as** expenditure on **plant and machinery**:

(a) regardless of whether the software is supplied in a tangible form (such as a disk) or transmitted electronically; and

(b) regardless of whether the purchaser acquires the software or only a licence to use it.

Disposal proceeds are brought into account in the normal way, except that if the fee for the grant of a licence is taxed as income of the licensor, no disposal proceeds are taken into account in computing the licensee's capital allowances.

2.30 Where someone has incurred expenditure qualifying for capital allowances on computer software (or the right to use software), and receives a capital sum in exchange for allowing someone else to use the software, that sum is brought into account as disposal proceeds. However, the cumulative total of disposal proceeds is not allowed to exceed the original cost

BPP PUBLISHING

of the software, and any proceeds above this limit are ignored for capital allowances purposes (although they may lead to chargeable gains).

2.31 If software is expected to have a useful economic life of less than two years, its cost may be treated as revenue expenditure.

3 ALLOWANCES ON PLANT AND MACHINERY

Writing down allowances

> **KEY TERM**
>
> **A writing down allowance (WDA)** is given on expenditure incurred on most plant and machinery **at the rate of 25% a year** (on a reducing balance basis). The WDA is calculated on the written down value (WDV) on all plant on a 'pool' basis, after adding the current period's additions and taking out the current period's disposals.

3.1 It is unnecessary to keep track of individual written down values.

3.2 Allowances are claimed in the tax return. Any company can claim less than the full allowances.

3.3 If less than the full allowances are claimed, higher capital allowances will then be available in later years because the WDV carried forward will be higher.

3.4 When plant is sold the proceeds (but limited to a maximum of the original cost) are taken out of the pool of qualifying expenditure. Provided that the trade is still being carried on, the balance remaining is written down in the future by writing down allowances, even if there are no assets left.

3.5 **Writing down allowances are 25% × months/12** where the accounting period is shorter than 12 months (a company's accounting period for tax purposes is never longer than 12 months), or where the trade concerned started in the accounting period and was therefore carried on for fewer than 12 months.

3.6 Expenditure on plant and machinery by a company about to begin a trade is treated as incurred on the first day of trading. Assets previously owned by an individual and then brought into the trade (at the start of trading or later) are treated as bought for their market values at the times when they are brought in.

First year allowances

Spending by small and medium sized enterprises

3.7 **Expenditure incurred on plant and machinery** (other than leased assets, cars, sea going ships or railway assets) after 2 July 1998 **by small and medium sized enterprises qualifies for a first year allowance** (FYA) of 40%.

3.8 The above expenditure qualified for a FYA of 50% if it was incurred in the year to 1 July 1998. In addition, expenditure on long life assets in this period qualify for a 12% FYA. Long life assets are considered further below.

Exam focus point
The rates of FYAs will be given to you on the exam paper.

KEY TERM

A **small or medium sized enterprise,** is a company that either satisfies at least two of the following conditions in the chargeable period/financial year in which the expenditure is incurred.

(a) **Turnover not more than £11.2 million**
(b) **Assets not more than £5.6 million**
(c) **Not more than 250 employees**

or which was small or medium sized in the previous year. A company must not be a member of a large group when the expenditure is incurred.

Spending by small enterprises on information and communication technology

3.9 Expenditure by **small enterprises on information and communication technology equipment** (computers, software and internet enabled mobile phones) **in the three year period from 1 April 2000 to 31 March 2003 qualifies for a 100% FYA.**

3.10 Equipment acquired for leasing does not qualify for the 100% FYA.

KEY TERM

A **small enterprise** is a company, which satisfies at least two of the following conditions in the chargeable period/financial year in which the expenditure is incurred:

(a) **Turnover not more than £2.8 million**
(b) **Assets not more than £1.4 million**
(c) **Not more than 50 employees**

or which was small in the previous year. If a company is a member of a group, the group must also be small when the expenditure is incurred

Calculation

3.11 For FYA purposes, the provisions which treat capital expenditure incurred prior to the commencement of trading as incurred on the first day of trading do not apply.

3.12 **First year allowances are given in the place of writing down allowances.** For subsequent years a WDA is given on the balance of expenditure at the normal rate. You should therefore transfer the balance of the expenditure to the pool at the end of the first period.

Question: Calculation of schedule D case I profits

Walton Ltd starts a trade on 1 March 1997, and has the following results (before capital allowances).

Period of account	Profits £
1.3.97 - 31.7.98	42,500
1.8.98 - 31.7.99	36,800
1.8.99 - 31.7.00	32,000

Plant (none of which is information or communication technology equipment) is bought as follows.

Date	Cost £
1.3.97	13,000
1.6.97	8,000
1.6.99	5,000
31.7.00	2,000

On 1 May 1999, plant which cost £7,000 is sold for £4,000.

Walton Ltd's business is a small or medium sized enterprise for FYA purposes.

Show the Schedule D Case I profits arising as a result of the above.

Answer

The seventeen month period of account must be split into two accounting periods for corporation tax purposes. The first period is the twelve months to 28.2.98 and the second period is the five months to 31.7.98.

The capital allowances are as follows.

	FYA £	Pool £	Allowances £
1.3.97 – 28.2.98			
Additions		21,000	
WDA 25%		(5,250)	5,250
1.3.98 – 31.7.98		15,750	
WDA 25% × 5/12		(1,641)	1,641
		14,109	
1.8.98 – 31.7.99			
Disposals		(4,000)	
		10,109	
WDA 25%		(2,527)	2,527
		7,582	
Addition (1.6.99)	5,000		
FYA 40%	(2,000)		2,000
		3,000	4,527
		10,582	
1.8.99 – 31.7.00			
WDA 25%		(2,646)	2,646
		7,936	
Addition (31.7.00)	2,000		
FYA 40%	(800)		800
		1,200	-
TWDV c/f		9,136	
			3,446

The profits of the accounting periods are as follows.

Period of account	Working	Profits £
1.3.97 – 28.2.98	£(42,500 × 12/17 – 5,250)	24,750
1.3.98 – 31.7.98	£(42,500 × 5/17 – 1,641)	10,859
1.8.98 – 31.7.99	£(36,800 – 4,527)	32,273
1.8.99 – 31.7.00	£(32,000 – 3,446)	28,554

3.13 FYAs are given for incurring expenditure. It is irrelevant whether the accounting period of expenditure is twelve months or less. FYAs are not scaled up or down by reference to the length of the period.

Exam focus point

Note the tax planning opportunities available. It may be important to buy plant just before an accounting date, so that allowances become available as soon as possible. On the other hand, it may be worthwhile to claim less than the maximum allowances so as to even out the annual assessments and avoid paying higher rates of corporation tax.

The disposal value of assets

3.14 **The most common disposal value at which assets are entered in a capital allowances computation is the sale proceeds.** But there are a number of less common situations.

3.15 **Where the asset is sold at below market value** (or is given away) **the market value is used instead of the actual sale proceeds.** This general rule has two exceptions. The actual proceeds of sale are used:

(a) where the buyer will be able to claim capital allowances on the expenditure;

(b) where an employee acquires an asset from his employer at undervalue (or as a gift) and so faces a charge under the Schedule E benefit-in-kind rules.

If the asset is demolished, destroyed or otherwise lost, the disposal value is taken to be the actual sale proceeds from any resulting scrap, plus any insurance or other compensation moneys.

3.16 With all these rules, there is an overriding rule that the capital allowances **disposal value cannot exceed the original purchase price.**

Balancing charges and allowances

3.17 **Balancing charges occur when the disposal value deducted exceeds the balance remaining in the pool. The charge equals the excess and is effectively a negative capital allowance,** increasing profits. Most commonly this happens when the trade ceases and the remaining assets are sold. It may also occur, however, whilst the trade is still in progress.

3.18 In certain circumstances it may be worthwhile to not claim first year allowances on expenditure, but instead to include the expenditure in the general pool and thus avoid (or reduce) a balancing charge that would otherwise arise.

3.19 **Balancing allowances on the capital allowance pools of expenditure arise only when the trade ceases.** The balancing allowance is equal to the remaining unrelieved expenditure after deducting the disposal value of all the assets. Balancing allowances also arise on items which are not pooled (see below) whenever those items are disposed of.

Long life assets

KEY TERM

Long life assets are assets with an expected working life of 25 years or more.

BPP PUBLISHING

3.20 The writing down allowance available on such assets is 6% per annum on a reducing balance basis. Expenditure on such assets must be kept in a pool that is separate from the general pool.

First year allowances at 12% are given to small and medium sized enterprises (see above) for expenditure incurred on long life assets in the 12 months to 1 July 1998.

3.21 The following are not **treated as long life assets** (and therefore (with the exception of expensive cars: see below) still qualify for writing down allowances of 25% per annum):

 (a) **Plant and machinery in dwelling houses, retail shops, showrooms, hotels and offices.**

 (b) **Motor cars**

 (c) **Ships and railways assets** bought before 1 January 2011

 (d) Any asset in respect of which expenditure was either incurred before 26 November 1996 or was incurred before 1 January 2001 under a contract entered into before 26 November 1996

 (e) **Second-hand machinery in respect of which the vendor obtained allowances at 25%**

3.22 The **long life asset rules do not apply to companies whose total expenditure on long life assets in a chargeable period is £100,000,** or less. If the expenditure exceeds £100,000, the whole of the expenditure qualifies for allowances at 6% per annum only. For this purpose all expenditure incurred under a contract is treated as incurred in the first chargeable period to which that contract relates.

3.23 The £100,000 limit is reduced or increased proportionately in the case of a chargeable period of less or more than 12 months. In the case of groups of companies, the limit must be divided between the number of associated companies in the group (See Chapter 7).

3.24 The £100,000 exclusion is not available in respect of leased assets, second-hand assets where the vendor was only able to claim allowances of 6%, or assets where the trader has only bought a share.

Cars

3.25 **Cars** (but not lorries, vans, short-term hire cars, taxis and vehicles unsuitable for private use) **have a special capital allowance treatment.** There are two categories of cars. **Cars costing more than £12,000 are dealt with on an individual basis (see below). Cars costing £12,000 or less are pooled.**

3.26 **Prior to Finance Act 2000 the car pool was a separate one to that used for general plant and machinery.** However, the separate pool for cars costing £12,000 or less is abolished for companies for accounting periods ending after 31 March 2000. The balance that was brought forward on the separate pool at the end of the last period before the abolition is transferred to the main pool.

3.27 Companies can choose to delay the abolition of the separate car pool until the first accounting period ending after 31 March 2001. You should assume this choice is not made, unless you are specifically told otherwise.

3.28 FYAs are not available on cars.

Assets which are not pooled

3.29 Some items are not pooled. A separate record of allowances and WDV must be kept for each such asset and when it is sold a balancing allowance or charge emerges. The items are:

(a) **motor cars costing more than £12,000** where the maximum WDA is £3,000 a year. The limit is £3,000 × months/12 for accounting periods of less than twelve months.

(b) **short-life assets** for which an election has been made (see below).

Assets not wholly used for business purposes

3.30 An asset with some private use by an employee of a company, suffers no restriction in capital allowances. The employee may be taxed on a benefit in kind so the company gets capital allowances on the full cost of the asset.

Employees' capital allowances

3.31 An employee who provides plant and machinery necessarily for use in the performance of his duties may claim capital allowances, to set against his employment income (see later in this text). If there is any private use of the asset concerned the capital allowances given are restricted to the proportion of the allowances that reflects the business use of the asset. In the case of cars, the provision of the car need not be necessary for the employment. Employees who use their own bicycles for business travel may also claim capital allowances.

The cessation of a trade

3.32 **When a company ceases to trade no FYAs or WDAs are given in the final accounting period**. Each asset is deemed to be disposed of on the date the trade ceased (usually at the then market value). Additions in the relevant period are brought in and then the disposal proceeds (limited to cost) are deducted from the balance of qualifying expenditure. If the proceeds exceed the balance then a balancing charge arises. If the balance of qualifying expenditure exceeds the proceeds then a balancing allowance is given.

4 SHORT-LIFE ASSETS

4.1 **A company can elect that specific items of plant be kept separately from the general pool. The election is irrevocable and must be made within** two years of the end of the accounting period of the expenditure. **Any asset subject to this election is known as a 'short-life asset'**, and the election is known as a 'de-pooling election'.

> **KEY TERM**
>
> Provided that the asset is disposed of within four years of the end of the accounting period in which it was bought, it is a **short life asset** and a balancing charge or allowance is made on its disposal.

4.2 The receipt of a capital sum in return for the right to use computer software does not count as a disposal for this purpose. If the asset is not disposed of in the correct time period, its tax written down value is added to the general pool at the end of that time.

4.3 The election should be made for assets likely to be sold within four years for less than their tax written down values. It should not be made for assets likely to be sold within four years for more than their tax written down values. (These are, of course, only general guidelines based on the assumption that a company will want to obtain allowances as quickly as possible. There may be other considerations eg a desire to even out annual taxable profits.

4.4 An election should not necessarily be made if including the expenditure in the general pool would reduce a balancing charge that would otherwise arise.

Question: Short life assets

Caithin Ltd bought an asset on 1 July 1996 for £12,000 and elected for de-pooling. The accounting period end is 31 March. Calculate the capital allowances due if:

(a) the asset is scrapped for £300 in August 2000;
(b) the asset is scrapped for £200 in August 2001.

Answer

(a)

	£
Year to 31.3.97	
Cost	12,000
WDA 25%	(3,000)
	9,000
Year to 31.3.98	
WDA 25%	(2,250)
	6,750
Year to 31.3.99	
WDA 25%	(1,688)
	5,062
Year to 31.3.00	
WDA 25%	(1,266)
	3,796
Year to 31.3.01	
Disposal proceeds	(300)
Balancing allowance	3,496

(b) If the asset is still in use at 31 March 2001, a WDA of 25% × £3,796 = £949 would be claimable in the year to 31 March 2001. The tax written down value of £3,796 - £949 = £2,847 would be added to the general pool at the beginning of the next accounting period. The disposal proceeds of £200 would be deducted from the general pool in that period's capital allowances computation.

4.5 Short-life asset treatment cannot be claimed for:

- motor cars;
- plant used partly for non-trade purposes;
- plant received by way of gift;
- plant in respect of which a subsidy is received;
- long life assets.

4.6 **Where a short-life asset is disposed of within the four year period to a connected person (see below):**

(a) the original owner receives a balancing allowance calculated as normal and the new owner receives WDAs on the cost to him; but

(b) **if both parties so elect, the asset is treated as being sold for its tax written down value at the start of the chargeable period in which the transfer takes place, so there is no balancing charge or allowance for the vendor.**

In both situations, the acquiring party will continue to 'de-pool' the asset up to the same date as the original owner would have done.

4.7   Companies are connected with anyone controlling them, with other companies under common control and with partnerships under common control.

5   HIRE PURCHASE AND LEASING

Assets on hire purchase

5.1   **Any asset (including a car) bought on hire purchase (HP) is treated as if purchased outright for the cash price.** Therefore:

   (a)   the buyer normally obtains **capital allowances on the cash price** when the agreement begins;

   (b)   he may write off the **finance charge as a trade expense** over the term of the HP contract.

Leased assets

5.2   **Under a lease, the lessee merely hires the asset over a period.**

5.3   An expensive car (one costing over £12,000) will attract WDAs limited to £3,000 a year if bought. If it is leased instead, the maximum allowable deduction from trading profits for lease rentals is

$$\frac{£12,000 + P}{2P} \times R$$

   where   P = the purchase price (if bought outright)
                   R = the annual rental

5.4   This restriction does not apply to the finance charges in hire purchase payments (which could be regarded as payment for the hire of the car), provided the amount payable to acquire the car at the end of the hire period is no more than 1% of the car's retail price when new.

5.5   EXAMPLE: LEASED CARS

A car is used by a business under a lease. The purchase price would have been £20,000. The annual rental is £5,000. The rental allowed for tax purposes is

$$\frac{£12,000 + £20,000}{2 \times £20,000} \times £5,000 = £4,000$$

Since £5,000 is deducted in the profit and loss account, £5,000 - £4,000 = £1,000 is added back in computing taxable profits.

5.6   A lessor of plant normally obtains the benefit of capital allowances although there are anti-avoidance provisions which deny or restrict capital allowances on certain finance leases. Leasing is thus an activity which attracts tax allowances and which can be used to defer tax liabilities where the capital allowances given exceed the rental income.

6   SUCCESSIONS

6.1   **Balancing adjustments arise on the cessation of a business.** No writing down allowances are given, but the final proceeds (limited to cost) on sales of plant are compared with the tax WDV to calculate balancing allowances or charges.

6.2   **Balancing charges may be avoided where the trade passes from one connected person to another.** If a succession occurs both parties must elect if the avoidance of the balancing adjustments is required. **An election will result in the plant being transferred at its tax written down value for capital allowances purposes.** The predecessor can write down the plant for the period prior to cessation and the successor can write it down from the date of commencement. The election must be made within two years of the date of the succession.

6.3   If no election is made on a transfer of business to a connected person, assets are deemed to be sold at their market values. If an election is made the limit on proceeds to be brought into account on a later sale of an asset is the original cost of the asset, not the deemed transfer price.

7   INDUSTRIAL BUILDINGS - TYPES

Types of building

7.1   A special type of capital allowance (an **industrial buildings allowance** or IBA) is available in respect of **expenditure on certain types of building**. The types of building are:

- general industrial buildings;
- hotels;
- buildings in enterprise zones (not examinable).

7.2   The allowance is available to:

- trading companies (taxable under Schedule D Case I);
- companies that let qualifying buildings to traders.

7.3   Trading companies can choose whether to segregate expenditure on long life assets in buildings and claim plant and machinery allowances or whether to claim industrial buildings allowances on the expenditure.

General industrial buildings

> **KEY TERM**
>
> **Industrial buildings** include:
>
> (a)   all factories and ancillary premises used in:
>
> > (i)   a manufacturing business;
> > (ii) a trade in which goods and materials are subject to any process;
> > (iii) a trade in which goods or raw materials are stored;
>
> (b)   staff welfare buildings (such as workplace nurseries and canteens, but not directors' restaurants) where the trade is qualifying;
>
> (c)   sports pavilions in any trade;
>
> (d)   buildings in use for a transport undertaking, agricultural contracting, mining or fishing;
>
> (e)   roads operated under highway concessions. The operation of such roads is treated as a trade for capital allowances purposes. The operator is treated as occupying the roads.

7.4 The key term in (a) (ii) above is 'the subjection of goods to any process'.

- The unpacking, repacking and relabelling of goods in a wholesale cash and carry supermarket did not amount to a 'process' but was a mere preliminary to sale (*Bestway Holdings Ltd v Luff 1998*).

- The mechanical processing of cheques and other banking documents was a process but pieces of paper carrying information were not 'goods' and thus the building housing the machinery did not qualify (*Girobank plc v Clarke 1998*).

7.5 Estate roads on industrial estates qualify, provided that the estate buildings are used wholly or mainly for a qualifying purpose.

7.6 Dwelling houses, retail shops, showrooms and offices are not industrial buildings.

7.7 Warehouses used for storage often cause problems in practice. A warehouse used for storage which is merely a transitory and necessary incident of the conduct of the business is not an industrial building. Storage is only a qualifying purpose if it is an end in itself.

7.8 Any building is an industrial building if it is constructed for the welfare of employees of a company whose trade is a qualifying one (that is, the premises in which the trade is carried on are industrial buildings).

7.9 Sports pavilions provided for the welfare of employees qualify as industrial buildings. In this case, it does not matter whether the taxpayer is carrying on a trade in a qualifying building or not. Thus a retailer's sports pavilion would qualify for IBAs.

7.10 Drawing offices which serve an industrial building are regarded as industrial buildings themselves (*CIR v Lambhill Ironworks Ltd 1950*).

Hotels

7.11 Allowances on hotels are given as though they were industrial buildings.

> **KEY TERM**
>
> For a building to qualify as a '**hotel**' for industrial buildings allowance purposes:
>
> (a) it must have at least ten letting bedrooms;
>
> (b) it must have letting bedrooms as the whole or main part of the sleeping accommodation;
>
> (c) it must offer ancillary services including at least:
>
>   (i) breakfast;
>   (ii) evening meals;
>   (iii) the cleaning of rooms; and
>   (iv) the making of beds; and
>
> (d) it must be open for at least four months during the April to October season.

Eligible expenditure

7.12 **Capital allowances are computed on the amount of eligible expenditure incurred on qualifying buildings.** The eligible expenditure is:

- the original cost of a building if built by the trader; or
- the purchase price if the building was acquired from a person trading as a builder.

If the building was acquired other than from a person trading as a builder, the eligible expenditure is the lower of the purchase price and the original cost incurred by the person incurring the construction expenditure.

If a building is sold more than once before being brought into use, the last buyer before the building is brought into use obtains the allowances. If, in such cases, the building was first sold by someone trading as a builder, the eligible expenditure is the lower of the price paid by the first buyer and the price paid by the last buyer.

In all cases where a building is sold before use and artificial arrangements have increased the purchase price, it is reduced to what it would have been without those arrangements.

7.13 **Where part of a building qualifies as an industrial building and part does not, the whole cost qualifies for IBAs, provided that the cost of the non-qualifying part is not more than 25% of the total expenditure.** If the non-qualifying part of the building does cost more than 25% of the total, its cost must be excluded from the capital allowances computation.

7.14 Difficulties arise where non-qualifying buildings (particularly offices and administration blocks) are joined to manufacturing areas. In *Abbott Laboratories Ltd v Carmody 1968* a covered walkway linking manufacturing and administrative areas was not regarded as creating a single building. The administrative area was treated as a separate, non-qualifying building.

7.15 The cost of land is disallowed but expenditure incurred in preparing land for building does qualify. The cost of items which would not be included in a normal commercial lease (such as rental guarantees) also does not qualify.

7.16 Professional fees, for example architects' fees, incurred in connection with the construction of an industrial building qualify. The cost of repairs to industrial buildings also qualifies, provided that the expenditure is not deductible as a trading expense.

8 ALLOWANCES ON INDUSTRIAL BUILDINGS

Writing down allowances

8.1 **A writing down allowance (WDA) is given to the person holding the 'relevant interest'.** Broadly, the relevant interest is the interest of the first acquirer of the industrial building and may be a freehold or leasehold interest.

8.2 Where a long lease (more than 50 years) has been granted on an industrial building, the grant may be treated as a sale so that allowances may be claimed by the lessee rather than the lessor. A claim must be made by the lessor and lessee jointly, within two years of the start of the lease. The election allows allowances to be claimed on industrial buildings where the lessor is not subject to tax (as with local authorities).

8.3 **The WDA is given for a period provided that the industrial building was in use as such on the last day of the accounting period concerned.**

8.4 **If the building was not in use as an industrial building at the end of the relevant period it may have been:**

- **unused** for any purpose; or

- **used for a non-industrial purpose.**

The distinction is important in ascertaining whether WDAs are due to the company. **If any disuse is temporary and previously the building had been in industrial use, WDAs may be claimed in exactly the same way as if the building were in industrial use.** The legislation does not define 'temporary' but in practice, any subsequent qualifying use of the building will usually enable the period of disuse to be regarded as temporary.

Non-industrial use has different consequences. **If this occurs a notional WDA is deducted from the balance of unrelieved expenditure but no WDA may be claimed by the company.**

8.5 **The WDA is 4%** of the eligible expenditure incurred by the company. For expenditure before 6 November 1962, the rate is 2%.

The allowance is calculated on a straight line basis (in contrast to WDAs on plant and machinery which are calculated on the reducing balance), starting when the building is brought into use.

8.6 **The WDA is 4%** (or 2%) × **months/12 if the accounting period is not 12 months long.**

8.7 Buildings always have a **separate computation for each building**. They are never pooled.

Balancing adjustments on sale

The tax life

8.8 **The 'tax life' of an industrial building is 25 years** (hence the 4% straight line WDA) after it is first used, or 50 years if constructed before 6 November 1962. (In such cases, allowances will stop when all the expenditure has been allowed, even if the tax life has not yet ended.) Balancing adjustments apply *only* if a building is sold within its tax life of 25 or 50 years.

8.9 On a sale between connected persons, the parties may jointly elect that the transfer price for IBAs purposes should be the lower of the market value and the residue of unallowed expenditure before the sale. This avoids a balancing charge unless there has been non-industrial use.

Sales without non-industrial use

8.10 **The seller's calculation is quite straightforward providing the building has not been put to non-industrial use at any time during his ownership.** It takes the following form.

	£
Cost	X
Less allowances previously given	(X)
Residue before sale	X
Less proceeds (limited to cost)	(X)
Balancing (charge)/allowance	(X)

8.11 **The buyer obtains annual straight line WDAs for the remainder of the building's tax life** (25 years if constructed after 5 November 1962). This life is calculated to the nearest month. The allowances are granted on the residue after sale which is computed thus.

	£
Residue before sale	X
Plus balancing charge or less balancing allowance	X
Residue after sale	X

This means that **the second owner will write off the lower of his cost or the original cost.**

Question - Calculation of IBAs

Frankie Ltd, which started to trade in 1995 preparing accounts to 31 December, bought an industrial building for £100,000 (excluding land) on 1 October 1996. The company brought the building into use as a factory immediately. On 1 September 2000 it sold the building for £120,000 to Holly Ltd. Holly Ltd's accounting date is 30 September and it brought the building into industrial use immediately. Show the IBAs available to Frankie Ltd and to Holly Ltd.

Answer

	£
Frankie Ltd	
Cost 1.10.96	100,000
Y/e 31.12.96 to y/e 31.12.99 WDA 4 × 4%	(16,000)
Residue before sale	84,000
Y/e 31.12.00 Proceeds (limited to cost)	(100,000)
Balancing charge	(16,000)
Holly Ltd	£
Residue before sale	84,000
Balancing charge	16,000
Residue after sale	100,000

The tax life of the building ends on 1.10.96 + 25 years = 30.9.2021
The date of Holly Ltd's purchase is 1.9.00
The unexpired life is therefore 21 years 1 month

	£
Y/e 30.9.00 WDA £100,000/21.083333	4,743
Next 20 accounting periods at £4,743 a year	94,860
Y/e 30.9.21 (balance)	397
	100,000

Exam focus point

The Inland Revenue allow IBA's equal to the fall in value of a building over the company's use of that building. As a general rule if an industrial building is sold for more than its original cost a balancing charge equal to the allowances given to date will arise. This is because there was no fall in value so no allowances are actually due.

If it is sold for less than original cost we could calculate the fall in value of the building and that would equal the allowances available for this building. If we compare this to the allowances already given, the difference would be the balancing adjustment due on the sale.

In the above question if Frankie Ltd sold the building Holly Ltd for £90,000:

	£
Fall in value (£100,000 – £90,000) = allowances due	10,000
Less: allowances already given to Frankie Ltd	16,000
Balancing adjustment = Balancing charge	6,000

Over the use of the building by Frankie Ltd £16,000 of IBA's were claimed. On the sale of the building the fall in value is calculated as £10,000. Thus Frankie Ltd should only have received £10,000 of allowances not £16,000. So £6,000 is paid back as a balancing charge.

Sales after non-industrial use

8.12 If at the end of a period, an industrial building was in non-industrial use, then the owner will not have been able to claim WDAs, but the building will have been written down by notional WDAs.

8.13 **If, following a period of non-industrial use, an industrial building is sold for more than its original cost, the balancing charge is the actual allowances given. The residue after sale is the original cost minus the notional allowances.**

Question - Non-industrial use

The facts are as in the above question except that on 1 October 1997 Frankie Ltd ceases manufacturing in the building, letting it out as a theatrical rehearsal studio. On 1 June 1999 he recommences manufacturing in the building and, as before, sells it to Holly Ltd for £120,000 on 1 September 2000. Show the IBAs available to Frankie Ltd and to Holly Ltd.

Answer

	£
Frankie Ltd	
Cost 1.10.96	100,000
Y/e 31.12.96 WDA 4%	(4,000)
	96,000
Y/e 31.12.97 and y/e 31.12.98 No WDA since not in industrial use at the ends of the accounting periods, but deduct notional allowances 2 × 4%	(8,000)
	88,000
Y/e 31.12.99 WDA 4%	(4,000)
Residue before sale	84,000
Balancing charge for y/e 31.12.00: real (not notional) allowances £(4,000 + 4,000)	£(8,000)

	£
Holly Ltd	
Residue before sale	84,000
Add: balancing charge	8,000
Residue after sale	92,000

	£
Y/e 30.9.00 WDA £92,000/21.083333	4,364
Next 20 account periods at £4,364 a year	87,280
Y/e 30.9.21 (balance)	356
	92,000

8.14 Sales at less than original cost following a period of non-industrial use are not examinable.

Chapter roundup

- Statutory rules generally exclude specified items from treatment as plant, rather than include specified items as plant.

- There are several cases on the definition of plant. To help you to absorb them, try to see the function/setting theme running through them.

- With capital allowances computations, the main thing is to get the layout right. Having done that, you will find that the figures tend to drop into place.

- Most expenditure on plant and machinery qualifies for a WDA at 25% every 12 months.

- First year allowances (FYA) may be available for certain expenditure.

- Short life asset elections can bring forward the allowances due on an asset.

- The computations for industrial buildings are a little more complicated than those for plant and machinery, but there is less case law to learn.

- Basically allowances equal to the fall in value of the building whilst it was being used industrially are available to the company.

Quick quiz

1   For what periods are capital allowances calculated? (see para 1.3)

2   What are the main cases on the meaning of 'plant'? (2.12 - 2.27)

3   What writing down allowances are given in an accounting period of less than 12 months? (3.5)

4   When do balancing allowances arise? (3.19)

5   Which assets cannot be treated as short-life assets? (4.5)

6   What is the formula for restricting allowable lease payments for expensive cars? (5.3)

7   Which buildings cannot be industrial buildings? (7.6)

8   Are drawing offices industrial buildings? (7.10)

9   What are the conditions for a hotel to qualify for allowances? (7.11 Key term)

10   How is the balancing adjustment computed on a sale where there been non-industrial use? (8.13)

Now try the questions below from the Exam Question Bank

Number	Level	Marks	Time
3	Exam	10	20 mins
4	Exam	16	29 mins

Chapter 4

LOAN RELATIONSHIPS. SCHEDULE D CASE III. SCHEDULE A

Topic list	Syllabus reference
1 Loan relationships (borrowing and lending)	1c(v)
2 Schedule D Case III income	1c(v)
3 Schedule A income	1c(iv)

Introduction

When a company borrows or lends money it has a loan relationship. In this chapter we see how loan relationships affect a company's CT liability. We also see how to compute various other types of investment income that we must include in calculating a company's profits chargeable to corporation tax.

Study guide

Loan relationships. Schedule D Case III. Schedule A

- Explain how profits from loan relationships and interest received are assessed under Schedule D Case III

- Compute the Schedule A profit

- Explain the treatment of a premium received for the grant of a short lease

- Explain how relief for a Schedule A loss is given

Exam guide

These are part of section 1c and so are key topics. One or more of these topics will appear in Question 1 in Section A and may also be part of Question 7 in Section B.

1   LOAN RELATIONSHIPS (BORROWING AND LENDING)

1.1   **If a company borrows or lends money, including issuing or investing in debentures or buying gilts, it has a loan relationship. This can be a creditor relationship** (where the company lends or invests money) **or a debtor relationship** (where the company borrows money or issues securities).

Treatment of trading loan relationships

1.2   If the company is a party to a **loan relationship for trade purposes, any debits – ie interest paid or other debt costs – charged through its accounts are allowed as a trading expense** and are therefore deductible in computing Schedule D Case I profits.

1.3 Similarly **if any credits – ie interest income or other debt returns – arise on a trading loan these are treated as a trading receipt and are taxable under Schedule D Case I.** This is not likely to arise unless the trade is one of money lending.

Treatment of non-trading loan relationships

1.4 **If a loan relationship is not one to which the company is a party for trade purposes any debits or credits must be pooled. A net credit on the pool is chargeable as income under Schedule D Case III. A net deficit on the pool may be relieved in certain ways, but this is not in your syllabus.**

Accounting methods

1.5 The following bases are acceptable for recognising debits or credits.

   (a) the accruals basis; or
   (b) the mark to market basis.

The mark to market basis places a fair value on the loan relationship for each accounting period and determines the credit or debit on the change in the value.

If neither the accruals or mark to market method is used in the accounts, the accruals basis must be used for tax purposes. In this study text, we assume that the accruals basis applies. The mark to market basis is only likely to be used by companies in the financial sector such as banks.

Incidental costs of loan finance

1.6 Under the loan relationship rules expenses (debits) are allowed if incurred directly:

   (a) in bringing a loan relationship into existence;

   (b) entering into or giving effect to any related transactions;

   (c) making payment under a loan relationship or related transactions; or

   (d) taking steps to ensure the receipt of payments under the loan relationship or related transaction.

A related transaction means any disposal or acquisition (in whole or in part) of rights or liabilities under the relationship, including any arising from a security issue in relation to the money debt in question .

The above categories of incidental costs are also allowable even if the company does not enter into the loan relationship (ie abortive costs). Cost directly incurred in varying the terms of a loan relationship are also allowed.

Other matters

1.7 It is not only the interest costs of borrowing that are allowable or taxable. The capital costs are treated similarly. Thus if a company issues a loan at a discount and repays it eventually at par, the capital cost is allowed either on redemption (if the accruals basis is adopted) or period by period (if it is accounted for on a mark to market basis).

1.8 Relief for pre-trading expenditure extends to expenses incurred on trading loan relationships in accounting periods ending within seven years of the company starting to trade. An expense that would have been a trading debit if it was incurred after the trade had commenced, is treated as a trading debit of the first trading period. An election has to be made within two years of the end of the first trading period.

1.9 Short interest or interest to a UK bank is payable gross while yearly interest is payable net of 20% tax. The tax withheld must be dealt with under the CT61 quarterly accounting system (see later in this text).

1.10 Interest charged on underpaid tax is allowable and interest received on overpaid tax is assessable under the loan relationship rules.

2 SCHEDULE D CASE III

2.1 Interest received on non-trading loan relationships is taxed under Schedule D Case III (see above).

2.2 UK companies receive interest gross from banks (including the European Investment bank) and **building societies**. It is taxable on the company under Schedule D Case III.

2.3 **Interest on most gilt edged securities** is received gross but in certain limited circumstances it is received net of tax at 20%. In both cases, the gross amount is taxable under Schedule D Case III.

2.4 Interest received from another UK company (such as debenture or loan stock interest) is received net of tax at 20%. Income tax suffered at source is dealt with through the quarterly accounting system (see later in this text). The gross equivalent is taxed under Schedule D Case III.

3 SCHEDULE A INCOME

3.1 **Income from land and buildings in the UK, including caravans and houseboats which are not moved, is taxed under Schedule A.**

3.2 **A company with rental income is treated as running a Schedule A business. All the rents and expenses for all properties are pooled, to give a single profit or loss. Profits and losses are computed in the same way as trading profits are computed for Schedule D Case I purposes,** on an accruals basis (see Chapter 2). The Schedule D Case I rules on post-cessation receipts and expenses apply.

3.3 **Interest paid on a loan taken out to buy a property is dealt with under the loan relationship rules (see above).** It is not deducted in computing Schedule A income.

3.4 **Capital allowances are given on plant and machinery used in the Schedule A business and on industrial buildings, in the same way as they are given for a Schedule D Case I business.** Capital allowances are not normally available on plant or machinery used in a dwelling (although in certain cases, they may exceptionally be available on radiators and boilers). A company that lets property furnished cannot claim capital allowances on the furniture. However, it can choose instead between the renewals basis and the 10% wear and tear allowance.

- Under the *renewals* basis, there is no deduction for the cost of the first furniture provided, but the cost of replacement furniture is treated as a revenue expense. However, the part of the cost attributable to improvement, as opposed to simple replacement, is not deductible.

BPP PUBLISHING

- Under the *10% wear and tear* basis, the actual cost of furniture is ignored. Instead, an annual deduction is given of 10% of rents. The rents are first reduced by amounts which are paid by the landlord but are normally a tenant's burden. These amounts include any water rates and council tax paid by the landlord.

3.5 If plant and machinery is used partly in a dwelling house and partly for other purposes a just and reasonable apportionment of the expenditure can be made.

3.6 Rent for furniture supplied with premises is taxed as part of the rent for the premises, unless there is a separate trade of renting furniture.

Loss relief

3.7 Schedule A losses are first set off against non-Schedule A income and gains of the company for the current period and any excess is:

(a) carried forward as a Schedule A loss of the following accounting period provided that the Schedule A business has not ceased; or

(b) available for surrender as group relief (see later in this text).

Premiums on leases

3.8 **When a premium or similar consideration is received on the grant** (that is, by a landlord to a tenant) **of a short lease (50 years or less), part of the premium is treated as rent received in the year of grant**. A lease is considered to end on the date when it is most likely to terminate.

The premium taxed under Schedule A is the whole premium, less 2% of the premium for each complete year of the lease, except the first year.

This rule does not apply on the *assignment* of a lease (one tenant selling his entire interest in the property to another).

Premiums paid

3.9 **Where a trading company (taxed under Schedule D Case I) pays a premium for a lease it may deduct an amount from his taxable profits in each year of the lease. The amount deductible is the figure treated as rent received by the landlord divided by the number of years of the lease.** For example, suppose that B Ltd, pays A Ltd a premium of £30,000 for a ten year lease. A Ltd is treated as receiving £30,000 – (£30,000 × (10 – 1) × 2%) = £24,600. B Ltd can therefore deduct £24,600/10 = £2,460 in each of the ten years. The company starts with the accounting period in which the lease starts and apportions the relief to the nearest month.

Premiums for granting subleases

3.10 **A tenant may decide to sublet property and to charge a premium on the grant of a lease to the subtenant. This premium is treated as rent received in the normal way** (because this is a grant and not an assignment, the original tenant retaining an interest in the property). **Where the tenant originally paid a premium for his own head lease, this deemed rent is reduced by:**

$$\text{Rent part of premium for head lease} \times \frac{\text{duration of sub} - \text{lease}}{\text{duration of head lease}}$$

If the relief exceeds the part of the premium for the sub-lease treated as rent (including cases where there is a sub-lease with no premium), the balance of the relief is treated as rent payable by the head tenant, spread evenly over the period of the sub-lease. This rent payable is an expense, reducing the overall Schedule A profit.

Question: Taxable premium received

C Ltd granted a lease to D Ltd on 1 March 1990 for a period of 40 years. D Ltd paid a premium of £16,000. On 1 June 2000 D Ltd granted a sublease to E Ltd for a period of ten years. E Ltd paid a premium of £30,000. Calculate the amount treated as rent out of the premium received by D Ltd.

Answer

	£
Premium received by D Ltd	30,000
Less £30,000 × 2% × (10-1)	(5,400)
	24,600
Less allowance for premium paid	
(£16,000 - (£16,000 × 39 × 2%)) × 10/40	(880)
Premium treated as rent	23,720

Chapter roundup

* Interest arising on a non-trading loan relationship is taxable, normally on an accruals basis, under Schedule D Case III

* Income from land is taxed under Schedule A. Schedule A profits are computed on an accruals basis in the same way as Schedule D Case I profits

Quick quiz

1   How is tax relief obtained for interest paid on a non-trading loan relationship (see para 1.4)

2   What interest income is received gross by companies? (2.2)

3   How are Schedule A profits computed? (3.2)

4   What relief is given when a lessee who paid a premium grants a sublease for a premium? (3.10)

Now try the question below from the Exam Question Bank

Number	Level	Marks	Time
5	Exam	11	20 mins

BPP PUBLISHING

Chapter 5

CHARGEABLE GAINS

Topic list		Syllabus reference
1	Taxing a company's chargeable gains	1e(i)
2	Chargeable persons, disposals and assets	1e(i)
3	Computing a gain or loss	1e(ii)
4	The indexation allowance	1e(ii)
5	Share matching rules for companies	1e(ii)
6	The FA 1985 pool	1e(ii)
7	Alterations of share capital	1e(ii)
8	Rollover relief	1e(iii)

Introduction

Companies can have both income and capital gains. If, for example, a company buys a factory for £10,000, uses the factory for 20 years and then sells it for £200,000, it will have a capital gain. In this chapter we see when a chargeable gain will arise and how to compute a chargeable gain.

We then look at shares and securities. Shares and securities need a special treatment because a company may hold several shares or securities in the same company, bought at different times for different prices but otherwise identical.

Finally, we consider how a company may defer a gain when it sells a business asset.

Study guide

Chargeable gains

- Prepare a basic capital gains computation
- Explain the treatment of capital losses
- State the allowable deductions
- Calculate the indexation allowance
- Explain the identification rules for disposals of shares and securities
- Apply the pooling provisions for shares and securities
- Explain the treatment following a bonus issue, rights issue, or takeover
- Explain and apply rollover relief

Exam guide

Although section 1e is not a key topic, the examiner has indicated that it may form part of Question 1 in Section A for a maximum of 10 marks.

Question 4 (15 marks) in Section B will be on capital gains (either for an incorporated or unincorporated business).

1 TAXING A COMPANY'S CHARGEABLE GAINS

1.1 Since its introduction by the Finance Act 1965, the taxation of chargeable gains has undergone significant amendment. As some knowledge of the history of taxing gains may help you understand the present rules, we summarise the main changes below:

1965	The taxation of chargeable gains was introduced.
1982	An indexation allowance was introduced to give some relief in respect of gains due to inflation.
1985	There were major amendments to the calculation of the indexation allowance.
1988	The base date for taxing gains was generally moved from 1965 to 1982, the tax charge being confined to gains accruing from 31 March 1982. You will not have to deal with gains or losses on assets acquired before 31 March 1982.
1992	Legislation concerning the taxation of gains was consolidated into the Taxation of Chargeable Gains Act 1992 (TCGA 1992).
1993	The use of the indexation allowance to create or increase a loss ended.

Losses

1.2 A company's net chargeable gains (gains less losses) for an accounting period are included within the computation of profits chargeable to corporation tax. A company, therefore, pays CT on its net chargeable gains. Any overall allowable loss in an accounting period is carried forward to set against the first chargeable gains arising in future accounting periods. Capital losses cannot be set against income.

Timing of disposals

1.3 From a tax planning point of view it is important to realise that a badly timed disposal (near the end of the accounting period) can raise the 'profits' of a company into a higher rate band of CT. In addition, from a cash flow point of view, by delaying a disposal into the next accounting period the payment date for CT on the gain is delayed for twelve months.

2 CHARGEABLE PERSONS, DISPOSALS AND ASSETS

Exam focus point

For a chargeable gain to arise there must be:

- a chargeable person; and
- a chargeable disposal; and
- a chargeable asset

otherwise no charge to tax occurs.

Chargeable persons

2.1 A company is a chargeable person.

Chargeable disposals

2.2 The following are chargeable disposals.

- Sales of assets or parts of assets
- Gifts of assets or parts of assets
- Receipts of capital sums following the surrender of rights to assets
- The loss or destruction of assets
- The appropriation of assets as trading stock

2.3 **A chargeable disposal occurs on the date of the contract** (where there is one, whether written or oral), or the date of a conditional contract becoming unconditional. This may differ from the date of transfer of the asset. However, when a capital sum is received on a surrender of rights or the loss or destruction of an asset, the disposal takes place on the day the sum is received.

Where a disposal involves an acquisition by someone else, the date of acquisition is the same as the date of disposal.

Transfers to and from trading stock

2.4 When a company acquires an asset other than as trading stock and then uses it as trading stock, the appropriation to trading stock normally leads to an immediate chargeable gain or allowable loss, based on the asset's market value at the date of appropriation. The asset's cost for Schedule D Case I purposes is that market value.

2.5 Alternatively, the company can elect to have no chargeable gain or allowable loss: if it does so, the cost for Schedule D Case I purposes is reduced by the gain or increased by the loss. The time limit for the election is two years after the end of the accounting period of appropriation.

2.6 When an asset which is trading stock is appropriated to other purposes, the company is treated for Schedule D Case I purposes as selling it for its market value, and for those other purposes as having bought it at the time of the appropriation for the same value.

Chargeable assets

2.7 **All forms of property, wherever in the world they are situated, are chargeable assets unless they are specifically designated as exempt.**

2.8 The following are exempt assets (thus gains are not taxable and losses on their disposal are not in general allowable losses).

- Motor vehicles suitable for private use
- Certain chattels (eg racehorses)
- Debts (except debts on a security)

3 COMPUTING A GAIN OR LOSS

3.1 **A chargeable gain (or an allowable loss) is generally calculated as follows.**

	£
Disposal consideration (or market value)	45,000
Less incidental costs of disposal	(400)
Net proceeds	44,600
Less allowable costs	(21,000)
Unindexed gain	23,600
Less indexation allowance	(8,500)
Indexed gain	15,100

3.2 **Incidental costs of disposal** may include:

- valuation fees (but not the cost of an appeal against the Revenue's valuation);
- estate agency fees;
- advertising costs;
- legal costs.

These costs should be deducted separately from any other allowable costs (because they do not qualify for any indexation allowance if it was available on that disposal).

3.3 **Allowable costs** include:

- the original cost of acquisition;
- incidental costs of acquisition;
- capital expenditure incurred in enhancing the asset.

Incidental costs of acquisition may include the types of cost listed above as incidental costs of disposal, but acquisition costs do qualify for indexation allowance (from the month of acquisition) if it is available on the disposal.

3.4 **Enhancement expenditure** is capital expenditure which enhances the value of the asset and is reflected in the state or nature of the asset at the time of disposal, or expenditure incurred in establishing, preserving or defending title to, or a right over, the asset. Excluded from this category are:

- costs of repairs and maintenance;
- costs of insurance;
- any expenditure deductible for Schedule D Case I purposes;
- any expenditure met by public funds (for example council grants).

Enhancement expenditure may qualify for indexation allowance from the month in which it becomes due and payable.

The consideration for a disposal

3.5 **Usually the disposal consideration is the proceeds of sale of the asset, but a disposal is deemed to take place at market value:**

(a) where the disposal is **not a bargain at arm's length**;
(b) where the disposal is made for a **consideration which cannot be valued**;
(c) where the disposal is by way of a **gift**.

Valuing assets

3.6 Quoted shares and securities are valued using prices in The Stock Exchange Daily Official List, taking the lower of:

- lower quoted price + 0.25 × (higher quoted price - lower quoted price);

- the average of the highest and lowest marked bargains (ignoring bargains marked at special prices).

Question: Calculation of CGT value

Shares in A plc are quoted at 100-110p. The highest and lowest marked bargains were 99p and 110p. What would be the market value for CGT purposes?

Answer

The value will be the lower of:

(a) $100 + 0.25 \times (110 - 100) = 102.5$;

(b) $\dfrac{110 + 99}{2} = 104.5$.

The market value for CGT purposes will therefore be 102.5p per share.

3.7 Unquoted shares are harder to value than quoted shares. The Revenue have a special office, the Shares Valuation Division, to deal with the valuation of unquoted shares.

3.8 **Where market value is used in a chargeable gains computation, the value to be used is the price which the assets in question might reasonably be expected to fetch on a sale in the open market.**

4 THE INDEXATION ALLOWANCE

4.1 The purpose of having an indexation allowance is to remove the inflationary element of a gain from taxation.

4.2 **Companies are entitled to an indexation allowance from the date of acquisition until the date of disposal of an asset.**

4.3 EXAMPLE: INDEXATION ALLOWANCE

J Ltd bought a painting on 2 January 1987 and sold it on 19 November 2000.

Indexation allowance is available from January 1987 until November 2000.

Exam formula

The indexation factor is:

$$\frac{\text{RPI for month of disposal} - \text{RPI for month of acquisition}}{\text{RPI for month of acquisition}}$$

The calculation is expressed as a decimal and is rounded to three decimal places.

The indexation factor is multiplied by the cost of the asset to calculate the indexation allowance. If the RPI has fallen, the indexation allowance is zero: it is not negative.

RPI values are given in the Rates and Allowances Tables in this text, including estimated values for January 2000 onwards.

Question: The indexation allowance

An asset is acquired by a company on 15 February 1983 (RPI = 83.0) at a cost of £5,000. Enhancement expenditure of £2,000 is incurred on 10 April 1984 (RPI = 88.6). The asset is sold for £20,500 on 20 December 2000 (RPI 173.0). Incidental costs of sale are £500. Calculate the chargeable gain arising.

Answer

The indexation allowance is available until December 2000 and is computed as follows.

	£
$\dfrac{173.0 - 83.0}{83.0} = 1.084 \times £5,000$	5,420
$\dfrac{173.0 - 88.6}{88.6} = 0.953 \times £2,000$	1,906
	7,326

The computation of the chargeable gain is as follows.

	£
Proceeds	20,500
Less incidental costs of sale	(500)
Net proceeds	20,000
Less allowable costs £(5,000 + 2,000)	(7,000)
Unindexed gain	13,000
Less indexation allowance (see above)	(7,326)
Chargeable gain	5,674

Indexation and losses

4.4 **The indexation allowance cannot create or increase an allowable loss.** If there is a gain before the indexation allowance, the allowance can reduce that gain to zero, but no further. If there is a loss before the indexation allowance, there is no indexation allowance.

5 SHARE MATCHING RULES FOR COMPANIES

5.1 Quoted and unquoted shares and securities and units in a unit trust present special problems when attempting to compute gains or losses on disposal. For instance, suppose that a company buys some quoted shares in X plc as follows.

Date	Number of shares	Cost
		£
5 May 1983	100	150
17 January 1985	100	375
10 June 2000	50	300

On 15 June 2000, it sells 120 of its shares for £1,450. To determine its chargeable gain, we need to be able to work out which shares were actually sold.

5.2 We therefore need **matching rules**. These **allow us to decide which shares have been sold and so work out what the allowable cost on disposal should be.**

5.3 **At any one time, we will only be concerned with shares or securities of the same class in the same company.** If a company owns both ordinary shares and preference shares in X plc, we will deal with the two classes of share entirely separately, because they are distinguishable.

5.4 In what follows, we will use 'shares' to refer to both shares and securities.

5.5 **For companies the matching of shares** sold is in the following order.

(a) Shares acquired on the **same day**
(b) Shares acquired in the **previous nine days**, taking earlier acquisitions first
(c) Shares from the **FA 1985 pool**

If a company owns 2% or more of another company, disposals are matched (after same day acquisitions) with shares acquired within one month before or after the disposal (for Stock Exchange transactions) or six months (in other cases) before being matched with shares from the FA 1985 pool.

5.6 Where shares are disposed of within nine days of acquisition, **no indexation allowance is available** even if the acquisition and the disposal fall in different months. Acquisitions matched with disposals under the nine day rule never enter the FA 1985 pool.

5.7 The composition of the FA 1985 pool is explained below.

> ### Exam focus point
>
> Learn the 'matching rules' because a crucial first step to getting a shares question right is to correctly match the shares sold to the original shares purchased.

6 THE FA 1985 POOL

6.1 For companies we treat shares as a 'pool' which grows as new shares are acquired and shrinks as they are sold. **The FA 1985 pool** (so called because it was introduced by rules in the Finance Act 1985) **comprises the following shares of the same class in the same company.**

- **Shares held by a company on 1 April 1985 and acquired by that company on or after 1 April 1982.**

- **Shares acquired by that company on or after 1 April 1985.**

6.2 In making computations which use the FA 1985 pool, we must keep track of:

(a) the **number** of shares;
(b) the **cost** of the shares ignoring indexation;
(b) the **indexed cost** of the shares.

6.3 Each FA 1985 **pool is started by aggregating the cost and number of shares acquired between 1 April 1982 and 1 April 1985** inclusive. In order to calculate the indexed cost of these shares, an indexation allowance, computed from the relevant date of acquisition of the shares to April 1985, is added to the cost.

6.4 EXAMPLE: THE FA 1985 POOL

Oliver Ltd bought 1,000 shares in Judith plc for £2,750 in August 1984 and another 1,000 for £3,250 in December 1984. The FA 1985 pool at 1 April 1985 is as follows.

6.5 SOLUTION

	No of shares	Cost £	Indexed cost £
August 1984 (a)	1,000	2,750	2,750
December 1984 (b)	1,000	3,250	3,250
	2,000	6,000	6,000
Indexation allowance			
$\dfrac{94.8 - 89.9}{89.9} = 0.055 \times £2,750$			151
$\dfrac{94.8 - 90.9}{90.9} = 0.043 \times £3,250$			140
Indexed cost of the pool at 1 April 1985			6,291

6.6 Disposals and acquisitions of shares which affect the indexed value of the FA 1985 pool are termed 'operative events'. **Prior to reflecting each such operative event within the FA 1985 share pool, a further indexation allowance (described as an indexed rise) must be computed up to the date of the operative event concerned from the date of the last such operative event** (or from the later of the first acquisition and April 1985 if the operative event in question is the first one).

6.7 **Indexation calculations within the FA 1985 pool** (after its April 1985 value has been calculated) **are not rounded to three decimal places.** This is because rounding errors would accumulate and have a serious effect after several operative events.

If there are several operative events between 1 April 1985 and the date of a disposal, the indexation procedure described above will have to be performed several times over.

Question: Value of FA 1985 pool

Following on from the above example, assume that Oliver Ltd acquired 2,000 more shares on 10 July 1986 at a cost of £4,000. Recalculate the value of the FA 1985 pool on 10 July 1986 following the acquisition.

Answer

	No of shares	Cost £	Indexed cost £
Value at 1.4.85	2,000	6,000	6,291
Indexed rise			
$\dfrac{97.5 - 94.8}{94.8} \times £6,291$			179
	2,000	6,000	6,470
Acquisition	2,000	4,000	4,000
Value at 10.7.86	4,000	10,000	10,470

6.8 **In the case of a disposal, following the calculation of the indexed rise to the date of disposal, the cost and the indexed cost attributable to the shares disposed of are deducted from the amounts within the FA 1985 pool. The proportions of the cost and indexed cost to take out of the pool should be computed by using the proportion of cost that the shares disposed of bear to the total number of share held.**

6.9 The indexation allowance is the indexed cost taken out of the pool minus the cost taken out. As usual, the indexation allowance cannot create or increase a loss.

Question: the FA 1985 pool

Continuing the above exercise, suppose that Oliver Ltd sold 3,000 shares on 10 July 2000 for £17,000. Compute the gain, and the value of the FA 1985 pool following the disposal.

Answer

	No of shares	Cost £	Indexed cost £
Value at 10.7.86	4,000	10,000	10,470
Indexed rise			
$\dfrac{170.5 - 97.5}{97.5} \times £10,470$			7,839
	4,000	10,000	18,309
Disposal	(3,000)		
Cost and indexed cost $\dfrac{3,000}{4,000} \times £10,000$ and £18,309		(7,500)	(13,732)
Value at 10.7.00	1,000	2,500	4,577

The gain is computed as follows:

	£
Proceeds	17,000
Less cost	(7,500)
	9,500
Less indexation allowance £(13,732 – 7,500)	(6,232)
Chargeable gain	3,268

6.10 When shares are transferred on a no gain no/loss basis between group companies, thereby creating or adding to an FA 1985 pool belonging to the acquiring company, the usual rules on no gain/no loss disposals and later disposals set out in Chapter 7 do not apply. The disposing company still has no gain and no loss, but the acquiring company takes the shares into their FA 1985 pool at original cost to the disposing company plus (in the indexed cost column) indexation up to the date of transfer.

Exam focus point

The examiner has said that a question will not be set which requires a detailed calculation of the 1985 pool.

7   ALTERATIONS OF SHARE CAPITAL

Bonus issues (scrip issues)

7.1 **When a company issues bonus shares all that happens is that the size of the original holding is increased. Since bonus shares are issued at no cost there is no need to adjust the original cost. Instead the numbers purchased at particular times are increased by the bonus.**

Rights issues

7.2 **The difference between a bonus issue and a rights issue is that in a rights issue the new shares are paid for and this results in an adjustment to the original cost. For the purposes of calculating the indexation allowance, expenditure on a rights issue is taken as being incurred on the date of the issue and not on the date of acquisition of the original holding.**

As with bonus issues, rights shares derived from the 1985 pool shares go into that pool rather than being treated as a new acquisition. This would be important if shares are sold within nine days of the rights issue as the usual '9 day' rule would not apply to the rights issue shares.

7.3 In an **open offer** shareholders have a right to subscribe for a minimum number of shares based on their existing holdings and may buy additional shares. Subscriptions up to the minimum entitlement are treated as a rights issue. Additional subscriptions are treated as new purchases of shares.

Question: Rights issues

J Ltd had the following transactions in the shares of T plc.

July 1985	Purchased 1,000 shares for £3,000
May 1986	Took up one for four rights issue at £4.20 per share
October 2000	Sold 1,250 shares for £10,000

Compute the chargeable gain or allowable loss arising on the sale in October 2000.

Answer

The FA 1985 pool

	No of shares	Cost £	Indexed cost £
July 1985	1,000	3,000	3,000
Indexed rise to May 1986			
$\dfrac{97.8 - 95.2}{95.2} \times £3,000$			82
May 1986 one for four rights	250	1,050	1,050
	1,250	4,050	4,132
Indexed rise to October 2000			
$\dfrac{172.0 - 97.8}{97.8} \times £4,132$			3,135
	1,250	4,050	7,267
Disposal in October 2000	(1,250)	(4,050)	(7,267)

The chargeable gain

	£
Proceeds	10,000
Less cost	(4,050)
	5,950
Less indexation allowance £(7,267 – 4,050)	(3,217)
Chargeable gain	2,733

Reorganisations

7.4 **A reorganisation takes place where new shares or a mixture of new shares and debentures are issued in exchange for the original shareholdings. The new shares take the place of the old shares.** The problem is how to apportion the original cost between the different types of capital issued on the reorganisation.

7.5 If the new shares and securities are quoted, then the cost is apportioned by reference to the market values of the new types of capital on the first day of quotation after the reorganisation. No amendment to the indexation process occurs unless further consideration is contributed, when indexation will be computed as for rights issues: indexation on new consideration will run from the time when it is contributed.

Question: Reorganisations

An original quoted shareholding is made up of 3,000 ordinary shares purchased in 1985 for £13,250.

In 2000 there is a reorganisation whereby each ordinary share is exchanged for two 'A' ordinary shares (quoted at £2 each) and one preference share (quoted at £1 each). Show how the original costs will be apportioned.

Answer

The new holding will be as follows.

	Value
	£
6,000 new 'A' ordinary shares at £2	12,000
3,000 preference shares at £1	3,000
	15,000

The costs will be apportioned between the new 'A' ordinary shares and the preference shares in the ratio of 12,000:3,000 = 4:1 as follows.

FA 1985 pools	£
6,000 new 'A' ordinary shares, deemed acquired in 1985 ($^4/_5$ x £13,250)	10,600
3,000 preference shares, deemed acquired in 1985 ($^1/_5$ x £13,250)	2,650
	13,250

7.6 Where a reorganisation takes place and the new shares and securities are unquoted, the cost of the original holding is apportioned using the values of the new shares and securities when they come to be disposed of. Further consideration is treated in the same way as for quoted shares.

7.7 For both quoted and unquoted shares and securities, any incidental costs (such as professional fees) are treated as additional consideration for the new shares and securities.

Takeovers

7.8 **A chargeable gain does not arise on a 'paper for paper' takeover,** that is, one where shares or securities in the old company are exchanged for shares or securities in the new company which has taken over the old company. **The cost of the original holding is passed on to the new holding** which takes the place of the original holding. The same rules apply as for reorganisations (above) in relation to the apportionment of the original base costs.

The takeover rules apply where the company issuing the new shares ends up with more than 25% of the ordinary share capital of the old company or the majority of the voting power in the old company, or the company issuing the new shares makes a general offer to shareholders in the other company which is initially made subject to a condition which, if satisfied, would give the first company control of the second company.

Question: Takeovers

Le Bon Ltd held 20,000 £1 shares out of a total number of issued shares of one million bought for £2 each in Duran plc. In 2000 the board of Duran plc agreed to a takeover bid by Spandau plc under which shareholders in Duran received three ordinary Spandau shares plus one preference share for every four shares held in Duran plc. Immediately following the takeover, the ordinary shares in Spandau plc were quoted at £5 each and the preferences shares at 90p. Show the unindexed base costs of the ordinary shares and the preference shares.

Answer

The total value due to Le Bon Ltd on the takeover is as follows.

		£
Ordinary	20,000 × 3/4 × £5	75,000
Preference	20,000 × 1/4 × 90p	4,500
		79,500

The base costs are therefore:

	£
Ordinary shares: 75,000/79,500 × 20,000 × £2	37,736
Preference shares: 4,500/79,500 × 20,000 × £2	2,264
	40,000

8 ROLLOVER RELIEF

8.1 **A gain may be 'rolled over' (deferred) where it arises on the disposal of a business asset which is replaced.** This is **rollover relief**. A claim cannot specify that only part of a gain is to be rolled over.

8.2 All the following conditions must be met.

- **The old asset sold and the new asset bought are both used only in the trade** or trades carried on **by the company claiming rollover relief.** Where part of a building is in non-trade use for all or a substantial part of the period of ownership, the building (and the land on which it stands) can be treated as two separate assets, the trade part (qualifying) and the non-trade part (non-qualifying). This split cannot be made for other assets.

- **The old asset and the new asset both fall within one** (but not necessarily the same one) **of the following classes.**

  (i)   Land and buildings (including parts of buildings) occupied as well as used only for the purpose of the trade

  (ii) Fixed (that is, immovable) plant and machinery

  (iii) Ships, aircraft and hovercraft

  (iv) Goodwill

  (v)   Satellites, space stations and spacecraft

  (vi) Milk quotas, potato quotas and ewe and suckler cow premium quotas

  (vii) Fish quota

- **Reinvestment of the proceeds of the old asset takes place in a period beginning one year before and ending three years after the date of the disposal.**

- **The new asset is brought into use in the trade on its acquisition** (not necessarily immediately, but not after any significant and unnecessary delay).

8.3 The new asset can be for use in a different trade from the old asset.

8.4 A rollover claim is not allowed when a company buys premises, sells part of the premises at a profit and then claims to roll over the gain into the part retained (*Watton v Tippet 1997*). However, a rollover claim is allowed (by concession) when the proceeds of the old asset are spent on improving a qualifying asset which the company already owns. The improved asset must already be in use for a trade, or be brought into trade use immediately the improvement work is finished.

8.5 **Deferral is obtained by deducting the chargeable gain from the cost of the new asset. For full relief, the whole of the consideration for the disposal must be reinvested. Where only part is reinvested, a part of the gain equal to the lower of the full gain and the amount not reinvested will be liable to tax immediately.**

8.6 The new asset will have a base 'cost' for chargeable gains purposes, of its purchase price less the gain rolled over into its acquisition.

8.7 If a company expects to buy new assets, it can make a provisional rollover claim on its tax return which includes the gain on the old asset. The gain is reduced accordingly. If new assets are not actually acquired, the Revenue collect the tax saved by the provisional claim.

Question: Rollover relief

A freehold factory was purchased by X Ltd in August 1995. It was sold in December 2000 for £70,000, giving rise to an indexed gain of £17,950. A replacement factory was purchased in June 2001 for £60,000. Compute the base cost of the replacement factory, taking into account any possible rollover gain from the disposal in December 2000.

Answer

	£
Total gain	17,950
Less: amount not reinvested, immediately chargeable £(70,000 – 60,000)	(10,000)
Rollover gain	7,950
Cost of new factory	60,000
Less rolled over gain	(7,950)
Base cost of new factory	52,050

8.8 Where an old asset has not been used in the trade for a fraction of its period of ownership, the amount of the gain that can be rolled over is reduced by the same fraction. If the proceeds are not fully reinvested the restriction on rollover by the amount not reinvested is also calculated by considering only the proportion of proceeds relating to the part of the asset used in the trade or the proportion relating to the period of trade use.

Question: Assets with non-business use

Y Ltd bought a factory in July 1990 for £100,000. It sold the factory in November 2000 for £215,000. The company let out a quarter of the factory on commercial terms for the entire period of ownership. Y Ltd bought a replacement factory in August 2000 for £165,000, which was used wholly for its trade.

Calculate the chargeable gain in the first factory and the base cost of the second factory.

Answer

Gain on 1st factory

	Business (75%) £	Non business (25%) £
Proceeds	161,250	53,750
Less: cost	(75,000)	(25,000)
	86,250	28,750
Less: indexation allowance		
$\dfrac{172.5-126.8}{126.8}$ (= 0.360) × £75,000/25,000	(27,000)	(9,000)
Indexed gain	59,250	19,750

The gain of £19,750 is chargeable.

Base cost of 2nd factory

All of business proceeds are reinvested so full relief is available.

	£
Cost	165,000
Less: rolled over gain	(59,250)
Base cost	105,750

8.9 **Where the replacement asset is a depreciating asset, the gain is not rolled over by reducing the cost of the replacement asset. Rather it is deferred until it crystallises on the earliest of:**

- the disposal of the replacement asset;
- ten years after the acquisition of the replacement asset;
- the date the replacement asset ceases to be used in the trade.

KEY TERM

An asset is a **depreciating asset** if it is, or within the next ten years will become, a wasting asset. Thus, any asset with an expected life of 60 years or less is covered by this definition. Plant and machinery (including ships, aircraft, hovercraft, satellites, space stations and spacecraft) is always treated as depreciating unless it becomes part of a building: in that case, it will only be depreciating if the building is held on a lease with 60 years or less to run.

Question: Deferred gain on investment into depreciating asset

N Ltd bought a factory for use in its business in June 1999 for £125,000. The factory was sold it for £140,000 on 1 August 2000. On 10 July 2000, N Ltd bought some fixed plant and machinery for use in its business, costing £150,000. The company sold the plant and machinery for £167,000 on 19 November 2001. Show N Ltd's chargeable gains position.

Answer

Gain deferred

	£
Proceeds of shop	140,000
Less cost	(125,000)
Gain	15,000
Less indexation $\frac{171.0 - 165.6}{165.6} = 0.033 \times £125,000$	(4,125)
	10,875

This gain is deferred in relation to the purchase of the plant and machinery. Sale of plant and machinery

	£
Proceeds	167,000
Less cost	(150,000)
Gain	17,000
Less indexation $\frac{178.5 - 170.5}{170.5} = 0.047 \times £150,000$	(7,050)
	9,950
Total gain chargeable on sale (gain on plant and machinery plus deferred gain) £(9,950 + 10,875)	£20,825

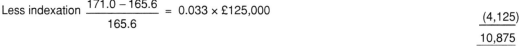

8.10 Where a gain on disposal is deferred against a replacement depreciating asset it is possible to transfer the deferred gain to a non-depreciating asset provided the non-depreciating asset is bought before the deferred gain has crystallised.

Question: Transfer of deferred gain into non-depreciating asset

In July 1990, Julius Ltd sold a warehouse used in its trade, realising a gain of £30,000. The company invested the whole of the proceeds of sale of £95,000 into fixed plant and machinery in January 1991 and made a claim to defer the gain on the warehouse.

In August 2000, Julius Ltd bought a freehold shop for use in its business costing £100,000. Julius Ltd has not bought any other assets for use in the business and wishes to minimise chargeable gains arising in its accounting period to 31.3.01. What advice would you give Julius Ltd?

Answer

Julius Ltd should claim to transfer the deferred gain of £30,000 to the purchase of the shop. If it does not do so, the deferred gain will be chargeable in January 2001, at the latest (10 years after the acquisition of the plant and machinery).

The effect of the claim will be to reduce the base cost of the shop to £(100,000 - 30,000) = £70,000.

Chapter roundup

- A chargeable gain is computed by taking the proceeds and deducting both the costs and the indexation allowance.

- When dealing with shares held by companies, we usually need to construct a FA 1985 pool.

- On an alteration of share capital the pooled base cast of the original shares needs to be apportioned, if more than one type of share is acquired.

- When assets falling within certain classes are sold and other such assets are bought, it is possible to 'rollover' the gains on the assets sold.

- A rolled over gain is deducted from the base cost of the asset acquired.

- When the replacement asset is a depreciating asset, the gain on the old asset is deferred rather than rolled over.

Quick quiz

1 What enhancement expenditure is allowable? (see para 3.4)

2 How are quoted shares valued? (3.6)

3 In what order are acquisitions of shares matched with disposals (5.5)

4 What shares are included in the FA 1985 pool? (6.1)

5 How is a rights issue dealt with? (7.2)

6 What assets are eligible for rollover relief on the replacement of a business assets? (8.2)

7 What deferral of a gain is available when a business asset is replaced with a depreciating business asset? (8.9)

Now try the questions below from the Exam Question Bank

Number	Level	Marks	Time
6	Introductory	5	9 mins
7	Exam	15	27 mins

Chapter 6

LOSSES

Topic list	Syllabus reference
1 Reliefs for losses	1c(iii)
2 Loss relief against future trading income: s 393 (1) ICTA 1988	1c(iii)
3 Loss relief against total profits: s 393A(1) ICTA 1988	1c(iii)
4 Restrictions on loss relief	1c(iii)
5 The choice between loss reliefs	1c(iii)

Introduction

In this chapter we see how a company may obtain relief for losses.

Study guide

Losses

- Explain how trading losses can be carried forward

- Explain how trading losses can be claimed against income of the current or previous accounting periods

- State the factors that will influence the choice of loss relief claim

Exam guide

This is part of section 1c which is a key topic area. You should expect to see losses in either Question 1 in Section A or in Question 7 in Section B.

1 RELIEFS FOR LOSSES

Trading losses

1.1 **In summary, the following reliefs are available for trading losses incurred by a single company.**

(a) **Set-off against current profits**
(b) **Carry back against earlier profits**
(c) **Carry forward against future trading profits**

Reliefs (a) and (b) must be claimed, and are given in the order shown. Relief (c) is given for any loss for which the other reliefs are not claimed.

Capital losses

1.2 **Capital losses can only be set against capital gains in the same or future accounting periods,** never against income. Capital losses must be set against the first available gains.

Schedule D Case V losses

1.3 In the case of a trade which is controlled outside the UK **any loss made in an accounting period can only be set against trading income from the same trade in later accounting periods.**

Schedule D Case VI losses

1.4 Where in an accounting period a company makes a loss in a transaction taxable under Schedule D Case VI, **the company can set the loss against any income from other transactions taxable under Case VI in the same or later accounting periods.** The loss must be set against the earliest income available.

Schedule A losses

1.5 Schedule A losses are first set off against non-Schedule A income and gains of the company for the current period. Any excess is then:

(a) carried forward as if a Schedule A loss arising in the later accounting period for offset against future income (of all descriptions); or

(b) available for surrender as group relief.

2 LOSS RELIEF AGAINST FUTURE TRADING INCOME: S 393(1) ICTA 1988

2.1 **A company must set off a trading loss, not otherwise relieved, against income from the same trade in future accounting periods. Relief is against the first available profits.**

2.2 Further relief (under s 393(9) ICTA 1988) is available for trade charges which are unrelieved in an accounting period. These **unrelieved trade charges are carried forward and set off against future trading profits in the same way** as a s 393(1) loss. In practice, such unrelieved trade charges are added to any trading losses being carried forward under s 393(1). Computations can then include a single line for 's 393(1)(9) relief'.

2.3 Relief under s 393(9) is only available in respect of payments made wholly and exclusively for the purposes of the trade (such as patent royalties). Payments not made wholly and exclusively for trading purposes (such as gift aid payments) are set against current year profits before trade charges in the first instance, but if a loss is brought back under s 393A(1) (see below) and trade charges have already been set against profits, those trade charges are not set free to carry forward.

Question: Carrying forward losses

A Ltd has the following results for the three years to 31 March 2001.

	Year ended		
	31.3.99	*31.3.00*	*31.3.01*
	£	£	£
Trading profit/(loss)	(8,000)	3,000	6,000
Non-trade charges	300	400	700
Trade charges	400	150	200

Calculate the profits chargeable to corporation tax for all three years showing any losses available to carry forward at 1 April 2001.

Answer

	Year ended		
	31.3.99	*31.3.00*	*31.3.01*
	£	£	£
Schedule D Case I	0	3,000	6,000
Less: s 393(1) loss relief		(3,000)	(5,550)
non-trade charges			(450)
PCTCT	0	0	0
Unrelieved non-trade charges	300	400	250

Loss memorandum

	£
Loss for y/e 31.3.99	8,000
Unrelieved trade charges y/e 31.3.99	400
Loss carried forward at 1.4.99	8,400
Less s 393(1)(9) relief y/e 31.3.00	3,000
	5,400
Unrelieved trade charges y/e 31.3.00	150
Loss carried forward at 1.4.00	5,550
Less s 393(1)(9) relief y/e 31.3.01	5,550
	0
Unrelieved trade charges y/e 31.3.01	200
Loss carried forward at 1.4.01	200

3 LOSS RELIEF AGAINST TOTAL PROFITS: S 393A(1) ICTA 1988

3.1 **A company may claim to set a trading loss** (arising in a Schedule D Case I trade, not a Schedule D Case V trade controlled abroad) **incurred in an accounting period against total profits (before deducting any charges) of the same accounting period.** The result may be that trade charges become unrelieved, and available to carry forward.

3.2 **Such a loss may then be carried back and set against total profits (after deducting trade charges but before deducting non-trade charges) of an accounting period falling wholly or partly within the 12 months of the start of the period in which the loss was incurred.**

In each such period, enough profits must be left to match against trade charges, so that trade charges do not become unrelieved and available to carry forward.

If a period falls partly outside the 12 months, loss relief is limited to the proportion of the period's profits (before all charges) equal to the proportion of the period which falls within the 12 months.

3.3 **The 12 month carry back period is extended to 36 months where the trading loss arose in the 12 months immediately before the company ceased to trade.**

3.4 Any possible s 393A(1) claim for the period of the loss must be made before any excess loss can be carried back to a previous period.

Any carry-back is to more recent periods before earlier periods. Relief for earlier losses is given before relief for later losses.

3.5 A claim for relief against current or prior period profits must be made within two years of the end of the accounting period in which the loss arose. Any claim must be for the *whole* loss (to the extent that profits are available to relieve it). The loss can however be reduced by not claiming full capital allowances, so that higher capital allowances are given (on higher tax written down values) in future years. Any loss remaining unrelieved may be carried forward under s 393(1) to set against future profits of the same trade.

Question: S393A loss relief

Helix Ltd has the following results.

	Year ended			
	30.9.98	30.9.99	30.9.00	30.9.01
	£	£	£	£
Trading profit/(loss)	2,000	11,500	10,000	(35,000)
Bank interest	400	500	500	500
Chargeable gains	800	0	0	4,000
Charges on income:				
Trade charges	0	1,000	1,000	1,000
Non-trade charges	250	250	250	250

Show the PCTCT for all the years affected assuming that s 393A(1) loss relief is claimed. Assume the provisions of FA 2000 continue to apply.

Answer

The loss of the year to 30.9.01 is relieved under s 393A ICTA 1988 against current year profits and against profits of the previous twelve months.

	Year ended			
	30.9.98	30.9.99	30.9.00	30.9.01
	£	£	£	£
Schedule D Case I	2,000	11,500	10,000	0
Schedule D Case III	400	500	500	500
Chargeable gains	800	0	0	4,000
	3,200	12,000	10,500	4,500
Less s 393A current period relief	0	0	0	(4,500)
	3,200	12,000	10,500	0
Less: trade charges	0	(1,000)	(1,000)	0
	3,200	11,000	9,500	0
Less s 393A carryback relief	0	0	(9,500)	0
	3,200	11,000	0	0
Less: Non-trade charges	(250)	(250)	0	0
PCTCT	2,950	10,750	0	0
Unrelieved non-trade charges			250	250

S 393A (1) loss memorandum	
	£
Loss incurred in y/e 30.9.01	35,000
Less s 393A (1): y/e 30.9.01	(4,500)
y/e 30.9.00	(9,500)
Remaining loss	21,000
Unrelieved trade charges y/e 30.9.01	1,000
Loss available to carry forward under s 393(1)(9)	22,000

3.6 If, in the accounting period in which a trade ceases, there are unrelieved trade charges which could (if the trade had continued) have been carried forward under s 393(9) ICTA 1988, they are added to a loss to be claimed under s 393A(1). Don't forget that when a company ceases to trade the loss for the final 12 months of trading can be carried back for up to three years.

Question: Ceasing to trade

Loser Ltd had always made up accounts to 31 December, but ceased to trade on 31 December 2001. Results had been as follows.

	Year ended			
	31.12.98	*31.12.99*	*31.12.00*	*31.12.01*
	£	£	£	£
Schedule D Case I/(loss)	25,000	30,000	27,000	(60,000)
Trade charges	2,000	2,000	2,000	1,200
Non-trade charges	170	170	170	80

Show the profits chargeable to corporation tax for all years after relief for the loss. Assume that the FA 2000 provisions continue to apply.

Answer

	Year ended			
	31.12.98	*31.12.99*	*31.12.00*	*31.12.01*
	£	£	£	£
Schedule D Case I	25,000	30,000	27,000	0
Less trade charges	2,000	2,000	2,000	0
	23,000	28,000	25,000	0
Less: s 393A carryback	(8,200)	(28,000)	(25,000)	0
	14,800	0	0	0
Less: non-trade charges	(170)	0	0	0
	14,630	0	0	0
Unrelieved non-trade charges		170	170	80

The loss available is £(60,000 + 1,200) = £61,200

4 RESTRICTIONS ON LOSS RELIEF

The continuity of trades

4.1 **Relief under s 393(1) and (9) is only available against future profits arising from the same trade as that in which the loss arose.**

4.2 The continuity of trade for this purpose was considered in a case involving a company trading as brewers: *Gordon & Blair Ltd v CIR 1962*. It ceased brewing but continued to bottle and sell beer. The company claimed that it carried on the same trade throughout so that its losses from brewing could be set off against profits from the bottling trade. The company lost their case and were prevented from obtaining any further relief for losses in the brewing trade under s 393(1)(9).

The disallowance of loss relief following a change in ownership

4.3 **No relief is available for trading losses in accounting periods on one side of (before or after) a change in ownership of a company if the loss making accounting period is on the other side of (after or before) the change in ownership and either:**

- there is a major change in the nature or conduct of the trade within three years before or three years after the change in ownership; or

- after the change in ownership there is a considerable revival of the company's trading activities which at the time of the change had become small or negligible.

4.4   Examples of a major change in the nature or conduct of a trade include changes in:

- the type of property dealt in (for example a company operating a dealership in saloon cars switching to a dealership in tractors);

- the services or facilities provided (for example a company operating a public house changing to operating a discotheque);

- customers;

- outlets or markets.

However, changes to keep up to date with technology or to rationalise existing ranges of products are unlikely to be regarded as major. The Revenue consider both qualitative and quantitative issues in deciding if a change is major.

4.5   If the change in ownership occurs in (and not at the end of) an accounting period, that period is notionally divided into two periods, one up to and one after the change, for the purposes of this rule, with profits and losses being time-apportioned.

4.6   A change in ownership is disregarded for this purpose if both immediately before and immediately after the change the company is a 75% subsidiary of the same company.

Uncommercial trades

4.7   **A loss made in a trade which is not conducted on a commercial basis and with a view to the realisation of gain cannot be set off against the company's profits in the same or previous accounting periods under s 393A(1). Such losses are only available to carry forward under s 393(1) and (9) against future profits of the same trade.**

Farming and market gardening

4.8   A company carrying on the trade of farming or market gardening is treated in the same way as one that trades on an uncommercial basis in any accounting period if, in the five successive years immediately before that accounting period, the trade made a loss (before capital allowances).

5   THE CHOICE BETWEEN LOSS RELIEFS

5.1   **Several alternative loss reliefs may be available. In making a choice consider:**

- **The rate at which relief will be obtained:**

  (i)   30% at the full rate (FY 2000);
  (ii)   20% at the small companies' rate (FY 2000);
  (iii)   10% at the starting rate (FY 2000)
  (iv)   22.5% if the starting rate marginal relief applies (FY 2000);
  (v)   32.5% if SCR marginal relief applies (FY 2000);

  Remember that the rates of corporation tax were different in earlier financial years.

- **How quickly relief will be obtained**: s 393A(1) relief is quicker than s 393(1) relief.

- **The extent to which relief for non-trade charges might be lost.**

Question: The choice between loss reliefs

M Ltd has had the following results.

			Year ended 31 March		
	1997	1998	1999	2000	2001
	£	£	£	£	£
Schedule D Case I/(loss)	5,000,000	20,000	(1,000,000)	200,000	200,000
Chargeable gains	0	35,000	750,000	0	0
Trade charges	30,000	18,000	22,000	40,000	40,000
Non-trade charges	20,000	20,000	20,000	20,000	20,000

Recommend appropriate loss relief claims, and compute the mainstream corporation tax for all years based on your recommendations. Assume that future years' profits will be similar to those of the year ended 31 March 2001 and that future rates of tax remain at FY 2000 levels.

Answer

A s 393A(1) claim for the year ended 31 March 1999 will save tax partly in the marginal relief band and partly at the small companies rate, and will waste non-trade charges of £20,000. The trade charges of £22,000 will save tax at the small companies rate in future accounts since it is carried forward.

A s 393A(1) carry back claim will save tax at the small companies rate on £(20,000 + 35,000 – 18,000) = £37,000 in the year ended 31 March 1998, with £20,000 of non-trade charges being wasted. The balance of the loss, £(1,000,000 – 750,000 – 37,000) = £213,000, is carried forward. Added to the carried forward amount is the £22,000 of unrelieved trade charges mentioned above. Then £200,000 of the £235,000 loss carried forward is relieved in y/e 31.3.2000 but this results in unrelieved trade charges of £40,000 to add to the loss carried forward from the 2000 to the 2001 period. The balance of loss, now totalling £75,000 is offset in full in the 2001 period.

If no s 393A(1) claim is made, £200,000 of the loss will save tax at the small companies rate in the year ended 31 March 2000, with £20,000 of non-trade charges being wasted. The remaining £800,000 of the loss, together with £40,000 of trade charges, would be carried forward to the year ended 31 March 2001 and later years to save tax at the small companies rate and at the starting rate.

So to conclude S 393A(1) claims should be made for both the year of the loss and previous year. £40,000 of non-trade charges would be wasted, but much of the loss would save tax at the marginal corporation tax rate and relief would be obtained quickly.

The final computations are as follows.

	1997 £	1998 £	1999 £	2000 £	2001 £
			Year ended 31 March		
Schedule D Case I	5,000,000	20,000	0	200,000	200,000
Less s 393(1)(9) relief	0	0	0	(200,000)	(75,000)
	5,000,000	20,000	0	0	125,000
Chargeable gains	0	35,000	750,000	0	0
	5,000,000	55,000	750,000	0	125,000
Less: s 393A current relief		0	(750,000)	0	0
	5,000,000	55,000	0	0	125,000
Less: trade charges	(30,000)	(18,000)	0	0	(40,000)
	4,970,000	37,000	0	0	85,000
Less: S 393A c/b		(37,000)			
	4,970,000	0	0	0	85,000
Less: non-trade charges	(20,000)	0	0	0	(20,000)
Profits chargeable to corporation tax	4,950,000	0	0		65,000
MCT at 33%/20%	1,633,500	0	0	0	13,000
Unrelieved non-trade charges	0	20,000	20,000	20,000	0

Chapter roundup

- Trading losses may be relieved against current total profits, against total profits of earlier periods or against future trading income.
- There are several restrictions on loss relief and there are many factors to consider when selecting a loss relief.

Quick quiz

1 Against what profits may trading losses carried forward be set? (see para 2.1)

2 What charges may be carried forward? (2.2, 2.3)

3 To what extent may losses be carried back? (3.2, 3.3)

4 How may loss relief be restricted on a change in ownership of a company? (4.3)

Now try the question below from the Exam Question Bank

Number	Level	Marks	Time
8	Exam	10	18 mins

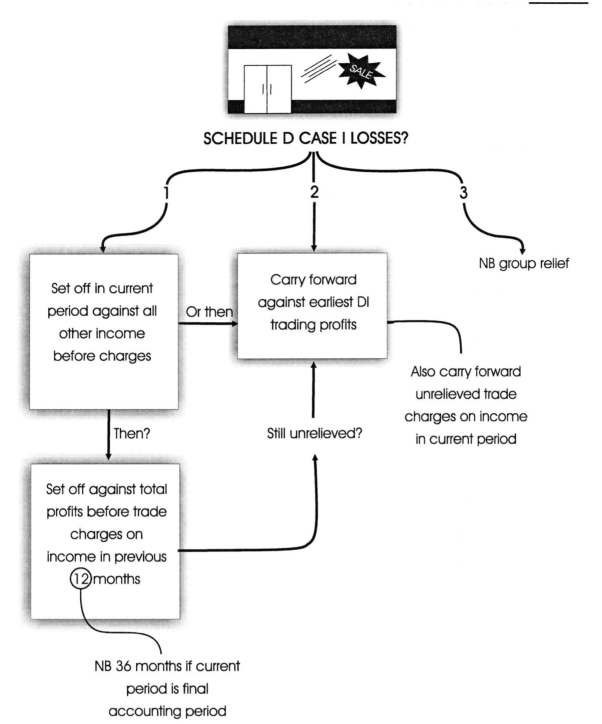

SCHEDULE D CASE I LOSSES?

Set off in current period against all other income before charges

Or then →

Carry forward against earliest DI trading profits

NB group relief

Then?

Still unrelieved?

Also carry forward unrelieved trade charges on income in current period

Set off against total profits before trade charges on income in previous (12) months

NB 36 months if current period is final accounting period

Chapter 7

GROUPS

Topic list		Syllabus reference
1	Types of group	1h
2	Group interest and charges	1h
3	Group relief	1h
4	Chargeable gains	1h

Introduction

In this chapter we consider the extent to which tax law recognises group relationships between companies. Companies in a group are still separate entities with their own tax liabilities, but tax law recognises the close relationship between group companies. They can, if they meet certain conditions, share their losses, pass assets between each other without chargeable gains and pay each other interest and charges without accounting for income tax.

Study guide

Groups

- Define an associated company

- Define a 51% group and explain the benefits of making a group election

- Define a 75% group

- Explain and apply the reliefs available to members of a 75% group

- Define a 75% capital gains group

- Explain and apply the reliefs available to members of a 75% capital gains group

Exam guide

Question 5 in Section B will either be on groups of companies or overseas aspects.

1 TYPES OF GROUP

1.1 A group exists for taxation purposes where one company is a subsidiary of another. The percentage shareholding involved determines the taxation consequences of the fact that there is a group.

1.2 The four types of relationship for tax purposes relevant to your syllabus are:

- **associated companies;**
- **51% subsidiaries;**
- **75% subsidiaries;**

- groups for chargeable gains purposes (75% capital gains groups).

Associated companies

1.3 **Two companies are associated with each other for taxation purposes if one is under the control of the other, or both are under the control of a third party.** Control for these purposes means entitlement to more than 50% of any one of:

- the share capital;
- the votes;
- the income;
- the net assets on a winding up.

1.4 **The number of associated companies determines the limits for the starting rate of corporation tax, the small companies rate and marginal relief.**

2 GROUP INTEREST AND CHARGES

2.1 **An election can be made under s 247 ICTA 1988 to enable interest and charges to be paid gross between members of a 51% group (ie without deducting income tax at source).** This election has a potential cash flow benefit for the group as a whole. It cannot be set aside for individual payments. To make a payment outside the election, the election must be revoked (and remade if required). Note that amounts can be paid to or from a subsidiary, or between subsidiaries.

> **KEY TERM**
>
> For there to be a 51% group, one company must hold more than 50% of the ordinary share capital of a second company and be entitled to more than 50% of:
>
> - any profits available for distribution; and
> - any assets available for distribution on a winding-up.
>
> Both companies must be UK resident.

2.2 If, for example, A owns 60% of B and 2% of C, and B owns 60% of C, A's effective interest in C would be only 60% × 60% + 2% = 38% and A and C would not be member of the same 51% group. However, B and C are members of a 51% group and gross payments of interest and charges can be made between them.

3 GROUP RELIEF

3.1 **The group relief provisions enable companies within a 75% group to transfer trading losses to other companies within the group,** in order to set these against taxable profits and reduce the group's overall corporation tax liability.

KEY TERM

For one company to be a **75% subsidiary** of another, the holding company must have:

- at least 75% of the ordinary share capital of the subsidiary;
- a right to at least 75% of the distributable income of the subsidiary; and
- a right to at least 75% of the net assets of the subsidiary were it to be wound up.

Two companies are members of a group for group relief purposes where one is a 75% subsidiary of the other, or both are 75% subsidiaries of a third company. Ordinary share capital is any share capital other than fixed dividend preference shares.

Two companies are in a group only if there is a 75% effective interest. Thus an 80% subsidiary (T) of an 80% subsidiary (S) is not in a group with the holding company (H), because the effective interest is only 80% × 80% = 64%. However, S and T are in a group and can claim group relief from each other. S *cannot* claim group relief from T and pass it on to H; it can only claim group relief for its own use.

3.2 A group relief group may include non-UK resident companies. **However, losses may generally only be surrendered between UK resident companies.**

The relief

3.3 A **claimant company** is assumed to use its own current year losses or losses brought forward in working out the profits against which it may claim group relief, even if it does not in fact claim s 393A relief for current losses. Furthermore, **group relief is against profits after all other reliefs for the current period or brought forward from earlier periods,** including charges. Group relief is given before relief for any amounts brought back from later periods.

3.4 **A surrendering company may group relieve a loss before setting it against its own profits for the period of the loss, and may specify any amount to be surrendered.** This is important for tax planning as it enables the surrendering company to leave profits in its own computation to be charged to corporation tax at the small companies rate or starting rate, while surrendering its losses to other companies to cover profits which would otherwise fall into a marginal relief band or be taxed at the full rate. Note that profits in the small companies marginal relief band are taxed at the marginal rate of 32.5%. Profits in the starting rate marginal relief band are taxed at the marginal rate of 22.5%.

Question: Group relief of losses

In a group of four companies, the results for the year ended 31 March 2001 are as follows.

	Profit/(loss) £
A Ltd	2,000
B Ltd	212,500
C Ltd	1,000,000
D Ltd	(400,000)

How should the loss be allocated to save as much tax as possible? How much tax is saved?

Answer

The upper and lower limits for small companies' marginal relief are £1,500,000/4 = £375,000 and £300,000/4 = £75,000 respectively. The upper and lower limits for starting rate marginal relief are £50,000/4 = £12,500 and £10,000/4 = £2,500 respectively.

	A Ltd	B Ltd	C Ltd
	£	£	£
Profits before group relief (note)	2,000	212,500	1,000,000
Less group relief	0	(137,500)	(262,500)
PCTCT	2,000	75,000	737,500

Tax saved
£137,500 × 32.5%		44,688	
£262,500 × 30%			78,750
Total £(44,688 + 78,750) = £123,438			

Note: We wish to save the most tax possible for the group.

Since A Ltd is in the starting rate band any loss given to it will only save 10% tax.

B Ltd is in the marginal relief for small companies rate band. Therefore, any loss given to B saves the effective marginal rate of 32.5% until the profits fall to £75,000 (the small companies lower limit). After this only 20% is saved.

C Ltd is in the full rate band of 30% until profits fall to £375,000 (the small companies upper limit).

So to conclude it is best to give B Ltd £137,500 of loss and save 32.5% tax on the profits in the marginal relief band. The balance of the loss is then given to C Ltd to save 30% tax.

3.5 **A company may surrender to other group companies trading losses, excess Schedule A losses and excess charges on income, including non-trading charges.** Charges can only be group-relieved to the extent that they exceed profits before taking account of losses brought forward or back from other accounting periods.

3.6 Capital losses cannot be group relieved. However, see paragraph 4.5 below for details of how a group may net off its gains and losses.

3.7 **Only current period losses are available for group relief. Furthermore, they must be set against profits of a corresponding accounting period.** If the accounting periods of a surrendering company and a claimant company are not the same this means that both the profits and losses must be apportioned so that only the results of the period of overlap may be set off. Apportionment is on a time basis. However, in the period when a company joins or leaves a group, an alternative method may be used if the result given by time-apportionment would be unjust or unreasonable.

Question: corresponding accounting periods

	£
S Ltd incurs a trading loss for the year to 30 September 2000	(15,000)
H Ltd makes taxable profits:	
for the year to 31 December 1999	20,000
for the year to 31 December 2000	10,000

What group relief can H Ltd claim from S Ltd?

Answer

	£
H Ltd can claim group relief as follows.	
For the year ended 31 December 1999 profits of the corresponding accounting period (1.10.99 - 31.12.99) are £20,000 × 3/12	5,000
Losses of the corresponding accounting period are £15,000 × 3/12	3,750
A claim for £3,750 of group relief may be made against H Ltd's profits	
For the year ended 31 December 2000 profits of the corresponding accounting period (1.1.00 - 30.9.00) are £10,000 × 9/12	7,500
Losses of the corresponding accounting period are £15,000 × 9/12	11,250
A claim for £7,500 of group relief may be made against H Ltd's profits	

3.8 If a claimant company claims relief for losses surrendered by more than one company, the total relief that may be claimed for a period of overlap is limited to the proportion of the claimant's profits attributable to that period. Similarly, if a company surrenders losses to more than one claimant, the total losses that may be surrendered in a period of overlap is limited to the proportion of the surrendering company's losses attributable to that period.

3.9 **A claim for group relief is normally made on the claimant company's tax return.** It is ineffective unless a notice of consent is also given by the surrendering company.

3.10 A claimant company may not amend a group relief claim but it may withdraw it and replace it with a new claim. The time limit for making or withdrawing a claim is the latest of:

(a) the first anniversary of the filing date for the CT return.

(b) 30 days after the completion of an enquiry into a return.

(c) 30 days after the amendment of a self assessment by the Revenue following the completion of an enquiry.

(d) 30 days after the settlement of an appeal against an amendment to the self assessment made by the Revenue following an enquiry.

The Revenue has discretion to accept a late claim/withdrawal.

3.11 Group wide claims/surrenders can be made as one person can act for two or more companies at once.

3.12 Any payment by the claimant company for group relief, up to the amount of the loss surrendered, is ignored for all corporation tax purposes.

Question: Group relief

C Ltd has one wholly owned subsidiary, D Ltd. The results of both companies for the four years ended 31 March 2001 are shown below.

	12 months to 31 March			
	1998	*1999*	*2000*	*2001*
	£	£	£	£
C Ltd				
Trading profit (loss)	200	(1,700)	100	(2,000)
Schedule A	800	800	800	800
Trade charges paid	(40)	(50)	0	(60)
D Ltd				
Trading profit (loss)	(2,300)	2,000	(870)	2,400
Interest on gilts (non-trading investment) (gross)	1,800	0	1,200	1,300
Trade charges paid	(600)	(400)	(300)	(500)

Show the profits chargeable to corporation tax for both companies for all years shown, assuming that loss relief and group relief are claimed as early as possible.

Answer

C Ltd

	Accounting periods to 31 March			
	1998	*1999*	*2000*	*2001*
	£	£	£	£
Schedule D Case I	200	0	100	0
Schedule A	800	800	800	800
	1,000	800	900	800
Less s 393A(1) - current period relief		(800)	0	(800)
		0	900	0
Less charges paid	(40)	0	0	0
	960	0	900	0
Less s 393A - carryback	0	0	(900)	0
	960	0	0	0
Less group relief claim	(960)	0	0	0
PCTCT	0	0	0	0

Loss memorandum

Loss		(1,700)		(2,000)
S 393A(1) claim: current year		800		800
		(900)		(1,200)
S 393A(1) claim: carry back				900
				(300)
Excess charges		(50)		(60)
		(950)		(360)
Group relief surrender		950		360
		0		0

D Ltd

Schedule D Case I	0	2,000	0	2,400
Less s 393(1)(9)		(140)		
		1,860		
Schedule D Case III	1,800	0	1,200	1,300
	1,800	1,860	1,200	3,700
Less s 393A(1) - current period relief	(1,800)		(870)	
	0		330	
Less trade charges paid	0	(400)	(300)	(500)
	0	1,460	30	3,200
Less group relief claim		(950)		(360)
PCTCT	0	510	30	2,840

	Accounting periods to 31 March	
	1998	2000
Loss memorandum	£	£
Loss	(2,300)	(870)
S 393A(1) claim	1,800	870
	(500)	0
Excess charges	(600)	
	(1,100)	
Group relief surrender	960	
	(140)	
S 393(1)(9) claim	140	
	0	

Tax planning for group relief

3.13   Here are some tax planning points to bear in mind when dealing with a group.

(a) Group relief should first be given in this order:

1st: To companies in the small companies marginal relief band paying 32.5% tax (but only sufficient loss to bring profits down to the SCR limit)

2nd To companies paying the full rate of tax at 30%

3rd To companies in the starting rate marginal relief band paying 22.5% tax (but only sufficient loss to bring profits down to the starting rate limit)

4th To companies paying SCR at 20%

5th To companies paying starting rate at 10%

(b) Similarly, a company should make a s 393A(1) claim to use a loss itself rather than surrender the loss to other group companies if the s 393A(1) claim would lead to a tax saving at a higher rate.

(c) Companies with profits may benefit by reducing their claims for capital allowances in a particular year. This may leave sufficient profits to take advantage of group relief which may only be available for the current year. The amount on which writing-down allowances can be claimed in later years is increased accordingly.

4 CHARGEABLE GAINS

Intra-group transfers

4.1 Companies are in a capital gains group if:

(a) at each level, there is a 75% holding; and
(b) the top company has an effective interest of over 50% in the group companies.

If A holds 75% of B, B holds 75% of C and C holds 75% of D, then A, B and C are in such a group, but D is outside the group because A's interest in D is only $75\% \times 75\% \times 75\% = 42.1875\%$. Furthermore, D is not in a group with C, because the group must include the top company (A).

4.2 **Companies in a capital gains group make intra-group transfers of chargeable assets without a chargeable gain or an allowable loss arising.** No election is needed, as this relief is compulsory. The assets are deemed to be transferred at such a price as will give the transferor no gain and no loss, that is cost plus indexation allowance to the date of the transfer.

4.3 **Non-UK resident companies are included as members of a capital gains group. Provided the assets transferred do not result in a potential leakage of UK corporation tax, no gain/no loss transfers are possible within a worldwide (global) group of companies.** This means that it may be possible to make no gain/no loss transfers to non-UK resident companies with a branch or agency in the UK.

Exceptions to the 'no gain/no loss' transfer price

4.4 **There are exceptions to the 'no gain no loss' transfer price for intra-group transfers of capital assets. There will be an immediate chargeable disposal:**

• where an intra-group **transfer is in satisfaction of a debt;**
• on the **disposal of an interest in shares in a group company by way of a capital distribution;**
• where **cash or other assets are received upon the redemption of shares in another company.**

In addition, when an asset is transferred between two group companies and is trading stock for one of those companies but not for the other, it is treated as appropriated to or from trading stock by the company for which it is trading stock. This may give rise to an immediate chargeable gain, allowable loss or trading profit or loss (see Chapter 5).

Matching group gains and losses

4.5 Capital losses cannot be included in a group relief claim. However, **two members of a capital gains group can elect that an asset that has been disposed of outside the group is treated as if it had been transferred between them immediately before disposal.** The deemed transferee company is then treated as having made the disposal. This election may be made within two years of the end of the accounting period in which the disposal took place.

Rollover relief

4.6 **If a member of a capital gains group disposes of an asset eligible for capital gains rollover or holdover relief it may treat all of the group companies as a single unit for the purpose of claiming such relief. Acquisitions by other group members within the qualifying period** of one year before the disposal to three years afterwards may therefore **be matched with the disposal.** However, both the disposing company and the acquiring company must make the claim. If an asset is transferred at no gain and no loss between group members, that transfer does not count as the acquisition of an asset for rollover or holdover relief purpose.

4.7 Claims may also be made by non-trading group members which hold assets used for other group members' trades.

> **Exam focus point**
>
> Try to remember the following summary - it will be of great help in the exam.
>
> Parent Co **controls** over 50% of subsidiary
>
> - associated companies for upper and lower limits
>
> Parent Co **owns** over 50% of subsidiary
>
> - pay charges and interest gross
>
> Parent Co **owns** 75% or more of subsidiary
>
> - surrender trading losses, Schedule A losses, excess charges to companies with some PCTCT for same time period
>
> Parent Co **owns** 75% or more of subsidiary and subsidiary owns 75% or more of its subsidiaries
>
> - transfer assets between companies automatically at no gain/no loss
> - capital gains and losses can be matched between group member companies
> - all companies treated as one for rollover relief purposes.

Chapter roundup

- Associated companies affect the limits for starting rate, small companies rate and marginal relief.

- Within a 51% group charges and interest can be paid gross.

- Within a 75% group, trading losses can be surrendered between UK companies.

- Group relief is available where the existence of a group is established through companies resident anywhere in the world.

- Within a capital gains group, assets are transferred at no gain and no loss.

- Rollover relief is available in a capital gains group.

Quick quiz

1   What is the effect of a s 247 ICTA 1988 election? (see para 2.1)

2   What sorts of losses may be group relieved? (3.5 - 3.7)

3   When may assets be transferred intra-group at no gain and no loss? (4.1 - 4.4)

Now try the questions below from the Exam Question Bank

Number	Level	Marks	Time
9	Exam	20	36 mins
10	Exam	15	27 mins

Chapter 8

OVERSEAS ASPECTS OF CORPORATE TAXATION

Topic list	Syllabus reference
1 Branch or subsidiary abroad	1g(i)
2 Double taxation relief (DTR)	1g(ii)
3 Transfer pricing	1g(iii)

Introduction

In this chapter we look at UK companies trading abroad. We see how relief may be given for overseas taxes suffered and how the transfer pricing legislation applies.

Study guide

Overseas aspects of corporate taxation

- Compare the UK tax treatment of an overseas branch to an overseas subsidiary

- Calculate double taxation relief for withholding tax and underlying tax

- Explain and apply the transfer pricing rules

Exam guide

Question 5 in Section B will either be on groups of companies or overseas aspects.

1   BRANCH OR SUBSIDIARY ABROAD

Taxation of foreign income and gains

1.1 **A UK resident company is subject to corporation tax on its worldwide profits.** It is also (unlike a non-resident company) entitled to the starting rate of corporation tax, the small companies rate and to marginal relief.

1.2 **If a UK resident company makes investments abroad it will be liable to corporation tax on the profits made, the taxable amount being before the deduction of any foreign taxes.** The profits may be any of the following.

(a) Interest and dividends received through paying agents.

(b) Schedule D Case I: profits of an overseas branch or agency controlled from the UK

(c) Schedule D Case III: income from foreign securities, for example debentures in overseas companies

     (d)   Schedule D Case V: income from other overseas possessions including:

         (i)   dividends from overseas subsidiaries;

         (ii)   profits of an overseas branch or agency controlled abroad

     (e)   Capital gains on disposals of foreign assets

Overseas dividends and interest received by a company are taxed at normal corporation tax rates.

1.3   A company may be subject to overseas taxes as well as to UK corporation tax on the same profits. Double taxation relief (see below) is available in respect of the foreign tax suffered.

Taxation of foreign branches and foreign subsidiaries

1.4   Where a foreign country has a lower rate of company taxation than the UK, it can be beneficial for the UK company to conduct its foreign activities through a **non-UK resident subsidiary** if profits are anticipated, and through a **branch if losses are likely to arise**.

1.5   The **profits of a foreign branch** are treated as part of the profits of the UK company and are normally included in its computation of Schedule D Case I trading profits. If, however, the operations of the overseas branch amount to a separate trade which is wholly carried on overseas, the profits are assessed under Schedule D Case V.

1.6   **Losses of a foreign branch can be surrendered as group relief** to the extent the loss cannot be relieved against profits in the overseas country. Alternatively a Schedule D Case V loss can be carried forward to set against future profits of the same trade. A Schedule D Case I loss is first set against other Schedule D Case I profits. The usual loss reliefs are then available.

1.7   The profits of a non-resident **foreign subsidiary** are only liable to UK tax when remitted to the UK, for example in the form of dividends (Schedule D Case V income). However, no relief can be obtained against the UK parent's profits for any overseas losses of a non-resident subsidiary.

Incorporation of a foreign branch

1.8   Where a foreign operation is likely to show a loss in the early years followed by a profit it may be worthwhile to trade through a foreign branch whilst losses arise (these are usually then automatically netted off against the company's UK profits) and then later to convert the branch into a non-UK resident subsidiary company (so that profits can be accumulated at potentially lower rates of foreign tax).

1.9   This conversion of a foreign branch into a non-UK resident subsidiary has some important implications and the tax effects both in the UK and the overseas country need to be considered. Firstly, it may be necessary to secure the consent of the Treasury for the transaction. It is illegal for a UK resident company to cause or permit a non-UK resident company over which it has control to create or issue any shares or debentures. It is also illegal for a UK resident company to transfer to any person, or cause or permit to be transferred to any person, any shares or debentures of a non-UK resident company over which it has control.

1.10   The Treasury have published General Consents which permit certain intra-group transactions and third party transactions provided full consideration is given. Additionally certain movements of capital between EEA states are allowed automatically. Thus in practice specific Treasury consent may not be required for a transaction of the type presently under consideration.

1.11 Secondly, the conversion will constitute a disposal of the assets of the branch giving rise to a chargeable gain or loss in the hands of the UK company. A chargeable gain can be postponed where:

(a) the trade of the foreign branch is transferred to the non-UK resident company with all the assets used for that trade except cash; and

(b) the consideration for the transfer is wholly or partly securities (shares or shares and loan stock); and

(c) the transferring company owns at least 25% of the ordinary share capital of the non-resident company; and

(d) a claim for relief is made.

There is full postponement of the net gains arising on the transfer where the consideration is wholly securities. Where part of the consideration is in a form other than securities, eg cash, that proportion of the net gains is chargeable immediately.

The postponement may be indefinite. The gain becomes chargeable only when:

(a) the transferor company at any time disposes of any of the securities received on the transfer; or

(b) the non-UK resident company within six years of the transfer disposes of any of the assets on which a gain arose at the time of the transfer.

1.12 The 'global group' concept applies to certain intra group transfers of assets. Such asset transfers are on a no gain/no loss basis provided the assets transferred do not result in a potential leakage of UK corporation tax.

European Community companies

1.13 **If all or part of a trade carried on in the UK by a company resident in one EC state is transferred to a company resident in another EC state, then the transfer is deemed to be at a price giving no gain and no loss,** if all the following conditions are fulfilled.

(a) The transfer is wholly in exchange for shares or securities.

(b) The company receiving the trade would be subject to UK corporation tax on any gains arising on later disposals of the assets transferred.

(c) Both parties claim this special treatment.

(d) The transfer is for bona fide commercial reasons. Advance clearance that this condition is satisfied may be obtained.

2 DOUBLE TAXATION RELIEF (DTR)

2.1 In the UK, relief for foreign tax suffered by a company is available in three ways:

(a) **Treaty relief**

Under a treaty entered into between the UK and the overseas country, a treaty may exempt certain profits from taxation in one of the countries involved, thus completely avoiding double taxation. More usually treaties provide for credit to be given for tax suffered in one of the countries against the tax liability in the other.

(b) **Unilateral credit relief**

Where no treaty relief is available, unilateral relief may be available in the UK giving credit for the foreign tax against the UK tax.

(c) **Unilateral expense relief**

Not examined in your syllabus.

Treaty relief

2.2 A tax treaty based on the OECD model treaty may use either the exemption method or the credit method to give relief for tax suffered on income from a business in country B by a resident of country R.

(a) Under the **exemption method**, the income is not taxed at all in country R, or if it is dividends or interest (which the treaty allows to be taxed in country R) credit is given for any country B tax against the country R tax.

(b) Under the **credit method**, the income is taxed in country R, but credit is given for any country B tax against the country R tax.

Under either method, any credit given is limited to the country B tax attributable to the income.

Unilateral credit relief

2.3 **Relief is available for overseas tax suffered on branch profits, dividends, interest and royalties, up to the amount of the UK corporation tax (at the company's average rate) attributable to that income.** The tax that is deducted overseas is usually called withholding tax. The gross income including the withholding tax is included within the profits chargeable to corporation tax.

Question: Unilateral credit relief

In the year ended 31 March 2001, AS plc receives a dividend from Bola of £60,000. This has been paid subject to 40% withholding tax. AS plc has UK trading income of £2,000,000. Show that the Schedule D Case V income is £100,000 and compute the corporation tax payable.

Answer

	Total £	UK £	Overseas £
Schedule D Case I	2,000,000	2,000,000	
Schedule D Case V(W)	100,000		100,000
PCTCT	2,100,000	2,000,000	100,000
Corporation tax at 30%	630,000	600,000	30,000
Less DTR: lower of:			
(a) overseas tax: £40,000; or			
(b) UK tax on overseas income: £30,000	(30,000)		(30,000)
MCT	600,000	600,000	0

DTR of £10,000 is lost. The excess cannot be reclaimed in the UK or relieved in any other manner.

Working: Schedule D Case V

£60,000 × 100/(100 − 40) = £100,000.

Underlying tax relief

2.4 **In addition to the relief available for withholding tax shown above, relief is available for underlying tax relating to a dividend received from a foreign company in which the UK company owns at least 10% of the voting power, either directly or indirectly. The underlying tax is the tax attributable to the relevant profits out of which the dividend was paid.** Underlying tax is calculated as

$$\text{Gross dividend income} \times \frac{\text{foreign tax paid}}{\text{after} - \text{tax accounting profits}}$$

Relief for underlying tax is not available to individuals.

2.5 We may need to decide which accounting profits have been used to pay a dividend. If the dividend is declared for a particular year, the set of accounts for that year are used. If this information is not given, the relevant profits are those of the period of account immediately before that in which the dividend was payable.

2.6 There is an anti-avoidance provision which restricts relief for underlying tax in certain circumstances where there is a scheme the purpose, or one of the main purposes, of which is to obtain relief for underlying tax.

Question: Underlying tax relief

A Ltd, a UK company with no associated companies, holds 30,000 out of 90,000 voting ordinary shares in B Inc (resident in Lintonia).

The profit and loss account of B Inc for the year to 31 March 2001 is as follows (converted into sterling).

		£	£
Trading profit			1,000,000
Less taxation:	provided on profits	300,000	
	transfer to deferred tax account	100,000	
			400,000
			600,000
Less dividends:	net	240,000	
	withholding tax (20%)	60,000	
			300,000
Retained profits			300,000

The actual tax paid on the profits for the year to 31 March 2001 was £270,000.

Apart from the net dividend of £80,000 received from B Inc the only other taxable profit of A Ltd for its year to 31 March 2001 was £610,000 UK trading profit. A Ltd paid no dividends during the year and received no UK dividends.

Calculate A Ltd's UK corporation tax liability after double taxation relief.

Answer

A LTD: UK CORPORATION TAX LIABILITY

	£	£
Schedule D Case I		610,000
Schedule D Case V		
Net dividend	80,000	
Withholding tax at 20%		
£80,000 × 20/80	20,000	
Gross dividend	100,000	
Underlying tax		
£100,000 × $\dfrac{270,000}{600,000}$	45,000	
Gross income		145,000
PCTCT		755,000

	Total £	UK £	Overseas £
Schedule D Case I	610,000	610,000	
Schedule D Case V	145,000		145,000
PCTCT	755,000	610,000	145,000

Corporation tax £755,000 × 30%			226,500
Less marginal relief £(1,500,000 − 755,000) × 1/40			(18,625)
			207,875

The average rate of corporation tax is
£207,875/£755,000 = 27.53311%.

Corporation tax at the average rate	207,875	167,952	39,923
Less DTR: lower of:			
(a) overseas tax £(20,000 + 45,000) = £65,000;			
(b) UK tax on overseas income £39,923	(39,923)		(39,923)
	167,952	167,952	0

Corporation tax of £167,952 is payable. £(65,000 − 39,923) = £25,077 of overseas tax is lost.

2.7   One further factor affects the computation of UK tax on overseas income against which credit for overseas tax may be claimed. This is the allocation of charges and losses relieved against total profits under s 393A(1).

2.8   **A company may allocate its charges and losses relieved under s 393A(1) in whatever manner it likes for the purpose of computing double taxation relief. It should set the maximum amount against any UK profits, thereby maximising the corporation tax attributable to the foreign profits and hence maximising the double taxation relief available.**

     If a company has several sources of overseas profits, then charges and losses should be allocated first to UK profits, and then to overseas sources which have suffered the **lowest** rates of overseas taxation.

     Losses relieved under s 393(1) must in any case be set against the first available profits of the trade which gave rise to the loss.

2.9   A company with a choice of loss reliefs should consider the effect of its choice on double taxation relief. For example, a s 393A(1) claim might lead to there being no UK tax liability, or a very small liability, so that foreign tax would go unrelieved. S 393(1) relief might avoid this problem and still leave very little UK tax to pay for the period of the loss.

3 TRANSFER PRICING

3.1 Companies which have subsidiaries resident in countries with lower corporate tax rates than the UK may attempt to divert profits by inter-company pricing arrangements. For example, a UK company has contracted to sell goods with an invoice value of £20,000 to a foreign customer:

UK selling company ——— Goods Invoice value : £20,000 ⟶ Foreign buying company

In this case all the profit on the sale arises to the UK company; alternatively the sale could be rearranged.

UK selling company —— Goods Invoice value : £16,000 ⟶ Tax haven subsidiary company —— Goods Invoice value : £20,000 ⟶ Foreign buying company

In this case £4,000 of the profit has been diverted to a subsidiary operating in a low-tax country (tax haven).

3.2 **The transfer pricing legislation restricts the freedom of a company to buy and sell goods at whatever price it wishes.** The legislation applies where property is sold between **associated persons (under control of each other or under common control). Where the sale is at an undervalue the seller must be treated as selling at market value, and if at an overvalue the buyer is treated likewise.**

3.3 **The transfer pricing legislation does not apply to transactions between two UK resident traders.**

3.4 The legislation applies not only to transactions in goods, but also to 'lettings and hirings of property ... and the giving of the business facilities of whatever kind'. This latter phrase includes the situation where a UK resident company makes an **interest-free or low interest rate loan to a foreign company under common control.** The company is deemed to have received interest at a market rate on the loan.

3.5 A transfer pricing adjustment to the profits of a UK company could lead to double taxation as it may not necessarily be matched by an adjustment to the profits of the overseas company. There is, however, an Arbitration Convention to avoid double taxation arising between EC members.

3.6 **Companies must self-assess their liability to tax under the transfer pricing rules and pay any corporation tax due. A statutory procedure exists for advance pricing arrangements (APAs) whereby a company can agree in advance that its transfer pricing policy is acceptable to the Revenue** – ie, not requiring a self-assessment adjustment. The APA facility is voluntary but companies may feel the need to use the facility as it provides necessary advance confirmation that their approach to transfer pricing in their self-assessment is acceptable.

Chapter roundup

- A UK resident company intending to do business abroad must choose between a branch and a subsidiary. If a subsidiary is chosen, it must bear in mind the rules on trading at artificial prices.

- A company may obtain double taxation relief for overseas withholding tax, and also (if its investment is large enough) for underlying tax. The allocation of charges and losses can affect the relief available.

- The transfer pricing legislation restricts the freedom of a company to buy and sell goods at whatever price it wishes between associate persons.

Quick quiz

1. A UK company is planning to set up a new operation in Australia that will initially be loss making. Should it set up as a branch or a subsidiary of the UK company? (see para 1.4)

2. How is underlying tax calculated? (2.4)

3. How should charges be allocated in computing credit relief for foreign tax? (2.8)

4. What steps can be taken against the use of artificial transfer prices? (3.2)

Now try the question below from the Exam Question Bank

Number	Level	Marks	Time
11	Exam	16	29 mins

Chapter 9

PAYMENT OF TAX BY COMPANIES

Topic list	Syllabus reference
1 Returns, records, enquiries, assessments and claims	1i(i)
2 Payment of tax and interest	1i(i)
3 Income tax suffered or withheld from charges and interest	1i(ii)

Introduction

In this chapter we look at the self assessment system for CT.

We also see how income tax is accounted for. Companies are not supposed to pay income tax so the effects of deducting income tax at source need to be neutralised.

Study guide

Payment of tax by companies

- Describe the features of self-assessment

- Calculate interest on overdue tax

- Explain how the Inland Revenue can enquire into a self-assessment return

- Explain how large companies are required to account for corporation tax on a quarterly basis

- Explain how companies account for income tax on a quarterly basis on form CT61

Exam guide

This is section 1i which is a key topic. You should expect to see payment of tax by companies in either Question 1 in Section A or in Question 7 in Section B.

1   RETURNS, RECORDS, ENQUIRIES, ASSESSMENTS AND CLAIMS

1.1   **A company's tax return (CT 600) must include a self assessment of any tax payable.**

Returns

1.2   **An obligation to file a return arises only when the company receives a notice requiring a return.** A return is required for each accounting period ending during or at the end of the period specified in the notice requiring a return. A company also has to file a return for certain other periods which are not accounting periods (eg for a period when the company is dormant).

BPP PUBLISHING

1.3 A company that does not receive a notice requiring a return must, if it is chargeable to tax, **notify the Revenue within twelve months of the end of the accounting period**. Failure to do so results in a maximum penalty equal to the tax unpaid twelve months after the end of the accounting period.

1.4 A notice to file a return may also require other information, accounts and reports. For a UK resident company the requirement to deliver accounts normally extends only to the accounts required under the Companies Act.

1.5 A return is due on or before the filing date. This is the later of:

(a) **12 months after the end of the period to which the return relates;**

(b) **if the relevant period of account is not more than 18 months long, 12 months from the end of the period of account;**

(c) **if relevant the period of account is more than 18 months long, 30 months from the start of the period of account; and**

(d) **three months from the date on which the notice requiring the return was made.**

The relevant period of account is that in which the accounting period to which the return relates ends.

Question: Filing date

A Ltd prepares accounts for the eighteen months to 30 June 2000. A notice requiring a return for the year ended 30 June 2000 was issued to A Ltd on 1 September 2000. State the periods for which A Ltd must file a tax return and the filing dates.

Answer

The company must file a return for the two accounting periods ending in the period specified in the notice requiring a return. The first accounting period is the twelve months to 31 December 1999 and the second is the six months to 30 June 2000. The filing date is twelve months after the end of the relevant period of account, 30 June 2001.

1.6 **There is a £100 penalty for a failure to submit a return on time, rising to £200 if the delay exceeds three months. These penalties become £500 and £1,000 respectively when a return was late (or never submitted) for each of the preceding two accounting periods.**

1.7 **An additional tax geared penalty is applied if a return is more than six months late. The penalty is 10% of the tax unpaid six months after the return was due if the total delay is up to 12 months, and 20% of that tax if the return is over 12 months late.**

1.8 There is a tax geared penalty for a fraudulent or negligent return and for failing to correct an innocent error without unreasonable delay. The maximum penalty is equal to the tax that would have been lost had the return been accepted as correct. The Revenue can mitigate this penalty. If a company is liable to more than one tax geared penalty, the total penalty is limited to the maximum single penalty that could be charged.

1.9 A company may amend a return within twelve months of the filing date. The Revenue may amend a return to correct obvious errors within nine months of the day the return was filed, or if the correction is to an amended return, within nine months of the filing of an amendment. The company may amend its return so as to reject the correction. If the time limit for amendments has expired, the company may reject the correction by giving notice within three months.

Records

1.10   Companies must keep records until the latest of:

(a)   six years from the end of the accounting period;

(b)   the date any enquiries are completed;

(c)   the date after which enquiries may not be commenced.

All business records and accounts, including contracts and receipts, must be kept.

1.11   If a return is demanded more than six years after the end of the accounting period, any records which the company still has must be kept until the later of the end of any enquiry and the expiry of the right to start an enquiry.

1.12   Failure to keep records can lead to a penalty of up to £3,000 for each accounting period affected. However, this penalty does not apply when the only records which have not been kept are ones which could only have been needed for the purposes of claims, elections or notices not included in the return.

1.13   The Revenue do not generally insist on original records being kept but original records of the following must be preserved:

(a)   Qualifying distributions and tax credits

(b)   Gross and net payments and tax deducted for payments made net of tax

(c)   Details of foreign tax paid, although the Revenue will accept photocopies or foreign tax assessments when calculating underlying tax on dividends from abroad

Enquiries

1.14   A return or an amendment need not be accepted at face value by the Revenue. **They may enquire into it, provided that they first give written notice that they are going to enquire.** The notice must be given by a year after the later of:

(a)   The filing date;

(b)   The 31 January, 30 April, 31 July or 31 October next following the actual date of delivery of the return or amendment.

Only one enquiry may be made in respect of any one return or amendment.

1.15   If a notice of an enquiry has been given, the Revenue may demand that the company produce documents for inspection and copying. However, documents relating to an appeal need not be produced and the company may appeal against a notice requiring documents to be produced.

1.16   If the Revenue demand documents, but the company does not produce them, there is a penalty of £50. There is also a daily penalty, which applies for each day from the day after the imposition of the £50 penalty until the documents are produced. The daily penalty may be imposed by the Revenue, in which case it is £30. If, however, the Revenue ask the Commissioners to impose the penalty, it is £150.

1.17   The Revenue may amend a self assessment at any time during an enquiry if they believe there might otherwise be a loss of tax. The company may appeal against such an amendment within 30 days. The company may itself make amendments during an enquiry under the normal rules for amendments. No effect will be given to such amendments during the enquiry but they may be taken into account in the enquiry.

1.18　An enquiry ends when the Revenue give notice that it has been completed and notify what they believe to be the correct amount of tax payable. Before that time, the company may ask the Commissioners to order the Revenue to notify the completion of its enquiry by a specified date. Such a direction will be given unless the Revenue can demonstrate that they have reasonable grounds for continuing the enquiry.

1.19　The company has 30 days from the end of an enquiry to amend its self assessment in accordance with the Revenue's conclusions. If the Revenue are not satisfied with the company's amendments, they have a further 30 days to amend the self assessment. The company then has another 30 days in which it may appeal against the Revenue's amendments.

Determinations and discovery assessments

1.20　If a return is not delivered by the filing date, the Revenue may issue a determination of the tax payable within the five years from the filing date. This is treated as a self assessment and there is no appeal against it. However, it is automatically replaced by any self assessment made by the company by the later of five years from the filing date and 12 months from the determination.

1.21　If the Revenue believe that not enough tax has been assessed for an accounting period they can make a discovery assessment to collect the extra tax. However, when a tax return has been delivered this power is limited as follows.

(a)　No discovery assessment can be made on account of an error or mistake as to the basis on which the tax liability ought to be computed, if the basis generally prevailing at the time when the return was made was applied.

(b)　A discovery assessment can only be made if either:

(i)　the loss of tax is due to fraudulent or negligent conduct by the company or by someone acting on its behalf; or

(ii)　the Revenue could not reasonably be expected to have been aware of the loss of tax, given the information so far supplied to them, when their right to start an enquiry expired or when they notified the company that an enquiry had finished.

1.22　The time limit for raising a discovery assessment is six years from the end of the accounting period but this is extended to 21 years if there has been fraudulent or negligent conduct. The company may appeal against a discovery assessment within 30 days of issue.

Claims

1.23　Wherever possible claims must be made on a tax return or on an amendment to it and must be quantified at the time the return is made.

1.24　If a company believes that it has paid excessive tax because of an error in a return, an error or mistake claim may be made within six years from the end of the accounting period. An appeal against a decision on such a claim must be made within 30 days. An error or mistake claim may not be made if the return was made in accordance with a generally accepted practice which prevailed at the time.

1.25 Other claims must be made by six years after the end of the accounting period, unless a different time limit is specified. If an error or mistake is made in a claim, a supplementary claim may be made within the time limit for the original claim.

1.26 If the Revenue amend a self assessment or issue a discovery assessment then the company has a further period to make, vary or withdraw a claim (unless the claim is irrevocable) even if this is outside the normal time limit. The period is one year from the end of the accounting period in which the amendment or assessment was made, or one year from the end of the accounting period in which the enquiry was closed if the amendment is the result of an enquiry. The relief is limited where there has been fraudulent or negligent conduct by the company or its agent.

2 PAYMENT OF TAX AND INTEREST

2.1 Corporation tax is due for payment by small and medium sized companies **nine months after the end of the accounting period.**

2.2 **Interest is charged on corporation tax paid late and interest is paid to companies on corporation tax overpaid or paid early. This interest paid/received is dealt with under Schedule D Case III as interest paid /received on a non trading loan relationship (See earlier in this text).**

2.3 Other points to note in respect of interest on overpaid corporation tax or corporation tax paid early are:

- the earliest date from which interest can be calculated is the date for the first instalment payment of corporation tax by large companies (see below);

- interest is paid from the day after the end of the accounting period if the refund is in respect of income tax suffered on payments received (see below);

- there will be a recovery, without assessment, of interest paid to companies where subsequent events show it ought not to have been paid; and

- there are restrictions on the amount of interest paid to companies (or the amount by which interest due from companies is reduced) where reliefs are carried back.

Quarterly payments of corporation tax liabilities

2.4 A system of quarterly payments on account for corporation tax liabilities is being phased in over a four year period. **For the first accounting period ending after 30.6.99 a 'large' company paid 60% of its corporation tax by four equal instalments each of 15% with the remaining 40% as a balancing payment nine months after the accounting end. Then:**

- **72% in instalments (4 × 18%), 28% as a balance in year 2;**
- **88% in instalments (4 × 22%), 12% as a balance in year 3;**
- **100% in instalments (4 × 25%) in year 4 and thereafter.**

2.5 **Instalments are due on the 14th day of the month, starting in the seventh month. Provided that the accounting period is twelve months long subsequent instalments are due in the tenth month during the accounting period and in the first and fourth months after the end of the accounting period. If an accounting period is less than twelve months long subsequent instalments are due at three monthly intervals but with the final payment being due in the fourth month of the next accounting period.**

2.6 EXAMPLE

X Ltd is a large company with a 31 December accounting year end. Instalments of corporation tax will be due to be paid by X Ltd on:

- 14 July and 14 October in the accounting period;
- 14 January and 14 April after the accounting period ends

Thus for the year ended 31 December 2000 instalment payments are due on 14 July 2000, 14 October 2000, 14 January 2001 and 14 April 2001.

2.7 Instalments are based on the estimated corporation tax liability for the current period (not the previous period). This means that it will be extremely important for companies to forecast their tax liabilities accurately. Large companies whose directors are poor at estimating may find their company's incurring significant interest charges. The amount of each instalment is computed by:

(a) working out $3 \times CT/n$ where CT is the amount of the estimated corporation tax liability payable in instalments for the period and n is the number of months in the period;

(b) allocating the smaller of that amount and the total estimated corporation tax liability to the first instalment;

(c) repeating the process for later instalments until the amount allocated is equal to the corporation tax liability. This gives four equal instalments for 12 month accounting periods and also caters for periods which end earlier than expected.

The company is therefore required to estimate its corporation tax liability before the end of the accounting period, and must revise its estimate each quarter.

Question: Short accounting period

A company has a CT liability of £1,000,000 for the eight month period to 30 November 2000. Accounts had previously always been prepared to 31 March. Show when the CT liability is due for payment.

Answer

72% of £1,000,000 = £720,000 must be paid in instalments.

The amount of each instalment is $3 \times \dfrac{£720,000}{8}$ = £270,000 = £270,000

The due dates are:

	£
14 October 2000	270,000
14 January 2001	270,000
14 March 2001	180,000 (balance)

The final payment of £280,000 is due for payment on 1 September 2001.

2.8 **Broadly, a 'large company' is a company that pays corporation tax at the full rate** (profits exceed £1.5 million where there are no associated companies). For this purpose only, a company will be regarded as an associated company where it was an associated company at the START of an accounting period. (This differs from the normal approach in CT where being an associated company for any part of the AP affects the thresholds of both companies for the whole of the AP).

2.9 A company is not required to pay instalments in the first year that it is 'large', unless its profits exceed £10 million (reduced proportionately if there are associated companies).

2.10   There is a de minimis limit in that any company whose liability for its accounting period ending on or after 1 July 2000 does not exceed £10,000 need not pay by instalments.

2.11   Interest runs from the due date on over/underpaid instalments. The position is looked at cumulatively after the due date for each instalment. The Revenue calculate the interest position after the company submits its corporation tax return.

2.12   EXAMPLE

X plc prepared accounts to 31.12.00. The company has always prepared accounts to 31 December each year. It paid CT instalments of:

Date	Amount
	£
14.7.00	3.5m
14.10.00	6.5m
14.01.01	3.5m
14.4.01	3.5m
	17.0m

X plc's CT return showed a CT liability of £25m. The £8m balance was paid on 1.10.01. £18m (72% × £25m) should have been paid in instalments. The under(over) payments were:

Date	Paid	Correct	Under(over) paid
	£	£	£
14.7.00	3.5m	4.5m	1m
14.10.00	6.5m	4.5m	
	10.0m	9.0m	(1m)
14.1.01	3.5m	4.5m	
	13.5m	13.5m	-
14.4.01	3.5m	4.5m	
	17.0m	18.0m	1m

Interest would be charged (received) as follows.

14.7.00 - 13.10.00	Interest charged on £1m
14.10.00 - 13.1.01	Interest received on £1m
14.1.01 - 13.4.01	No interest
14.4.01 - 30.9.01	Interest charged on £1m

2.13   The rate of interest charged on underpayments of corporation tax under the quarterly instalment arrangements is one percentage point above base rate. For overpayments the interest rate is one quarter of a percentage point below base rate. The interest rates applying after the normal due date (ie nine months and one day after the end of the accounting period) are two and half percentage points above base rate for underpayments and one percentage point below base rate for overpayments.

2.14   There are penalties if a company deliberately and flagrantly fails to pay instalments of sufficient size. After a company has filed its return or the Revenue has determined its liability, the Revenue may wish to establish the reason for inadequate instalment payments. It can do this by asking the company to produce relevant information or records (presumably to decide if a penalty applies). The failure to supply these will lead to an initial fixed penalty which may also be followed by a daily penalty which may continue until the information/records are produced.

2.15   Companies can have instalments repaid if they later conclude they ought not to have been paid.

3 INCOME TAX SUFFERED OR WITHHELD FROM CHARGES AND INTEREST

3.1 **Companies may receive some income which has suffered 20% or 22% income tax at source.** This is known as taxed income, or unfranked investment income (UFII). The cash income plus the income tax suffered, that is the gross figure, forms part of a company's profits chargeable to corporation tax. The income tax suffered is deductible from the corporation tax liability.

3.2 **When the company pays interest or a charge on income it deducts the gross amount in its corporation tax computation. For items paid net** (such as debenture interest and patent royalties), **it acts as an agent for the Revenue and retains income tax at 20% (interest) or 22% (charges) on the gross amount for payment to the Revenue.** The *net* amount is then payable to the payees (for example the debenture holders).

3.3 **Income tax is accounted for on amounts paid and received. However, interest is dealt with on an accruals basis in working out profits chargeable to corporation tax.**

3.4 A company must deduct 20% tax from interest paid unless it is short interest (interest on a loan for a year or less) or interest payable to a bank.

Quarterly accounting for income tax

3.5 **Income tax is accounted for by companies on a quarterly basis on a return form CT 61. Returns are made for each of the quarters to 31 March, 30 June, 30 September and 31 December.** If the end of a company's accounting period does not coincide with one of these dates, a fifth return must be made to the end of the accounting period (and a new return period started at the beginning of the company's next accounting period).

Question: Quarterly returns

S Ltd makes up accounts to 31 May each year. Show the income tax quarterly return periods for this company for the year to 31 May 2001.

Answer

(a) 1 June 2000 to 30 June 2000
(b) 1 July 2000 to 30 September 2000
(c) 1 October 2000 to 31 December 2000
(d) 1 January 2001 to 31 March 2001
(e) 1 April 2001 to 31 May 2001

3.6 **Each quarterly return has details of income tax suffered and income tax withheld from interest and charges.** (*Note: not the gross income and payment figures.*)

3.7 **The company must account to the Revenue for any income tax payable 14 days after the end of the return period. Interest runs from this date.**

3.8 The overall amount of income tax due is reduced by that suffered on income received.

3.9 **If a company has tax suffered on income exceeding its tax deducted from payments, it can reclaim the income tax suffered by recovering income tax payments already made through the quarterly accounting system or by reducing its corporation tax liability.** If appropriate a repayment of income tax will be made after the corporation tax computation has been submitted. There is no limit on the amount which can be set off.

Question: Quarterly accounting for income tax

Income plc has the following income and payments for the year to 31 March 2001.

		£
30.4.00	Patent royalty paid	10,000
30.9.00	Debenture interest received	14,000
30.11.00	Debenture interest paid	10,000
5.3.01	Patent royalty received	18,000

All of the above figures are gross.

Set out the relevant CT 61 income tax returns.

Answer

Return period	Tax on payments	Tax on income	Income tax Due	Income tax Repayable	Due date
	£	£	£	£	
1.4.00 - 30.6.00	2,200	0	2,200	0	14.7.00
1.7.00 - 30.9.00	0	2,800	0	(2,200) (a)	14.10.00
1.10.00 - 31.12.00	2,000	0	1,400 (b)	0	14.1.01
1.1.01 - 31.3.01	0	3,960	0	(1,400) (a)	14.4.01
	4,200	6,760			
		4,200			
		2,560 (c)			

Notes

(a) The repayment is restricted to income tax already paid in the same accounting period. The return is due by the date shown, but there is no set date by which the Revenue must make the repayment.

(b) Up to the end of the previous quarter, the net tax suffered is £(2,800 2,200) = £600. The tax to be accounted for is therefore £(2,000 – 600) = £1,400.

(c) £2,560, the net income tax suffered over the year, will be set against the company's corporation tax liability. If that liability is less than £2,560, the company will receive a repayment of income tax suffered.

Chapter roundup

- CT 600 returns must, in general, be filed within twelve months of the end of an accounting period.

- The Revenue can enquire into returns.

- In general, corporation tax is due nine months after the end of an accounting period but large companies must pay their corporation tax in four quarterly instalments.

- Income tax is accounted for quarterly, but income tax suffered is always recovered in full for each accounting period

BPP PUBLISHING

Quick quiz

1   What are the penalties for failure to deliver a corporation tax return on time? (see paras 1.6-1.7)

2   For how long must a company keep records? (1.10)

3   When must the Revenue give notice that it is going to start an enquiry? (1.14)

4   State the due dates for the payment of quarterly instalments of corporation tax. (2.5)

5   Which companies must pay quarterly instalments of their corporation tax liability? (2.4, 2.8)

6   For which periods are CT61s due? (3.5)

7   How do companies account for income tax? (3.5 - 3.9)

Now try the questions below from the Exam Question Bank

Number	Level	Marks	Time
12	Exam	21	35 mins
13	Exam	30	54 mins

Chapter 10

VALUE ADDED TAX 1

Topic list	Syllabus reference
1 Basic principles	1j, 2e
2 The scope of VAT	1j, 2e
3 Registration	1j, 2e
4 Accounting for VAT	1j, 2e
5 VAT invoices and records	1j, 2e
6 The valuation of supplies	1j, 2e
7 Administration	1j, 2e
8 Penalties	1j, 2e

Introduction

In this and the next chapter, we study value added tax (VAT). VAT is a tax on turnover rather than on profits. It applies to both corporate and unincorporated businesses so may be tested under Sections 1 or 2 of the syllabus.

As the name of the tax suggests, it is charged (usually at 17.5%) on the value added. If someone in a chain of manufacture or distribution buys goods for £1,000 and sells them for £1,200 he has increased their value by £200. (He may have painted them, packed them or distributed them to shops to justify his mark-up, or he may simply be good at making deals to buy cheaply and sell dearly.) Because he has added value of £200, he collects VAT of £200 × 17.5% = £35 and pays this over to the government. The VAT is collected bit by bit along the chain and finally hits the consumer who does not add value, but uses up the goods.

VAT is a tax with simple computations but many detailed rules to ensure its enforcement. You may find it easier to absorb the detail if you ask yourself, in relation to each rule, exactly how it helps to enforce the tax.

Study guide

Value Added Tax

- Describe the scope of VAT
- State the circumstances in which a person must register for VAT, and explain the advantages of voluntary VAT registration
- Explain how a person can deregister for VAT
- Explain how the tax point is determined
- State the circumstances in which pre-registration input VAT can be recovered
- Explain how VAT is accounted for and administered
- List the information that must be given on a VAT invoice
- Describe the principles that apply to the valuation of supplies
- State the circumstances in which the default surcharge, a serious misdeclaration penalty and default interest will be applied

---

Exam guide

Question 3 (15 marks) in Section B will be on Value Added Tax (either for an incorporated business or an unincorporated business).

---

1 BASIC PRINCIPLES

1.1 The legal basis of value added tax (VAT) is to be found in the Value Added Tax Act 1994 (VATA 1994), supplemented by regulations made by statutory instrument and amended by subsequent Finance Acts. VAT is administered by HM Customs & Excise. In legal proceedings they are called 'the Commissioners of Customs & Excise'.

1.2 VAT is a tax on turnover, not on profits. The basic principle is that the VAT should be borne by the final consumer. Registered traders may deduct the tax which they suffer on supplies to them (input VAT) from the tax which they charge to their customers (output VAT) at the time this is paid to HM Customs & Excise. Thus, at each stage of the manufacturing or service process, the net VAT paid is on the value added at that stage.

1.3 EXAMPLE: THE VAT CHARGE

A forester sells wood to a furniture maker for £100 plus VAT. The furniture maker uses this wood to make a table and sells the table to a shop for £150 plus VAT. The shop then sells the table to the final consumer for £300 plus VAT. VAT will be accounted for to HM Customs & Excise as follows.

	Cost	Input VAT 17.5%	Net sale price	Output VAT 17.5%	Payable to HM Customs & Excise
	£	£	£	£	£
Forester	0	0	100	17.50	17.50
Furniture maker	100	17.50	150	26.25	8.75
Shop	150	26.25	300	52.50	26.25
					52.50

1.4 Because the traders involved account to HM Customs & Excise for VAT charged less VAT suffered, their profits for income tax or corporation tax purposes are based on sales and purchases net of VAT.

2 THE SCOPE OF VAT

2.1 **VAT is charged on taxable supplies of goods and services made in the UK by a taxable person in the course or furtherance of any business carried on by him.**

KEY TERM

A **taxable supply** is a supply of goods or services made in the UK, other than an exempt supply.

2.2 A taxable supply is either standard rated or zero rated. The standard rate is 17.5% (although on certain supplies, for example the supply of domestic fuel and power, a lower rate is charged of 5%) and zero rated supplies are taxed at 0%. An exempt supply is not chargeable to VAT. The categories of zero rated and exempt supplies are listed in the next chapter.

104

Supplies of goods

2.3 **Goods are supplied if exclusive ownership of the goods passes to another person.** The following are also supplies of goods.

- The supply of any form of power, heat, refrigeration or ventilation, or of water

- The grant, assignment or surrender of a major interest (the freehold or a lease for over 21 years) in land

- Taking goods permanently out of the business for the non-business use of a taxable person or for other private purposes including the supply of goods by an employer to an employee for his private use

- Transfers under an agreement contemplating a transfer of ownership, such as a hire purchase agreement

2.4 **Gifts of goods are normally treated as sales at cost** (so VAT is due). **However, business gifts are not supplies of goods if:**

  (a) **the cost to the donor is £15 or less** and the gift is not part of a series of gifts made to the same person; or

  (b) **the gift is a sample.** However, if two or more identical samples are given to the same person, all but one of them are treated as supplies.

Supplies of services

2.5 Apart from a few specific exceptions, **any supply which is not a supply of goods as** defined above **and which is done for a consideration is a supply of services**. A consideration is any form of payment in money or in kind, including anything which is itself a supply.

2.6 A supply of services also takes place if:

- goods are lent to someone for use outside the business;
- goods are hired to someone;
- services bought for business purposes are used for private purposes.

2.7 The European Court of Justice has ruled that restaurants supply services rather than goods.

Taxable persons

2.8 **The term 'person' includes individuals, partnerships** (which are treated as single entities, ignoring the individual partners), **companies, clubs, associations and charities. If a person is in business making taxable supplies, then the value of these supplies is called the taxable turnover. If a person's taxable turnover exceeds certain limits then he is a taxable person and should be registered for VAT.**

3 REGISTRATION

Compulsory registration

3.1 **A person making taxable supplies becomes liable to register for VAT if**, in any period of up to 12 consecutive calendar months, **the value of his taxable supplies** (excluding VAT) **exceeds £52,000** (from 1 April 2000 onwards). The person is required to notify HM Customs & Excise within 30 days of the end of the 12 month period. HM Customs & Excise will then register the person with effect from the end of the month following the 12 month period, or from an earlier date if they and the trader agree.

Registration under this rule is not required if HM Customs & Excise are satisfied that the value of the trader's taxable supplies (excluding VAT) in the year starting at the end of the 12 month period will not exceed £50,000 (from 1 April 2000 onwards).

3.2 A person is also liable to register at any time if there are reasonable grounds for believing that his taxable supplies (excluding VAT) in the following 30 days will exceed £52,000. HM Customs & Excise must be notified by the end of the 30 day period and registration will be with effect from the beginning of that period.

3.3 **When determining the value of a person's taxable supplies for the purposes of registration, supplies of goods and services that are *capital assets* of the business are to be disregarded,** except for non-zero rated supplies of interests in land.

Question: VAT registration

Fred started to trade in cutlery on 1 January 2000. Sales (excluding VAT) were £4,325 a month for the first nine months and £7,100 a month thereafter. From what date should Fred be registered for VAT?

Answer

	£
Sales to 31 October 2000	46,025
Sales to 30 November 2000	53,125 (exceeds £52,000)

Fred must notify his liability to register by 30 December 2000 (not 31 December) and will be registered from 1 January 2001 or from an agreed earlier date.

3.4 When a person is liable to register in respect of a past period, it is his responsibility to pay VAT. If he is unable to collect it from those to whom he made taxable supplies, the VAT burden will fall on him. A person must start keeping VAT records and charging VAT to customers as soon as it is known that he is required to register. However, VAT should not be shown separately on any invoices until the registration number is known. The invoice should show the VAT inclusive price and customers should be informed that VAT invoices will be forwarded once the registration number is known. Formal VAT invoices should then be sent to such customers within 30 days of getting the registration number.

3.5 **Notification of liability to register must be made on form VAT 1.** Simply writing to, or telephoning, a local VAT office is not enough. On registration the VAT office will send the trader a certificate of registration. This shows the VAT registration number, the date of registration, the end of the first VAT period and the length of later VAT periods.

3.6 If a trader makes a supply before becoming liable to register, but gets paid after registration, VAT is not due on that supply.

Voluntary registration

3.7 **A person may decide to become registered even though his taxable turnover falls below the registration limit. Unless a person is registered he cannot recover the input VAT he pays on supplies to him.**

3.8 Voluntary registration is advantageous where a person wishes to recover input VAT on supplies to him. For example, consider a trader who has one input during the year which cost £1,000 plus £175 VAT; he works on the input which becomes his sole output for the year and he decides to make a profit of £1,000.

(a) If he is not registered he will charge £2,175 and his customer will obtain no relief for any VAT.

(b) If he is registered he will charge £2,000 plus VAT of £350. His customer will have input VAT of £350 which he will be able to recover if he, too, is registered.

If the customer is a non-taxable person he will prefer (a) as the cost to him is £2,175. If he is taxable he will prefer (b) as the net cost is £2,000. Thus, a decision whether or not to register voluntarily may depend upon the status of customers. It may also depend on the status of the outputs and the image of his business the trader wishes to project (registration may give the impression of a substantial business). The administrative burden of registration should also be considered.

Intending trader registration

3.9 **Providing that a trader satisfies HM Customs & Excise that he is carrying on a business, and intends to make taxable supplies, he is entitled to be registered if he chooses.** But, once registered, he is obliged to notify HM Customs & Excise within 30 days if he no longer intends to make taxable supplies.

Exemption from registration

3.10 **If a person makes only zero rated supplies, he may request exemption from registration.** The trader is obliged to notify HM Customs & Excise of any material change in the nature of his supplies

HM Customs & Excise may also allow exemption from registration if only a small proportion of supplies are standard rated, provided that the trader would normally receive repayments of VAT if registered.

Deregistration

Voluntary deregistration

3.11 **A person is eligible for voluntary deregistration if HM Customs & Excise are satisfied that the value of his taxable supplies** (net of VAT and excluding supplies of capital assets) **in the following one year period will not exceed £50,000 (from 1 April 2000).** However, voluntary deregistration will not be allowed if the reason for the expected fall in value of taxable supplies is the cessation of taxable supplies or the suspension of taxable supplies for a period of 30 days or more in that following year.

3.12 HM Customs & Excise will cancel a person's registration from the date the request is made or from an agreed later date.

Compulsory deregistration

3.13 **Traders may be compulsorily deregistered.** Failure to notify a requirement to deregister may lead to a penalty. Compulsory deregistration may also lead to HM Customs & Excise reclaiming input VAT which has been wrongly recovered by the trader since the date on which he should have deregistered.

3.14 Other points to note are:

- If HM Customs & Excise are misled into granting registration then the registration is treated as void from the start.

- A person may be compulsorily deregistered if HM Customs & Excise are satisfied that he is no longer making nor intending to make taxable supplies.

- Changes in legal status also require cancellation of registration. For example:
  - (i)   a sole trader becoming a partnership;
  - (ii) a partnership reverting to a sole trader;
  - (iii) a business being incorporated;
  - (iv) a company being replaced by an unincorporated business.

The consequences of deregistration

3.15 **On deregistration, VAT is chargeable on all stocks and capital assets in a business on which input VAT was claimed,** since the registered trader is in effect making a taxable supply to himself as a newly unregistered trader. If the VAT chargeable does not exceed £1,000, it need not be paid.

3.16 **This special VAT charge does not apply if the business** (or a separately viable part of it) **is sold as a going concern to another taxable person** (or a person who immediately becomes a taxable person as a result of the transfer). **Such transfers are outside the scope of VAT** (except for assets being transferred which are 'new' or opted buildings and the transferee does not make an election to waive exemption - refer to the section on land in the next chapter). If the original owner ceases to be taxable, the new owner of the business may also take over the existing VAT number. If he does so, he takes over the rights and liabilities of the transferor as at the date of transfer.

3.17 On a transfer of a business as a going concern the transferee must include the turnover of the business before the transfer when looking at his own turnover for registration purposes.

Pre-registration input VAT

3.18 **VAT incurred before registration can be treated as input VAT and recovered from HM Customs & Excise subject to certain conditions.**

3.19 If the claim is for input VAT suffered on goods purchased prior to registration then the following conditions must be satisfied.

(a) The goods were acquired for the purpose of the business which either was carried on or was to be carried on by him at the time of supply.

(b) The goods have not been supplied onwards or consumed before the date of registration (although they may have been used to make other goods which are still held).

(c) The VAT must have been incurred in the three years prior to the effective date of registration.

3.20 If the claim is for input VAT suffered on the supply of services prior to registration then both of the following conditions must be satisfied.

(a) The services were supplied for the purposes of a business which either was carried on or was to be carried on by him at the time of supply.

(b) The services were supplied within the six months prior to the date of registration.

3.21 Input tax attributable to supplies made before registration is not deductible even if the input VAT concerned is treated as having been incurred after registration.

4 ACCOUNTING FOR VAT

VAT periods

4.1 **The VAT period (also known as the tax period) is the period covered by a VAT return. It is usually three calendar months.** The return shows the total input and output VAT for the tax period and must be submitted (along with any VAT due) within one month of the end of the period. (Businesses who pay VAT electronically automatically receive a seven day extension to this time limit.)

4.2 HM Customs & Excise allocate VAT periods according to the class of trade carried on (ending in June, September, December and March; July, October, January and April; or August, November, February and May), to spread the flow of VAT returns evenly over the year. When applying for registration a trader can ask for VAT periods which fit in with his own accounting year. It is also possible to have VAT periods to cover accounting systems not based on calendar months.

4.3 A registered person whose input VAT will regularly exceed his output VAT can elect for a one month VAT period, but will have to balance the inconvenience of making 12 returns a year against the advantage of obtaining more rapid repayments of VAT.

4.4 Certain small businesses may submit an annual VAT return (see the next chapter).

The tax point

4.5 **The tax point of each supply is the deemed date of supply. The basic tax point is the date on which the goods are removed or made available to the customer, or the date on which services are completed.**

4.6 The tax point determines the VAT period in which output VAT must be accounted for and credit for input VAT will be allowed. The tax point also determines which rate applies if the rate of VAT or a VAT category changes (for example when a supply ceases to be zero rated and becomes standard rated).

4.7 **If a VAT invoice is issued or payment is received before the basic tax point, the earlier of these dates automatically becomes the tax point. If the earlier date rule does not apply and if the VAT invoice is issued within 14 days after the basic tax point, the invoice date becomes the tax point** (although the trader can elect to use the basic point for all his supplies if he wishes). This period may be extended to accommodate, for example, monthly invoicing; the tax point is then the VAT invoice date or the end of the month, whichever is applied consistently.

4.8 **Goods supplied on sale or return are treated as supplied on the earlier of adoption by the customer or 12 months after despatch. Continuous supplies of services paid for periodically have tax points on the earlier of the receipt of each payment and the issue of each VAT invoice,** unless one invoice covering several payments is issued in advance for up to a year. The tax point is then the earlier of each due date or date of actual payment.

The VAT return

4.9 The regular VAT return to HM Customs & Excise is made on form VAT 100. The boxes on a VAT return which a trader must fill in are as follows.

(a) Box 1: the VAT due on sales and other outputs

(b) Box 2: the VAT due on acquisitions from other EC member states

(c) Box 3: the total of boxes 1 and 2

(d) Box 4: the VAT reclaimed on purchases and other inputs

(e) Box 5: the net VAT to be paid or reclaimed: the difference between boxes 3 and 4

(f) Box 6: the total value (before cash discounts) of sales and all other outputs, excluding VAT but including the total in box 8

(g) Box 7: the total value (before cash discounts) of purchases and all other inputs, excluding VAT but including the total in box 9

(h) Box 8: the total value of all sales and related services to other EC member states

(i) Box 9: the total value of all purchases and related services from other EC member states

4.10 Input and output VAT figures must be supported by the original or copy tax invoices, and records must be maintained for six years.

Internet filing of VAT returns

4.11 Customs are currently developing systems to allow businesses to file their VAT returns via the Internet.

4.12 From April 2001, for one year only, approved small businesses that file their VAT returns via the Internet and pay the tax due electronically will receive a one-off discount of £50. Such businesses must have a turnover below £600,000.

Substantial traders

4.13 **If a trader does not make monthly returns, and the total VAT liability over 12 months to the end of a VAT period exceeds £2,000,000, he must make payments on account of each quarter's VAT liability during the quarter.** Payments are due a month before the end of the quarter and at the end of the quarter, with the final payment due at the usual time, a month after the end of the quarter. An electronic payment system must be used, not a cheque through the post.

4.14 For a trader who exceeds the £2,000,000 limit in the 12 months to 30 September, 31 October or 30 November, the amount of each of the two payments on account is 1/24 of the total VAT liability of those 12 months. The obligation to pay on account starts with the first VAT period starting *after* 31 March.

4.15 A trader who first exceeds the £2,000,000 limit in 12 months ending at some other time must pay 1/24 of the VAT liability for the first 12 months in which he exceeded the £2,000,000 limit. His obligation starts with the first VAT period which starts after those 12 months, unless he first went over the £2,000,000 limit in the 12 months to 31 December: in that case, his obligation starts with the VAT period starting on 1 April.

4.16 If the total VAT liability for any later 12 months is less than 80% of the total liability for the 12 months used to compute the payments on account, the trader can apply to use 1/24 of that later total. A later total can even be used if the 12 months have not ended, so long as HM Customs & Excise are satisfied that it will be below the 80% limit. A trader can leave the scheme if the latest 12 months' VAT liability was less than £1,600,000.

4.17 If a trader's total annual liability increases to 120% or more of the amount used to calculate the payments on account, then the new higher annual liability is used to calculate new payments on account. The increase applies from the end of the 12 months with the new higher annual liability.

4.18 Once a trader is in the scheme, the payments on account are also recomputed annually, using the liability in the 12 months to 30 September, 31 October or 30 November, even if the change is less than ± 20%. The new figure first applies to the first VAT period starting after 31 March.

4.19 Traders can choose to switch from making quarterly to monthly returns instead of paying the interim amounts calculated by Customs. For example, the actual return and liability for January would be due at the end of February.

4.20 Traders can also choose to pay their actual monthly liability without having to make monthly returns. Customs can refuse to allow a trader to continue doing this if they find he has abused the facility by not paying enough. The trader will then either have to pay the interim amount or switch to making monthly returns.

4.21 A trader does have the right to appeal to a VAT tribunal if Customs and Excise refuse to allow him to make monthly payments of his actual liability.

Refunds of VAT

4.22 **There is a three year time limit on the right to reclaim overpaid VAT.** This time limit does not apply to input VAT which a business could not have reclaimed earlier because the supplier only recently invoiced the VAT, even though it related to a purchase made some time ago. Nor does it apply to overpaid VAT penalties.

4.23 If a taxpayer has overpaid VAT and has overclaimed input tax by reason of the same mistake, HM Customs and Excise can set off any tax, penalty, interest or surcharge due to them against any repayment due to the taxpayer and repay only the net amount. In such cases the normal three year time limit for recovering VAT, penalties, interest, etc by assessment does not apply.

4.24 **HM Customs and Excise can refuse to make any repayment which would unjustly enrich the claimant.** They can also refuse a repayment of VAT where all or part of the tax has, for practical purposes, been borne by a person other than the taxpayer (eg by a customer of the taxpayer) except to the extent that the taxpayer can show loss or damage to any of his businesses as a result of mistaken assumptions about VAT.

4.25 In *Marks and Spencer plc v CCE (1998)* chocolate teacakes which had been treated as standard rated were later found to be zero-rated. M&S sought a repayment of the overpaid VAT but the Tribunal thought that had M&S been aware of the true VAT position it would have remained in the same economic position by varying its prices to maintain a similar margin. It followed that M&S had, in effect, passed on most of the VAT to its customers without suffering economic loss, and it would be unjustly enriched if more than ten per cent of the overpaid VAT was repaid to it. M&S are so unhappy with this decision that the case has now gone to the European Court of Justice.

5   VAT INVOICES AND RECORDS

5.1   **A taxable person making a taxable supply to another person registered for VAT must supply a VAT invoice within 30 days of the time of supply, and must keep a copy.** The invoice must show:

(a)   the supplier's name, address and registration number;

(b)   the date of issue, the tax point and an invoice number;

(c)   the name and address of the customer;

(d)   the type of supply (sale, hire purchase, loan, exchange, hire, goods made from the customer's materials, sale on commission, sale or return, etc);

(e)   a description of the goods or services supplied, giving for each description the quantity, the rate of VAT and the VAT exclusive amount;

(f)   the rate of any cash discount;

(g)   the total invoice price excluding VAT (with separate totals for zero rated and exempt supplies);

(h)   each VAT rate applicable, the amount of VAT at each rate and the total amount of VAT.

5.2   If an invoice is issued, and a change in price then alters the VAT due, a credit note or debit note to adjust the VAT must be issued.

5.3   Credit notes must give the reason for the credit (such as 'returned goods'), and the number and date of the original VAT invoice. If a credit note makes no VAT adjustment, it should state this.

5.4   **A less detailed VAT invoice may be issued by a retailer where the invoice is for a total including VAT of up to £100.** Such an invoice must show:

(a)   the supplier's name, address and registration number;
(b)   the date of the supply;
(c)   a description of the goods or services supplied;
(d)   the rate of VAT chargeable;
(e)   the total amount chargeable including VAT.

Zero rated and exempt supplies must not be included in less detailed invoices.

5.5   **VAT invoices are not required for payments of up to £25 including VAT which are for telephone calls or car park fees or are made through cash operated machines. In such cases, input VAT can be claimed without a VAT invoice.**

5.6   **Every VAT registered trader must keep records for six years,** although HM Customs & Excise may sometimes grant permission for their earlier destruction. They may be kept on paper, on microfilm or microfiche or on computer. However, there must be adequate facilities for HM Customs & Excise to inspect records.

5.7   All records must be kept up to date and in a way which allows:

- the calculation of VAT due;
- officers of HM Customs & Excise to check the figures on VAT returns.

5.8   The following records are needed.

- Copies of VAT invoices, credit notes and debit notes issued

- A summary of supplies made

- VAT invoices, credit notes and debit notes received

- A summary of supplies received

- A VAT account

- Order and delivery notes, correspondence, appointment books, job books, purchases and sales books, cash books, account books, records of takings (such as till rolls), bank paying-in slips, bank statements and annual accounts

- Records of zero rated and exempt supplies, gifts or loans of goods, taxable self-supplies and any goods taken for non-business use

6   THE VALUATION OF SUPPLIES

6.1   **The value of a supply is the VAT-exclusive price on which VAT is charged. The consideration for a supply is the amount paid in money or money's worth.** Thus with a standard rate of 17.5%:

Value + VAT = consideration
£100 + £17.50 = £117.50

The VAT proportion of the consideration is known as the 'VAT fraction'. It is

$$\frac{\text{rate of tax}}{100 + \text{rate of tax}} = \frac{17.5}{100 + 17.5} = \frac{7}{47}$$

6.2   Provided the consideration for a bargain made at arm's length is paid in money, the value for VAT purposes is the VAT exclusive price charged by the trader. If it is paid in something other than money, as in a barter of some goods or services for others, it must be valued and VAT will be due on the value.

6.3   If the price of goods is effectively reduced with money off coupons, the value of the supply is the amount actually received by the taxpayer.

Mixed supplies and composite supplies

6.4   **Different goods and services are sometimes invoiced together at an inclusive price (a mixed supply).** Some items may be chargeable at the standard rate and some at the zero rate. **The supplier must account for VAT separately on the standard rated and zero rated elements by splitting the total amount payable in a fair proportion between the different elements and charging VAT on each at the appropriate rate.** There is no single way of doing this: one method is to split the amount according to the cost to the supplier of each element, and another is to use the open market value of each element.

6.5   **If a supply cannot be split into components, there is a composite supply, to which one VAT rate must be applied.** The rate depends on the nature of the supply as a whole.

6.6   A supply of air transport including an in-flight meal has been held to be a single, composite supply of transport (zero rated) rather than a supply of transport (zero rated) and a supply of a meal (standard rated). Contrast this with where catering is included in the price of leisure travel - there are two separate supplies: standard rated catering and zero rated passenger transport.

6.7   Broadly, a composite supply occurs when one element of the supply is merely incidental to the main element. A mixed supply occurs where different elements of the supply are the subject of separate negotiation and customer choice giving rise to identifiable obligations on the supplier.

Discounts

6.8   **Where a discount is offered for prompt payment, VAT is chargeable on the net amount, regardless of whether the discount is taken up** (except that for imports from outside the EC, the discount is ignored unless it is taken up). Supplies made on contingent discount terms (for example depending on the level of purchases) must be invoiced with VAT based on the full amount, an adjustment being made when the discount is earned. When goods are sold to staff at a discount, VAT is only due on the discounted price.

6.9   Goods supplied under a hire purchase agreement are chargeable on the cash selling price at the start of the contract.

6.10   If a trader charges different prices to customers paying with credit cards and those paying by other means, the VAT due in respect of each standard rated sale is the full amount paid by the customer × the VAT fraction.

6.11   **When goods are permanently taken from a business for non-business purposes VAT must be accounted for on their market value.** If services bought for business purposes are used for non-business purposes (without charge), then VAT must be accounted for on their cost, but the VAT to be accounted for is not allowed to exceed the input VAT deductible on the purchase of the services.

7   ADMINISTRATION

Local VAT offices

7.1   **Local VAT offices are responsible for the local administration of VAT and for providing advice to registered persons whose principal place of business is in their area.** They are controlled by regional collectors.

7.2   **Completed VAT returns should be sent to the VAT Central Unit at Southend,** not to a local VAT office.

7.3   **From time to time a registered person will be visited by staff from a local VAT office (a control visit)** to ensure that the law is understood and is being applied properly. If a trader disagrees with any decision as to the application of VAT given by HM Customs & Excise he can ask his local VAT office to reconsider the decision. It is not necessary to appeal formally to a tribunal while a case is being reviewed in this way. Where an appeal can be settled by agreement before being heard by a tribunal, a written settlement has the same force as a tribunal decision.

7.4   **HM Customs & Excise may issue assessments of VAT due to the best of their judgement if they believe that a trader has failed to make returns or if they believe those returns to be incorrect or incomplete.** The time limit for making assessments is normally three years after the end of a VAT period, but this is extended to 20 years in the case of fraud, dishonest conduct, certain registration irregularities and the unauthorised issue of VAT invoices.

HM Customs & Excise sometimes write to traders, setting out their calculations, before issuing assessments. The traders can then query the calculations.

Appeals to VAT and duties tribunals

7.5 **VAT and duties tribunals, which are independent of HM Customs & Excise, provide a method of dealing with disputes.** Provided that VAT returns and payments shown thereon have been made, appeals can be heard.

A tribunal can waive the requirement to pay all VAT shown on returns before an appeal is heard in cases of hardship. It cannot allow an appeal against a purely administrative matter such as Customs refusal to apply an extra statutory concession.

There may be a dispute over the deductibility of input VAT which hinges on the purposes for which goods or services were used, or on whether they were used to make taxable supplies. The trader must show that HM Customs & Excise acted unreasonably in refusing a deduction, if the goods or services are luxuries, amusements or entertainment.

Time limits

7.6 **An appeal must be lodged with the tribunal (not the local VAT office) within 30 days of the date of any decision by HM Customs & Excise. If instead the trader would like the local VAT office to reconsider their decision he should apply within 30 days of the decision to the relevant VAT office.** The local VAT office may either:

- confirm the original decision, in which case the taxpayer has a further 21 days from the date of that confirmation in which to lodge an appeal with a tribunal; or

- send a revised decision, in which case the taxpayer will have a further 30 days from the date of the revised decision in which to lodge an appeal with a tribunal.

7.7 Tribunal hearings are normally in public, and decisions are published. If one of the parties is dissatisfied with a decision on a point of law he may appeal to the courts. Tribunals may award costs.

The Adjudicator

7.8 **The Adjudicator for the Inland Revenue, Customs & Excise and the Contributions Agency is independent of these bodies.** The Adjudicator considers complaints about the way in which taxpayers' affairs are handled, for example complaints about delays or the exercise of officials' discretion. The Adjudicator does not consider complaints where there are alternative channels of appeal, such as exist for appeals against assessments.

Tax avoidance and evasion

7.9 Significant resources are deployed to tackle fraud, tax evasion and avoidance. To assist in this Customs & Excise, the Revenue and the DSS can pass information to each other.

8   PENALTIES

The default surcharge

8.1   A default occurs when a trader either submits his VAT return late, or submits the return on time but pays the VAT late. It also occurs when a payment on account from a substantial trader is late. **If a trader defaults, HM Customs & Excise will serve a surcharge liability notice on the trader. The notice specifies a surcharge period running from the date of the notice to the anniversary of the end of the period for which the trader is in default.**

8.2   If a further default occurs in respect of a return period ending during the specified surcharge period the original surcharge period will be extended to the anniversary of the end of the period to which the new default relates. In addition, if the default involves the late payment of VAT (as opposed to simply a late return) a surcharge is levied.

8.3   The surcharge depends on the number of defaults involving late payment of VAT which have occurred in respect of periods ending in the surcharge period, as follows.

Default involving late payment of VAT in the surcharge period	Surcharge as a percentage of the VAT outstanding at the due date
First	2%
Second	5%
Third	10%
Fourth and over	15%

Surcharges at the 2% and 5% rates are not normally demanded unless the amount due would be at least £200 but for surcharges calculated using the 10% or 15% rates there is a minimum amount of £30 payable.

If a substantial trader is late with more than one payment (on account or final) for a return period, this only counts as one default. The total VAT paid late is the total of late payments on account plus the late final payment.

8.4   A trader must submit one year's returns on time and pay the VAT shown on them on time in order to break out of the surcharge liability period and the escalation of surcharge percentages.

8.5   A default will be ignored for all default surcharge purposes if the trader can show that the return or payment was sent at such a time, and in such a manner, that it was reasonable to expect that HM Customs & Excise would receive it by the due date. Posting the return and payment first class the day before the due date is generally accepted as meeting this requirement. A default will also be ignored if the trader can demonstrate a reasonable excuse (see above) for the late submission or payment.

The misdeclaration penalty

8.6   The making of a return which understates a person's true liability or overstates the repayment due to him incurs a penalty of 15% of the VAT which would have been lost if the return had been accepted as correct. The same penalty applies when HM Customs & Excise issue an assessment which is too low and the trader fails to notify the error within 30 days from the issue of the assessment. **These penalties apply only where the VAT which would have been lost is at least £1,000,000 or is at least 30% of the sum of the true input VAT and the true output VAT. This sum is known as the gross amount of tax (GAT).** (In the case of an incorrect assessment 30% of the true amount of tax, the VAT actually due from or to the trader, is used instead of 30% of the GAT.) The penalty may be mitigated.

8.7 **Errors on a VAT return of up to £2,000 (net: underdeclaration minus overdeclaration) may be corrected on the next return without giving rise to a misdeclaration penalty or interest.**

8.8 This penalty does not apply if the trader can show reasonable excuse (see above) for his conduct, or if he made a full disclosure when he had no reason to suppose that HM Customs & Excise were enquiring into his affairs.

Default interest

8.9 **Interest** (not deductible in computing taxable profits) **is charged on VAT which is the subject of an assessment** (where returns were not made or were incorrect), **or which could have been the subject of an assessment but was paid before the assessment was raised. It runs from the reckonable date until the date of payment.** This interest is sometimes called 'default interest'.

8.10 **The reckonable date is when the VAT should have been paid** (one month from the end of the return period), or in the case of VAT repayments, seven days from the issue of the repayment order. However, where VAT is charged by an assessment interest does not run from more than three years before the date of the assessment; and where the VAT was paid before an assessment was raised, interest does not run for more than three years before the date of payment.

8.11 In practice, interest is only charged when there would otherwise be a loss to the Exchequer. It is not, for example, charged when a company failed to charge VAT but if it had done so, another company would have been able to recover the VAT.

Repayment supplement

8.12 **Where a person is entitled to a repayment of VAT and the original return was rendered on time but HM Customs & Excise do not issue a written instruction for the repayment to be made within 30 days of the receipt of the return, then the person will receive a supplement of the greater of £50 and 5% of the amount due.**

8.13 **If the return states a refund due which differs from the correct refund due by more than the greater of 5% of the correct refund and £250, no supplement is added.**

8.14 Days spent in raising and answering reasonable enquiries in relation to the return do not count towards the 30 days allowed to HM Customs & Excise to issue an instruction to make the repayment. The earliest date on which the 30 days can start is the day following the end of the prescribed accounting period.

Interest on overpayments due to official errors

8.15 **If VAT is overpaid or a credit for input VAT is not claimed because of an error by HM Customs & Excise, then the trader may claim interest on the amount eventually refunded, running from the date on which he paid the excessive VAT** (or from the date on which HM Customs & Excise might reasonably be expected to have authorised a VAT repayment) **to the date on which HM Customs & Excise authorise a repayment.**

8.16 Interest must be claimed within three years of the date on which the trader discovered the error or could with reasonable diligence have discovered it. Interest is not available where a repayment supplement is available. Interest does not run for periods relating to reasonable enquiries by HM Customs & Excise into the matter in question.

Chapter roundup

- VAT is charged on turnover at each stage in a production process, but in such a way that the burden is borne by the final consumer.

- A trader may be required to register for VAT because of the level of his turnover, or he may register voluntarily.

- VAT is accounted for on regular returns. Extensive records must be kept.

- VAT is administered by HM Customs & Excise, and independent tribunals hear appeals. There is an extensive regime of penalties to ensure compliance with VAT law.

Quick quiz

1 On what transactions will VAT be charged? (see para 2.1)

2 What is a taxable person? (2.8)

3 When must a person register for VAT? (3.1, 3.2)

4 When may a person be deregistered? (3.11, 3.13)

5 How is the tax point determined? (4.5, 4.7, 4.8)

6 What must be shown on a VAT invoice? (5.1, 5.4)

7 How do discounts affect the computation of VAT due? (6.8)

8 Within what time limit must an appeal to a tribunal be lodged? (7.6)

9 What is a default? (8.1)

Now try the question below from the Exam Question Bank

Number	Level	Marks	Time
14	Exam	12	22 mins

Chapter 11

VALUE ADDED TAX 2

Topic list	Syllabus reference
1 Zero rated and exempt supplies	1j, 2e
2 The deduction of input VAT	1j, 2e
3 Special schemes	1j, 2e

Introduction

This chapter concentrates on matters which do not apply to every trader. We start by looking at zero rated and exempt supplies. We then consider the deduction of input tax and relief for bad debts.

Finally, we look at two special schemes.

Study guide

Value Added Tax

- List the principal zero-rated and exempt supplies

- Describe the relief that is available for bad debts

- State the circumstances in which input VAT is non-deductible

- Describe the cash accounting and the annual accounting schemes

Exam guide

Question 3 (15 marks) in Section B will be on Value Added Tax (either for an incorporated business or an unincorporated business).

1   ZERO RATED AND EXEMPT SUPPLIES

1.1   **Zero rated supplies are taxable at 0%.** A taxable supplier whose outputs are zero rated but whose inputs are standard rated will obtain repayments of the VAT paid on purchases.

1.2   Exempt supplies are not so advantageous. In exactly the same way as for a non-registered person, a **person making exempt supplies is unable to recover VAT on inputs**.

The exempt supplier thus has to shoulder the burden of VAT. Of course, he may increase his prices to pass on the charge, but he cannot issue a VAT invoice which would enable a taxable customer to obtain a credit for VAT, since no VAT is chargeable on his supplies.

BPP PUBLISHING

1.3   EXAMPLE: STANDARD RATED, ZERO RATED AND EXEMPT SUPPLIES

Here are figures for three traders, the first with standard rated outputs, the second with zero rated outputs and the third with exempt outputs. All their inputs are standard rated.

	Standard rated £	Zero rated £	Exempt £
Inputs	20,000	20,000	20,000
VAT	3,500	3,500	3,500
	23,500	23,500	23,500
Outputs	30,000	30,000	30,000
VAT	5,250	0	0
	35,250	30,000	30,000
Pay/(reclaim)	1,750	(3,500)	0
Net profit	10,000	10,000	6,500

Zero rated supplies

1.4   The following supplies are zero rated.

(a)   Human and animal food, although pet food and certain luxury foods are standard rated. Food supplied in the course of catering (which includes all hot takeaways) is standard rated. Most beverages are standard rated, but milk, tea (excluding iced tea), coffee and cocoa are zero rated unless supplied in the course of catering

(b)   Sewerage services and water (but services supplied for industrial activities and supplies of heated water are standard rated)

(c)   Printed matter used for reading (eg books, newspapers) but anything used for writing is standard rated (eg diaries/address books with blank pages to be filled in).

(d)   Supplies to charities in respect of 'talking books' for the blind and sound recording equipment and cassette recorders used or loaned by charities caring for the blind and severely handicapped

(e)   New construction work or the sale of the freehold of or a lease over 21 years (at least 20 years in Scotland) of new buildings by builders, where the buildings are to be used for residential or non-business charitable purposes (not repairs, enlargements to existing buildings or alterations, apart from the conversion of non-residential buildings to new residential accommodation and enlargements which create new dwellings)

(f)   Sales of substantially reconstructed listed buildings, and alterations to such buildings, where such buildings are to be used for residential or charitable purposes. Certain buildings which are the subject of an immunity certificate granting exemption from listing are treated as though they are listed for this purpose

(g)   Services of making arrangements to perform services outside the EC and certain services in relation to goods to be exported from the EC

(h)   A wide range of services relating to ships and aircraft, and the transport of goods and passengers. In relation to passenger transport, zero-rating generally applies where the vehicle is designed or adapted to carry at least 12 passengers. However, certain types of transport are specifically excluded from zero-rating. The effect is that VAT at the standard rate applies to:

•   rides at attractions such as theme parks and museums;
•   transport services provided in conjunction with airport car parking;
•   recreational flights, eg. in a hot air balloon.

(i) Caravans and houseboats; the hire or sale of houseboats and certain caravans is zero-rated. However, the supply of holiday accommodation in either is excluded, and this applies regardless of the purpose of the accommodation.

(j) Gold held in the UK is zero-rated when supplied between central banks and members of the London Gold market. EU investors can purchase gold bars, wafers and gold bullion coins exempt from VAT. There is an option for taxation for some suppliers of gold for industrial purposes and a limited right to input tax deduction for some traders.

(k) Bank notes

(l) Drugs and medicines on prescription or provided in private hospitals. Prosthesis fixed by surgical intervention and certain aids, building alterations, vehicles etc for the handicapped. Incontinence products supplied directly to the disabled or to a charity

(m) Exports of goods to outside the EC, and certain supplies to VAT registered traders in other EC states (see below). Exports by charities to outside the EC are treated as zero rated business supplies even if there is no consideration

(n) Specialised equipment used by rescue/first aid services. Sales to health authorities/ medical institutions of certain medical equipment paid for with charitable funds.

(o) Sales or hire by a charity (or by another person who has made a written agreement or other obligation to transfer all the profits of the sale to a charity) of goods donated for sale or hire, provided the goods are either sold to the general public or are unsuitable for sale to the general public or are offered for sale only to disabled people or to people receiving means tested benefits.

(p) Clothing and footwear for young children and certain protective clothing eg motor cyclists' crash helmets

(q) The service of treating or processing someone else's goods, if the result is zero-rated goods or if a supply of the resultant goods by the processor to the other person would be zero-rated

(r) Certain supplies (eg advertising services) to certain charitable institutions

Exempt supplies

1.5 The following supplies are exempt.

(a) Sales of freeholds of 'old' buildings and leaseholds of land and buildings of any age including a surrender of a lease. A building is 'old' if it is three years or more since its construction in general.

(b) Transactions in buildings (other than a sale by the builder) where the building is to be used for residential or charitable purposes including renting, leasing or hiring, except short-term accommodation at hotels and boarding houses and camping and parking facilities

(c) Financial services, although credit management and most processing services are standard rated. Investment advice is also standard rated

(d) Insurance. If insurance is supplied with other goods and services that are liable to VAT, the insurance is only exempt if disclosed separately to the customer

(e) Postal services provided by the Post Office

(f) Betting and gaming, except admission charges and subscriptions

(g) Certain education and vocational training

(h) Health services. Medical products are also exempt if supplied in connection with the provision of care, or treatment in any hospital or other institution which is either registered or exempt from registration

(i) Burial and cremation services

(j) Supplies to members by trade unions and professional bodies if in consideration only for a membership subscription

(k) Entry fees to non-profit making sports competitions and services closely related to sport and physical education supplied by non-profit making bodies to members (not visitors). It has been held that pigeon racing does not qualify as a sport for this purpose because the individual concerned does not take part in the main activity. However, berthing rights granted to members of a yachting club have been held to qualify

(l) Disposals of works of art and other items to public bodies in lieu of capital taxes

(m) Welfare services supplied by charities

(n) Supplies by charities, philanthropic bodies, trade unions, professional associations and non-profit making sports bodies in connection with fund raising events

(o) Residential care services

(p) Admission charges to certain cultural events or places

(q) Supplies of training, retraining and work experience paid for using further education funding council funds

(r) Investment gold although traders dealing in investment gold can opt to tax supplies.

(s) The supply of goods on which input tax was irrecoverable on purchase.

Standard rated supplies

1.6 **There is no list of standard rated supplies. If a supply is not zero rated and is not exempt then it is treated as standard rated.** Standard rated supplies normally have a 17.5% VAT charge but some supplies are subject to a lower rate of VAT. For example fuel and power for domestic or charity use (except fuel for motor vehicles) is taxed at 5%. VAT is also charged at 5% on the installation of certain energy saving materials in all homes, the grant funded installation, maintenance and repair of central heating systems and home security goods in the homes of qualifying pensioners and the grant funded installation of heating system measures in the homes of the less well off.

From 1 January 2001 VAT will also be charged at 5% on women's sanitary products.

Land and buildings

1.7 The construction of new dwellings or buildings to be used for residential or charitable purposes is zero rated. The construction of new residential accommodation by the conversion of non-residential buildings is also zero rated. Zero rating extends to the construction of homes for children, the elderly, students and the armed forces, but not to hospitals, prisons or hotels, to which the standard rate applies. The sale of the freehold of a 'new' commercial building is standard rated. The definition of 'new' is less than three years old. The construction of commercial buildings is also standard rated.

1.8 Other sales and also grants, variations and surrenders of leases (including reverse surrenders, when the tenant pays the landlord) are exempt. The provision of holiday accommodation is standard rated.

2   THE DEDUCTION OF INPUT VAT

2.1   **For input VAT to be deductible, the payer must be a taxable person, with the supply being to him in the course of his business. In addition a VAT invoice must be held (except for payments of up to £25 including VAT which are for telephone calls or car park fees or which are made through cash operated machines).**

Capital items

2.2   **The distinction between capital and revenue** which is important in other areas of tax **does not apply to VAT**. Thus a manufacturer buying plant subject to VAT will be able to obtain a credit for all the VAT immediately. The plant must of course be used to make taxable supplies, and if it is only partly so used only part of the VAT can be reclaimed. Conversely if plant is sold secondhand then VAT should be charged on the sale and is output VAT in the normal way. But VAT need not be charged on the sale of a secondhand car except on any profit element (which, of course, is rare), unless input VAT on the original purchase of the car was recoverable.

Non-deductible input VAT

2.3   **The following input VAT is not deductible even for a taxable person with taxable outputs.**

(a)   **VAT on motor cars** not used wholly for business purposes. This is never reclaimable unless a car is acquired new for resale or is acquired for use in or leasing to a taxi business, a self-drive car hire business or a driving school. Private use by a proprietor **or an employee** is non-business use (regardless of any benefit in kind charge) unless the user pays a full commercial hire charge (not just a reimbursement of costs). However, VAT on accessories such as car radios is deductible if ordered on a separate purchase order and fitted after delivery of the car. The VAT charged when a car is hired for business purposes is reclaimable, but if there is some non-business use and the hire company has reclaimed VAT on the original purchase of the car, only 50% of the VAT on hire charges can be reclaimed by the hirer. A hiring for five days or less is assumed to be for wholly business use;

(b)   **VAT on business entertaining** where the cost of the entertaining is not a deductible Schedule D Case I expense. If the items bought are used partly for such entertaining and partly for other purposes, the proportion of the VAT relating to the entertainment is non-deductible.

In *Ernst & Young v CCE* the Tribunal held that staff entertaining was wholly for business purposes and a full input tax recovery was allowed. Customs accept this decision in respect of staff entertainment but maintain that following the case *KPMG v CCE* input tax on entertaining guests at a staff party is non-deductible.

(c)   **VAT on expenses incurred on domestic accommodation for directors;**

(d)   **VAT on non-business items passed through the business accounts.** However, when goods are bought partly for business use, the purchaser may:

(i)   deduct all the input VAT, and account for output VAT in respect of the private use; or

(ii)   deduct only the business proportion of the input VAT.

Where services are bought partly for business use, only method (ii) may be used. If services are initially bought for business use but the use then changes, a fair proportion of the input VAT (relating to the private use) is reclaimed by HM Customs & Excise by making the trader account for output VAT.

A business that provides employees with mobile phones for business use can, regardless of any private use, deduct all the VAT incurred on purchase and on standing charges provided the charges do not contain any element for calls.

If a business allows its employees to make private calls without charge, then it must apportion the VAT incurred on the call charges. Any method of apportionment may be used, eg a sample of bills over a reasonable time, providing the method produces a fair and reasonable result. Apportionment must be made where the phone package allows the business to make a certain quantity of calls for a fixed monthly payment and there is no standing payment, or where the contract is for the purchase of the phone and the advance payment of a set amount of call time for a single charge.

If a business imposes clear rules prohibiting private calls, and enforces them, Customs allows a deduction of all of the VAT incurred on the call charges. Similarly, if a business tolerates only a small amount of calls, Customs allow all of the input tax incurred to be deducted.

(e) VAT which does not relate to the making of supplies by the buyer in the course of a business.

Irrecoverable VAT

2.4 Where all (as with many cars) of the input VAT on a purchase is not deductible, the **non-deductible VAT is included in the cost for income tax, corporation tax, capital allowance or capital gains purposes. Deductible VAT is omitted from costs, so that only net amounts are included in accounts. Similarly, sales** (and proceeds in chargeable gains computations) **are shown net of VAT**, because the VAT is paid over to HM Customs & Excise.

Motoring expenses

Cars

2.5 **The VAT incurred on the purchase of a car not used wholly for business purposes is not recoverable** (except as in Paragraph 2.3(a) above). If accessories are fitted after the original purchase and a separate invoice is raised then the VAT on the accessories can be treated as input tax so long as the accessories are for business use.

If a car is used wholly for business purposes (including leasing, so long as the charges are at the open market rate), the input VAT is recoverable but the buyer must account for VAT when he sells the car. **If a car is leased, the lessor recovered the input VAT when the car was purchased and the lessee makes some private use of the car** (for example private use by employees), **the lessee can only recover 50% of the input VAT on the lease charges.**

If a car is used for business purposes then any VAT charged on repair and maintenance costs can be treated as input VAT. No apportionment has to be made for private use.

If an employee accepts a reduced salary in exchange for being allowed to use his employer's car privately, or pays his employer for that use, there is no supply, so VAT is not due on the salary reduction. However, VAT is due on charges for running costs. VAT is also due on charges for employee use in the rare cases where the charge is a full commercial rate so that the employer has recovered input VAT on the cost or on leasing charges in full.

Fuel for business use

2.6 **The VAT incurred on fuel used for business purposes is fully deductible as input VAT.** If the fuel is bought by employees who are reimbursed for the actual cost or by a mileage allowance, the employer may deduct the input VAT.

Fuel for private use

2.7 **When fuel is supplied for an individual's private use at less than the cost of that fuel to the business, all input VAT incurred on the fuel is allowed but the business must account for output VAT using set scale charges per VAT return period, based on the cylinder capacity of the car's engine.** The scale figures will be stated in the exam if required. However, take care to note whether the examiner has given you the VAT inclusive or the VAT exclusive scale figure. The VAT inclusive scale charges are reproduced in the tax rates and allowances tables in this text. The output VAT is the VAT inclusive scale charge $\times$ 7/47 or the VAT exclusive scale charge $\times$ 17.5%.

If the employee has to pay the full cost of fuel (or more than its cost) to the employer, the employer must account for VAT on the amount paid, rather than on the scale charge.

Relief for bad debts

2.8 **Relief is available for VAT on bad debts if the debt is over six months old (measured from when payment is due) and has been written off in the creditor's accounts.** Where a supplier of goods or services has accounted for VAT on the supply and the customer does not pay, the supplier may claim a refund of VAT on the amount unpaid. Where payments on account have been received, they are attributed to debts in chronological order. If the debtor later pays all or part of the amount owed, a corresponding part of the VAT repaid must be paid back to HM Customs & Excise.

2.9 **Bad debt relief claims must be made within three years.** The creditor must have a copy of the VAT invoice, and records to show that the VAT in question has been accounted for and that the debt has been written off. The VAT is reclaimed on the creditor's VAT return.

2.10 The supplier must notify any debtor who is a taxable person of his claim within seven days of the claim. The notification must state:

- the date of issue of the notice;
- the date and amount of the claim;
- the date and number of any VAT invoice issued in relation to each relevant supply;
- the consideration due for each supply written off as a bad debt.

The supplier must keep a copy of the notification along with other records relating to the bad debt relief claim.

2.11 **Debtors must repay any VAT reclaimed which has not been paid and on which the supplier has claimed bad debt relief.** The debtor is required to make the repayment by means of a negative entry in the VAT allowable portion of his VAT account for the period in which the bad debt relief was claimed by the supplier. The debtor's entitlement to input VAT credit is restored when payment is made to the supplier and his bad debt relief claim is reversed.

2.12 There is anti-avoidance legislation to counter abuse through assigning debts to third parties in order to reduce the amount of VAT due or to claim too much bad debt relief.

BPP PUBLISHING

Self-supply

2.13 As we have seen, a person making exempt supplies is unable to reclaim input VAT charged on goods and services purchased in relation to those supplies. This could lead to distortion of competition, as some businesses with exempt outputs could obtain a VAT advantage by producing their own goods or making use of their own services rather than buying them. The Treasury has power to deal with such distortion by making regulations taxing self-supplies. Regulations made include regulations covering certain stationery in excess of £52,000 a year (the stationery regulation does not apply to fully taxable persons) and cars.

2.14 **The effect is that the trader is treated as supplying the goods or services to himself** (in general, at market value). **Output VAT is due to HM Customs & Excise, but if the trader is wholly or partly exempt** (or the cars have some non-business use) **all or some of that VAT cannot be recovered as input VAT.** Thus the business suffers a VAT cost.

2.15 Regulations prevent the input VAT being fully recovered by the trader saying it is attributable to the (taxable) supply of the goods or services concerned to himself. However, the VAT on materials bought to make self-supplies is fully recoverable.

2.16 The amount of the self-supply is excluded from both the numerator and the denominator of the fraction used in the partial exemption calculation.

3 SPECIAL SCHEMES

The cash accounting scheme

3.1 **The cash accounting scheme enables businesses to account for VAT on the basis of cash paid and received.** That is, the date of payment or receipt determines the return in which the transaction is dealt with. **The scheme can only be used by a trader whose annual taxable turnover (exclusive of VAT) does not exceed £350,000.** A trader can join the scheme only if all returns and VAT payments are up to date (or arrangements have been made to pay outstanding VAT by instalments).

3.2 If the value of taxable supplies exceeds £437,500 in the 12 months to the end of a VAT period a trader must leave the cash accounting scheme immediately.

The annual accounting scheme

3.3 **The annual accounting scheme is only available to traders** who regularly pay VAT to Customs and Excise, not to traders who normally get repayments. It is available for traders **whose taxable turnover (exclusive of VAT) for the 12 months starting on their application to join the scheme is not expected to exceed £300,000.** Traders cannot apply to join until they have been registered for at least 12 months. The year for which each return is made may end at the end of any calendar month.

3.4 **Under the annual accounting scheme traders file annual VAT returns but throughout the year they must make payments on account of their VAT liability by direct debit.** If annual turnover is £100,000 or more, the trader must pay 90% of the previous year's net VAT liability during the year by means of nine monthly payments commencing at the end of the fourth month of the year. If taxable turnover in the previous year was up to £100,000, quarterly payments are required, each of 20% of the previous year's net VAT liability. In this case the payments are made at the end of the fourth, seventh and tenth months of the year. However, if the sum due does not exceed £400, the trader need not make the quarterly interim payment.

Late payment of instalments is not a default for the purposes of the default surcharge.

3.5 **An annual VAT return must be submitted to HM Customs & Excise along with any payment due within two months of the end of the year.**

3.6 It is not possible to use the annual accounting scheme if input VAT exceeded output VAT in the year prior to application. In addition, all returns must have been made up to date. Annual accounting is not available where VAT registration is in the name of a VAT group or a division.

3.7 If the expected value of a trader's taxable supplies exceeds £375,000 notice must be given to HM Customs & Excise within 30 days and he may then be required to leave the scheme. If the £375,000 limit is in fact exceeded, the trader must leave the scheme.

If a trader fails to make the regular payments required by the scheme or the final payment for a year, or has not paid all VAT shown on returns made before joining the scheme, he may be expelled from the scheme. Customs can also prevent a trader using the scheme 'if they consider it necessary to do so for the protection of the revenue'.

3.8 Advantages of annual accounting:

- Only one VAT return each year so fewer occasions to trigger a default surcharge

- Ability to manage cash flow more accurately

- Avoids need for quarterly calculations for partial exemption purposes and input tax recovery

3.9 Disadvantages of annual accounting:

- Need to monitor future taxable supplies to ensure turnover limit not exceeded

- Timing of payments have less correlation to turnover (and hence cash received) by business

- Payments based on previous year's turnover may not reflect current year turnover which may be a problem if the scale of activities have reduced

Chapter roundup

- Some supplies are taxable (either standard rated or zero rated). Others are exempt.

- Not all input VAT is deductible, eg VAT on most motor cars.

- Special schemes include the cash accounting scheme and the annual accounting scheme. These schemes are supposed to make VAT accounting easier for certain types of trader.

BPP PUBLISHING

Quick quiz

1   Give some examples of zero rated supplies. (see para 1.4)

2   What input VAT is never deductible? (2.3)

3   What relief is available for bad debts? (2.8, 2.9)

4   What is self-supply? (2.13, 2.14)

5   Which traders may use cash accounting? (3.1)

Now try the questions below from the Exam Question Bank

Number	Level	Marks	Time
15	Exam	10	18 mins
16	Exam	15	27 mins

Part B
Unincorporated businesses

Chapter 12

AN OUTLINE OF INCOME TAX

Topic list	Syllabus reference
1 The aggregation of income	2a
2 Income taxed at source	2a
3 Charges on income	2a
4 Personal allowance	2a
5 The layout of personal tax computations	2a

Introduction

We look here at income tax, which is a tax on what individuals make from their jobs, their businesses and their savings. We see how to collect together all of an individual's income in a personal tax computation, and then work out the tax on that income.

In later chapters, we look at particular types of income in more detail.

Study guide

An outline of income tax

- Prepare a basic income tax computation

- Explain the treatment of savings income and dividends

- Explain the treatment of business charges on income

Exam guide

This is section 2a and a key topic. Question 2 (about 25 marks) in Section A will be on an unincorporated business and/or employees. The topic may also appear in Question 7 in Section B.

1 THE AGGREGATION OF INCOME

1.1 **An individual's income from all sources is brought together in a personal tax computation**. Three columns are needed. Here is an example. All items are explained later in this text.

RICHARD: INCOME TAX COMPUTATION 2000/01

	Non-savings income £	Savings (excl dividend) income £	Dividend income £	Total £
Income from employment	38,000			
Building society interest		1,320		
UK dividends			1,000	
	38,000	1,320	1,000	
Less charges on income	(2,000)			
Statutory total income (STI)	36,000	1,320	1,000	38,320
Less personal allowance	(4,385)			
Taxable income	31,615	1,320	1,000	33,935

Income tax	£	£
Non savings income		
£1,520 × 10%		152
£26,880 × 22%		5,914
£3,215 × 40%		1,286
		7,352
Savings (excl. dividend) income		
£1,320 × 40%		528
Dividend income		
£1,000 × 32.5%		325
		8,205
Add basic rate tax withheld on charges		
paid net £2,000 × 22%		440
Tax liability		8,445
Less tax suffered		
PAYE tax on salary (say)	6,226	
Tax on building society interest	264	
Tax credit on dividend income	100	
		(6,590)
Tax payable		1,855

KEY TERM

The **tax liability** is the amount which must be accounted for to the Inland Revenue. **Tax payable** is the balance of the liability still to be settled in cash. **Statutory total income** (STI) is all income before deducting the personal allowance.

1.2 Income tax is charged on the figures of 'taxable income'. **There is only one set of income tax bands to be used for all three types of income.** Non-savings income is dealt with first, then savings (excl. dividend) income and then dividend income.

1.3 **For non-savings income, the first £1,520 is taxed at the starting rate (10%), the next £26,880 is taxed at the basic rate (22%) and the rest at the higher rate (40%).**

1.4 Savings (excl. dividend) income is taxed as the next slice of income after non-savings income has been taxed. Any savings (excl. dividend) income falling within the starting rate band is taxed at the starting rate (10%). **Any savings (excl. dividend) income that falls within the basic rate band is taxed at 20% (not 22%)** whilst any such income in excess of the basic rate threshold of £28,400 is taxed at 40%.

1.5 **Any dividend income falling within the starting or basic rate bands is taxed at 10%. Dividend income in excess of the basic rate threshold is taxed at 32.5%.**

1.6 Any tax already suffered and the tax credit on dividend income comes off the tax liability. However, the tax credit on dividend income cannot be repaid.

1.7 The remainder of this chapter gives more details of the income tax computation.

2 INCOME TAXED AT SOURCE

2.1 **Some income is received after deduction of tax. This is income taxed at source.** The taxable income for a tax year (6 April in one year to 5 April in the next) is the **gross** amount (that is, adding back any tax deducted at source). The tax deducted at source is deducted in computing tax payable and may be repaid.

2.2 Dividends on UK shares are received net of a 10% tax credit. The taxable income for a tax year is the gross dividend; that is the dividends received multiplied by 100/90.

The schedular system for individuals

2.3 **As for companies, income received by an individual is usually taxed under a set of rules known as a schedule.**

The following schedules (and cases) are examinable in detail:

Schedule D
  Case I   Profits of trades

  Case II   Profits of professions or vocations

Schedule E   Income from an office or employment including salaries, bonuses, benefits in kind and pensions. Most tax is collected under the PAYE system.

Schedule F   UK dividends.

Savings income received net of 20% tax

2.4 The following savings income is received net of 20% tax. The amount received is grossed up by multiplying by 100/80 and included gross in the income tax computation.

(a) Interest paid by UK companies on debentures and loan stocks
(b) Bank and building society interest paid to individuals
(c) The income portion of a purchased annuity

> **Exam focus point**
>
> In examinations you may be given either the net or the gross amount of such income: read the question carefully. If you are given the net amount (the amount received or credited), you should gross up the figure at the rate of 20%. For example, net building society interest of £160 is equivalent to gross income of £160 × 100/80 = £200 on which tax of £40 (20% of £200) has been suffered.

Dividends on UK shares

2.5 **Dividends on UK shares are received net of a 10% tax credit.** This means a dividend of £90 has a £10 tax credit, giving gross income of £100. The tax credit cannot be repaid to non-taxpayers.

Exempt income

2.6 **Some income is exempt from income tax.** Several of these exemptions are mentioned at places in this text where the types of income are described in detail, but you should note the following types of exempt income now.

(a) Scholarships (exempt as income of the scholar. If paid by a parent's employer, a scholarship may be taxable income of the parent)

(b) Betting and gaming winnings, including premium bond prizes

(c) Interest or terminal bonus on National Savings Certificates

(d) Many social security benefits, although the jobseeker's allowance, the state pension and certain incapacity benefits are taxable

(e) Gifts

(f) Damages and payments for personal injury. The exemption applies to lump sum and periodical payments, including payments made via trusts and payments made by buying annuities. Payments under annuities are made gross (unlike most annuities)

(g) Payments under insurance policies to compensate for loss of income on illness or disability (permanent health insurance) or while out of work (eg policies to pay interest on mortgages), so long as the person benefiting paid the premiums and did not get tax relief for them

(h) The amount by which a pension awarded on a retirement due to a disability caused at work, by a work related illness or by war wounds exceeds the pension that would have been payable if the retirement had been on ordinary ill health grounds. This exemption only applies to pensions paid under non-approved pension schemes.

(i) Interest on amounts repaid to borrowers under the income contingent student loans scheme

(j) Payments made under the 'new deal 50 plus' scheme and payments made under the employment zones programme.

Exam focus point

Learn the different types of exempt income. They are popular items in the exam. Always state on your exam script that such income is exempt (do not ignore it) to gain an easy half mark.

3 CHARGES ON INCOME

3.1 **Charges on income are deducted in computing taxable income.**

KEY TERM

A **charge on income** is a payment by the taxpayer which income tax law allows as a deduction.

3.2 Examples of charges on income are:

(a) eligible interest;
(b) patent royalties.
(c) copyright royalties

3.3   Charges on income paid in money fall into two categories: those from which basic rate (22%) income tax is first deducted by the payer (charges paid net) and those which are paid gross (without any tax deduction). Always deduct the gross figure in the payer's tax computation.

3.4   Patent royalties are an example of a charge on income which is paid net. Eligible interest and copyright royalties are paid gross.

3.5   In the personal tax computation of someone who *receives* a charge, for example the owner of a patent who gets royalties from someone who exploits the patent you should:

(a)   Include the **gross** amount under non-savings income. If the charge is paid gross, the gross amount is the amount received. If it is paid net, the gross amount is the amount received $\times$ 100/78.

(b)   If the charge was received net, then under the heading 'less tax suffered' (between tax liability and tax payable) include the tax deducted. This is the gross amount $\times$ 22%.

Eligible interest

3.6   **Interest qualifies for tax relief as a charge if the loan concerned is used for a qualifying purpose:**

(a)   **The purchase of an interest in a partnership, or contribution to the partnership of capital or a loan.** The borrower must be a partner (other than a limited partner), and relief ceases when he ceases to be one.

(b)   **The purchase of ordinary shares in a close company** (other than a close investment holding company) or the loan of money to such a company for use in its business, provided that when the interest is paid the individual either has (with any associates) a material (more than 5%) interest in the close company, or holds (ignoring associates) **some** ordinary share capital and works full time as a manager or director of the company. A close company is (broadly) a company controlled by its shareholder-directors or by five or fewer shareholders.

(c)   **Investment in a co-operative.** This provision applies to investment in shares or through loans to the co-operative. The borrower must work for the greater part of his time in the co-operative.

(d)   **The purchase of shares in an employee-controlled company.** The company must be an unquoted trading company resident in the UK with at least 50% of the voting shares held by employees.

(e)   **The purchase by a partner of plant or machinery used in the business.** Interest is allowed only until three years from the end of the tax year in which the loan was taken out. If the plant is used partly for private purposes, then the allowable interest is proportionately reduced.

(f)   **The purchase by an employee of plant or machinery used by him in the performance of his duties.** The interest is allowable only until three years from the end of the tax year in which the loan was taken out.

(g)   The replacement of other loans qualifying under (a) to (f) above.

Interest on a loan within (a) to (d) above continues to be allowable if a partnership is succeeded by a new partnership or is incorporated into a close company, a co-operative or an employee controlled company, or if shares in a company of one of these kinds are exchanged for shares in a company of another of these kinds, provided that interest on a new loan (to make the loan to or buy the shares in the new entity) would have qualified.

Interest is never allowed if it is payable under a scheme or arrangement of which the expected sole or main benefit was tax relief on the interest. Interest on an overdraft or on a credit card debt does not qualify. Relief under (a) to (d) above is reduced or withdrawn if capital is withdrawn from the business.

Business interest

3.7 **A taxpayer paying interest wholly and exclusively for business purposes can deduct such interest in computing his Schedule D Case I profit, instead of as a charge.** The interest need not fall into any of the categories outlined above, and it may be on an overdraft or a credit card debt.

3.8 **If interest is allowable as a Schedule D Case I deduction, the amount payable (on an accruals basis) is deducted. Only interest paid in the tax year may be set against total income as a charge.**

Charges in personal tax computations

3.9 **The gross amount of any charge is deducted from the taxpayer's income to arrive at STI. Deduct charges from non-savings income, then from savings (excl dividend) income and lastly from dividend income.**

3.10 If a charge has been paid net, the basic rate income tax deducted (22% of the gross charge) is added to any tax liability. The taxpayer obtained tax relief because the charge reduced his income: he cannot keep the basic rate tax as well, but must pay it to the Inland Revenue.

3.11 **If charges paid net exceed total income** (ignoring charges paid net) **minus allowances deductible from STI, the payer of the charge must, under s 350 ICTA 1988, pay the Inland Revenue the tax withheld when the excess charge was paid.** In other words, the Revenue ensure that you do not get tax relief for charges if you are not a payer of tax.

3.12 EXAMPLE

Three taxpayers have the following schedule D Case I income and allowances for 2000/01. Taxpayers A and B pay a patent royalty of £176 (net). Taxpayer C pays a patent royalty of £1,248 (net).

	A £	B £	C £
Schedule D Case I Income	5,000	3,000	34,615
Less: charge on income (□ 100/78)	(226)	(226)	(1,600)
	4,774	2,774	33,015
Less: personal allowance	(4,385)	(4,385)	(4,385)
Taxable income	389	–	28,630
Income tax			
10% on £389/-/£1,520	39	–	152
22% on -/-/£26,880			5,914
40% on -/-/£230			92
	39	–	6,158
Add: 22% tax retained on charge	50	50	352
Tax payable	89	50	6,510

4 PERSONAL ALLOWANCE

4.1 Once taxable income from all sources has been aggregated and any charges on income deducted, the remainder is the taxpayer's statutory total income (STI). An allowance, the personal allowance, is deducted from STI. Like charges, it comes off non savings income first, then off savings (excl. dividend) income and lastly off dividend income.

4.2 **All persons (including children) are entitled to the personal allowance of £4,385.**

4.3 A person aged 65 or over receives an age allowance (not examinable).

Question: Calculation of taxable income

Susan (aged 36) has an annual salary of £27,000. She has a loan of £7,000 at 10% interest to buy shares in her employee-controlled company. She receives building society interest of £2,000 a year. What is her taxable income for 2000/01?

Answer

	Non-savings	Savings (excl dividend)	Total
	£	£	£
Salary	27,000		
Building society interest £2,000 × 100/80		2,500	
	27,000	2,500	
Less charge £7,000 × 10%	(700)		
STI	26,300	2,500	28,800
Less personal allowance	(4,385)		
Taxable income	21,915	2,500	24,415

---

5 THE LAYOUT OF PERSONAL TAX COMPUTATIONS

Non-savings income, savings (excl. dividend) income and dividend income

5.1 **We need three columns in a personal tax computation. One for non-savings income, one for savings (excl. dividend) income and one for dividend income. Non savings income is treated as the first tranche of income. Savings (excl. dividend) income is dealt with next. Dividend income is treated as the top slice of income.**

5.2 **The first £1,520 of savings (excl. dividend) income is taxed at the starting rate of 10%. If savings (excl. dividend) income falls within the basic rate band it is taxed at 20% (not 22%). When the income is paid net (for example building society interest), the tax already deducted may match the tax payable, so there will be no extra tax to pay. If, however, the income falls within the 40% band, it is taxable at 40% and there is extra tax to pay and if the income falls within the 10% band the taxpayer may need to claim a repayment.**

5.3 **If dividend income falls within the starting or basic rate bands it is taxed at 10% (never 20% or 22%). The tax credit attached to the dividend will match the tax payable, so there will be no extra tax to pay. If, however, the dividend income exceeds the basic rate threshold of £28,400, it is taxable at 32.5% and there is extra tax to pay.**

5.4   EXAMPLES: PERSONAL TAX COMPUTATIONS

(a)   Kathe has a salary of £10,000 and receives dividends of £4,500.

	Non-savings £	*Dividends* £	*Total* £
Schedule E	10,000		
Dividends £4,500 × 100/90		5,000	
STI	10,000	5,000	15,000
Less personal allowance	(4,385)		
Taxable income	5,615	5,000	10,615

	£
Income tax	
Non savings income	
£1,520 × 10%	152
£4,095 × 22%	901
Dividend income	
£5,000 × 10%	500
Tax liability	1,553
Less tax credit on dividend	(500)
Tax payable	1,053

Some of the tax payable has probably already been paid on the salary under PAYE.

The dividend income falls within the basic rate band so it is taxed at 10% (*not* 22%).

(b)   Jules has a salary of £20,000, business profits of £30,000, net dividends of £6,750 and building society interest of £3,000 net. He pays gross charges of £2,000.

	Non-savings £	*Savings (excl dividend)* £	*Dividends* £	*Total* £
Schedule D Case I	30,000			
Schedule E	20,000			
Dividends £6,750 × 100/90			7,500	
Building society interest £3,000 × 100/80		3,750		
	50,000	3,750	7,500	
Less charges	(2,000)			
STI	48,000	3,750	7,500	59,250
Less personal allowance	(4,385)			
Taxable income	43,615	3,750	7,500	54,865

	£
Income tax	
Non savings income	
£1,520 × 10%	152
£26,880 × 22%	5,914
£15,215 × 40%	6,086
	12,152
Savings (excl. dividend) income	
£3,750 × 40%	1,500
Dividend income	
£7,500 × 32.5%	2,438
Less tax credit on dividend income	(750)
Less tax suffered on building society interest	(750)
Tax payable	14,590

Savings (excl. dividend) income and dividend income fall above the basic rate threshold so they are taxed at 40% and 32.5% respectively.

(c) Jim does not work. He receives net bank interest of £38,000. He pays gross charges of £2,000.

	Savings (excl dividend) £	Total £
Bank interest × 100/80	47,500	
Less charges	(2,000)	
STI	45,500	45,500
Less personal allowance	(4,385)	
	41,115	41,115

	£
Savings (excluding dividend) income	
£1,520 × 10%	152
£26,880 × 20%	5,376
£12,715 × 40%	5,086
Tax liability	10,614
Less tax suffered	(9,500)
Tax payable	1,114

Savings (excl. dividend) income within the basic rate band is taxed at 20% (*not* 22%).

What is savings income?

5.5 **'Savings income'** does not include everything you might expect it to. Here are lists of savings and non-savings income.

5.6 **Savings income**

(a) **Interest** (including interest from banks and buildings societies)

(b) **Dividends**

(c) The income part of a purchased life annuity. This is an annuity which lasts for a period depending on someone's lifespan, and which is bought for a lump sum. Part of each payment is treated as income and is paid net of 20% tax, while the rest is treated as a return of capital and is tax-free.

5.7 **Non-savings income**

Income from a job
Income from running a business (alone or as a partner)
Rental income
Charges **received** (other than interest)

The complete proforma

5.8 Here is a complete proforma computation of taxable income. It is probably too much for you to absorb at this stage, but refer back to it as you come to the chapters dealing with the types of income shown.

	Non-savings £	Savings (excl dividend) £	Dividend £	Total £
Business profits	X			
Less losses set against business profits	(X)			
	X			
Less pension contributions	(X)			
	X			
Wages less pension contributions	X			
Other non-savings (as many lines as necessary)	X			
Building society interest (gross)		X		
Other savings (excl. dividends) (gross)		X		
(as many lines as necessary)				
Dividends (gross)			X	
	X	X	X	
Less charges (gross)	(X)	(X)	(X)	
	X	X	X	
Less losses set against general income	(X)	(X)	(X)	
STI	X	X	X	X
Less personal allowance	(X)	(X)	(X)	
Taxable income	X	X	X	X

Chapter roundup

- In this chapter we have covered the basic rules for working out the income tax an individual must pay.

- In a personal income tax computation, we bring together income from all sources, splitting the sources into non-savings, savings (excl. dividend) and dividend income. We deduct charges, and then the personal allowance. Finally, we work out income tax on the taxable income, and take account of tax retained on charges and tax already suffered.

Quick quiz

1 At what rates is income tax charged? (see paras 1.3 - 1.5)

2 What types of savings income are received net of 20% tax? (2.4)

3 Give an example of a charge on income paid net. (3.4)

4 How is dividend income taxed? (5.3)

Now try the questions below from the Exam Question Bank

Number	Level	Marks	Time
17	Introductory	7	13 mins
18	Exam	10	18 mins

Chapter 13

SCHEDULE D CASES I AND II

Topic list	Syllabus reference
1 The badges of trade	2c(i)
2 The computation of trading income	2c(ii)
3 Basis periods	2c(iii)
4 Change of accounting date	2c(iv)
5 Capital allowances for unincorporated businesses	2c(v)

Introduction

We are now going to look at the computation and taxation of profits or unincorporated businesses. We work out a business's profit as if it were a separate entity (the separate entity concept familiar to you from basic bookkeeping) but as an unincorporated business has no legal existence apart from its proprietor, we cannot tax it separately. We have to feed its profit into the proprietor's personal tax computation.

Study guide

Schedule D Cases I and II

- Describe and apply the badges of trade

- State the expenditure that is allowable in calculating the tax-adjusted profit

- Explain how relief can be obtained for pre-trading expenditure

- Explain the basis of assessment

- Compute the assessable profits on commencement and cessation

- State the factors that will influence the choice of accounting date

- State the conditions that must be met for a change of accounting date to be valid

- Compute the assessable profits on a change of accounting date

- Define plant and machinery for capital allowances purposes

- Calculate writing down allowances and first year allowances

- Compute balancing allowances and charges

- Explain the treatment of motor cars

- Explain the treatment of short life assets and long life assets

- Define an industrial building for industrial buildings allowance purposes

- Calculate industrial buildings allowance for new and second-hand buildings

- Compute the balancing adjustment on the disposal of an industrial building

> **Exam guide**
>
> This is part of section 2c which is a key topic. Question 2 in Section A will be on an unincorporated businesses and/or employees. It may also appear in Question 7 in Section B.

1 THE BADGES OF TRADE

> **KEY TERM**
>
> A trade is defined in the legislation only in an unhelpful manner as including every trade, manufacture, adventure or concern in the nature of a trade. It has therefore been left to the courts to provide guidance. This guidance is often summarised in a collection of principles known as the **'badges of trade'**. These are set out below. They apply to both corporate businesses and unincorporated businesses.

1.1 Trading income is subject to tax under Schedule D Case I.

The subject matter

1.2 **Whether a person is trading or not may sometimes be decided by examining the subject matter of the transaction.** Some assets are commonly held as investments for their intrinsic value: an individual buying some shares or a painting may do so in order to enjoy the income from the shares or to enjoy the work of art. A subsequent disposal may produce a gain of a capital nature rather than a trading profit. But **where the subject matter of a transaction is such as would not be held as an investment** (for example 34,000,000 yards of aircraft linen (*Martin v Lowry 1927*) or 1,000,000 rolls of toilet paper (*Rutledge v CIR 1929*)), **it is presumed that any profit on resale is a trading profit.**

The frequency of transactions

1.3 Transactions which may, in isolation, be of a capital nature will be interpreted as trading transactions where their **frequency indicates the carrying on of a trade**. It was decided that whereas normally the purchase of a mill-owning company and the subsequent stripping of its assets might be a capital transaction, where the taxpayer was embarking on the same exercise for the fourth time he must be carrying on a trade (*Pickford v Quirke 1927*).

The length of ownership

1.4 The courts may infer adventures in the nature of **trade where items purchased are sold soon afterwards.**

Supplementary work and marketing

1.5 **When work is done to make an asset more marketable,** or steps are taken to find purchasers, the courts will be more ready to ascribe a trading motive. When a group of accountants bought, blended and recasked a quantity of brandy they were held to be taxable on a trading profit when the brandy was later sold (*Cape Brandy Syndicate v CIR 1921*).

A profit motive

1.6 The absence of a profit motive will not necessarily preclude a Schedule D Case I assessment, but its presence is a strong indication that a person is trading. The purchase and resale of £20,000 worth of silver bullion by the comedian Norman Wisdom, as a hedge against devaluation, was held to be a trading transaction (*Wisdom v Chamberlain 1969*).

The way in which the asset sold was acquired

1.7 **If goods are acquired deliberately, trading may be indicated.** If goods are acquired unintentionally, for example by gift or inheritance, their later sale is unlikely to be trading.

The taxpayer's intentions

1.8 Where a transaction is clearly trading on objective criteria, **the taxpayer's intentions are irrelevant**. If, however, a transaction has (objectively) a dual purpose, the taxpayer's intentions may be taken into account. An example of a transaction with a dual purpose is the acquisition of a site partly as premises from which to conduct another trade, and partly with a view to the possible development and resale of the site.

This test is not one of the traditional badges of trade, but it may be just as important.

2 THE COMPUTATION OF TRADING INCOME

The adjustment of profits

2.1 As for companies, although the net profit before taxation shown in the accounts is the starting point in computing the taxable trading profit, many adjustments may be required to find the profit taxable under Schedule D Case I. The same rules apply to Case II (profits of a profession or vocation), and we will just refer to Case I from now on. Many of the same rules apply to both corporate and unincorporated businesses. Where appropriate, reference is made to the appropriate paragraphs in Chapter 2.

Accounting policies

2.2 **As a rule, accounts drawn up on normal accepted accounting principles are acceptable for tax purposes.** Two special points are worth noting.

- If there is a legal action in progress, the best estimate of the cost should be debited, not the most prudent estimate.

- Under SSAP 9, a loss on a long-term contract is recognised as soon as it is foreseen. Anticipating a loss in this way is not acceptable for tax purposes, so the debit to profit and loss must be added back.

2.3 The taxable profits of a trade, profession or vocation must normally be computed on a basis which gives a true and fair view, subject to adjustments permitted or required by tax law.

There are rules to deal with the consequences of a change in accounting basis. An uplift is calculated, broadly recognising receipts (together with trading stock and work in progress) which might fall out of account on a change of basis, less expenses which might similarly fall out of account. The uplift, if positive, is charged to tax (under Schedule D Case VI) and, if negative, is allowed as a deduction in computing the profits of the business.

Where the change is from a basis previously acceptable to the Revenue (eg cash basis) to a 'true and fair' basis the uplift charge is spread over ten years; in the first nine years the amount charged to tax is one tenth of the total uplift or ten per cent of the taxable profits of the business for that year.

BPP PUBLISHING

Rounding

2.4 Where an individual or a partnership has an annual turnover of at least £5,000,000 and prepares its accounts with figures rounded to at least the nearest £1,000, figures in computations of adjusted profits may generally be rounded to the nearest £1,000.

Deductible and non-deductible expenditure

Payments contrary to public policy and illegal payments

2.5 Based on case law, **fines and penalties are not deductible.** However, **the Revenue usually allow employees' parking fines incurred in parking their employer's cars while on their employer's business. Fines relating to proprietors, however, are never allowed.**

A payment is (by statute) not deductible if making it constitutes an offence by the payer. This covers protection money paid to terrorists, and also bribes. Statute also prevents any deduction for payments made in response to blackmail or extortion.

Capital expenditure

2.6 The principles in Chapter 2 paragraphs 2.3 and 2.4 also apply to unincorporated businesses.

2.7 **Two exceptions to the 'capital' rule** are worth noting.

   (a) The costs of **registering patents and trade marks** are deductible.

   (b) **Incidental costs of obtaining loan finance,** or of attempting to obtain or redeeming it, are deductible other than a discount on issue or a premium on redemption (which are really alternatives to paying interest).

Appropriations

2.8 **Salary or interest on capital paid to a proprietor, and also depreciation, amortisation and general provisions are not deductible.** A specific provision against a particular trade debt is deductible if it is a reasonable estimate of the likely loss.

The private proportion of payments for motoring expenses, rent, heat and light and telephone expenses of a proprietor is not deductible. Where the payments are to or on behalf of employees, the full amounts are deductible but the employees are taxed on benefits in kind.

Charges

2.9 **Charges (such as royalties) are dealt with in the personal tax computation. They are not also deducted in computing trading profits.**

Entertaining and gifts

2.10 The principles in Chapter 2 paragraphs 2.8 to 2.11 also apply to unincorporated businesses.

Expenditure not wholly and exclusively for the purposes of the trade

2.11 **Expenditure is not deductible if it is not for trade purposes (the remoteness test), or if it reflects more than one purpose (the duality test). If an exact apportionment is possible (as with motor expenses) relief is given on the business element.** The cases in Chapter 2 paragraphs 2.13 and 2.14 also apply to unincorporated businesses.

2.12   However, the cost of overnight accommodation when on a business trip may be deductible and reasonable expenditure on an evening meal and breakfast in conjunction with such accommodation is then also deductible.

Subscriptions and donations

2.13   **The general 'wholly and exclusively' rule determines the deductibility of expenses. Subscriptions and donations are not deductible unless the expenditure is for the benefit of the trade.** The following are the main types of subscriptions and donations you may meet and their correct treatments.

- Trade subscriptions (such as to a professional or trade association) are generally deductible.

- Charitable donations are deductible only if they are small and to local charities.

- Political subscriptions and donations are generally not deductible.

- When a business makes a gift of equipment manufactured, sold or used in the course of its trade to an educational establishment or for a charitable purpose, nothing need be brought into account as a trading receipt or (if capital allowances had been obtained on the asset) as disposal proceeds, so full relief is obtained for the cost. The donor must claim the relief. The time limit for the claim for unincorporated businesses is the 31 January which is 22 months after the end of the tax year in whose basis period the gift is made. The value of any benefit to the donor from the gift is taxable on him.

- Where a donation represents the most effective commercial way of disposing of stock (for example, where it would not be commercially effective to sell surplus perishable food), the donation can be treated as for the benefit of the trade and the disposal proceeds taken as £Nil. In other cases, the amount credited to the accounts in respect of a donation of stock should be its market value.

Legal and professional charges/bad and doubtful debts

2.14   The principles in Chapter 2 paragraphs 2.16 to 2.19 also apply to unincorporated businesses.

Interest

2.15   **Interest paid by an individual on borrowings for trade purposes is deductible as a trading expense on an accruals basis, so no adjustment to the accounts figure is needed.**

2.16   Individuals cannot deduct interest on overdue tax.

Pre-trading expenditure and other miscellaneous deductions

2.17   The principles in Chapter 2 paragraphs 2.23 – 2.26 also apply to unincorporated businesses.

Miscellaneous deductions

2.18   Here is a list of various other items that you may meet.

Item	Treatment	Comment
Educational courses for staff	Allow	
Educational courses for proprietor	Allow	If to update existing knowledge or skills, not if to acquire new knowledge or skills

BPP PUBLISHING

Item	Treatment	Comment
Removal expenses (to new business premises)	Allow	Only if not an expansionary move
Travelling expenses to the trader's place of business	Disallow	*Ricketts v Colquhoun 1925*: unless an itinerant trader (*Horton v Young 1971*)
Contribution to expenses of agents under the payroll deduction scheme	Allow	
Redundancy pay in excess of the statutory amount	Allow	If the trade ceases, the limit on allowability is $3 \times$ the statutory amount (in addition to the statutory amount)
Compensation for loss of office and ex gratia payments	Allow	If for benefit of trade: *Mitchell v B W Noble Ltd 1927*
Counselling services for employees leaving employment	Allow	If qualify for exemption from Schedule E charge on employees

Contributions to any of:
  local enterprise agencies;
  training and enterprise councils;
  local enterprise companies;
  business link organisations;
  individual learning accounts (ILA)
	Allow	The ILA must qualify for a discount or grant and contributions must be available to all employees generally.

Pension contributions (to schemes for employees and company directors)	Allow	If paid, not if only provided for; special contributions may be spread over the year of payment and future years

Premiums for insurance:
  against an employee's death or illness
  to cover locum costs or fixed overheads
  whilst the policyholder is ill
	Allow	Receipts are taxable

Payments to employees for restrictive undertakings	Allow	Taxable on employee
Damages paid	Allow	If not too remote from trade: *Strong and Co v Woodifield 1906*
Preparation and restoration of waste disposal sites	Allow	Spread preparation expenditure over period of use of site. Pre-trading expenditure is treated as incurred on the first day of trading. Allow restoration expenditure in period of expenditure
Improving an individual's personal security	Allow	Provision of a car, ship or dwelling is excluded

Income taxable under Schedule D Case I but excluded from the accounts

2.19 **The usual example is when a proprietor takes goods for his own use. In such circumstances the normal selling price of the goods is added to the accounting profit.** In other words, the proprietor is treated for tax purposes as having made a sale to himself (*Sharkey v Wernher 1955*). This rule does not apply to supplies of services, which are treated as sold for the amount (if any) actually paid (but the cost of services to the trader or his household is not deductible).

Accounting profits not taxable under Schedule D Case I

2.20 The principles in Chapter 2 paragraphs 3.1 to 3.3 also apply to unincorporated businesses.

Deductible expenditure not charged in the accounts

2.21 The principles in Chapter 2 paragraphs 4.1 and 4.2 also apply to unincorporated businesses.

The cessation of trades

2.22 **Post-cessation receipts** (including any releases of debts incurred by the trader) **are taxable under Schedule D Case VI**. If they are received in the tax year of cessation or the next six tax years, the trader can elect that they be treated as received on the day of cessation. The time limit for electing is the 31 January which is 22 months after the end of the tax year of receipt.

2.23 **Post-cessation expenses can be deducted so long as they would have been deductible had the trade continued,** and they did not arise as a result of the cessation. Capital allowances which the trader was entitled to immediately before the discontinuance but which remain unrelieved can also be deducted.

Post-cessation expenses set against total income

2.24 If an individual trader or a partner incurs expenses within the seven years after ceasing to trade and no deduction from post-cessation receipts is possible, he can claim to **deduct them from his total income for the year of payment**. The deduction should be made in the personal tax computation after deductions for charges and post-employment expenses, and before deductions for trading losses set against income as a whole. The trader cannot, of course, claim to the extent that an accrual for the expenses was allowed in computing his trading profits.

2.25 This relief is only available for the following expenses.

- Certain costs incurred in connection with defects. Any corresponding amounts received, for example under an insurance policy, are treated as taxable post-cessation receipts for the later of the tax year of receipt and the tax year of the corresponding payment.

- Insurance against the above costs. Any sum received under the insurance policy or as a return of premiums is treated as a taxable post-cessation receipt for the later of the tax year of receipt and the tax year of the corresponding payment.

- The cost of collecting a debt which was taken into account in computing the profits of the former trade. Any sum recovered for the cost of collection is treated as a taxable post-cessation receipt for the later of the tax year of receipt and the tax year of the corresponding payment.

- The amount of a debt which was taken into account in computing the profits of the former trade, but which later proves to be bad or is released under a voluntary arrangement under the Insolvency Act 1986 or a compromise or arrangement under section 425 of the Companies Act 1985. If any amount is later received in respect of such a debt, it is treated as a taxable post-cessation receipt.

2.26 The relief is only available for expenses which cannot be set against post-cessation receipts. Expenses which do not fall within the categories in the above paragraph are set against those receipts first. The remaining expenses are eligible for relief against total income.

2.27 This relief must be claimed. A claim may be made or not made for each payment separately, but any one payment must be claimed in full or not at all. The time limit for claims is the 31 January which is nearly two years from the end of the tax year of payment (so 31 January 2003 for payments in 2000/01).

2.28 If the payments deductible in a tax year exceed total income, the excess cannot be carried back or forward to any other year. However, the ex-trader can claim to set the excess against his chargeable gains for the year. The gains against which the excess is set are the gains for the year minus the losses for the year, ignoring losses brought forward, the annual exempt amount and any relief for trading losses against capital gains. Payments may be claimed or not claimed individually, but any one payment must be claimed in full or not at all.

Valuing trading stock on cessation

2.29 **When a trade ceases, the closing stock must be valued**. The higher the value, the higher the profit for the final period of trading will be.

2.30 If the stock is sold to a UK trader who will deduct its cost in computing his taxable profits, it is valued under the following rules.

   (a) If the seller and the buyer are unconnected, take the actual price.

   (b) If the seller and the buyer are connected, take what would have been the price in an arm's length sale.

   (c) However, if the seller and the buyer are connected, the arm's length price exceeds both the original cost of the stock and the actual transfer price, and both the seller and the buyer make an election, then take the greater of the original cost of the stock and the transfer price. The time limit for election for unincorporated business is the 31 January which is 22 months after the end of the tax year of cessation.

2.31 In all cases covered above, the value used for the seller's computation of profit is also used as the buyer's cost.

> **KEY TERM**
>
> An individual is **connected** (connected person) with his spouse, with the relatives (brothers, sisters, ancestors and lineal descendants) of himself and his spouse, and with the spouses of those relatives. He is also connected with his partners (except in relation to bona fide commercial arrangements for the disposal of partnership assets), with their spouses and relatives and with a company he controls. Partners are connected with their partnerships, two partnerships are connected if they have any member in common.

2.32 If the stock is not transferred to a UK trader who will be able to deduct its cost in computing his profits, then it is valued at its open market value as at the cessation of trade.

3 BASIS PERIODS

3.1 **A tax year runs from 6 April to 5 April**, but most businesses do not have periods of account ending on 5 April. **Thus there must be a link between a period of account of a business and a tax year.** The procedure is to **find a period to act as the basis period for a tax year. The profits for a basis period are taxed in the corresponding tax year.** If a basis period is not identical to a period of account, the profits of periods of account are time-apportioned as required. We will assume that profits accrue evenly over a period of account. We will also apportion to the nearest month, since this is required in the examination.

3.2 We will now look at the basis period rules that apply in the opening, continuing and closing years of a business when there is no change of accounting date. Special rules are needed when the trader changes his accounting date. We will look at these rules in the next section.

3.3 The first tax year is the year during which the trade commences. For example, if a trade commences on 1 June 2000 the first tax year is 2000/01.

The first tax year

3.4 The **basis period for the first tax year runs from the date the trade starts to the next 5 April** (or to the date of cessation if the trade does not last until the end of the tax year).

The second tax year

3.5 **If the accounting date falling in the second tax year is at least 12 months after the start of trading, the basis period is the 12 months down to that accounting date.**

3.6 **If the accounting date falling in the second tax year is less than 12 months after the start of trading, the basis period is the first 12 months of trading.**

3.7 **If there is no accounting date falling in the second tax year**, because the first period of account is a very long one which does not end until a date in the third tax year, **the basis period for the second tax year is the year itself (from 6 April to 5 April).**

3.8 The following flowchart may help you determine the basis period for the second tax year.

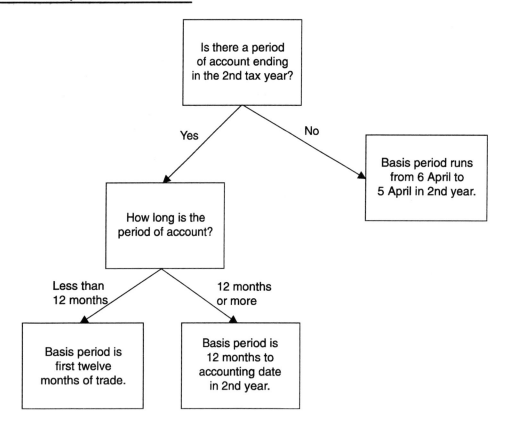

The third tax year

3.9   **If there is an accounting date falling in the second tax year, the basis period for the third tax year is the period of account ending in the third tax year.**

3.10 If there is no accounting date falling in the second tax year, the basis period for the third tax year is the 12 months down to the accounting date falling in the third tax year.

Later tax years

3.11 For later tax years, except the year in which the trade ceases, **the basis period is the period of account ending in the tax year.** This is known as the **current year basis of assessment.**

The final year

3.12 If a trade starts and ceases in the same tax year, the basis period for that year is the whole lifespan of the trade.

3.13 If the final year is the second year, the basis period runs from 6 April at the start of the second year to the date of cessation. This rule overrides the rules that normally apply for the second year.

3.14 If the final year is the third year or a later year, **the basis period runs from the end of the basis period for the previous year to the date of cessation.** This rule overrides the rules that normally apply in the third and later years.

Overlap profits

KEY TERM

Profits which have been taxed more than once are called **overlap profits**.

3.15   When a business starts, some profits may be taxed twice because the basis period for the second year includes some or all of the period of trading in the first year or because the basis period for the third year overlaps with that for the second year.

3.16   **Overlap profits may be deducted on a change of accounting date (see below). Any overlap profits unrelieved when the trade ceases are deducted from the final year's taxable profits.** Any deduction of overlap profits may create or increase a loss. The usual loss reliefs (covered later in this text) are then available.

3.17   EXAMPLE: ACCOUNTING DATE IN 2ND YEAR AT LEAST 12 MONTHS

Jenny trades from 1 July 1995 to 31 December 2000, with the following results.

Period	Profit
	£
1.7.95 - 31.8.96	7,000
1.9.96 - 31.8.97	12,000
1.9.97 - 31.8.98	15,000
1.9.98 - 31.8.99	21,000
1.9.99 - 31.8.00	18,000
1.9.00 - 31.12.00	5,600
	78,600

The profits to be taxed in each tax year from 1995/96 to 2000/01, and the total of these taxable profits are calculated as follows.

Year	Basis period	Working	Taxable profit
			£
1995/96	1.7.95 - 5.4.96	£7,000 × 9/14	4,500
1996/97	1.9.95 - 31.8.96	£7,000 × 12/14	6,000
1997/98	1.9.96 - 31.8.97		12,000
1998/99	1.9.97 - 31.8.98		15,000
1999/00	1.9.98 - 31.8.99		21,000
2000/01	1.9.99 - 31.12.00	£(18,000 + 5,600 − 3,500)	20,100
			78,600

The overlap profits are those in the period 1 September 1995 to 5 April 1996, a period of seven months. They are £7,000 × 7/14 = £3,500. Overlap profits are either relieved on a change of accounting date (see below) or are deducted from the final year's taxable profit when the business ceases. In this case the overlap profits are deducted when the business ceases. Over the life of the business, the total taxable profits equal the total actual profits.

BPP PUBLISHING

Question: Calculation of taxable profits for six tax years

Peter trades from 1 September 1995 to 30 June 2000, with the following results.

Period	Profit £
1.9.95 - 30.4.96	8,000
1.5.96 - 30.4.97	15,000
1.5.97 - 30.4.98	9,000
1.5.98 - 30.4.99	10,500
1.5.99 - 30.4.00	16,000
1.5.00 - 30.6.00	950
	59,450

Show the profits to be taxed in each year from 1995/96 to 2000/01, the total of these taxable profits and the overlap profits.

Answer

Year	Basis period	Working	Taxable profits £
1995/96	1.9.95 - 5.4.96	£8,000 × 7/8	7,000
1996/97	1.9.95 - 31.8.96	£8,000 + (£15,000 × 4/12)	13,000
1997/98	1.5.96 - 30.4.97		15,000
1998/99	1.5.97 - 30.4.98		9,000
1999/00	1.5.98 - 30.4.99		10,500
2000/01	1.5.99 - 30.6.00	£(16,000 + 950 - 12,000)	4,950
			59,450

The overlap profits are the profits from 1 September 1995 to 5 April 1996 (taxed in 1995/96 and in 1996/97) and those from 1 May 1996 to 31 August 1996 (taxed in 1996/97 and 1997/98).

	£
1.9.95 - 5.4.96 £8,000 × 7/8	7,000
1.5.96 - 31.8.96 £15,000 × 4/12	5,000
Total overlap profits	12,000

3.18 EXAMPLE: NO ACCOUNTING DATE IN THE SECOND YEAR

Thelma starts to trade on 1 March 1999. Her first accounts, covering the 16 months to 30 June 2000, show a profit of £36,000. The taxable profits for the first three tax years and the overlap profits are as follows.

Year	Basis period	Working	Taxable profits £
1998/99	1.3.99 - 5.4.99	£36,000 × 1/16	2,250
1999/00	6.4.99 - 5.4.00	£36,000 × 12/16	27,000
2000/01	1.7.99 - 30.6.00	£36,000 × 12/16	27,000

The overlap profits are the profits from 1 July 1999 to 5 April 2000: £36,000 × 9/16 = £20,250.

The choice of an accounting date

3.19 A new trader should consider which accounting date would be best. There are **three factors to consider** from the point of view of taxation.

- **If profits are expected to rise, a date early in the tax year** (such as 30 April) will delay the time when rising accounts profits feed through into rising taxable profits, whereas a date late in the tax year (such as 31 March) will accelerate the taxation of rising profits. This is because with an accounting date of 30 April, the taxable profits for each tax year are mainly the profits earned in the previous tax year. With an accounting date of 31 March the taxable profits are almost entirely profits earned in the current year.

- If the accounting date in the second tax year is less than 12 months after the start of trading, the taxable profits for that year will be the profits earned in the first 12 months. If the accounting date is at least 12 months from the start of trading, they will be the profits earned in the 12 months to that date. **Different profits may thus be taxed twice (the overlap profits)**, and if profits are fluctuating this can make a considerable difference to the taxable profits in the first few years. **It may be many years before relief for the overlap profits is obtained.**

- **The choice of an accounting date affects the profits shown in each set of accounts,** and this may affect the taxable profits.

Question: The choice of an accounting date

Christine starts to trade on 1 December 1998. Her monthly profits are £1,000 for the first seven months, and £2,000 thereafter. Show the taxable profits for the first three tax years with each of the following accounting dates (in all cases starting with a period of account of less than 12 months).

(a) 31 March
(b) 30 April
(c) 31 December

Answer

(a) *31 March*

Period of account	Working	Profits £
1.12.98 – 31.3.99	£1000 × 4	4,000
1.4.99 - 31.3.2000	£1,000 × 3 + £2,000 × 9	21,000
1.4.2000 – 31.3.2001	£2,000 × 12	24,000

Year	Basis period	Taxable profits £
1998/99	1.12.98 - 5.4.99	4,000
1999/2000	1.4.99 - 31.3.2000	21,000
2000/2001	1.4.2000 - 31.3.2001	24,000

(b) *30 April*

Period of account	Working	Profits £
1.12.98 – 30.4.99	£1,000 × 5	5,000
1.5.99 - 30.4.2000	£1,000 × 2 + £2,000 ×10	22,000

Year	Basis period	Working	Taxable profits £
1998/99	1.12.98 - 5.4.99	£5,000 × 4/5	4,000
1999/2000	1.12.98 - 30.11.99	£5,000 + £22,000 × 7/12	17,833
2000/2001	1.5.99 - 30.4.2000		22,000

(c) *31 December*

Period of account	Working	Profits £
1.12.98 – 31.12.98	£1,000 × 1	1,000
1.1.99 - 31.12.99	£1,000 × 6 + £2,000 × 6	18,000
1.1.2000 – 31.12.2000	£2,000 × 12	24,000

Year	Basis period	Working	Taxable profits £
1998/99	1.12.98 - 5.4.99	£1,000 + £18,000 × 3/12	5,500
1999/2000	1.1.99 - 31.12.99		18,000
2000/2001	1.1.2000 - 31.12.2000		24,000

4 CHANGE OF ACCOUNTING DATE

4.1 **A trader may change the date to which he prepares his annual accounts** for a variety of reasons. For example, he may wish to move to a calendar year end or to fit in with seasonal variations of his trade. Special rules normally apply for fixing basis periods when a trader changes his accounting date.

4.2 On a change of accounting date there may be

- One set of accounts covering a period of less than twelve months, or
- One set of accounts covering a period of more than twelve months, or
- No accounts, or
- Two sets of accounts

ending in a tax year. In each case, the basis period for the year relates to the new accounting date. We will look at each of the cases in turn.

One short period of account

4.3 **When a change of accounting date results in one short period of account ending in a tax year, the basis period for that year is always the 12 months to the new accounting date.**

4.4 EXAMPLE

Sue prepares accounts to 31 December each year until she changes her accounting date to 30 June by preparing accounts for the six months to 30 June 2000.

There is one short period of account ending during 2000/01. This means the basis period for 2000/01 is the twelve months to 30 June 2000.

Sue's basis period for 1999/00 was the twelve months to 31 December 1999. This means the profits of the six months to 31 December 1999 are overlap profits that have been taxed twice. These overlap profits must be added to any overlap profits that arose when the business began. The total is either relieved when the business ceases or it is relieved on a subsequent change of accounting date (see Paragraphs 4.6 and 4.10).

One long period of account

4.5 **When a change of accounting date results in one long period of account ending in a tax year, the basis period for that year ends on the new accounting date.** It begins immediately after the basis period for the previous year ends. This means the basis period will exceed 12 months.

4.6 **No overlap profits arise in this situation. However, more than twelve months worth of profits are taxed in one income tax year and to compensate for this, relief is available for brought forward overlap profits. The overlap relief can not reduce the number of months worth of profits taxed in the year to below twelve. So, if you have a fourteen month basis period you can give relief for up to two months worth of overlap profits.**

4.7 EXAMPLE

Zoe started trading on 1 October 1997 and prepared accounts to 30 September until she changed her accounting date by preparing accounts for the fifteen months to 31 December 2000. Her results were as follows

Year to 30 September 1998	£24,000
Year to 30 September 1999	£48,000
Fifteen months to 31 December 2000	£75,000

The Schedule D Case I profits for 1997/98 to 2000/01 are:

Profits for the first three tax years of the business are

1997/98 (1.10.97 -5.4.98)	
6/12 × £24,000	£12,000
1998/99 (1.10.97 -30.9.98)	£24,000
1999/00 (1.10.98 -30.9.99)	£48,000

Overlap profits are £12,000. These arose in the six months to 5.4.98.

The change in accounting date results in one long period of account ending during 2000/01 which means the basis period for 2000/01 is the fifteen months to 31 December 2000. Three months worth of the brought forward overlap profits can be relieved.

	£
2000/01 (1.10.99 - 31.12.00)	75,000
Less: Overlap profits 3/6 × £12,000	(6,000)
	69,000

The unrelieved overlap profits of £6,000 (£12,000 − £6,000) are carried forward for relief either when the business ceases or on a further change of accounting date.

No accounting date ending in the year

4.8 **If a change of accounting date results in there being no period of account ending in a tax year** there is a potential problem because basis periods usually end on an accounting date. To get round this problem **you must manufacture a basis period by taking the new accounting date and deducting one year. The basis period is then the twelve months to this date.**

4.9 EXAMPLE

Anne had always prepared accounts to 31 March. She then changed her accounting date by preparing accounts for the thirteen months to 30 April 2001.

There is no period of account ending during 2000/01 so the basis period for this year is the manufactured basis period of the twelve months to 30 April 2000.

You've probably spotted that this produces an overlap with the previous basis period. The overlap period is 1 May 1999 to 31 March 2000. The overlap profits arising in this period are added to any other unrelieved overlap profits and are carried forward for future relief.

Two Accounting Dates Ending in the Year

4.10 **When two periods of account end in a tax year, the basis period for the year ends on the new accounting date. It begins immediately following the previous basis period. This means that the basis period will exceed 12 months and overlap relief can be allowed to ensure that only twelve months worth of profits are assessed in the tax year.**

BPP PUBLISHING

4.11 EXAMPLE

Elizabeth prepared accounts to 30 September until 2001 when she changed her accounting date by preparing accounts for the six months to 31 March 2001.

The new accounting date is 31 March 2001. This is the end of the basis period for 2000/01. The basis period for 1999/00 ended on 30 September 1999. The 2000/01 basis period is therefore the eighteen month period 1 October 1999 to 31 March 2001. Six months worth of overlap profits can be relieved in this year.

Conditions

4.12 The above changes in basis period automatically occur if the trader changes his accounting date during the first three tax years of his business.

4.13 In other cases **the following conditions must be met before a change in basis periods can occur:**

- the trader must notify the Revenue of the change by the 31 January, following the tax year in which the change is made. (By 31 January 2002 for a change made during 2000/01.)

- the period of account resulting from the change must not exceed 18 months

- in general, there must have been no previous change of accounting date in the last 5 tax years. However, a second change can be made within this period if the later change is for genuine commercial reasons. If the Revenue do not respond to a notification of a change of accounting date within 60 days of receiving it, the trader can assume that they are satisfied that the reasons for making the change are genuine commercial ones.

4.14 If the above conditions are not satisfied because the first period of account ending on the new date exceeds 18 months or the change of accounting date was not notified in time, but the 'five year gap or commercial reasons' condition is satisfied, then the basis period for the year of change is the 12 months to the *old* accounting date in the year of change. The basis period for the next year is then found using rules above as if it were the year of change.

4.15 **If the 'five year gap or commercial reasons' test is not satisfied, the old accounting date remains in force for tax purposes** (with the profits of accounts made up to the new date being time-apportioned as necessary) until there have been five consecutive tax years which were not years of change. The sixth tax year is then treated as the year of change to the new accounting date, and the rules above apply.

5 CAPITAL ALLOWANCES FOR UNINCORPORATED BUSINESSES

5.1 **Capital expenditure is not in itself an allowable Schedule D Case I deduction, but it *may* attract capital allowances. Capital allowances are treated as a trading expense and are deducted in arriving at Schedule D Case I profits. Balancing charges, effectively negative allowances, are added in arriving at those profits.**

5.2 For capital expenditure to qualify for capital allowances it must fall into one of the following categories:

- plant and machinery;
- industrial buildings.

5.3 **For unincorporated businesses, capital allowances are calculated for periods of account.** These are simply the periods for which the trader chooses to make up accounts.

5.4 The definition of plant is the same for both corporate and unincorporated businesses (see Chapter 3 Section 2).

Writing down allowances

5.5 Allowances are claimed in the tax return. Any business can claim less than the full allowances. This may be to its advantage, if, for example, the trader wants to avoid making such a large loss claim as to lose the benefit of the personal allowance. Higher capital allowances will then be available in later years because the WDV carried forward will be higher.

5.6 When plant is sold the proceeds (but limited to a maximum of the original cost) are taken out of the pool of qualifying expenditure. Provided that the trade is still being carried on, the balance remaining is written down in the future by writing down allowances, even if there are no assets left.

5.7 **Writing down allowances are 25% × months/12** for unincorporated businesses where the period of account is longer or shorter than 12 months.

5.8 Expenditure on plant and machinery by a person about to begin a trade is treated as incurred on the first day of trading. Assets previously owned by a trader and then brought into the trade (at the start of trading or later) are treated as bought for their market values at the times when they are brought in.

First year allowances

Spending by small and medium sized enterprises

5.9 **Expenditure incurred on plant and machinery** (other than leased assets, cars, sea going ships, railway assets or long life assets) after 2 July 1998 **by small and medium sized enterprises qualifies for a first year allowance** (FYA) of 40%.

5.10 The above expenditure qualified for a FYA of 50% if it was incurred in the year to 1 July 1998. In addition, expenditure on long life assets in this period qualified for a 12% FYA.

> **KEY TERM**
>
> A **small or medium sized enterprise,** is an individual or partnership that either satisfies at least two of the following conditions in the chargeable period/financial year in which the expenditure is incurred.
>
> (a) **Turnover not more than £11.2 million**
> (b) **Assets not more than £5.6 million**
> (c) **Not more than 250 employees**
>
> or which was small or medium sized in the previous year.

Spending by small enterprises on information and communication technology

5.11   Expenditure by **small enterprises on information and communication technology equipment** (computers, software and internet enabled mobile phones) **in the three year period from 1 April 2000 to 31 March 2003 qualifies for a 100% FYA.**

5.12   Equipment acquired for leasing does not qualify for the 100% FYA.

> **KEY TERM**
>
> **A small enterprise** is an individual or partnership, which satisfies at least two of the following conditions in the chargeable period/financial year in which the expenditure is incurred:
>
> (a)   **Turnover not more than £2.8 million**
> (b)   **Assets not more than £1.4 million**
> (c)   **Not more than 50 employees**
>
> or which was small in the previous year.

Calculation

5.13   For FYA purposes, the provisions which treat capital expenditure incurred prior to the commencement of trading as incurred on the first day of trading do not apply.

5.14   **First year allowances are given in the place of writing down allowances.** For subsequent years a WDA is given on the balance of expenditure at the normal rate. You should therefore transfer the balance of the expenditure to the pool at the end of the first period.

5.15   FYAs are given for incurring expenditure. It is irrelevant whether a basis period of expenditure is twelve months or less. FYAs are not scaled up or down by reference to the length of the period.

Question: Calculation of taxable profits

Eric starts a trade on 1 March 1997, and has the following results (before capital allowances).

Period of account	Profits
	£
1.3.97 - 31.7.98	42,500
1.8.98 - 31.7.99	36,800
1.8.99 - 31.7.00	32,000

Plant (none of which is information or communication technology equipment) is bought as follows.

Date	Cost
	£
1.3.97	13,000
1.6.97	8,000
1.6.99	5,000
31.7.00	2,000

On 1 May 1999, plant which cost £7,000 is sold for £4,000.

Eric's business is a small or medium sized enterprise for FYA purposes.

Show the Schedule D Case I profits arising in the above periods of account.

Answer

The capital allowances are as follows.

	FYA £	Pool £	Allowances £
1.3.97 – 31.7.98			
Additions		21,000	
WDA 25% × 17/12		(7,438)	7,438
		13,562	
1.8.98 – 31.7.99			
Disposals		(4,000)	
		9,562	
WDA 25%		(2,391)	2,391
		7,171	
Addition (1.6.99)	5,000		
FYA 40%	(2,000)		2,000
		3,000	4,391
		10,171	
1.8.99 – 31.7.00			
WDA 25%		(2,543)	2,543
		7,628	
Addition (31.7.00)	2,000		
FYA 40%	(800)		800
		1,200	
TWDV c/f		8,828	
			3,343

The profits of the first three periods of account are as follows.

Period of account	Working	Profits £
1.3.97 – 31.7.98	£(42,500 – 7,438)	35,062
1.8.98 – 31.7.99	£(36,800 – 4,391)	32,409
1.8.99 – 31.7.00	£(32,000 – 3,343)	28,657

Long life assets

5.16 The rules in Chapter 4 paragraphs 3.20 to 3.24 also apply to unincorporated businesses. **Individuals and partnerships spending less than £100,000 a year are also excluded** from the long life asset rules provided the individual, or at least half of the partners, works full time in the business.

Cars

5.17 **Cars** (but not lorries, vans, short-term hire cars, taxis and vehicles unsuitable for private use) **have a special capital allowance treatment.** There are two categories of cars. **Cars costing more than £12,000 are dealt with on an individual basis (see below). Cars costing £12,000 or less are pooled.**

5.18 **Prior to Finance Act 2000 the car pool was a separate one to that used for general plant and machinery.** For individuals, the separate car pool is abolished for periods of account ending after 5 April 2000. The balance that was brought forward on the separate pool at the end of the last period before the abolition is transferred to the main pool.

5.19 Businesses can choose to delay the abolition of the separate car pool until the first period of account ending after 5 April 2001. You should assume this choice is not made, unless you are specifically told otherwise.

5.20 FYAs are not available on cars.

Assets which are not pooled

5.21 Some items are not pooled. A separate record of allowances and WDV must be kept for each such asset and when it is sold a balancing allowance or charge emerges. The items are:

(a) **assets** not wholly used for business purposes (such as cars **with private use by the proprietor**);

(b) **motor cars costing more than £12,000,** where the maximum WDA is £3,000 a year. The limit is £3,000 × months/12:

(i) for short or long periods of account of unincorporated businesses;
(ii) for short accounting periods of companies.

(c) **short-life assets** for which an election has been made.

Assets not wholly used for business purposes

5.22 **Where an asset (for example, a car) is used partly for private purposes by a sole trader or a partner, make all calculations on the full cost but claim only the business use proportion of the allowances.** An asset with some private use by an employee (not a proprietor), however, suffers no such restriction. The employee may be taxed on a benefit in kind so the business gets capital allowances on the full cost of the asset.

Question: Capital allowances on a car

A trader started to trade on 1 July 1997, making up accounts to 31 December 1997 and each 31 December thereafter. On 1 August 1997 he bought a car for £15,500. The private use proportion is 10%. The car was sold in July 2000 for £4,000. What are the capital allowances?

Answer

	Car	Allowances 90%
	£	£
1.7.97 – 31.12.97		
Purchase price	15,500	
WDA 25% × 6/12 of £15,500 = £1,938,		
Limited to £3,000 × 6/12 = £1,500	(1,500)	1,350
	14,000	
1.1.98 – 31.12.98		
WDA 25% of £14,000 = £3,500,		
Limited to £3,000	(3,000)	2,700
	11,000	
1.1.99 – 31.12.99		
WDA 25% of £11,000	(2,750)	2,475
	8,250	
1.1.00 – 31.12.00		
Proceeds	(4,000)	
Balancing allowance	4,250	3,825

Employees' capital allowances

5.23 An employee who provides plant and machinery necessarily for use in the performance of his duties may claim the same allowances as a sole trader, to set against his Schedule E income. In the case of cars, the provision of the car need not be necessary. Employees who use their own bicycles for business travel may also claim capital allowances.

The cessation of a trade

5.24 **When a business ceases to trade no FYAs or WDAs are given in the final period of account.** Each asset is deemed to be disposed of on the date the trade ceased (usually at the then market value). Additions in the relevant period are brought in and then the disposal proceeds (limited to cost) are deducted from the balance of qualifying expenditure. If the proceeds exceed the balance then a balancing charge arises. If the balance of qualifying expenditure exceeds the proceeds then a balancing allowance is given.

Short life assets

5.25 The rules in Chapter 3 paragraphs 4.2 to 4.6 also apply to unincorporated businesses.

5.26 Connected persons for individuals are defined above.

Hire purchase and leasing

5.27 The rules in Chapter 3 paragraphs 5.1 to 5.6 also apply to unincorporated businesses.

Successions

5.28 **Balancing adjustments arise on the cessation of a business.** No writing down allowances are given, but the final proceeds (limited to cost) on sales of plant are compared with the tax WDV to calculate balancing allowances or charges.

5.29 **Balancing charges may be avoided where the trade passes from one connected person to another.** If a succession occurs both parties must elect if the avoidance of the balancing adjustments is required. **An election will result in the plant being transferred at its tax written down value for capital allowances purposes.** The predecessor can write down the plant for the period prior to cessation and the successor can write it down from the date of commencement. The election must be made within two years of the date of the succession.

5.30 If no election is made on a transfer of business to a connected person, assets are deemed to be sold at their market values.

5.31 Where a person succeeds to a business under a will or on intestacy, then even if he was not connected with the deceased he may elect to take over the assets at the lower of their market value and their tax written down value.

5.32 For both connected persons transfers and transfers on death, where the elections are made, the limit on proceeds to be brought into account on a later sale of an asset is the original cost of the asset, not the deemed transfer price.

Industrial buildings allowance

5.33 The principles in Chapter 3 Sections 7 and 8 also apply to unincorporated businesses. The allowance is only available to traders taxable under Schedule D Case I (not to those unincorporated businesses taxable under Schedule D Case II) and landlords who let qualifying buildings to traders. The building must be in use on the last day of the basis period for a WDA to be given. The WDA is 4% (or 2%) × months/12 if the basis period is not 12 months long.

Chapter roundup

- The badges of trade can be used to decide whether or not a trade exists. If one does exist, the accounts profits need to be adjusted in order to establish the taxable profits.

- Basis periods are used to link periods of account to tax years.

- In opening and closing years, special rules are applied so that a new trader can start to be taxed quickly, and a retiring trader need not be taxed long after his retirement.

- On a change of accounting date, special rules may apply for fixing basis periods.

- Capital allowances apply to unincorporated businesses with some special rules.

Quick quiz

1   What are the badges of trade? (see paras 1.1 - 1.8)

2   How is the basis period for the second tax year of a business found? (3.5 - 3.7)

3   How is the basis period for the third tax year of a business found? (3.9, 3.10)

4   How is the basis period for the final tax year of a business found? (3.12 - 3.14)

5   How do we find the basis period for a tax year, if following a change of accounting date, there is no period of account ending in the year? (4.8)

6   How is an asset which is partly used privately by the proprietor of a business dealt with for capital allowances? (5.22)

Now try the questions below from the Exam Question Bank

Number	Level	Marks	Time
19	Exam	15	27 mins
20	Exam	12	22 mins

Chapter 14

TRADING LOSSES

Topic list	Syllabus reference
1 Losses	2c(vi)
2 Relief for trading losses by carry forward: s 385 ICTA 1988	2c(vi)
3 Setting trading losses against total income: s 380 ICTA 1988	2c(vi)
4 Businesses transferred to companies: s 386 ICTA 1988	2c(vi)
5 Trade charges: s 387 ICTA 1988	2c(vi)
6 Losses in the early years of a trade: s 381 ICTA 1988	2c(vi)
7 Losses on the cessation of a trade: s 388 ICTA 1988	2c(vi)

Introduction

Traders sometimes make losses rather than profits. In this chapter we consider the reliefs available for losses.

A loss does not in itself lead to getting tax back from the Revenue. Relief is obtained by setting a loss against trading profits, against other income or against capital gains, so that tax need not be paid on them. An important consideration is the choice between different reliefs. The aim is to use a loss to save as much tax as possible, as quickly as possible.

Study guide

Trading losses

- Explain how trading losses can be carried forward

- Explain how trading losses can be claimed against total income and chargeable gains

- Explain the relief for trading losses in the early years of a trade

- Explain terminal loss relief

Exam guide

This is part of section 2c which is a key topic. Question 2 in Section A will be on an unincorporated business and/or employees. It was also given by the examiner as a specific example of an area which could be examined in Question 7 in Section B.

1   LOSSES

1.1   This chapter considers how losses are calculated and how a loss-suffering taxpayer can use a loss to reduce his tax liability. Most of the chapter concerns trading losses in respect of trades normally taxed under Schedule D Case I. Losses arising in professions and vocations (Schedule D Case II) are treated in exactly the same way.

1.2   **The rules in this chapter apply only to individuals,** trading alone or in partnership.

1.3   **Losses of one spouse cannot be relieved against income of the other spouse.**

1.4   When computing tax adjusted trading profits, profits may turn out to be negative, that is a loss has been made in the basis period. **A loss is computed in exactly the same way as a profit,** making the same adjustments to the accounts profit or loss.

1.5   **If there is a loss in a basis period, the taxable income for the tax year based on that basis period is nil.**

2   RELIEF FOR TRADING LOSSES BY CARRY FORWARD: S 385 ICTA 1988

2.1   A trading loss not relieved in any other way may be **carried forward to set against the first available profits of the same trade.** Losses may be carried forward for any number of years.

2.2   EXAMPLE: CARRYING FORWARD LOSSES

B has the following results.

Year ending	£
31 December 1998	(6,000)
31 December 1999	5,000
31 December 2000	11,000

B's taxable profits, assuming that he claims loss relief only under s 385 are:

	1998/99		*1999/00*		*2000/01*
	£		£		£
Schedule D Case I	0		5,000		11,000
Less s 385 relief	(0)	(i)	(5,000)	(ii)	(1,000)
Profits	0		0		10,000

Loss memorandum		£
Trading loss, y/e 31.12.98		6,000
Less: claim in y/e 31.12.99	(i)	(5,000)
claim in y/e 31.12.00 (balance of loss)	(ii)	(1,000)
		0

3   SETTING TRADING LOSSES AGAINST TOTAL INCOME: S 380 ICTA 1988

3.1   **Instead of carrying a loss forward against future trading income, it may be relieved against current income of all types.**

The computation of the loss

3.2   EXAMPLE

The loss for a tax year is the loss in the basis period for that tax year. However, if basis periods overlap then a loss in the overlap period is a loss for the earlier tax year only. Here is an example of a trader who starts to trade on 1 July 2000 and makes losses in opening years.

Period of account	*Loss*
	£
1.7.00 - 31.12.00	9,000
1.1.01 - 31.12.01	24,000

Tax year	Basis period	Working	Loss for the tax year
			£
2000/01	1.7.00 - 5.4.01	£9,000 + (£24,000 × 3/12)	15,000
2001/02	1.1.01 - 31.12.01	£24,000 - (£24,000 × 3/12)	18,000

3.3 EXAMPLE

The same rule against using losses twice applies when losses are netted off against profits in the same basis period. Here is an example, again with a commencement on 1 July 2000 but with a different accounting date.

Period of account	(Loss)/profit
	£
1.7.00 - 30.4.01	(10,000)
1.5.01 - 30.4.02	24,000

Tax year	Basis period	Working	(Loss)/Profit
			£
2000/01	1.7.00 - 5.4.01	£(10,000) × 9/10	(9,000)
2001/02	1.7.00 - 30.6.01	£24,000 × 2/12 + £(10,000) × 1/10	3,000

Relieving the loss

3.4 **Relief under s 380 is against the income of the tax year in which the loss arose. In addition or instead,** relief may be claimed **against the income of the preceding year.**

If there are losses in two successive years, and relief is claimed against the first year's income both for the first year's loss and for the second year's loss, relief is given for the first year's loss before the second year's loss.

3.5 A claim for a loss must be made by the 31 January which is 22 months after the end of the tax year of the loss: thus by 31 January 2003 for a loss in 2000/01.

3.6 The taxpayer cannot choose the amount of loss to relieve: thus the loss may have to be set against income, part of which would have been covered by the personal allowance. However, the taxpayer can choose whether to claim full relief in the current year and then relief in the preceding year for any remaining loss, or the other way round.

Set the loss against non-savings income then against savings (excluding dividend) income and finally against dividend income.

3.7 Relief is available by carry forward under s 385 for any loss not relieved under s 380.

Question: s 380 relief

Janet has a loss in her period of account ending 31 December 2000 of £25,000. Her other income is £18,000 interest income a year, and she wishes to claim loss relief for the year of loss and then for the preceding year. Show her taxable income for each year, and comment on the effectiveness of the loss relief. Assume that tax rates and allowances for 2000/01 have always applied.

Answer

The loss-making period ends in 2000/01, so the year of the loss is 2000/01.

	1999/00	2000/01
	£	£
Income	18,000	18,000
Less s 380 relief	(7,000)	(18,000)
STI	11,000	0
Less personal allowance	(4,385)	(4,385)
Taxable income	6,615	0

In 2000/01, £4,385 of the loss has been wasted because that amount of income would have been covered by the personal allowance. If Janet claims s 380 relief, there is nothing she can do about this waste of loss relief. However, Janet might have been best advised to claim relief in 1999/00 before making a claim in 2000/01. This would have had the effect of moving the taxable income to 2000/01 and delaying the payment of the associated income tax.

Capital allowances

3.8 The trader may adjust the size of the total s 380 claim by not claiming all the capital allowances he is entitled to: a reduced claim will increase the balance carried forward to the next year's capital allowances computation.

Trading losses relieved against capital gains

3.9 Where relief is claimed against total income of a given year, the taxpayer may include **a further claim to set the loss against his chargeable gains for the year** less any allowable capital losses for the same year or for previous years. This amount of net gains is computed ignoring taper relief and the annual exempt amount (see later).

3.10 **The trading loss is first set against total income of the year of the claim, and only any excess of loss is set against capital gains. The taxpayer cannot specify the amount to be set against capital gains, so the annual exempt amount may be wasted.**

Question: Loss relief against income and gains

Sibyl had the following results for 2000/01.

	£
Loss available for relief under s 380	27,000
Income	19,500
Capital gains less current year capital losses	10,000
Annual exemption for capital gains tax purposes	7,200
Capital losses brought forward	4,000

Assume no taper relief is due.

Show how the loss would be relieved against income and gains.

Answer

	£
Income	19,500
Less loss relief	(19,500)
STI	0

	£
Capital gains	10,000
Less loss relief: lower of £(27,000 – 19,500) = £7,500 (note 1) and	
£(10,000 - 4,000) = £6,000 (note 2)	(6,000)
	4,000
Less annual exemption	(4,000)
	0

Note 1   This equals the loss left after the S380 claim
Note 2   This equals the gains left after losses b/fwd but ignoring taper relief and the annual exemption.

A trading loss of £(7,500 – 6,000) = £1,500 is carried forward. Sibyl's personal allowance and £(7,200 – 4,000) = £3,200 of her capital gains tax annual exemption are wasted. Her capital losses brought forward of £4,000 are carried forward to 2001/02. Although we deducted this £4,000 in working out how much trading loss we were allowed to use in the claim, we do not actually use any of the £4,000 unless there are gains remaining after the annual exemption.

Restrictions on s 380 relief

3.11   **Relief cannot be claimed under s 380 unless a business is conducted on a commercial basis with a view to the realisation of profits;** this condition applies to all types of business. In addition, relief cannot be claimed for a loss in farming or market gardening if, in all of the five previous tax years, there was a loss even ignoring capital allowances.

The choice between loss reliefs

3.12   **When a trader has a choice between loss reliefs, he should aim to obtain relief both quickly and at the highest possible tax rate.** However, do consider that losses relieved against income which would otherwise be covered by the personal allowance are wasted.

3.13   Another consideration is that a trading loss cannot be set against the capital gains of a year unless relief is first claimed under s 380 against income of the same year. It may be worth making the claim against income and wasting the personal allowance in order to avoid a CGT liability.

Question: The choice between loss reliefs

Felicity's trading results are as follows.

Year ended 30 September	Trading profit/(loss) £
1998	1,900
1999	(21,000)
2000	13,000

Her other income (all non-savings income) is as follows.

	£
1998/99	2,200
1999/00	25,330
2000/01	12,000

Show the most efficient use of Felicity's trading loss. The personal allowance was £4,195 in 1998/99, £4,335 in 1999/00 and £4,385 in 2000/01.

Answer

Relief could be claimed under s 380 for 1998/99 and/or 1999/00, with any unused loss being carried forward under s 385. Relief in 1998/99 would be against total income of £(1,900 + 2,200) = £4,100, all of which would be covered by the personal allowance anyway, so this claim should not be made. A s 380 claim should be made for 1999/00 as this saves tax quicker than a s 385 claim in 2000/01 would. The final results will be as follows:

	1998/99	1999/00	2000/01
	£	£	£
Schedule D Case I	1,900	0	13,000
Less s 385 relief	(0)	(0)	(0)
	1,900	0	13,000
Other income	2,200	25,330	12,000
	4,100	25,330	25,000
Less s 380 relief	(0)	(21,000)	(0)
STI	4,100	4,330	25,000
Less personal allowance	(4,195)	(4,335)	(4,385)
Taxable income	0	0	20,615

Exam focus point

Before recommending S 380 loss relief consider whether it will result in the waste of the personal allowance and any tax reducers. Such waste is to be avoided if at all possible.

4 BUSINESSES TRANSFERRED TO COMPANIES: S 386 ICTA 1988

4.1 **Although the set-off under s 385 is restricted to future profits of the same business, this is extended to cover income received from a company to which the business is sold under s 386.**

4.2 **The amount carried forward is the total unrelieved trading losses of the business. The set-off must be made against the first available income from the company. The order of set-off is:**

(a) against **salary** derived from the company by the former proprietor of the business; **then**

(b) against **interest and dividends** from the company.

4.3 The consideration for the sale must be wholly or mainly shares, which must be retained by the vendor throughout any tax year in which the loss is relieved; the Revenue treat this condition as being satisfied if 80% or more of the consideration consists of shares.

5 TRADE CHARGES: S 387 ICTA 1988

5.1 Annual charges such as patent royalties, although they may be paid out wholly and exclusively for business purposes, are nevertheless not deducted in arriving at the adjusted Schedule D Case I profit or loss.

But it is possible to suffer a 'loss' if STI is reduced to zero by such a charge because the Revenue will collect the tax withheld from the charge under s 350 ICTA 1988. **Excess trade charges can be carried forward against future profits from the same trade** in the same way as losses under s 385. Non-trade charges, however cannot be relieved in this way. However, non-trade charges can be relieved first against profits, resulting in a greater amount of trade charges eligible for relief under s 387.

5.2 EXAMPLE: EXCESS TRADE CHARGES

A taxpayer has the following results for 2000/01.

	£
Schedule D Case I	4,000
Other income	1,000
	5,000
Less patent royalty	(7,000)
STI	0

Basic rate tax would be due on the unrelieved £2,000, so that the taxpayer accounted for 22% × £2,000 = £440, but the taxpayer could then carry forward the £2,000 against future profits from the trade.

6 LOSSES IN THE EARLY YEARS OF A TRADE: S 381 ICTA 1988

6.1 S 381 relief is available for **trading losses incurred in the first four tax years of a trade.**

6.2 Relief is obtained by **setting the allowable loss against total income in the three years preceding the year of loss,** applying the loss to the earliest year first. Thus a loss arising in 2000/01 may be set off against income in 1997/98, 1998/99 and 1999/00 in that order.

6.3 A claim under s 381 applies to all three years automatically, provided that the loss is large enough. The taxpayer cannot choose to relieve the loss against just one or two of the years, or to relieve only part of the loss.

6.4 Do not double-count a loss. If basis periods overlap, a loss in the overlap period is treated as a loss for the earlier tax year only. This is the same rule as applies for s 380 purposes.

6.5 Claims for the relief must be made by the 31 January which is 22 months after the end of the tax year in which the loss is incurred.

6.6 The 'commercial basis' test is stricter for loss relief under s 381 than under s 380. The trade must be carried on in such a way that profits could reasonably have been expected to be realised in the period of the loss or within a reasonable time thereafter.

Question: S381 loss relief

Mr A is employed as an auditor until 1 January 1999. On that date he starts up his own business as a scrap metal merchant, making up his accounts to 30 June each year.

His taxable income as an auditor is as follows.

	£
1995/96	5,000
1996/97	6,000
1997/98	7,000
1998/99 (nine months)	6,000

His trading results as a scrap metal merchant are as follows.

	Profit/(Loss) £
Six months to 30 June 1999	(3,000)
Year to 30 June 2000	(1,500)
Year to 30 June 2001	(1,200)
Year to 30 June 2002	0

Assuming that loss relief is claimed as early as possible, show the final Schedule E and Schedule D Case I income for each of the years 1995/96 to 2001/02 inclusive.

Answer

Since reliefs are to be claimed as early as possible, s 381 ICTA 1988 is applied. The losses available for relief are as follows.

	£	£	*Years against which relief is available*
1998/99 (basis period 1.1.99 - 5.4.99)			
3 months to 5.4.99			
£(3,000) × 3/6		(1,500)	1995/96 to 1997/98
1999/00 (basis period 1.1.99 - 31.12.99)			
3 months to 30.6.99			
(omit 1.1.99 - 5.4.99: overlap)			
£(3,000) × 3/6	(1,500)		
6 months to 31.12.99			
£(1,500) × 6/12	(750)		
		(2,250)	1996/97 to 1998/99
2000/2001 (basis period 1.7.99 - 30.6.00)			
6 months to 30.6.00			
(omit 1.7.99 - 31.12.99: overlap)			
£(1,500) × 6/12		(750)	1997/98 to 1999/00
2001/2002 (basis period 1.7.00 - 30.6.01)			
12 months to 30.6.01		(1,200)	1998/99 to 2000/01

The revised Schedule E income is as follows.

	£	£
1995/96		
Original	5,000	
Less 1998/99 loss	(1,500)	
		3,500
1996/97		
Original	6,000	
Less 1999/00 loss	(2,250)	
		3,750
1997/98		
Original	7,000	
Less 2000/01 loss	(750)	
		6,250
1998/99		
Original	6,000	
Less 2001/02 loss	(1,200)	
		4,800

The Schedule D Case I income for 1998/99 to 2001/02 will all be zero, because there were losses in the basis periods.

7   LOSSES ON THE CESSATION OF A TRADE: S 388 ICTA 1988

7.1   S 380 relief will often be insufficient on its own to deal with a loss incurred in the last months of trading. For this reason there is a special relief, **terminal loss relief, which allows a loss on cessation to be carried back for relief in previous years.**

Computing the terminal loss

7.2   A terminal loss under s 388 is **the loss of the last 12 months of trading**.

7.3   It is built up as follows.

		£
(a)	The actual trading loss for the tax year of cessation (calculated from 6 April to the date of cessation)	X
(b)	The actual trading loss for the period from 12 months before cessation until the end of the penultimate tax year	X
(c)	Any excess trade charges for the tax year of cessation	X
(d)	A proportion of any excess trade charges for the penultimate tax year	X
	Total terminal loss	X

7.4   If either (a) or (b) above yields a profit as opposed to a loss, the profit is regarded as zero for this purpose.

The terminal loss cannot include any amounts for which relief has already been given. Make sure that computations exclude any amounts claimed under s 380 and also any losses which have been set off in computing the taxable profits for the final tax year.

The proportion mentioned in (d) above is needed to ensure that only trade charges of the last 12 months are included. The figure included in the terminal loss is limited to the total trade charges multiplied by:

$$\frac{\text{number of months in item (b) in the computation}}{12}$$

7.5   Any unrelieved overlap profits may be deducted in the tax year of cessation and should, therefore, be included within (a) above.

Relieving the terminal loss

7.6   The income against which the terminal loss can be set in any one year is computed as follows.

	£
Schedule D Case I income	X
Less the excess of the gross amount of charges paid net of tax over other income *	(X)
Available for s 388 relief	X

*   This amount also comes off the terminal loss available for relief in earlier years to the extent that it is charges which are non-trade *and* do not give rise to a s 350 charge.

7.7   **Relief is given in the tax year of cessation and the three preceding years, later years first.**

BPP PUBLISHING

Question: Terminal loss relief

Set out below are the results of a business up to its cessation on 30 September 2000.

	Profit/(loss)
	£
Year to 31 December 1997	2,000
Year to 31 December 1998	400
Year to 31 December 1999	300
Nine months to 30 September 2000	(1,950)

Overlap profits on commencement were £450. These were all unrelieved on cessation.

Show the available terminal loss relief, and suggest an alternative claim if the trader had had other non-savings income of £10,000 in each of 1999/00 and 2000/01. Assume that 2000/01 tax rates and allowances apply to all years.

Answer

The terminal loss comes in the last 12 months, the period 1 October 1999 to 30 September 2000. This period is split as follows.

1999/00 Six months to 5 April 2000
2000/01 Six months to 30 September 2000

The terminal loss is made up as follows.

Unrelieved trading losses		£	£
1999/00			
3 months to 31.12.99	£300 × 3/12	75	
3 months to 5.4.00	£(1,950) × 3/9	(650)	
			(575)
2000/01			
6 months to 30.9.00	£(1,950) × 6/9		(1,300)
Overlap relief	£(450)		(450)
			(2,325)

Schedule D Case I profits will be as follows.

Year	Basis period	Profits	Terminal loss relief	Final taxable profits
		£	£	£
1997/98	Y/e 31.12.97	2,000	1,625	375
1998/99	Y/e 31.12.98	400	400	0
1999/00	Y/e 31.12.99	300	300	0
2000/01	1.1.99 - 30.9.00	0	0	0
			2,325	

If the trader had had £10,000 of other income in 1999/00 and 2000/01, we would have had to consider s 380 claims for these two years, using the loss of £(1,950 + 450) = £2,400 for 2000/01. From a cash flow point of view it is better to claim relief in the earlier year than in the later year.

The final results would be as follows. (We could alternatively claim loss relief in 2000/01.)

	1997/98	*1998/99*	*1999/00*	*2000/01*
	£	£	£	£
Schedule D Case I	2,000	400	300	0
Other income	0	0	10,000	10,000
	2,000	400	10,300	10,000
Less s 380 claims	0	0	(2,400)	0
STI	2,000	400	7,900	10,000

Chapter roundup

- Trading losses may be relieved against future profits of the same trade, against total income and against capital gains.

- In opening years, a special relief involving the carry back of losses against total income is available. On the cessation of trade, a loss may be carried back against trading profits.

- It is important for a trader to choose the right loss relief, so as to save tax at the highest possible rate and so as to obtain relief reasonably quickly.

Quick quiz

1   Against what income may losses carried forward be set off? (see para 2.1)

2   When a loss is to be relieved against total income, how are losses linked to particular tax years? (3.2)

3   Against which years' total income may a loss be relieved under s 380 ICTA 1988? (3.4)

4   What relief for past losses is available following the incorporation of a business? (4.1 - 4.3)

5   What is the relief available under s 381 ICTA 1988? (6.1 - 6.3)

6   How is a terminal loss calculated? (7.3 - 7.5)

Now try the question below from the Exam Question Bank

Number	Level	Marks	Time
21	Exam	15	27 mins

BPP PUBLISHING

Chapter 15

PARTNERSHIPS

Topic list	Syllabus reference
1 Partnerships	2c(vii)

Introduction

We now see how the income tax rules for traders are adapted to deal with partnerships. On the one hand, a partnership is a single trading entity, making profits as a whole. On the other hand, each partner has a personal tax computation, so the profits must be apportioned to the partners. The general approach is to work out the profits of the partnership, then tax each partner as if he were a sole trader running a business equal to his slice of the partnership (for example 25% of the partnership).

Study guide

Partnership

* Explain how a partnership is assessed to tax

* Allocate assessable profits between the partners following a change in the profit sharing ratio or a change in the members of the partnership

* Describe the alternative loss relief claims that are available to partners

Exam guide

This is part of section 2c which is a key topic. Question 2 in Section A will be on an unincorporated business and/or employees. It was also given by the examiner as a specific example of an area which could be examined in Question 7 in Section B.

1   PARTNERSHIPS

1.1   **A partnership is treated like a sole trader for the purposes of computing its profits.** (As usual, 'trade' in this chapter includes professions and vocations.) Partners' salaries and interest on capital are not deductible expenses and must be added back in computing profits, because they are a form of drawings.

1.2   **Once the partnership's profits for a period of account have been computed, they are shared between the partners according to the profit sharing arrangements for that period of account.**

The tax positions of individual partners

1.3   **Each partner is taxed like a sole trader** who runs a business which:

* starts when he joins the partnership;

174

- finishes when he leaves the partnership;

- has the same periods of account as the partnership (except that a partner who joins or leaves during a period will have a period which starts or ends part way through the partnership's period);

- makes profits or losses equal to the partner's share of the partnership's profits or losses.

Changes in membership

1.4 **When a trade continues but partners join or leave** (including cases when a sole trader takes in partners or a partnership breaks up leaving only one partner as a sole trader), **the special rules for basis periods in opening and closing years do not apply to the people who were carrying on the trade both before and after the change. They carry on using the period of account ending in each tax year as the basis period for the tax year. The commencement rules only affect joiners, and the cessation rules only affect leavers.**

1.5 However, when no-one carries on the trade both before and after the change, as when a partnership transfers its trade to a completely new owner or set of owners, the cessation rules apply to the old owners and the commencement rules apply to the new owners.

Loss reliefs

1.6 **Partners are entitled to the same loss reliefs as sole traders.** A partner is entitled to s 381 relief for losses in the four tax years starting with the year in which he is treated as starting to trade and he is entitled to terminal loss relief when he is treated as ceasing to trade. This is so even if the partnership trades for many years before the partner joins or after he leaves. Loss relief under s 380 and s 385 is also available to partners. Different partners may claim loss reliefs in different ways.

1.7 When a partnership business is transferred to a company, each partner can carry forward his share of any unrelieved losses against income from the company under s 386 ICTA 1988.

Assets owned individually

1.8 **Where the partners own assets (such as their cars) individually, a capital allowances computation must be prepared for each partner in respect of the assets he owns** (not forgetting any adjustment for private use). **The capital allowances must go into the partnership's tax computation.**

1.9 EXAMPLE: A PARTNERSHIP

Alice and Bertrand start a partnership on 1 July 1997, making up accounts to 31 December each year. On 1 May 1999, Charles joins the partnership. On 1 November 2000, Charles leaves. On 1 January 2001, Deborah joins. The profit sharing arrangements are as follows.

	Alice	Bertrand	Charles	Deborah
1.7.97 - 31.1.98				
Salaries (per annum)	£3,000	£4,500		
Balance	3/5	2/5		
1.2.98 - 30.4.99				
Salaries (per annum)	£3,000	£6,000		
Balance	4/5	1/5		
1.5.99 - 31.10.00				
Salaries (per annum)	£2,400	£3,600	£1,800	
Balance	2/5	2/5	1/5	
1.11.00 - 31.12.00				
Salaries (per annum)	£1,500	£2,700		
Balance	3/5	2/5		
1.1.01 onwards				
Salaries (per annum)	£1,500	£2,700		£600
Balance	3/5	1/5		1/5

Profits and losses as adjusted for tax purposes are as follows.

Period	Profit(loss)
	£
1.7.97 - 31.12.97	22,000
1.1.98 - 31.12.98	51,000
1.1.99 - 31.12.99	39,000
1.1.00 - 31.12.00	15,000
1.1.01 - 31.12.01	(18,000)

Show the taxable profits for each partner for 1997/98 to 2000/01, and outline the loss reliefs available to the partners in respect of the loss in the year ending 31 December 2001. Assume that the partnership will continue to trade with the same partners until 2011.

1.10 SOLUTION

We must first share the profits and losses for the periods of account between the partners, remembering to adjust the salaries for periods of less than a year.

	Total	Alice	Bertrand	Charles	Deborah
	£	£	£	£	£
1.7.97 - 31.12.97					
Salaries	3,750	1,500	2,250		
Balance	18,250	10,950	7,300		
Total (P/e 31.12.97)	22,000	12,450	9,550		
1.1.98 - 31.12.98					
January					
Salaries	625	250	375		
Balance	3,625	2,175	1,450		
Total	4,250	2,425	1,825		
February to December					
Salaries	8,250	2,750	5,500		
Balance	38,500	30,800	7,700		
Total	46,750	33,550	13,200		
Total for y/e 31.12.98	51,000	35,975	15,025		
1.1.99 - 31.12.99					
January to April					
Salaries	3,000	1,000	2,000		
Balance	10,000	8,000	2,000		
Total	13,000	9,000	4,000		
May to December					
Salaries	5,200	1,600	2,400	1,200	
Balance	20,800	8,320	8,320	4,160	
Total	26,000	9,920	10,720	5,360	
Total for y/e 31.12.99	39,000	18,920	14,720	5,360	
1.1.00 - 31.12.00					
January to October					
Salaries	6,500	2,000	3,000	1,500	
Balance	6,000	2,400	2,400	1,200	
Total	12,500	4,400	5,400	2,700	
November and December					
Salaries	700	250	450		
Balance	1,800	1,080	720		
Total	2,500	1,330	1,170		
Total for y/e 31.12.00	15,000	5,730	6,570	2,700	
1.1.01 - 31.12.01					
Salaries	4,800	1,500	2,700		600
Balance	(22,800)	(13,680)	(4,560)		(4,560)
Total loss for y/e 31.12.01	(18,000)	(12,180)	(1,860)		(3,960)

1.11 The next stage is to work out the basis periods and hence the taxable profits for the partners. All of them are treated as making up accounts to 31 December, but Alice and Bertrand are treated as starting to trade on 1 July 1997, Charles as trading only from 1 May 1999 to 31 October 2000 and Deborah as starting to trade on 1 January 2001. Applying the usual rules gives the following basis periods and taxable profits.

Alice

Year	Basis period	Working	Taxable profits
			£
1997/98	1.7.97 - 5.4.98	£12,450 + (£35,975 × 3/12)	21,444
1998/99	1.1.98 - 31.12.98		35,975
1999/00	1.1.99 - 31.12.99		18,920
2000/01	1.1.00 - 31.12.00		5,730

Note that for 1997/98 we take Alice's total for the year ended 1998 and apportion that, because the partnership's period of account runs from 1 January to 31 December 1998. Alice's profits for 1997/98 are *not* £12,450 + £2,425 + (£33,550 × 2/11) = £20,975.

Alice will have overlap profits for the period 1 January to 5 April 1998 (£35,975 × 3/12 = £8,994) to deduct when she ceases to trade.

Bertrand

Year	Basis period	Working	Taxable profits
			£
1997/98	1.7.97 - 5.4.98	£9,550 + (£15,025 × 3/12)	13,306
1998/99	1.1.98 - 31.12.98		15,025
1999/00	1.1.99 - 31.12.99		14,720
2000/01	1.1.00 - 31.12.00		6,570

Bertrand's overlap profits are £15,025 × 3/12 = £3,756.

Charles

Year	Basis period	Working	Taxable profits
			£
1999/00	1.5.99 - 5.4.00	£5,360 + (£2,700 × 3/10)	6,170
2000/01	6.4.00 - 31.10.00	£2,700 × 7/10	1,890

Because Charles ceased to trade in his second tax year of trading, his basis period for the second year starts on 6 April and he has no overlap profits.

Deborah

Year	Basis period	Working	Taxable profits
			£
2000/01	1.1.01 - 5.4.01	A loss arises	0

1.12 Finally, we must look at the loss reliefs available to Alice, Bertrand and Deborah. Charles is not entitled to any loss relief, because he left the firm before any loss arose.

Alice and Bertrand

For 2001/02, Alice has a loss of £12,180 and Bertrand has a loss of £1,860. They may claim relief under s 380 or under s 385.

Deborah

Deborah's losses are as follows, remembering that a loss which falls in the basis periods for two tax years is only taken into account in the earlier year.

Year	Basis period	Working	Loss
			£
2000/01	1.1.01 - 5.4.01	£3,960 × 3/12	990
2001/02	1.1.01 - 31.12.01	£3,960 - £990 (overlap loss)	2,970

Deborah may claim relief for these losses under s 380, s 381 (because she has just started to trade) or s 385.

Exam focus point

Partners are effectively taxed in the same way as sole traders with just one difference. Before you tax the partner you need to take each set of accounts (as adjusted for tax purposes) and divide the profit (or loss) between each partner.

Then carry on as normal for a sole trader - each partner is that sole trader in respect of his profits for each accounting period.

Chapter roundup

- A partnership is simply treated as a source of profits and losses for trades being carried on by the individual partners.

- Commencement and cessation rules apply to partners individually when they join or leave.

Quick quiz

1   How are individual partners taxed on the partnership's profits? (see para 1.1 to 1.3)

2   What loss reliefs are partners entitled to? (1.6, 1.7)

Now try the questions below from the Exam Question Bank

Number	Level	Marks	Time
22	Exam	12	22 mins
23	Exam	15	27 mins

BPP PUBLISHING

Chapter 16

PERSONAL PENSIONS. NICs FOR THE SELF EMPLOYED

Topic list	Syllabus reference
1 Personal pension schemes	2c(viii)
2 National insurance contributions (NICs) for the self employed	2f

Introduction

Employees may be provided with pensions under an occupational pension scheme (dealt with in Chapter 21) or under a personal pension scheme. Tax relief is given for contributions to either type of pension scheme.

Self-employed individuals must make provision under a personal pension scheme.

The self-employed are required to make national insurance contributions in two ways: a flat rate contribution (Class 2) and a contribution based on profits (Class 4).

Study guide

Unincorporated businesses

*   Explain the relief given for contributions to a personal pension scheme

*   Calculate Class 2 NIC

*   Calculate Class 4 NIC

Exam guide

Personal pensions are part of section 2c and therefore a key topic. It is likely to be examined as part of Question 2 in Section A or Question 7 in Section B.

National insurance contributions are not a key topic, but may be asked for a maximum of ten marks, again in Question 2 or Question 7.

1   PERSONAL PENSION SCHEMES

KEY TERM

Personal pension schemes (PPSs) are a means of providing pensions to the self-employed and to those in non-pensionable employment (which includes employees who choose not to join their employer's occupational scheme; employees cannot be forced to join such a scheme).

1.1 **The taxpayer makes a contract with a life assurance company or other pension provider and pays premiums. An individual's employer may also contribute. Such a contribution is not a taxable emolument in the hands of the employee, to the extent that the employer's contribution is within the appropriate limit on premiums,** for example 17½% of earnings (see below). **The premiums go into a fund which is invested, and is ultimately used to provide a pension.**

1.2 The taxpayer may also use his PPS to contract out of the state earnings related pension scheme (SERPS). If he does so, the Department of Social Security pays premiums into his scheme, in addition to his own premiums and without reducing the maximum premiums he can pay. He must still pay full (not contracted out) national insurance contributions.

Tax reliefs

1.3 **The taxpayer may deduct his premium from his earnings, up to a percentage of 'net relevant earnings' (NRE) that depends on his age. Employees (but not the self-employed) pay PPS contributions net of basic rate tax. The allowable premium should be shown as a deduction from the appropriate source of income (Schedule D or Schedule E) in the individual's personal tax computation.** If a premium is paid net of basic rate tax, that tax must be added back in arriving at tax liability, just like the tax on charges paid net. However, if the result would be an amount owing to the Inland Revenue because the premium came out of income taxable only at 10% or covered by the personal allowance, the Inland Revenue do not collect the tax: the employee gets the benefit of basic rate relief. In such cases, to prevent double relief when finding tax liability, you should add back tax at the rates (0%, 10% and 22%, but *not* 40%) at which the premium has actually saved tax.

1.4 The pensions part of the life assurance company's business is tax exempt, so both capital gains on, and income from, investments bought with premiums are tax free.

Eligibility

1.5 To be eligible to take out a PPS the taxpayer must have relevant earnings. That is either he is self-employed or he has emoluments taxable under Schedule E which do not provide rights in an occupational pension scheme.

It is also possible for an individual in pensionable employment to have a PPS, provided that his scheme does not permit contributions from the employee or the employer. Thus the DSS contributions for someone contracting out of SERPS may be paid into a personal pension scheme.

1.6 Strictly an employee who is a member of an occupational pension scheme cannot contribute to a PPS in respect of earnings from the employment concerned. By concession, the Revenue will not withdraw tax relief on contributions made to a PPS if:

(a) the employer's scheme provides for only modest lump sums on retirement; and

(b) under the rules of the employer's scheme, the employee waives entitlement to the lump sum, or no such sums accrue, for the period in question.

Part B: Unincorporated businesses

Limits on contributions

1.7 The deductible percentages of net relevant earnings (NRE) are as follows.

Age at start of tax year	%
Up to 35	17½
36 - 45	20
46 - 50	25
51 - 55	30
56 - 60	35
61 or more	40

1.8 NRE is calculated thus.

	£	£
Earnings under Schedule D Cases I and II		X
Schedule E emoluments not providing pension scheme rights		X
		X
Less: the excess of trade charges over other income	X	
loss relief*	X	
Schedule E deductions	X	
		(X)
Net relevant earnings		X

* If, in any tax year for which an individual claims relief for a premium payment, a deduction for loss relief is made from income *other* than relevant earnings but that loss relates to activities any income from which *would* be relevant earnings, then the individual's NRE for the *next* tax year are treated as reduced by the loss. Any balance is carried forward to the third year and so on.

1.9 Non-trading charges are not deducted in arriving at NRE even if there is insufficient other income to deduct them from.

1.10 Some of the premium paid can be used to secure a lump sum or an annuity for a spouse or dependants in the event of death prior to retirement age. The limit (which forms part of the overall limit) for such premiums is 5% of NRE.

1.11 Net relevant earnings are restricted to the same earnings cap as applies for occupational schemes (£91,800 for 2000/01).

1.12 The maximum tax deductible premium payable by an employee is restricted if the employer also contributes. The employee's tax deductible limit is the limit that would apply for his age less the employer's contribution.

Relating back premiums

1.13 **Relief for a premium is given primarily against NRE of the tax year in which the premium is actually paid. An election may, however, be made for any premium to be treated as if paid in the previous tax year or, if NRE was nil in that previous year, as if paid in the year before that** (related back two years). This election is valuable to an individual whose income for the previous period was higher and taxed at a higher rate. The taxpayer can relate back any specified part of a premium. The time limit for the election is 31 January following the end of the tax year in which the premium was actually paid. Although the relief due is calculated as if the premium was carried back to an earlier year, the actual relief itself is given in the tax year in which the premium was actually paid.

Unused relief

1.14 **Unused relief is the amount by which premiums paid are less than the maximum calculated as a percentage of NRE. It can be carried forward for six years.** For example, in 2000/01 unused relief from 1994/95 (six years earlier) to 1999/00 can be taken into account to increase the maximum allowable premium.

The relief available for a particular tax year must be used before unused relief brought forward, and relief brought forward is used on a FIFO basis.

1.15 Any contributions in excess of the amount eligible for relief must be repaid to the taxpayer.

Question: Relief for premiums paid

An individual born in 1976 who took out a PPS on 1 July 1997 has the following NRE and paid the following gross premiums.

	NRE	17½% of NRE	Gross premiums
	£	£	£
1997/98	35,000	6,125	5,800
1998/99	33,000	5,775	5,700
1999/00	38,000	6,650	6,850
2000/01	43,000	7,525	8,000

Show the relief available for premiums paid.

Answer

1997/98	£
17½% of NRE	6,125
Less premium paid	(5,800)
Unused relief	325

1998/99	£
17½% of NRE	5,775
Less premium paid	(5,700)
Unused relief	75

1999/00	£
17½% of NRE	6,650
Unused relief 1997/98	200
	6,850
Less premium paid	(6,850)
Unused relief	0

2000/01	£
17½% of NRE	7,525
Unused relief: 1997/98 (balance)	125
1998/99	75
	7,725
Less premium paid	(8,000)
Unrelieved premium (must be repaid)	275

Benefits on retirement

1.16 Benefits can be taken under a PPS from the age of 50 (whether or not the recipient actually stops work) and must begin at age 75 at the latest. For certain occupations (such as a dancer or a cricketer) and in cases of ill health the Revenue may allow benefits to be taken earlier.

1.17 The taxpayer receives his pension in the form of an annuity bought with the savings built up in the scheme. This annuity is normally purchased from the same pension provider that has managed the fund before retirement but some pension plans allow the taxpayer to buy his annuity elsewhere. Part of the fund may, however, be used to produce a lump sum tax free cash payment. The maximum lump sum allowed is 25% of the value of the fund at the time.

The lump sum must be taken when the annuity starts or when any income withdrawals (see below) start.

1.18 Someone with a personal pension scheme may wish to start drawing benefits at a time when interest rates are low. If the fund were immediately used to buy an annuity, it would be correspondingly low. To help such people, taxpayers are allowed to start by making income withdrawals. The bulk of the fund continues to grow, tax-free, until the taxpayer decides to buy an annuity or reaches age 75 (when an annuity must be bought). In the meantime, some of the fund is paid out to the taxpayer in regular instalments. However, the only contributions which may be made to a scheme once an income withdrawal has been made are the contributions from the DSS where an employee uses a personal pension to contract out of SERPS.

1.19 Income withdrawals cannot start before the taxpayer is aged 50, unless he becomes incapable of carrying on his occupation at an earlier age (as with sportsmen). The annual total of income withdrawals must be between 35% and 100% of the annual amount of the annuity which the taxpayer could have bought with his fund. This annuity amount is first computed when the taxpayer first elects for income withdrawals. It is recomputed every three years, using annuity rates computed by the Government Actuary.

1.20 Annuities and income withdrawals are paid under PAYE so as to take account of the pensioner's allowances, and are taxed under Schedule E.

1.21 It is often sensible to take the maximum lump sum permitted, even if the pensioner would prefer a regular income, as the lump sum can then be used to buy an annuity to last for his life. Part of each annuity payment bought in this way will be treated as a return of capital and will therefore be tax free, and the balance will qualify as savings income (unlike the annuity bought with the rest of the fund).

Pension sharing on divorce

1.22 There are provisions to ensure that the parties to a divorce can share pension rights on divorce without affecting the tax approved status of the pension scheme.

Investments

1.23 A PPS may be a self-invested personal pension (SIPP). This means that the scheme member can direct how his contributions are invested. (Unquoted shares are, however, forbidden.) No investments may be acquired from or sold to the scheme member, though the scheme may let commercial property to the scheme member's business on commercial terms.

Transfer of funds

1.24 Personal pension scheme members who enter pensionable employment can, if they wish, transfer their pension fund from the PPS to either their employer's scheme or to a free standing additional voluntary contribution scheme.

2   NATIONAL INSURANCE CONTRIBUTIONS (NICS) FOR THE SELF EMPLOYED

2.1   Four classes of contribution exist, as set out below.

    (a)   **Class 1.** This is divided into:

        (i)   **Primary,** paid by employees;

        (ii)   **Secondary, Class 1A and Class 1B** paid by employers

    (b)   **Class 2.** Paid by the self-employed

    (c)   **Class 3. Voluntary contributions** (paid to maintain rights to certain state benefits)

    (c)   **Class 4.** Paid by the self-employed

National insurance contribution for employees are considered later in this text.

2.2   The Contributions Agency, which is part of the Inland Revenue, examine employers' records and procedures to ensure that the correct amounts of NICs are collected.

2.3   **The self employed** (sole traders and partners) **pay NICs in two ways. Class 2 contributions are payable at a flat rate.** It is possible, however, to be excepted from payment of Class 2 contributions (or to get contributions already paid repaid) if annual profits are less than £3,825. **The Class 2 rate for 2000/01 is £2.00 a week.**

2.4   Additionally, **the self employed pay Class 4 NICs, based on the level of the individual's business profits.**

2.5   **Class 4 NICs are calculated by applying a fixed percentage (7% for 2000/01) to the individual's profits between the lower limit (£4,385 for 2000/01) and the upper limit (£27,820 for 2000/01).**

2.6   EXAMPLE: CLASS 4 CONTRIBUTIONS

If a sole trader had profits of £13,740 for 2000/01 his Class 4 NIC liability would be as follows.

	£
Profits	13,740
Less lower limit	(4,385)
	9,355

Class 4 NICs = 7% × £9,355 = £654.85

2.7   If an individual's profits exceed the upper limit, no Class 4 NICs are due on the excess. Thus the maximum payable in 2000/01 is as follows.

	£
Profits (upper limit)	27,820
Less lower limit	(4,385)
	23,435

Class 4 NICs = 7% × £23,435 = £1,640.45.

2.8   **For Class 4 NIC purposes, profits are the business profits taxable under Schedule D Case I or II profits, less:**

- **trading losses;**
- **trade charges on income.**

There is no deduction for personal pension premiums.

2.9 **Class 4 NICs are collected by the Inland Revenue.** They are paid **at the same time as the associated income tax liability.** Interest is charged on overdue contributions.

Chapter round up

- Personal pension schemes may be used by the self employed or employees who are not in an occupational pension scheme

- Contributions are based on net relevant earnings, up to an earnings cap

- Benefits may be taken under an personal pensions scheme from the age of 50

- The self employed pay Class 2 and Class 4 NICs

Quick quiz

1 What tax relief is available for contributions to a personal pension scheme? (see para 1.3)

2 What are the rules on relating back premiums? (1.13)

3 Between what ages must benefits be taken from a personal pension scheme? (1.16)

4 How are Class 4 NICs calculated? (2.5)

Now try the question below from the Exam Question Bank

Number	Level	Marks	Time
24	Exam	7	13 mins

Chapter 17

CAPITAL GAINS TAX

Topic list	Syllabus reference
1 Chargeability of individuals to CGT	2d(i)
2 Calculating CGT	2d(i), 2d(ii)
3 Share and securities	2d(ii)
4 Gifts of business assets ('holdover' relief)	2d(iii)
5 Incorporation relief	2d(iii)
6 Rollover relief	2d(iii)

Introduction

In this chapter we see what gains are taxed on individuals and how to work out the tax on an individual's taxable gains. We also look at the rules on shares and securities and three deferral reliefs.

Study guide

Capital gains tax

- Prepare a basic capital gains computation

- Explain the treatment of capital losses

- State the allowable deductions

- Define a business asset for the purposes of taper relief

- Compute taper relief (including non-business assets)

- Explain the identification rules for disposals of shares and securities

- Apply the pooling provisions for shares and securities

- Explain the treatment following a bonus issue, rights issue, or takeover

- Explain and apply rollover relief

- Explain and apply holdover relief for the gift of business assets

- Explain and apply the relief available when a business is transferred to a limited company

Exam guide

Although section 2d is not a key topic, the examiner has indicated that it may form part of Question 2 in Section A for a maximum of 10 marks.

Question 4 (15 marks) in Section B will be on capital gains (either for an incorporated or unincorporated business).

BPP PUBLISHING

1 CHARGEABILITY OF INDIVIDUALS TO CGT

1.1 Individuals are chargeable persons and are charged to capital gains tax on their gains arising from investments and from assets used in an unincorporated business. Partners are chargeable on their share of gains of partnership assets (but details of partnership capital gains are not in your syllabus).

1.2 CGT was introduced for individuals in 1965. The base date for taxing gains was generally moved from 1965 to 1982 in 1988. You will not be asked to deal with gains or losses on assets acquired before 31 March 1982.

For individuals, indexation allowance was abolished from April 1998 and a new relief, taper relief, was introduced. This is dealt with later in this chapter.

The rules on shares and securities held by individuals was also changed from April 1998 as the result of the introduction of taper relief. Again, these rules are dealt with later in this chapter.

1.3 The rules about chargeable assets and disposals are broadly the same for companies and individuals, so you should look again at Chapter 5 section 2.

The rules on transfers of trading stock in Chapter 5 paragraphs 2.4-2.6 apply to individuals. The time limit for the election to have no chargeable gains or allowable loss is the 31 January which is 22 months after the end of the tax year which included the end of the period of account of appropriation.

The following are exempt assets with particular reference to individuals:

- motor vehicles suitable for private use
- national savings certificates and premium bonds
- foreign currency for private use
- decorations for valour unless acquired by purchase
- damages for personal or professional injury
- life assurance policies (only exempt in the hands of the original beneficial owner)
- certain chattels
- debts (except debts on a security)
- pension and annuity rights

Transfers of assets on death are not chargeable to capital gains tax. The heirs of the estate inherit assets as if they bought them at death for the then market values.

2 CALCULATING CGT

2.1 **Individuals are generally liable to CGT on the disposal of assets situated anywhere in the world.**

2.2 An individual pays CGT on any taxable gains arising in the tax year. **Taxable gains are the net chargeable gains (gains minus losses) of the tax year reduced by unrelieved losses brought forward from previous years, taper relief and the annual exemption.**

2.3 **There is an annual exemption for each tax year.** For 2000/01 it is £7,200. It is the last deduction to be made in the calculation of taxable gains.

Calculating CGT

2.4 Taxable gains are chargeable to capital gains tax as if the gains were an extra slice of savings (excl dividend) income for the year of assessment concerned. This means that CGT may be due at 10%, 20% or 40%.

2.5 The rate bands are used first to cover income and then gains.

Question: Rates of CGT

In 2000/01, Carol, a single woman, has the following income, gains and losses. Find the CGT payable.

	£
Sch DI profit	32,080
Chargeable gains (not eligible for taper relief - see later)	25,400
Allowable capital losses	8,000

Answer

(a) Carol's taxable income is as follows.

	£
Sch DI	32,080
Less personal allowance	(4,385)
Taxable income	27,695

(b) The gains to be taxed are as follows.

	£
Gains	25,400
Less losses	(8,000)
	17,400
Less annual exemption	(7,200)
Taxable gains	10,200

(c) The tax bands are allocated as follows.

	Total	Income	Gains
Lower rate	1,520	1,520	0
Basic rate	26,880	26,175	705
Higher rate	9,495	0	9,495
		27,695	10,200

(d) The CGT payable is as follows.

	£
£705 × 20%	141
£9,495 × 40%	3,798
Total CGT payable	3,939

Allowable losses

2.6 **Deduct allowable capital losses from chargeable gains in the tax year in which they arise. Any loss which cannot be set off is carried forward to set against future chargeable gains. Losses must be used as soon as possible** (subject to the following paragraph). Losses may not normally be set against income.

2.7 Allowable losses brought forward are only set off to reduce current year chargeable gains less current year allowable losses to the annual exempt amount. No set-off is made if net chargeable gains for the current year do not exceed the annual exempt amount.

2.8 EXAMPLE: THE USE OF LOSSES

(a) George has chargeable gains for 2000/01 of £10,000 and allowable losses of £6,000. As the losses are *current year losses* they must be fully relieved against the £10,000 of gains to produce net gains of £4,000, despite the fact that net gains are below the annual exemption.

(b) Bob has gains of £11,400 for 2000/01 and allowable losses brought forward of £6,000. Bob restricts his loss relief to £4,200 so as to leave net gains of £(11,400 – 4,200) = £7,200, which will be exactly covered by his annual exemption for 2000/01. The remaining £1,800 of losses will be carried forward to 2001/02.

(c) Tom has chargeable gains of £5,000 for 2000/01 and losses brought forward from 1999/00 of £4,000. He will leapfrog 2000/01 and carry forward all of his losses to 2001/02. His gains of £5,000 are covered by his annual exemption for 2000/01.

Taper relief

2.9 **Taper relief may be available to reduce gains realised after 5 April 1998 by individuals. It replaced indexation allowance which was frozen at April 1998. You will not be expected to calculate indexation allowance for individuals to April 1998.** You will either be given an indexed based cost at April 1998 or the actual amount of indexation allowance that is available.

2.10 **Taper relief reduces the percentage of the gain chargeable according to how many complete years the asset had been held since acquisition or 6 April 1998 if earlier. Taper relief is more generous for business assets than for non-business assets.**

2.11 The percentages of gains which remain chargeable after taper relief for disposals after 5 April 2000 are set out below.

Business assets Number of complete years after 5.4.98 for which asset held	% of gain chargeable	Non business assets No of complete years after 5.4.98 for which asset held	% of gain chargeable
0	100	0	100
1	87.5	1	100
2	75	2	100
3	50	3	95
4 or more	25	4	90
		5	85
		6	80
		7	75
		8	70
		9	65
		10 or more	60

Exam focus point

You will be given the above percentages in your exam.

2.12 **Non-business assets acquired before 17 March 1998 qualify for an addition of 1 year (a 'bonus year') to the period for which they are actually held after 5 April 1998.**

2.13 EXAMPLE: COMPLETE YEARS HELD FOR TAPER RELIEF

Peter buys a non business asset on 1 January 1998 and sells it on 1 July 2002. For the purposes of the taper Peter is treated as if he had held the asset for 5 complete years (four complete years after 5 April 1998 plus one additional year).

If the asset had been a business asset, Peter holds the asset for four years only.

2.14 **Taper relief is applied to net chargeable gains after the deduction of current year and brought forward losses. The annual exemption is then deducted from the tapered gains.**

2.15 EXAMPLE: USE OF LOSSES AND TAPER RELIEF

Ruby sold a business asset in July 2000 which she had purchased in January 1999. She realised a chargeable gain (before taper relief) of £17,300. She also sold a painting in 2000/01 realising a capital loss of £6,000. She has a capital loss brought forward from 1998 of £10,000.

Losses are dealt with **before** taper relief. However losses brought forward are only deducted from net current gains to the extent that the gains exceed the CGT annual exemption:

	£
Gain	17,300
Loss	(6,000)
Current net gains	11,300
Less: brought forward loss	(4,100)
Gains before taper relief	7,200
Gains after taper relief (1 year ownership) £7,200 × 87.5%	6,300
Less: annual exemption	(7,200)
Taxable gains	Nil

Note that the benefit of the taper relief is effectively wasted since the brought forward loss reduces the gain down to the annual exemption amount but the taper is then applied to that amount reducing it further.

The loss carried forward is £5,900 (£10,000 – £4,100).

2.16 Allocate losses to gains in the way that produces the lowest tax charge. Losses should therefore be deducted from the gains attracting the lowest rate of taper (ie where the highest percentage of the gain remains chargeable).

2.17 EXAMPLE: ALLOCATION OF LOSSES TO GAINS

Alastair made the following capital losses and gains in 2001/2002:

	£
Loss	10,000
Gains (before taper relief)	
Asset A (non-business asset)	25,000
Asset B (business asset)	18,000

Asset A was purchased in December 1997 and sold in January 2002. Taper relief reduces the gain to 90% of the original gain (4 years including additional year; non-business asset). Asset B was purchased on 5 November 1998 and sold on 17 December 2001. Taper relief reduces the gain to 50% of the original gain (3 years; business asset).

The best use of the loss is to offset it against the gain on the non-business asset:

	£	£
Gain – Asset A	25,000	
Less loss	(10,000)	
Net gain before taper relief	15,000	
Gain after taper relief (£15,000 × 90%)		13,500
Gain – Asset B	18,000	
Gain after taper relief £18,000 × 50%		9,000
Gains after taper relief		22,500
Less annual exemption (say)		(8,000)
Taxable gains		14,500

2.18 Where gains have been relieved under a provision which reduces the cost of the asset in the hands of a new owner (such as gift relief, see later in this chapter) the taper will operate by reference to the holding period of the new owner.

Business assets

2.19 **A business asset is:**

- an asset **used for the purposes of a trade** carried on by an individual (either alone or in partnership) or by a qualifying company of that individual;

- an asset **held for the purposes of any office or employment** held by that individual with a person carrying on a trade;

- **shares in a qualifying company** held by an individual.

2.20 **A qualifying company** is a trading company (or holding company of a trading group) where:

(a) the company is **not listed** on a recognised stock exchange nor is a 51% subsidiary of a listed company (companies listed on the Alternative Investment Market (AIM) are unlisted for this purpose); or

(b) the shareholder is an **officer or employee** of the company (full-time or part-time), or of a 51% group company, or a company which is under common control with the company in which the shares are held and carries on a complementary business which can reasonably be regarded as one composite undertaking; or

(c) the shareholder holds at least **5% of the voting rights** in the company.

2.21 If an asset qualifies as a business asset for part of the time of ownership, and part not, the business part and the non-business part are treated as separate assets calculated by time apportionment over the period of ownership of the assets (not just complete years). However if the asset was acquired before 6 April 1998, only use on or after that date is taken into account. If the asset is owned for more than ten years after 5 April 1998, only the use in the **last ten years** of ownership is taken into account. Taper relief applies to each gain separately.

Question: Mixed asset

Robert bought a warehouse on 5 August 1998. He used the whole of the building for his trade until 4 April 2002. The building was then let out as an investment until it was sold on 4 December 2004. The gain on sale was £140,000.

Show Robert's gain after taper relief.

Answer

	Business use	Non business use
Period between 5.8.98 - 4.4.02	44 months	
Period between 5.4.02 - 4.12.02		32 months

Number of complete years ownership is 5.8.98 – 4.8.04 = 6 years

Gain on business asset after taper relief is:

£140,000 × 44/76 × 25% (4+ years) = £20,263

Gain on non-business asset after taper relief is:

£140,000 × 32/76 × 80% (6 years) = £47,158

Total gain 20,263 + 47,158 = £67,421

3 SHARES AND SECURITIES

3.1 Up to 6 April 1998, the matching rules for shares and securities for companies and individuals were identical. **For individuals the pooling of shares ceased on 5 April 1998. This allows the time of each post April 1998 acquisition to be recorded so that the length of ownership of each share can be calculated for taper relief purposes.**

3.2 **For individuals, share disposals are matched with acquisitions in the following order.**

(a) Same day acquisitions.

(b) Acquisitions within the following 30 days (known as the 'bed and breakfast rule').

(c) Previous acquisitions after 5 April 1998 identifying the most recent acquisition first (a LIFO basis).

(d) Any shares in the FA 1985 pool at 5 April 1998 (the FA 1985 pool runs from 6 April 1982 (instead of 1 April 1982) to 5 April 1998 for individuals).

3.3 The 'bed and breakfast' rule stops shares being sold to crystallise a capital gain or loss and then being repurchased a day or so later. Without the rule a gain or loss would arise on the sale since it would be 'matched' to the original acquisition.

3.4 For all FA 1985 pools held by an individual at 5 April 1998 indexation allowance to April 1998 is calculated for the first disposal after 5 April 1998. No further indexation then applies.

> **Exam focus point**
>
> The examiner will state the value of the FA 1985 indexed pool at 5 April 1998 (including indexation to that date).

3.5 EXAMPLE: POST APRIL 1998 DISPOSALS FOR INDIVIDUALS

Ron acquired the following shares in First plc:

Date of acquisition	No of shares	Cost	Indexed to 5.4.98
9.11.90	10,000	25,000	31,269
4.8.99	3,000	11,400	n/a
15.7.00	5,000	19,000	n/a

He disposed of all his shares on 10 July 2000 for £80,000. The shares are not business assets for the purposes of taper relief. Calculate the chargeable gain arising.

3.6 SOLUTION:

Matching of shares

(a) Acquisition in 30 days after disposal:

	£
Proceeds $\dfrac{5,000}{20,000} \times £80,000$	20,000
Less cost	(19,000)
Gain	1,000

(b) Post 5.4.98 acquisitions

	£
Proceeds $\dfrac{3,000}{20,000} \times £80,000$	12,000
Less cost	(11,400)
Gain	600

Note. No taper relief is due against this gain since the period of ownership was only 11 months.

(c) FA 1985 pool

	Number of shares	Cost £	Indexed cost £
Pool at 5.4.98	10,000	25,000	31,269
7.00 sales	(10,000)	(25,000)	(31,269)

Gain

	£
Proceeds $\dfrac{10,000}{20,000} \times £80,000$	40,000
Less cost	(25,000)
	15,000
Less indexation from FA 1985 pool £(31,269 – 25,000)	(6,269)
Gain before taper relief	8,731

Gain after taper relief (6.4.98 – 5.4.00 = 2 years plus additional year = 3 years)

95% × £8,731	£8,294

Total gains £(1,000 + 600 + 8,294)	£10,684

3.7 Bonus and rights issues are dealt with in the same way as for companies (see Chapter 5 paragraphs 7.1. to 7.3).

Question: Rights issues after 5 April 1998 (individuals)

Simon (aged 36) had the following transactions in S Ltd, of which he has been a full time director since January 1995.

1.10.95	Bought 10,000 shares (10%) holding) for £15,000
11.9.98	Bought 2,000 shares for £5,000
1.2.99	Took up rights issue 1 for 2 at £2.75 per share
14.10.00	Sold 5,000 shares for £15,000

Compute the gain arising in October 2000, after taper relief (if applicable). The shares have always been a business asset for taper relief purposes.

Answer

(a) *Post 5.4.98 holding*

	Number	Cost £
Shares acquired 11.9.98	2,000	5,000
Shares acquired 1.2.99 (rights) 1:2 @ £2.75	1,000	2,750
	3,000	7,750

Gain

	£
Proceeds $\dfrac{3,000}{5,000} \times £15,000$	9,000
Less: cost	(7,750)
Gain	1,250

Taper relief (based on ownership of original holding 11.9.98 – 10.9.00)

75% (Two years: business asset) × £1,250   <u>£937</u>

(b)   *FA 1985 pool*

	Number	Cost £	Indexed cost £
1.10.95	10,000	15,000	15,000
IA to 4.98 $\dfrac{162.6 - 149.8}{149.8} \times £15,000$			1,282
Pool at 5.4.98	10,000	15,000	16,282
Rights issues 1.2.99	5,000	13,750	13,750
	15,000	28,750	30,032
14.10.00 Sale	(2,000)	(3,833)	(4,004)
c/f	13,000	24,917	26,028

Gain

	£
Proceeds $\dfrac{2,000}{5,000} \times £15,000$	6,000
Less: cost	(3,833)
Unindexed gain	2,167
Less: indexation £(4,004 – 3,833)	(171)
Indexed gain	1,996

Taper relief (based on original holding 6.4.98 – 5.4.00)

75% (Two years: business asset) × £1,996   <u>£1,497</u>

(c)   Total gains (after taper relief)

£(937 + 1,497)   <u>£2,434</u>

3.8   The rules on reorganisations and takeovers in Chapter 5 Paragraphs 7.4 to 7.8 also apply to individuals.

4   GIFTS OF BUSINESS ASSETS ('HOLDOVER' RELIEF)

4.1   **If an individual gives away a qualifying asset, the transferor and the transferee can jointly elect** by the 31 January which is nearly six years after the end of the tax year of the transfer, **that the transferor's gain be reduced to nil. The transferee is then deemed to acquire the asset for market value at the date of transfer less the transferor's deferred gain** (no taper relief given). The transferee will qualify for further indexation allowance (if available) on that reduced base cost from the date of the transfer. The transferee will start a new period for taper relief from the date of his acquisition.

4.2   **If a disposal involves actual consideration rather than being a pure gift but is still not a bargain made at arm's length** (so that the proceeds are deemed to be the market value of the asset), **then any excess of actual consideration over allowable costs** (excluding indexation allowance) **is chargeable immediately and only the balance of the gain is deferred**. Of course, the amount chargeable immediately is limited to the full gain after indexation allowance.

Qualifying assets

4.3   **Gift relief can be claimed on gifts or sales at undervalue** on transfers of **business assets** as described below. Note that the definition of what is a business asset for gift relief is not the same as for taper relief.

4.4   **Transfers of business assets** are transfers of assets

- Used in a trade, profession or vocation carried on:

    (1)   by the donor;

    (2)   if the donor is an individual, by his personal company or a member of a 51% trading group of which the holding company is his personal company (a personal company is one of which he holds at least 5% of voting rights).

    If the asset was used for the purposes of the trade, profession or vocation for only part of its period of ownership, the gain to be held over is the gain otherwise eligible × period of such use/total period of ownership.

    If the asset was a building or structure only partly used for trade, professional or vocational purposes, only the **part of the gain attributable to the part so used is eligible for gift relief**

- **Shares and securities in trading companies**, or holding companies of 51% trading groups, where:

    (1)   the shares or securities are **not listed on a recognised stock exchange** (but they may be on the AIM); or

    (2)   if the donor is an individual, the company concerned is his **personal company** (defined as above);

    If the company has chargeable non-business assets at the time of the gift, and (2) applied at any time in the last 12 months, **the gain to be held over is the gain otherwise chargeable × the value of the chargeable business assets/the value of the chargeable assets of the company.**

Question: Gift relief

On 6 December 2000 Angelo sold to his son Michael a freehold shop valued at £200,000 for £50,000, and claimed gift relief. Angelo had originally purchased the shop from which he had run his business in July 1982. Its indexed cost at April 1998 was £59,550. Michael continued to run a business from the shop premises but decided to sell the shop in March 2004 for £195,000. Compute any chargeable gains arising. Assume Finance Act 2000 continues to apply in March 2004.

Answer

(a)   *Angelo's CGT position (2000/01)*

	£
Proceeds	200,000
Less indexed cost	(59,550)
Indexed gain	140,450
Less gain deferred	
£140,450 – £(50,000 – 30,000)	(120,450)
Gain left in charge	20,000
Gain after taper relief (note)	£15,000

(b) *Michael's CGT position (2003/04)*	£
Proceeds	195,000
Less cost £(200,000 – 120,450)	(79,550)
Gain	115,450
Chargeable gain after taper relief (50%)	£57,725

Note: Taper relief is available for Angelo since the asset disposed of in December 2000 is a 'business asset'. The period of ownership is two complete years. Thus only 75% of the gain will be taxable.

5 INCORPORATION RELIEF

5.1 **If a person transfers his business to a company then he makes a disposal of the business assets for CGT purposes and realises chargeable gains on those assets.** (Note that the individual assets are disposed of. Contrast this with a sale of shares, when shares are disposed of but business assets remain the property of the company which issued the shares, and are not disposed of.) It is, however, clearly undesirable to discourage entrepreneurs from incorporating their businesses and so a relief is available.

5.2 **The relief (sometimes called Incorporation Relief) is compulsory** (so no claim need be made). **All or some of the gains are held over if all the following conditions are met.**

(a) The **business is transferred as a going concern.**

(b) **All its assets** (or all its assets other than cash) **are transferred.** If the relief is not wanted, it can therefore be avoided by not transferring some non-cash asset.

(c) **The consideration is wholly or partly in shares.**

5.3 **The amount held over is found by applying the fraction:**

$$\frac{\text{Value of shares received from the company}}{\text{Total value of consideration from the company}}$$

to the indexed gain. This amount is then deducted from the base cost of the shares received. The company is deemed to acquire assets transferred at their market values.

5.4 **Incorporation relief applies to the chargeable gain calculated before taper relief.**

Question: Incorporation relief

Mr P transferred his business to a company in May 2001, realising a gain after indexation allowance but before taper relief of £24,000 on the only business asset transferred (a factory). The consideration comprised cash of £15,000 and shares at a market value of £75,000.

(a) What is the gain on the transfer before taper relief?

(b) What is the base cost of the shares for any future disposal?

Answer

(a)

	£
Gain	24,000
Less held over $\dfrac{75,000}{15,000+75,000} \times £24,000$	(20,000)
Chargeable gain before taper relief	4,000

(b)

	£
Market value	75,000
Less gain held over	(20,000)
Base cost of shares	55,000

---

6 ROLLOVER RELIEF

6.1 The reliefs on the replacement of business assets apply to sole traders and partners. The conditions for the reliefs to apply are the same as for companies, as set out in Chapter 5 section 8.

6.2 **Rollover relief applies to the untapered gain. Any gain left in charge will then be eligible for taper relief.** When the replacement asset is sold taper relief on that sale will only be given by reference to the holding period for that asset (assuming further rollover relief is not claimed on this disposal). **Effectively, taper relief on the rolled over gain, for the period of ownership of the original asset, is lost.**

Question: Rollover relief and taper relief interaction

Karen is a sole trader who bought a business asset for £170,625 on 5 November 1991 and sold it on 31 December 2000 for £491,400. A replacement business asset was acquired on 1 November 2000 at a cost of £546,000. The new asset was sold on 3 September 2005 for £914,550. Karen made a claim for rollover relief on the first asset sale but not on the second asset sale.

Calculate the taxable gains for each asset disposal.

Answer

31 December 2000 disposal

	£
Sale proceeds	491,400
Cost (5.11.1991)	(170,625)
	320,775

Less: indexation allowance to April 1998

$$\frac{162.6 - 135.6}{135.6} = 0.199 \times £170,625$$ (33,954)

Chargeable gain before taper relief	286,821

Since the asset was sold for £491,400 and within the required time period a replacement asset was purchased for £546,000 there was a full reinvestment of the sale proceeds. Thus the full gain before taper relief of £286,821 is rolled over against the cost of the new asset.

3 September 2005 disposal

	£	£
Sale proceeds		914,550
Cost (1 November 2000)	546,000	
Less: rollover relief	(286,821)	
		(259,179)
Gain		655,371
Ownership period is 1 November 2000 to 3 September 2005		
= 4 complete years of ownership)		
Gain after taper relief		
Taxable gain (25%) for Karen		£163,843

6.3 Where the gain is deferred against the purchase of a depreciating asset, taper relief is applied to the original gain *before* it is deferred, in relation to the ownership of the original asset. No further relief is given for the time that the gain is deferred. Taper relief applies on the depreciating asset from the date of purchase in the normal way.

Question: Deferred gain on investment into depreciating asset

Norma bought a freehold shop for use in her business in June 1999 for £125,000. She sold it for £140,000 on 1 August 2000. On 10 July 2000, Norma bought some fixed plant and machinery to use in her business, costing £150,000. She then sells the plant and machinery for £167,000 on 19 November 2004. Show Norma's CGT position.

Answer

Gain deferred

	£
Proceeds of shop	140,000
Less cost	(125,000)
Gain	15,000

Gain after taper relief (1 year)

87.5% x £15,000 — £13,125

This gain is deferred in relation to the purchase of the plant and machinery.

Sale of plant and machinery

	£
Proceeds	167,000
Less cost	(150,000)
Gain	17,000

Gain on plant and machinery after taper relief (4 years)

£17,000 × 25% — £4,250

Total gain chargeable on sale (gain on plant and machinery plus deferred gain)

£(4,250 + 13,125) — £17,375

6.4 It is possible to transfer the deferred gain to a non-depreciating asset provided the non-depreciating asset is bought before the deferred gain has crystallised.

Chapter roundup

- Individuals pay CGT on their taxable gains.
- Individuals are entitled to taper relief and an annual exemption.
- Losses are set off before taper relief against gains of the same year or of future years.
- Shares and securities are not pooled for individuals after 5 April 1998. Each acquisition is treated separately.
- Gift relief can be claimed on gifts of business assets.
- A gain arising on the incorporation of a business can be deferred into the base cost of the shares acquired by incorporation relief.
- Reliefs on replacement of business assets are available to unincorporated businesses.

Quick quiz

1   At what rate or rates do individuals pay CGT? (2.4)

2   To what extent must allowable losses be set against chargeable gains? (2.6, 2.7)

3   Which types of shares are a business asset for the purpose of taper relief? (2.20)

4   What is the order of matching for disposals of shares by individuals? (3.2)

5   Who must elect for gift relief to apply and by when? (4.1)

6   What is the effect of non-share consideration being given on incorporation on incorporation relief? (5.3)

7   How does taper relief apply in relation to rollover relief? (6.2)

Now try the question below from the Exam Question Bank

Number	Level	Marks	Time
25	Exam	15	27 mins

Chapter 18

SELF ASSESSMENT FOR INDIVIDUALS AND PARTNERSHIPS

Topic list	Syllabus reference
1 Notification of liability to income tax and CGT	2b
2 Tax returns and keeping records	2b
3 Self assessment and claims	2b
4 Payment of income tax and capital gains tax	2b
5 Enquiries, determinations and discovery assessments	2b

Introduction

In this chapter we see how individuals (including partners) must 'self assess' their liability to income tax and capital gains tax.

Study guide

Self assessment system

- Describe the features of self-assessment

- Calculate payments on account and balancing payments/repayments

- Calculate interest on overdue tax and state the penalties that can be charged

- Explain how the Inland Revenue can enquire into a self-assessment return

Exam guide

This is section 2b which is a key topic. It may appear in Question 2 in Section A. It was also given by the examiner as a specific example of an area which could be examined in Question 7 in Section B.

1   NOTIFICATION OF LIABILITY TO INCOME TAX AND CGT

1.1   **Individuals who are chargeable to income tax or CGT for any tax year and who have not received a notice to file a return are required to give notice of chargeability to an officer of the Board within six months from the end of the year** ie by 5 October 2001 for 2000/01.

1.2   A person who has no chargeable gains and who is not liable to higher rate tax does not have to give notice of chargeability if all his income:

(a)   is taken into account under PAYE (see later);

(b)   is from a source of income not subject to tax under a self-assessment;

(c)   has had (or is treated as having had) income tax deducted at source; or

(d)   is chargeable to tax under Schedule F (eg a dividend).

The maximum mitigable penalty where notice of chargeability is not given is 100% of the tax assessed which is not paid on or before 31 January following the tax year.

2   TAX RETURNS AND KEEPING RECORDS

Tax returns

2.1   The tax return comprises a Tax Form, together with supplementary pages for particular sources of income. Taxpayers are sent a Tax Form and a number of supplementary pages depending on their known sources of income, together with a Tax Return Guide and various notes relating to the supplementary pages. Taxpayers with new sources of income may have to ask the orderline for further supplementary pages.

2.2   If a return for the previous year was filed electronically, or a computer generated substitute form used, the taxpayer may be sent a notice to file a return, rather than the official Revenue form. This is intended to reduce unnecessary waste of paper etc.

2.3   Partnerships must file a separate return which includes 'a partnership statement' showing the firm's profits, losses, and proceeds from the sale of assets and the division of all these amounts between partners. The partnership return must normally be made by the senior partner (or whoever else may be nominated by the partnership), but the Revenue have power to require any, all, or some of the partners (or their nominated successors) to submit the return.

2.4   A partnership return must include a declaration of the name, residence and tax reference of each partner, as well as the usual declaration that the return is correct and complete to the best of the signatory's knowledge.

2.5   Each partner must then include his share of partnership profits on his personal tax return.

Time limit for submission of tax returns

> **KEY TERM**
>
> The **filing due date for filing a tax return is the later of:**
>
> •   **31 January following the end of the tax year which the return covers.**
> •   **three months after the notice to file the return was issued.**

2.6   **If an individual wishes the Revenue to prepare the self-assessment on their behalf, earlier deadlines apply. The filing date is then the later of:**

•   **30 September following the tax year; eg for 2000/01, by 30 September 2001.**
•   **two months after notice to file the return was issued.**

Since a partnership return does not include a self-assessment these revised deadlines do not apply to partnership returns. This may, of course, create problems if one of the partners wishes the Revenue to complete his personal self-assessment.

Penalties for late filing

Individual returns

2.7 **The maximum penalties for delivering a tax return after the filing due date are:**

    (a) **Return up to 6 months late:**   **£100**

    (b) **Return more than 6 months but not more than 12 months late:**   **£200**

    (c) **Return more than 12 months late:**   **£200 + 100% of the tax liability**

2.8 In addition, the General or Special Commissioners can direct that a maximum penalty of £60 per day be imposed where failure to deliver a tax return continues after notice of the direction has been given to the taxpayer. In this case the additional £100 penalty, imposed under (b) if the return is more than six months late, is not charged.

2.9 The fixed penalties of £100/£200 can be set aside by the Commissioners if they are satisfied that the taxpayer had a reasonable excuse for not delivering the return. If the tax liability shown on the return is less than the fixed penalties, the fixed penalty is reduced to the amount of the tax liability. The tax geared penalty is mitigable by the Revenue or the Commissioners.

Partnership returns

2.10 The maximum penalties for late delivery of a partnership tax return are as shown above, save that there is no tax-geared penalty if the return is more than 12 months late. The penalties apply separately to each partner.

Reasonable excuse

2.11 A taxpayer only has a reasonable excuse for a late filing if a default occurred because of a factor outside his control. This might be non-receipt of the return by the taxpayer, an industrial dispute in the post office after the return was posted, serious illness of the taxpayer or a close relative, or destruction of records through fire and flood. Illness etc is only accepted as a reasonable excuse if the taxpayer was taking timeous steps to complete the return, and if the return is filed as soon as possible after the illness etc.

Returns rejected as incomplete

2.12 If a return, filed before the filing date, is rejected by the Revenue as incomplete later than 14 days before the filing deadline of 31 January, a late filing penalty will not be charged if the return is completed and returned within 14 days of the rejection. This only applies if the omission from the return was a genuine error. It does not apply if a return was deliberately filed as incomplete in the hope of extending the time limit.

Electronic lodgement of tax returns

2.13 The electronic lodgement of tax returns and other documents is possible if:

    (a) The information is transferred by persons approved by the Inland Revenue.

    (b) The information is transmitted using approved hardware and software.

(c)　A hard copy of the information (signed by the taxpayer etc) was made before the information is transmitted electronically and the fact that this has been done is signified as part of the transmission.

(d)　The information is accepted by the Inland Revenue's computer.

2.14　Where a return is filed electronically, supporting documents may be sent separately (eg. by post). Provided they are submitted within one month of the return and have been referred to in the return the Revenue accept that they 'accompany' the return.

Standard accounting information

2.15　'Three line' accounts (ie income less expenses equals profit) only need be included on the tax return of businesses with a turnover of less than £15,000 pa. This is not as helpful as it might appear, as underlying records must still be kept for tax purposes (disallowable items etc) when producing three line accounts.

2.16　Large businesses with a turnover of at least £5 million which have used figures rounded to the nearest £1,000 in producing their published accounts can compute their profits to the nearest £1,000 for tax purposes.

2.17　The tax return requires trading results to be presented in a standard format. Although there is no requirement to submit accounts with the return, accounts may be filed. If accounts accompany the return, the Revenue's power to raise a discovery assessment (see below) is restricted.

Keeping of records

2.18　All taxpayers must keep and retain all records required to enable them to make and deliver a correct tax return.

2.19　**Records must be retained until the later of:**

(a)　(i)　**5 years after the 31 January following the tax year where the taxpayer is in business** (as a sole trader or partner); or

(ii)　**1 year after the 31 January following the tax year otherwise;** or

(b)　provided notice to deliver a return is given before the date in (a):

(i)　**the time after which enquiries by the Inland Revenue into the return can no longer be commenced;** or

(ii)　**the date any such enquiries have been completed.**

2.20　Where a person receives a notice to deliver a tax return after the normal record keeping period has expired, he must keep all records in his possession at that time until no enquiries can be raised in respect of the return or until such enquiries have been completed.

2.21　**The maximum (mitigable) penalty for each failure to keep and retain records is £3,000 per tax year/accounting period.**

2.22　The duty to preserve records can generally be satisfied by retaining copies of original documents except that for documents which show tax deducted or creditable, the originals (eg dividend certificates) must be kept.

2.23 Record keeping failures are taken into account in considering the mitigation of other penalties. Where the record keeping failure is taken into account in this way, a penalty will normally only be sought in serious and exceptional cases where, for example, records have been destroyed deliberately to obstruct an enquiry or there has been a history of serious record keeping failures.

3 SELF-ASSESSMENT AND CLAIMS

3.1 **Every personal tax return must be accompanied by a self-assessment.**

> **KEY TERM**
>
> **A self assessment** is a calculation of the amount of taxable income and gains after deducting reliefs and allowances, and a calculation of the income tax and CGT payable after taking into account tax deducted at source and tax credits.

3.2 Although Tax Calculation Working Sheets are provided with the tax return there is no requirement for the taxpayer to use these in computing his self-assessment. It is sufficient to enter the appropriate figures on the tax return.

3.3 **The self-assessment calculation may either be made by the taxpayer or the Revenue.** If a return is filed within certain time limits (normally, 30 September following the tax year to which it relates, see above) an officer of the board must make a self-assessment on the taxpayer's behalf on the basis of the information contained in the return. He must send a copy of the assessment to the taxpayer. These assessments, even though raised by the Revenue, are treated as self-assessments.

3.4 If the taxpayer files a return after the above deadline but without completing the self-assessment, the Revenue will not normally reject the return as incomplete. However the Revenue are not then bound to complete the self-assessment in time to notify the taxpayer of the tax falling due on the normal due date (generally the following 31 January), and it is the taxpayer's responsibility to estimate and pay his tax on time.

3.5 **Within nine months of receiving a tax return, the Revenue can amend a taxpayer's self-assessment to correct any obvious errors or mistakes;** whether errors of principle, arithmetical mistakes or otherwise.

3.6 **Within 12 months of the due filing date (*not* the actual filing date), the taxpayer can give notice to an officer to amend his tax return and self-assessment.** Such amendments by taxpayers are not confined to the correction of obvious errors. They may not be made whilst the Revenue are making enquiries into the return.

3.7 The same rules apply to corrections and amendments of partnership statements and stand alone claims (see below).

Claims

3.8 **All claims and elections which can be made in a tax return must be made in this manner if a return has been issued. A claim for any relief, allowance or repayment of tax must be quantified at the time it is made.** These rules do not apply to claims involving two or more years or to claims that can be dealt with through the PAYE system (eg. by amending a code number).

3.9   Certain claims have a time limit that is longer than the time limit for filing or amending a tax return. A claim may therefore be made after the time limit for amending the tax return has expired. Claims not made on the tax return are referred to as **'stand alone' claims**.

3.10   Claims made on a tax return are subject to the administrative rules governing returns, for the making of corrections, enquiries etc.

Stand alone claims

3.11   Claims and elections not made in a tax return are governed by provisions which are similar to the rules governing the treatment of tax returns. The rules cover:

(a)   keeping supporting records. Records must be kept until enquiries may no longer be made into the claim, or until any enquiries which are made have been completed;

(b)   amending the claim. The Revenue's nine month time limit is unchanged, but the taxpayer has twelve months from the date the claim was made (see below);

(c)   giving effect to the claim (ie repaying the tax);

(d)   enquiring into the claim and making any necessary amendments (see below).

Claims involving more than one year

3.12   Self-assessment is intended to avoid the need to reopen earlier years, so relief should be given for the year of the claim. This rule can best be explained by considering a claim to carry back a trading loss to an earlier year of assessment:

(a)   the claim for relief is treated as made in relation to the year in which the loss was actually incurred;

(b)   the amount of any tax repayment due is calculated in terms of tax of the earlier year to which the loss is being carried back; and

(c)   any tax repayment etc is treated as relating to the later year in which the loss was actually incurred.

3.13   These rules apply not only to trading losses, but also to pension premiums carried back and to the carry back of post cessation receipts.

Time limits

3.14   **The time limit for making a claim is 5 years from 31 January following the tax year, unless a different limit is specifically set for the claim.** Many reliefs have a shorter time limit specifically set – of one year from the 31 January following the end of the tax year. These time limits are mentioned, where relevant, throughout this text.

3.15   Since a taxpayer needs to be able to calculate his tax liability under self-assessment a certain amount of formality in the claims procedure is needed. For example, capital losses are only allowable if notified to an officer of the Board and such notification is treated as a claim for relief for the year in which the loss accrues. Therefore, notification of such losses has to be made within 5 years from 31 January following the tax year in which they accrue.

Error or mistake claims

3.16 **An error or mistake claim may be made for errors in a return or partnership statement where tax would otherwise be overcharged.** The claim may not be made where the tax liability was computed in accordance with practice prevailing at the time the return or statement was made.

3.17 An error or mistake claim may not be made in respect of a claim. If a taxpayer makes an error or mistake in a claim, he may make a supplementary claim within the time limits allowed for the original claim.

3.18 The taxpayer may appeal to the Special Commissioners against any refusal of an error or mistake claim.

4 PAYMENT OF INCOME TAX AND CAPITAL GAINS TAX

4.1 The self-assessment system may result in the taxpayer making three payments of income tax and Class 4 NICs.

Date	Payment
31 January in the tax year	**1st payment on account**
31 July after the tax year	**2nd payment on account**
31 January after the tax	**Final payment to settle the remaining liability**

4.2 The Inland Revenue issue payslips/demand notes in a credit card type 'Statement of Account' format, but there is no statutory obligation for them to do so and **the onus is on the taxpayer to pay the correct amount of tax on the due date**

KEY TERM

Payments on account are usually required where the income tax and Class 4 NICs due in the previous year exceeded the amount of income tax deducted at source; this excess is known as '**the relevant amount**'. Income tax deducted at source includes tax suffered, PAYE deductions and tax credits on dividends.

4.3 **The payments on account are each equal to 50% of the relevant amount for the previous year.**

Question: Payments on account

Sue is a self employed writer who paid tax for 2000/01 as follows:

		£
Total amount of income tax charged		9,200
This included:	Tax deducted on savings income	3,200
She also paid;	Class 4 NIC	1,640
	Class 2 NIC	104
	Capital gains tax	4,800

How much are the payments on account for 2001/2002?

Answer

	£
Income tax:	
Total income tax charged for 2000/01	9,200
Less: tax deducted for 2000/01	(3,200)
	6,000
Class 4 NIC	1,640
'Relevant amount'	7,640
Payments on account for 2001/2002:	
31 January 2002 £7,640 x ½	3,820
31 July 2002 As before	3,820

There is no requirement to make payments on account of capital gains tax nor Class 2 NIC.

4.4   **Payments on account are not required if the relevant amount falls below a de minimis limit of £500. Also, payments on account are not required from taxpayers who paid 80% or more of their tax liability for the previous year through PAYE or other deduction at source arrangements.**

4.5   If the previous year's liability increases following an amendment to a self-assessment, or the raising of a discovery assessment, an adjustment is made to the payments on account due.

4.6   Payments on account are normally fixed by reference to the previous year's tax liability but if a taxpayer expects his liability to be lower than this **he may claim to reduce his payments on account to:**

(a)   **a stated amount,** or
(b)   **nil.**

The claim must state the reason why he believes his tax liability will be lower, or nil.

4.7   **If the taxpayer's eventual liability is higher than he estimated he will have reduced the payments on account too far. Although the payments on account will not be adjusted, the taxpayer will suffer an interest charge on late payment.**

4.8   A penalty of the difference between the reduced payment on account and the correct payment on account may be levied if the reduction was claimed fraudulently or negligently.

4.9   **The balance of any income tax and Class 4 NICs together with all CGT due for a year, is normally payable on or before the 31 January following the year.**

Question: Payments of tax

Giles made payments on account for 2000/01 of £6,500 each on 31 January 2001 and 31 July 2001, based on his 1999/00 liability. He then calculates his total income tax and Class 4 NIC liability for 2000/01 at £18,000 of which £2,750 was deducted at source. In addition he calculated that his CGT liability for disposals in 2000/01 is £5,120.

What is the final payment due for 2000/01?

Answer

Income tax and Class 4 NIC: £18,000 - £2,750 - £6,500 - £6,500 = £2,250. CGT = £5,120.

Final payment due on 31 January 2002 for 2000/2001 £2,250 + £5,120 = £7,370

4.10   In one case the due date for the final payment is later than 31 January following the end of the year. **If a taxpayer has notified chargeability by 5 October but the notice to file a tax return is not issued before 31 October, then the due date for the payment is three months after the issue of the notice.**

4.11   Tax charged in an amended self-assessment is usually payable on the later of:

   (a)   the normal due date, generally 31 January following the end of the tax year; and

   (b)   the day following 30 days after the making of the revised self-assessment.

4.12   Tax charged on a discovery assessment is due thirty days after the issue of the assessment.

Surcharges

> ### KEY TERM
>
> **Surcharges** are normally imposed in respect of amounts paid late:
>
> | *Paid* | *Surcharge* |
> |---|---|
> | (a) within 28 days of due date: | none |
> | (b) more than 28 days but not more than six months after the due date: | 5% |
> | (c) more than six months after the due date: | 10% |

4.13   Surcharges apply to:

   (a)   balancing payments of income tax and Class 4 NICs and any CGT under self-assessment or a determination;

   (b)   tax due on the amendment of a self-assessment;

   (c)   tax due on a discovery assessment

4.14   **The surcharge rules do not apply to late payments on account.**

4.15   No surcharge will be applied where the late paid tax liability has attracted a tax-geared penalty on the failure to notify chargeability to tax, or the failure to submit a return, or on the making of an incorrect return (including a partnership return).

Interest

4.16   **Interest is chargeable on late payment of both payments on account and balancing payments. In both cases interest runs from the due date until the day before the actual date of payment.**

4.17   Interest is charged from 31 January following the tax year (or the normal due date for the balancing payment, in the rare event that this is later), even if this is before the due date for payment on:

   (a)   tax payable following an amendment to a self-assessment;
   (b)   tax payable in a discovery assessment; and
   (c)   tax postponed under an appeal which becomes payable.

4.18 Since a determination (see below) is treated as if it were a self-assessment, interest runs from 31 January following the tax year.

4.19 If a taxpayer claims to reduce his payments on account and there is still a final payment to be made, interest is normally charged on the payments on account as if each of those payments had been the lower of:

(a) the reduced amount, plus 50% of the final income tax liability; and

(b) the amount which would have been payable had no claim for reduction been made.

Question: Interest

Herbert's payments on account for 2000/01 based on his income tax liability for 1999/00 were £4,500 each. However when he submitted his 1999/00 income tax return in January 2001 he made a claim to reduce the payments on account for 2000/01 to £3,500 each. The first payment on account was made on 29 January 2001, and the second on 12 August 2001.

Herbert filed his 2000/01 tax return in December 2001. The return showed that his tax liabilities for 2000/01 (before deducting payments on account) were income tax and Class 4 NIC: £10,000, capital gains tax: £2,500. Herbert paid the balance of tax due of £5,500 on 19 February 2002.

For what periods and in respect of what amounts will Herbert be charged interest?

Answer

Herbert made an excessive claim to reduce his payments on account, and will therefore be charged interest on the reduction. The payments on account should have been £4,500 each based on the 1999/00 liability (not £5,000 each based on the 2000/01 liability). Interest will be charged as follows:

(a) first payment on account

    (i)   on £3,500 - nil - paid on time

    (ii)   on £1,000 from due date of 31 January 2001 to day before payment, 18 February 2002

(b) second payment on account

    (i)   on £3,500 from due date of 31 July 2001 to day before payment, 11 August 2001

    (ii)   on £1,000 from due date of 31 July 2001 to day before payment, 18 February 2002

(c) balancing payment

    (i)   on £3,500 from due date of 31 January 2002 to day before payment, 18 February 2002

4.20 Where interest has been charged on late payments on account but the final balancing settlement for the year produces a repayment, all or part of the original interest is remitted.

4.21 If a taxpayer provided the Revenue in good time with the information needed to calculate the payment on account due on 31 January but did not receive a Statement of Account in time to make the correct payment by 31 January, it is Revenue practice to treat the due date for interest purposes as 30 days after the issue of the Statement.

Repayment of tax and repayment supplement

4.22 Tax is repaid when claimed unless a greater payment of tax is due in the following 30 days, in which case it is set-off against that payment.

4.23 Interest is paid on overpayments of:

(a) payments on account;

(b) final payments of income tax and Class 4 NICs and CGT, including tax deducted at source or tax credits on dividends; and

(c) penalties and surcharges.

4.24 Repayment supplement runs from the original date of payment (even if this was prior to the due date), until the day before the date the repayment is made. Income tax deducted at source and tax credits are treated as if they were paid on the 31 January following the tax year concerned.

4.25 Tax repaid is identified with tax payments in the following order:

(a) final balancing payment
(b) equally to the payments on account
(c) income tax deducted at source/tax credits
(d) if it is attributable to tax paid in instalments, to a later instalment before an earlier one.

5 ENQUIRIES, DETERMINATIONS AND DISCOVERY ASSESSMENTS

Enquiries into returns

5.1 **An officer of the Board has a limited period within which to commence enquiries into a return or amendment. The officer must give written notice of his intention by:**

(a) the **first anniversary of the due filing date (not the actual filing date);** or

(b) **if the return is filed after the due filing date, the quarter day following the first anniversary of the actual filing date. The quarter days are 31 January, 30 April, 31 July and 31 October.**

5.2 If the taxpayer amended the return after the due filing date, the enquiry 'window' extends to the quarter day following the first anniversary of the date the amendment was filed. Where the enquiry was not raised within the limit which would have applied had no amendment been filed, the enquiry is restricted to matters contained in the amendment.

5.3 Enquiries may be made into partnership returns (or amendments) upon which a partnership statement is based within the same time limits. A notice to enquire into a partnership return is deemed to incorporate a notice, to enquire into each individual partner's return.

5.4 Enquiries may also be made into stand alone claims, provided notice is given by the officer of the Board by the later of:

(a) The quarter day following the first anniversary of the making or amending of the claim;

(b) 31 January next but one following the tax year, if the claim relates to a tax year; or

(c) the first anniversary of the end of the period to which a claim relates if it relates to a period other than a tax year.

5.5 The procedures for enquiries into claims mirror those for enquiries into returns.

5.6 **The officer does not have to have, or give, any reason for raising an enquiry. In particular the taxpayer will not be advised whether he has been selected at random for an audit. Enquiries may be full enquiries, or may be limited to 'aspect' enquiries.**

5.7 In the course of his enquiries **the officer may require the taxpayer to produce documents, accounts or any other information required. The taxpayer can appeal to the Commissioners.**

5.8 During the course of his enquiries an officer may amend a self-assessment if it appears that insufficient tax has been charged and an immediate amendment is necessary to prevent a loss to the Crown. This might apply if, for example, there is a possibility that the taxpayer will emigrate.

5.9 If a return is under enquiry the Revenue may postpone any repayment due as shown in the return until the enquiry is complete. The Revenue have discretion to make a provisional repayment but there is no facility to appeal if the repayment is withheld.

5.10 At any time during the course of an enquiry, the taxpayer may apply to the Commissioners to require the officer to notify the taxpayer within a specified period that the enquiries are complete, unless the officer can demonstrate that he has reasonable grounds for continuing the enquiry.

5.11 An officer must issue a notice that the enquiries are complete, and a statement of the amount of tax that he considers should be included in the tax return, or the amounts which should be contained in the partnership statement, or the amount of the claim. The taxpayer then has thirty days to amend his self-assessment, partnership statement or claim to give effect to the officer's conclusions. He may also make any other amendments that he could have made had the enquiry not been commenced (amendments may not be made whilst enquiries are in progress).

5.12 If the officer is not satisfied with the taxpayer's amendment he has thirty days in which to amend the self-assessment, partnership statement or claim. Also if a claim has been disallowed, but does not affect the self-assessment, he must advise the taxpayer of the extent to which it has been disallowed.

   If the taxpayer is not satisfied with the officer's amendment he may, within 30 days, appeal to the Commissioners.

5.13 Once an enquiry is complete the officer cannot make further enquiries. The Revenue may, in limited circumstances, raise a discovery assessment if they believe that there has been a loss of tax (see below).

Determinations

5.14 The Revenue may only raise enquiries if a return has been submitted.

5.15 If notice has been served on a taxpayer to submit a return but the return is not submitted by the due filing date, an officer of the Board may make a determination of the amounts liable to income tax and CGT tax and of the tax due. Such a determination must be made to the best of the officer's information and belief, and is then treated as if it were a self-assessment. This enables the officer to seek payment of tax, including payments on account for the following year and to charge interest.

5.16 The determination must be made within the period ending 5 years after 31 January following the tax year. It may be superseded by a self-assessment made within the same period or, if later, within 12 months of the date of the determination.

Discovery assessments

5.17 If an officer of the Board discovers that profits have been omitted from assessment, that any assessment has become insufficient, or that any relief given is, or has become excessive, an assessment may be raised to recover the tax lost.

5.18 If the tax lost results from an error in the taxpayer's return but the return was made in accordance with prevailing practice at the time, no discovery assessment may be made.

5.19 A discovery assessment may only be raised where a return has been made if:

(a) there has been fraudulent or negligent conduct by the taxpayer or his agent; or

(b) at the time that enquiries into the return were completed, or could no longer be made, the officer did not have information to make him aware of the loss of tax.

5.20 Information is treated as available to an officer if:

(a) It is contained in the taxpayer's return for the period (or for either of the two preceding periods) or in any accompanying documents.

(b) It is contained in a claim made in respect of that period or in any accompanying documents;

(c) It is contained in any documents, produced in connection with an enquiry into a return (or claim) for the period or either of the two preceding periods;

(d) It is information, the existence and relevance of which, could reasonably be expected to be inferred by an officer from the information described above, or which was notified in writing by or on behalf of the taxpayer to an officer.

5.21 These rules do not prevent the Revenue from raising assessments in cases of genuine discoveries, but prevent assessments from being raised due to the Revenue's failure to make timely use of information or to a change of opinion on information made available.

Appeals and postponement of payment of tax

5.22 A taxpayer may appeal against an amendment to a self-assessment or partnership statement, or an amendment to or disallowance of a claim, following an enquiry, or against an assessment which is not a self-assessment, such as a discovery assessment.

5.23 **The appeal must normally be made within 30 days of the amendment or self-assessment.**

5.24 The notice of appeal must state the **grounds** of appeal. These may be stated in general terms. At the hearing the Commissioners may allow the appellant to put forward grounds not stated in his notice if they are satisfied that his omission was not wilful or unreasonable.

5.25 In some cases it may be possible to agree the point at issue by negotiation with the Revenue, in which case the appeal may be settled by agreement. If the appeal cannot be agreed, it will be heard by the General or Special Commissioners.

5.26 An appeal does not relieve the taxpayer of liability to pay tax on the normal due date unless he obtains a 'determination' of the Commissioners or agreement of the Inspector that payment of all or some of the tax may be postponed pending determination of the appeal. The amount not postponed is due 30 days after the determination or agreement is issued, if that is later than the normal due date.

BPP
PUBLISHING

5.27 If any part of the postponed tax becomes due a notice of the amount payable is issued and the amount is payable 30 days after the issue of the notice. Interest, however, is still payable from the normal due date.

Chapter roundup

- Individuals who do not receive a tax return must notify their chargeability to income tax or CGT.

- Although taxpayers must normally self assess their income tax, Class 4 NIC and CGT liabilities they can opt out of self assessment if they file their tax return by 30 September following the end of the tax year.

- Two payments on account and a final balancing payment of income tax and Class 4 NICs are due.

- All capital gains tax is due on 31 January following the end of the tax year.

- The Revenue can enquire into tax returns but strict procedural rules govern enquiries.

- Self assessment is enforced through a system of automatic surcharges, penalties and interest.

Quick quiz

1 By when must a taxpayer who has not received a tax return give notice of his chargeability to capital gains tax? (see para 1.1)

2 By when must a taxpayer who does not intend to calculate his own tax file a tax return? (2.7)

3 What are the normal payment dates for income tax and CGT? (4.1)

4 What surcharges are due in respect of late paid income tax? (4.13 – 4.15)

Now try the question below from the Exam Question Bank

Number	Level	Marks	Time
26	Exam	8	15 mins

Part C
Employees

Chapter 19

SCHEDULE E. PAYE

Topic list	Syllabus reference
1 The Schedule E charge	3a(i)
2 Allowable deductions	3a(ii)
3 The PAYE system	3a(iii)

Introduction

Most people have jobs, which pay them wages or salaries. This chapter starts by looking at the basis of assessment under the Schedule E charge.

Sometimes, the income for tax purposes is less than the total received from the employer. This may be because the employee can deduct some expenses. We look at the rules in Section 2.

The Revenue require employers to deduct tax at source from wages under the PAYE system. This system ensures that the Revenue get their money. We look at it in Section 3.

In the next chapter we look at benefits in kind assessable under Schedule E.

Study guide

Basis of assessment, allowable deductions and PAYE system

- State the factors that determine whether an engagement is treated as employment or self-employment

- Describe the income assessable

- Explain the basis of assessment

- List the allowable deductions, including travelling expenses

- Explain the use of the fixed profit car scheme

- Explain the PAYE system

Exam guide

This is part of section 3a which is a key topic. Question 2 in Section A will be on an unincorporated business and/or employees. It could also be examined in Question 7 in Section B.

BPP PUBLISHING

1 THE SCHEDULE E CHARGE

Taxable income

> **KEY TERM**
>
> **'Emoluments'** from an office or employment are taxed under Schedule E. The term 'emoluments' includes 'all salaries, fees, wages, perquisites and profits whatsoever'.

1.1 Emoluments include tips from customers and benefits in kind. Benefits in kind are converted into their cash equivalent using the rules set out in the next chapter. Employees must pay income tax on this amount.

1.2 **Earnings (or 'emoluments') are taxed in the year of receipt.** There is a general definition of 'receipt' and a wider one for directors (who are in a position to manipulate the timing of payments). **The general rule is that emoluments are treated as received on the earlier of:**

- **the time payment is made;**
- **the time entitlement to payment arises.**

1.3 The time of receipt for directors' earnings is the earliest of:

- the earlier of the two alternatives given in the general rule (above);
- when the amount is credited in the company's accounting records;
- the end of the company's period of account (if the amount was determined by then);
- when the amount is determined (if after the end of the company's period of account).

1.4 If an employee dies while employed, tax on earnings received after his death is charged on his personal representatives and is a liability of his estate.

1.5 The receipts basis does not apply to benefits in kind (see next chapter). Benefits are taxable when they are provided.

1.6 Pensions and taxable state benefits (such as the jobseeker's allowance) are also taxable under Schedule E. Unlike normal salary, however, the taxable amount is the amount accruing during the tax year, irrespective of whether or not it has actually been received in the tax year.

Employment and self employment

1.7 **The distinction between employment (Schedule E) and self employment (Schedule D) is a fine one. Employment involves a contract of service, whereas self employment involves a contract for services.** Taxpayers tend to prefer self employment, because the rules on deductions for expenses are more generous.

1.8 Factors which may be of importance include:

- the degree of control exercised over the person doing the work;
- whether he must accept further work;
- whether the other party must provide further work;
- whether he provides his own equipment;
- whether he hires his own helpers;
- what degree of financial risk he takes;
- what degree of responsibility for investment and management he has;

- whether he can profit from sound management;
- whether he can work when he chooses;
- the wording used in any agreement between the parties.

1.9 Relevant cases include:

(a) *Mitchell & Edon v Ross 1961*

A doctor with a private practice (assessable under Schedule D) also held a part-time appointment with a regional hospital board.

Held: the income from the part-time appointment was taxable under Schedule E.

(b) *Edwards v Clinch 1981*

A civil engineer acted occasionally as an inspector on temporary ad hoc appointments.

Held: there was no ongoing office which could be vacated by one person and held by another so the fees received were taxable under Schedule D and not under Schedule E.

(c) *Hall v Lorimer 1994*

A vision mixer was engaged under a series of short-term contracts.

Held: the vision mixer was self employed, not because of any one detail of the case but because the overall picture was one of self-employment.

(d) *Barnett v Brabyn 1996*

Mr Barnett worked under an oral agreement for a partnership. The parties agreed that Mr Barnett was self-employed and free to exploit other opportunities.

Held: Although a number of factors indicated employment, the deciding factors indicated self employment. The deciding factors were the agreement between the parties and that Mr Barnett could decide how much time he spent working for the partnership.

(e) *Carmichael and Anor v National Power plc 1999*

Individuals engaged as visitor guides on a casual 'as required' basis were not employees. An exchange of correspondence between the company and the individuals was not a contract of employment as there was no provision as to the frequency of work and there was flexibility to accept work or turn it down as it arose. Sickness, holiday and pension arrangements did not apply and neither did grievance and disciplinary procedures.

1.10 A worker's status also affects national insurance contributions. The self-employed generally pay less than employees.

2 ALLOWABLE DEDUCTIONS

2.1 **Certain types of expenditure are specifically deductible against Schedule E income:**

(a) **contributions** (within certain limits) **to an approved occupational pension scheme;**

(b) **premiums paid** (within certain limits) **for approved personal pension plans;**

(c) **subscriptions to professional bodies** on the list of bodies issued by the Inland Revenue (which includes most UK professional bodies), if relevant to the duties of the employment;

(d) payments for certain liabilities and for insurance against them.

2.2 Otherwise, **Schedule E deductions are notoriously hard to obtain. They are limited to:**

- **qualifying travel expenses** (see below);

- other expenses incurred wholly, exclusively and necessarily in the performance of the duties of the employment;

- capital allowances on plant and machinery necessarily provided for use in the performance of those duties and on bicycles used in carrying out the duties of the employment.

Liabilities and insurance

2.3 If a director or employee incurs a qualifying liability (see below) or pays for insurance against such a liability, the cost is a deductible expense. If the employer pays such amounts, there is no taxable benefit in kind.

2.4 A qualifying liability is one which is imposed in respect of the director's or employee's acts or omissions as director or employee. Thus, for example, liability for negligence would be covered. Related costs, for example the costs of legal proceedings, are included.

2.5 For insurance premiums to qualify, the insurance policy must:

(a) cover only qualifying liabilities, vicarious liability in respect of qualifying liabilities of other people, related costs and payments to the employee's own employees in respect of their qualifying liabilities and related costs, and

(b) it must not last for more than two years (although it may be renewed for up to two years at a time), and the insured person must not be not required to renew it.

Payments after employment ceases

2.6 The deduction is normally made from the emoluments of the directorship or employment. It cannot be made from other income, except as follows.

2.7 Payments made after the directorship or employment ceases, but which would have been deductible if it had continued, are deductible in computing statutory total income (STI) for the year in which the payments are made. They should be deducted in the same place as charges in the personal tax computation (and from non-savings income before savings income).

2.8 Payments are only deductible if they are made in the last tax year of the directorship or employment or in the following six tax years.

2.9 Amounts taken out of retirement or other post-employment benefits are deductible (so that only the remaining payments to the employee are taxable). Payments borne by the ex-employer are not deductible, but they are not taxable on the ex-director or employee.

2.10 If the amount deductible in a tax year exceeds total income, the excess cannot be carried back or forward to any other year. However, the employee can claim to set the excess against his chargeable gains for the year. The gains against which the excess is set are the gains for the year minus the losses for the year, ignoring losses brought forward, the annual exempt amount and any relief for trading losses against capital gains.

Travelling expenses

2.11 **Tax relief is not available for an employee's normal commuting costs**. This means relief is not available for any costs an employee incurs in getting from home to his normal place of work. However **employees are entitled to relief for 'qualifying travelling expenses' which**

basically are the full costs that they are obliged to incur in travelling in the performance of their duties or travelling to or from a place which they have to attend in the performance of their duties (other than the normal place of work). The Fixed Profit Car Scheme (FPCS) can be used as the basis for an expense claim. This scheme is dealt with in detail in the next chapter.

2.12 EXAMPLE: TRAVEL IN THE PERFORMANCE OF DUTIES

Judi is an accountant. She often travels to meetings at the firm's offices in the North of England returning to her office in Leeds after the meetings. Relief is available for the full cost of these journeys as the travel is undertaken in the performance of her duties.

Question: Relief for travelling costs

Zoe lives in Wycombe and normally works in Chiswick. Occasionally she visits a client in Wimbledon and travels direct from home. Distances are shown in the diagram below:

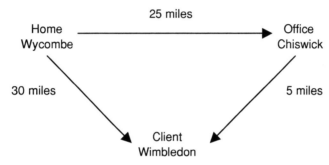

What tax relief is available for Zoe's travel costs?

Answer

Zoe is not entitled to tax relief for the costs incurred in travelling between Wycombe and Chiswick since these are normal commuting costs. However, relief is available for all costs that Zoe incurs when she travels from Wycombe to Wimbledon to visit her client.

2.13 To prevent manipulation of the basic rule normal commuting will not become a business journey just because the employee stops en-route to perform a business task (eg make a 'phone call'). Nor will relief be available if the journey is essentially the same as the employee's normal journey to work.

2.14 EXAMPLE: NORMAL COMMUTING

Judi is based at her office in Leeds City Centre. One day she is required to attend a 9.00 am meeting with a client whose premises are around the corner from her Leeds office. Judi travels from home directly to the meeting. As the journey is substantially the same as her ordinary journey to work relief is not available.

2.15 Site based employees (eg construction workers, management consultants etc) who do not have a permanent work place, are entitled to relief for the costs of all journeys made from home to wherever they are working. This is because these employees do not have an ordinary commuting journey or any normal commuting costs. However there is a caveat that the employee does not spend more than 24 months of continuous work at any one site.

2.16 Tax relief is available for travel, accommodation and subsistence expenses incurred by an employee who is working at a temporary location on a secondment expected to last up to 24 months. If a secondment is initially expected not to exceed 24 months, but it is extended, relief ceases to be due from the date the employee becomes aware of the change. When looking at how long a secondment is expected to last, the Revenue will consider not only the terms of the written contract but also any verbal agreement by the employer and other factors such as whether the employee buys a house etc.

Question: Temporary workplace

Philip works for Vastbank at its Newcastle City Centre branch. Philip is sent to work full-time at another branch in Morpeth for 20 months at the end of which he will return to the Newcastle branch. Morpeth is about 20 miles north of Newcastle.

What travel costs is Philip entitled to claim as a deduction?

Answer

Although Philip is spending all of his time at the Morpeth branch it will not be treated as his normal work place because his period of attendance will be less than 24 months. Thus Philip can claim relief in full for the costs of travel from his home to the Morpeth branch.

Other expenses

2.17 **The word 'exclusively' strictly implies that the expenditure must give no private benefit at all. If it does, none of it is deductible. In practice inspectors may ignore a small element of private benefit or make an apportionment between business and private use.**

2.18 **Whether an expense is 'necessary' is not determined by what the employer requires. The test is whether the duties of the employment could not be performed without the outlay.**

- *Sanderson v Durbridge 1955*
  The cost of evening meals taken when attending late meetings was not deductible because it was not incurred in the performance of the duties.

- *Nolder v Walters 1930*
  An airline pilot was liable to be called for duty at any time. He claimed a deduction for:

  (i)   travel to the airport;
  (ii) telephone costs;
  (iii) subsistence in excess of his employer's allowance.

  Held: (i) and (ii) were not deductible because they were not necessarily incurred in the performance of the duties. (iii) was deductible.

- *Blackwell v Mills 1945*
  As a condition of his employment, an employee was required to attend evening classes. The cost of his textbooks and travel was not deductible because it was not incurred in the performance of the duties.

- *Lupton v Potts 1969*
  Examination fees incurred by a solicitor's articled clerk were not deductible because they were incurred neither wholly nor exclusively in the performance of the duties, but in furthering the clerk's ambition to become a solicitor.

- *Brown v Bullock 1961*
  The expense of joining a club that was virtually a requisite of an employment was not deductible because it would have been possible to carry on the employment without the club membership, so the expense was not necessary.

- *Elwood v Utitz 1965*
  A managing director's subscriptions to two residential London clubs were claimed by him as an expense on the grounds that they were cheaper than hotels.

  The expenditure was deductible as it was necessary in that it would be impossible for the employee to carry out his London duties without being provided with first class accommodation. The residential facilities (which were cheaper than hotel accommodation) were given to club members only.

2.19   The cost of business telephone calls on a private telephone is deductible, but **no part of the line or telephone rental charges is deductible** (*Lucas v Cattell 1972*).

2.20   **The cost of clothes for work is not deductible,** except that for certain trades requiring protective clothing there are annual deductions on a set scale.

2.21   Where actors and other entertainers are treated as employed rather than self employed, agency fees calculated as a percentage of earnings (including those paid to a co-operative society) are deductible, up to 17½% of emoluments.

2.22   Journalists cannot claim a deduction for the cost of buying newspapers which they read to keep themselves informed, since they are merely preparing themselves to perform their duties (*Fitzpatrick v IRC 1994; Smith v Abbott 1994*).

2.23   **An employee required to work at home may be able to claim a deduction for an appropriate proportion of his or her expenditure on lighting, heating and** (if a room is used exclusively for work purposes) **the council tax.**

3   THE PAYE SYSTEM

3.1   **The objective of the PAYE system is to deduct the correct amount of tax over the year. Its scope is very wide. It applies to most cash payments, other than reimbursed business expenses, and to certain non cash payments.**

3.2   In addition to wages and salaries, PAYE applies to round sum expense allowances and payments instead of benefits in kind. It also applies to statutory sick pay, statutory maternity pay and any readily convertible asset.

3.3   A readily convertible asset is any asset which can effectively be exchanged for cash. The amount subject to PAYE is the amount taxable under Schedule E. This is usually the cost to the employer of providing the asset. Shares or rights over shares (eg options), in the employing company (or in a company controlling it) are not readily convertible assets if they are not marketable.

3.4   Tips paid direct to an employee are normally outside the PAYE system (although still assessable under Schedule E). An exception may apply in the catering trades where tips are often pooled. Here the PAYE position depends on whether a 'tronc', administered other than by the employer, exists.

3.5   **It is the employer's duty to deduct income tax from the pay of his employees,** whether or not he has been directed to do so by the Revenue. **If he fails to do this he** (or sometimes the employee) **must pay over the tax which he should have deducted and the employer may be subject to penalties.** Interest will also run from 14 days after the end of the tax year concerned on any underpaid PAYE. Officers of the Inland Revenue can inspect employer's records in order to satisfy themselves that the correct amounts of tax are being deducted and paid over to the Revenue.

Benefits in kind

3.6 **PAYE is not normally operated on benefits in kind; instead the employee's PAYE code is restricted** (see below).

3.7 However, PAYE must be applied to remuneration in the form of a taxable non-cash voucher if at the time it is provided:

(a) the voucher is capable of being exchanged for readily convertible assets; or
(b) the voucher can itself be sold, realised or traded.

3.8 PAYE must be normally operated on cash vouchers and on each occasion when a director/employee uses a credit-token (eg a credit card) to obtain money or goods which are readily convertible assets. However, a cash voucher or credit token which is used to defray expenses is not subject to PAYE.

How PAYE works

3.9 To operate PAYE the employer needs:

(a) deductions working sheets;
(b) codes for employees that reflect the tax allowances to which the employees are entitled;
(c) tax tables.

3.10 **The employer works out the amount of PAYE tax to deduct on any particular pay day by using the employees code number (see below) in conjunction with the PAYE tables. The tables are designed so that tax is normally worked out on a cumulative basis.** This means that with each payment of emoluments the running total of tax paid is compared with tax due on total emoluments to that date. The difference between the tax due and the tax paid is the tax to be deducted on that particular payday.

3.11 National insurance tables are used to work out the national insurance due on any payday.

3.12 Although PAYE is normally operated on a cumulative basis, an employee may have a week 1/month 1 code (see below). In this case the figures for pay and tax deducted are not cumulated, and the tax on each payday is worked out on the pay on that payday as if it were the first payday in the tax year (using week1/month 1 table).

3.13 If a K code applies there is a restriction on the amount of tax that can be deducted (see below). On a cumulative basis, this restriction will be recouped on a later payday (subject to the overriding limit on the later pay day). On a week 1/month 1 basis the restriction cannot be recouped, and will be dealt with by the Revenue after the end of the tax year.

Records

3.14 **The employer must keep records of each employee's pay and tax at each pay day.** The records must also contain details of National Insurance. The employer has a choice of three ways of recording and returning these figures:

(a) he may use the official deductions working sheet (P11);
(b) he may incorporate the figures in his own pay records using a substitute document;
(c) he may retain the figures on a computer.

These records will be used to make a return at the end of the tax year.

Payment under the PAYE system

3.15 **Under PAYE income tax and national insurance is normally paid over to the Inland Revenue monthly, 14 days after the end of each tax month.**

3.16 **If an employer's average monthly payments under the PAYE system are less than £1,500, the employer may choose to pay quarterly, within 14 days of the end of each tax quarter.** Tax quarters end on 5 July, 5 October, 5 January and 5 April. Payments can continue to be made quarterly during a tax year even if the monthly average reaches or exceeds £1,500, but a new estimate must be made and a new decision taken to pay quarterly at the start of each tax year. Average monthly payments are the average net monthly payments due to the Inland Revenue for income tax and NICs.

PAYE codes

3.17 **An employee is normally entitled to various allowances. Under the PAYE system an amount reflecting the effect of a proportion of these allowances is set against his pay each pay day. To determine the amount to set against his pay the allowances are expressed in the form of a code which is used in conjunction with the Pay Adjustment Tables** (Tables A).

3.18 An employee's code may be any one of the following:

  (a) a code of one, two or three numbers followed by a single suffix letter (a suffix code): for example 438L. The letter allows the Revenue to tell the employer how the code should be adjusted each year to take account of Budget changes;

  (b) the prefix D is usually followed by the number 0; these codes apply on a one-off basis and require the use of higher rate tax tables D;

  (c) code BR, which means that tax will be deducted at the basic rate with no tax free allowances;

  (d) code NT, which means that no tax is to be deducted;

  (e) a code with a K prefix, followed by one to four numbers.

3.19 **Generally, a tax code number is arrived at by deleting the last digit in the sum representing the employee's tax free allowances** (eg the personal allowance of £4,385 becomes 438).

The code number may also reflect other items. For example, **it will be restricted to reflect benefits in kind, small amounts of untaxed income** and **unpaid Schedule E tax from earlier years.** If an amount of tax is in point, it is necessary to gross up the tax in the code using the taxpayer's estimated marginal rate of income tax.

Question: PAYE codes

Adrian is a 40 year old single man (suffix letter L) who earns £15,000 pa. He has benefits in kind of £560 and his unpaid Schedule E tax for 1999/00 was £57.50.

What is Adrian's PAYE code for 2000/01?

BPP
PUBLISHING

Answer

	£
Personal allowance	4,385
Benefits in kind	(560)
Unpaid tax £57.50 × 100/22	(261)
Available allowances	3,564

Adrian's PAYE code is 356L

3.20 Codes are determined and amended by the Revenue. They are normally notified to the employer on a code list. The employer must act on the code notified to him until amended instructions are received from the Revenue, even if the employee has appealed against the code.

3.21 **By using the code number in conjunction with the tax tables, an employee is generally given 1/52nd or 1/12th of his tax free allowances against each week's/month's pay.** However because of the cumulative nature of PAYE, if an employee is first paid in, say, September, that month he will receive six months' allowances against his gross pay. In cases where the employee's previous PAYE history is not known, this could lead to under-deduction of tax. To avoid this, codes for the employees concerned have to be operated on a 'week 1/month1' basis, so that only 1/52nd or 1/12th of the employee's allowances are available each week/month.

3.22 **'K' codes increase taxable pay instead of reducing it.** This means benefits exceed allowances. The PAYE deducted under a K code could remove all of an employee's actual remuneration for a pay period. As this could cause hardship, **the PAYE deduced on any payday is not to exceed 50% of the amount of actual remuneration on that pay day.** (This overriding limit does not restrict the tax on non cash payments).

Employer's responsibilities: year end returns and employees leaving or joining

3.23 **At the end of each tax year, the employer must provide each employee with a form P60.** This shows total taxable emoluments for the year, tax deducted, code number, NI number and the employer's name and address. **The P60 must be provided by 31 May following the year of assessment** (so that the employee can complete his self-assessment tax return).

3.24 **Following the end of each tax year, the employer must send the Revenue:**

(a) **by 19 May;**

    (i) **End of year Returns P14** (showing the same details as the P60);

    (ii) **Form P35** (summary of tax and NI deducted).

(b) **by 6 July:**

    (i) **Forms P11D** (benefits in kind etc for directors and employees paid £8,500+ pa);

    (ii) **Forms P11D(b)** (return of Class 1A NICs (see below));

    (iii) **Forms P9D** (benefits in kind etc for other employees).

3.25 From April 2001 small employers will be able to file PAYE returns via the internet and pay tax electronically. One-off discounts of £50 will be available for using this new service. Small employers who pay the working families tax credit or the disabled persons tax credit to any of their employees in 2000/01, will be entitled to an additional £50 discount for internet filing.

3.26 **A copy of the form P11D (or P9D) must also be provided to the employee by 6 July.** The details shown on the P11D include the cash equivalent of all benefits, so that the employee may enter the details on his self-assessment tax return. Specific reference numbers for the entries on the P11D are also used on the employment supplementary pages of the self-assessment tax return.

3.27 **When an employee leaves, a certificate on form P45 (particulars of Employee Leaving) must be prepared. This form shows the employee's code and details of his income and tax paid to date and is a four part form. One part is sent to the Revenue, and three parts handed to the employee. One of the parts (part 1A) is the employee's personal copy. If the employee takes up a new employment, he must hand the other two parts of the form P45 to the new employer. The new employer will fill in details of the new employment and send one part to the Revenue, retaining the other.** The details on the form are used by the new employer to calculate the PAYE due on the next payday. If the employee dies a P45 should be completed, and the whole form sent to the Revenue.

3.28 If an employee joins with a form P45, the new employer can operate PAYE. If there is no P45 the employer still needs to operate PAYE. The employee is required to complete a form P46. If he declares that the employment is his first job since leaving education, or his only or main job and that he not in receipt of a pension, the emergency code (438L for 2000/01) applies, on a cumulative basis or week 1/month 1 basis respectively. Otherwise the employer must use code BR. The P46 is sent to the Revenue, unless the pay is below the PAYE and NIC thresholds, and the emergency code applies. In this case no PAYE is deductible until the pay exceeds the threshold.

Penalties

3.29 A form P35 is due on 19 May after the end of the year of assessment. In practice, a 7 day extension to the due date of 19 May is allowed.

3.30 **Where a form P35 is late, a penalty of £100 per month per 50 employees may be imposed.** This penalty cannot be mitigated. **This penalty ceases 12 months after the due date and a further penalty of up to 100% of the tax (and NIC) for the year which remains unpaid** at 19 April may be imposed. This penalty can be mitigated. The Revenue automatically reduce the penalty by concession to the greater of £100 and the total PAYE/NIC which should be reported on the return.

3.31 Where a person has fraudulently or negligently submitted an incorrect form P35 the penalty is 100% of the tax (and NIC) attributable to the error. This penalty can be mitigated.

PAYE settlement agreements

3.32 **PAYE settlement agreements (PSAs) are arrangements under which employers can make single payments to settle their employees' income tax liabilities on expense payments and certain benefits in kind.** Benefits may be included in a PSA if the Inspector considers them to be minor (eg small gifts), irregular (eg relocation payments of over £8,000) or benefits in respect of which it is impractical to apply PAYE or identify the amount attributable to a particular employee (eg free dental care). Items covered by a PSA do not have to be included on either Forms P9D or P11D or on the employee's tax return.

3.33 PSAs cannot be used to settle tax on:

(a) cash payments of salaries, wages or bonuses

(b) major benefits provided regularly for the sole use of individual employees (for example, company cars)

(c) round sum allowances

3.34 **Tax due under a PSA must be paid by 19 October following the end of the tax year.**

Charitable donations under the payroll deduction scheme

3.35 Employees can make tax deductible donations under the payroll deduction scheme to an approved charity of their choice by asking their employer to deduct the donation from their gross earnings prior to calculating PAYE due thereon. The government will pay a 10% supplement on all donations made under the scheme before 6 April 2003.

Chapter roundup

- The Schedule E charge has a very wide scope.
- Deductions for expenses are extremely limited.
- Most tax in respect of income is deducted under the PAYE system.

Quick quiz

1   On what basis are earnings taxed? (see paras 1.2 - 1.6)
2   What are the conditions for expenses to be deductible? (2.1, 2.2)
3   Give an example of a PAYE code. (3.18)

Now try the question below from the Exam Question Bank

Number	Level	Marks	Time
27	Exam	11	20 mins

Chapter 20

BENEFITS IN KIND

Topic list	Syllabus reference
1 Benefits in kind: all employees	3a(iv)
2 Benefits in kind: employees earning £8,500 or more a year and directors	3a(iv)

Introduction

In this chapter we look at the benefits assessable under Schedule E on employees. These fall into two categories. First, those assessable on all employees and second, those assessable on 'higher paid' employees and directors.

Study guide

Benefits in kind

- Identify P11D employees

- Explain how benefits in kind are assessed

Exam guide

This is part of section 2c which is a key topic. Question 2 in Section A will be on an unincorporated business and/or employees. It could also be examined in Question 2 in Section B.

1   BENEFITS IN KIND: ALL EMPLOYEES

1.1   **Generally, benefits in kind are taxable at the cost of providing them** (but only the marginal cost, where the benefit is also sold to non-employees). So if an employer spent £200 on a suit and gave it to an employee earning £9,000 a year, the taxable benefit would be £200.

1.2   **The above does not apply to employees who are not directors and earn less than £8,500 a year. For them benefits are taxed on their 'cash equivalent', the amount they would fetch if the employee were to dispose of them to a third party.** If, the employee above earned £7,000 a year, the benefit of the suit would be the secondhand value, which might be only £10.

1.3   **Several rules override the cost or secondhand value rule,** as follows.

Vouchers

1.4   If an employee:

(a)   receives cash vouchers (vouchers exchangeable for cash);

(b) uses a credit token (such as a credit card) to obtain money, goods or services; or

(c) receives exchangeable vouchers (such as book tokens), also called non-cash vouchers

he is taxed on the cost of providing the benefit, less any amount made good.

1.5 **The first 15p per working day of luncheon vouchers is not taxed.**

Entertainment

1.6 No benefit in kind arises on entertainment received by employees from third parties, even if it is provided by giving the employee a voucher. The exemption is intended to cover hospitality such as seats at sporting and cultural events. The exemption applies provided:

(a) neither the employer nor a connected person bears the cost;

(b) neither the employer nor a connected person procured the entertainment; and

(c) the entertainment is not provided in recognition of services which have been or are to be performed.

The exemption also covers gifts of goods (or vouchers exchangeable for goods) if the total cost (including VAT) of all gifts by the same donor to the same employee in the tax year is £150 or less. If the £150 limit is exceeded, the full amount is taxable, not just the excess.

Long service awards

1.7 Awards for long service are in general taxable. However non-cash awards are exempt if the period of service was at least 20 years, no similar award was made to the employee in the past 10 years and the cost is not more than £20 per year of service.

Suggestion schemes

1.8 Awards to employees under suggestion schemes are in general taxable, but an extra-statutory concession exempts awards when all the following conditions are satisfied.

(a) There is a formal scheme, open to all employees on equal terms.

(b) The suggestion is outside the scope of the employee's normal duties.

(c) Either the award is not more than £25, or the award is only made after a decision is taken to implement the suggestion.

(d) Awards over £25 reflect the financial importance of the suggestion to the business, and either do not exceed 50% of the expected net financial benefit during the first year of implementation or do not exceed 10% of the expected net financial benefit over a period of up to five years.

(e) Awards of over £25 are shared on a reasonable basis between two or more employees putting forward the same suggestion.

If an award exceeds £5,000, the excess is always taxable.

Share options

1.9 If an employee gains the right to acquire shares at less than their market value, he will be taxed on the difference between the market value of the shares on the date they are issued to him and the sum of the cost of acquiring the right and the cost of acquiring the shares.

Approved share option schemes receive more favourable treatment (details not in your syllabus).

Accommodation

1.10 **The taxable value of accommodation provided to any employee or director is the rent that would have been payable if the premises had been let at their annual value** (taken to be their **rateable value**, despite the abolition of domestic rates). **If the premises are rented** rather than owned by the employer, then **the taxable benefit is the higher of the rent actually paid and the annual value.** If property does not have a rateable value the Revenue estimate a value.

1.11 **Where the cost of any one property exceeds £75,000, an additional benefit in kind is chargeable upon the employee or director.** The additional benefit is

(Cost of providing the living accommodation - £75,000) × the official rate of interest.

Thus with an official rate of 10%, the total benefit for accommodation costing £90,000 and with an annual value of £2,000 would be £2,000 + £(90,000 – 75,000) × 10% = £3,500.

The 'cost of providing' the living accommodation is the aggregate of the cost of purchase and the cost of any improvements made before the start of the tax year for which the benefit is being computed. It is therefore not possible to avoid the charge by buying an inexpensive property requiring substantial repairs and improving it.

Where the property was acquired more than six years before first being provided to the employee, the market value when first so provided plus the cost of subsequent improvements is used as the cost of providing the living accommodation. However, unless the actual cost plus improvements up to the start of the tax year in question exceeds £75,000, the additional charge cannot be imposed, however high the market value.

> ### Exam focus point
> The 'official rate' of interest will be given to you in the exam.

1.12 **There is no taxable benefit in respect of job related accommodation.** Accommodation is job related if:

(a) residence in the accommodation is necessary for the proper performance of the employee's duties (as with a caretaker); or

(b) the accommodation is provided for the better performance of the employee's duties and the employment is of a kind in which it is customary for accommodation to be provided (as with a policeman); or

(c) the accommodation is provided as part of arrangements in force because of a special threat to the employee's security.

Directors can only claim exemptions (a) or (b) if:

(i) they have no material interest ('material' means over 5%) in the company; and

(ii) either they are full time working directors or the company is non-profit making or is a charity.

1.13 Any contribution paid by the employee is deducted from the annual value of the property and then from the additional benefit.

1.14 If there is some other way of taxing the benefit (for example taking the amount of salary which the employee could have had instead of the accommodation), ignore it and apply the above rules. Next tax the amount under the other way minus the amount already taxed (so we tax the higher figure).

1.15 **If an employer pays an employee's council tax, the amount paid is always a taxable benefit, unless the tax arises in connection with job-related accommodation.**

Removal expenses and benefits

1.16 An employer may pay removal expenses for an employee and his family. Legal and estate agents' fees, surveys, temporary accommodation, transport of property and interest on bridging loans are typical items. **There is no taxable benefit in respect of the first £8,000 of such expenses or benefits.** For this purpose, benefits are valued under the normal benefits rules for the employee concerned. **Payments above the £8,000 limit are taxable,** but PAYE need not be applied to them.

1.17 This exemption applies only if:

(a) The employee does not already live within a reasonable daily travelling distance of his new place of employment, but will do so after moving.

(b) The expenses are incurred or the benefits provided by the end of the tax year following the tax year of the start of employment at the new location.

Work related benefits

1.18 **If an employer runs a workplace nursery the cost is not a taxable benefit for the employees.** However, cash or vouchers given so that employees can obtain nursery facilities, are taxable.

1.19 **Sporting or recreational facilities available to employees generally and not to the general public do not give rise to taxable benefits,** unless they are provided on domestic premises, or they consist in an interest in or the use of any mechanically propelled vehicle or any overnight accommodation. Vouchers only exchangeable for such facilities also do not give rise to taxable benefits, but membership fees for sports clubs are taxable benefits.

1.20 Subject to certain exemptions for potentially high value benefits (eg cars and living accommodation), no taxable benefit arises on assets or services used in performing the duties of employment provided any private use of the item concerned is insignificant. This exempts, for example, the benefit arising on the private use of employer-provided tools.

1.21 Welfare counselling and other similar minor benefits are exempt if the benefit concerned is available to employees generally. Welfare counselling and small amounts of private use by employees of assets owned by employers are also not subject to Class 1A NICs (see below).

The fixed profit car scheme

1.22 If an employee uses his own car on his employer's business, he will normally be paid a mileage allowance. Strictly, this **mileage allowance is taxable and the employee is entitled to make a claim under S198 ICTA 1988 to deduct any motoring expenses incurred wholly, exclusively and necessarily in the performance of his duties.**

1.23 However, an employee can take advantage of the **Fixed Profit Car Scheme (FPCS)**. Under this scheme the Revenue have laid down mileage rates which are dependant on the engine capacity of the car and the number of business miles travelled. **The employee can receive tax free mileage allowances of up to the amounts laid down under the scheme.** Any excess allowance received is a taxable benefit. In general, the employee cannot also make a S198 ICTA 1988 claim in respect of any business motoring expenses actually incurred but exceptionally, a deduction for the business proportion of any interest paid on a loan taken out to buy the car may be claimed. FPCS rates for 2000/01 are set out in the Rates and Allowances Tables in this text.

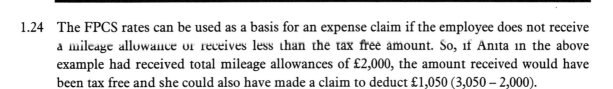

Question: FPCS

Anita travels 9,000 business miles in her own 1800cc car during 2000/01. Her employer pays a mileage allowance of 35p per mile for cars with up to 2000cc engines. What taxable benefit arises under the FPCS?

Answer

	£
Mileage allowance paid (9,000 × 35p)	3,150
FPCS tax free amount	
4,000 miles @ 45p	(1,800)
5,000 miles @ 25p	(1,250)
Taxable benefit	100

1.24 The FPCS rates can be used as a basis for an expense claim if the employee does not receive a mileage allowance or receives less than the tax free amount. So, if Anita in the above example had received total mileage allowances of £2,000, the amount received would have been tax free and she could also have made a claim to deduct £1,050 (3,050 − 2,000).

1.25 Self-employed taxpayers with turnover below the VAT registration threshold (see earlier in this text) may use the tax free mileage rates as an alternative to keeping detailed records of their actual expenditure.

Bicycles and motorcycles

1.26 **Employers can pay a tax free sum to employees who use their bicycle or motorcycle on business travel.** The tax free amount is 12p per mile for bicycles and 24p per mile for motorcycles. If an employer makes no payment, an employee can claim tax relief for the tax free amount (or he can claim relief on the balance up to the tax free amount if the employer pays less than this).

1.27 There is no taxable benefit in respect of bicycles or cycling safety equipment provided to enable employees to get to and from work or to travel between one workplace and another. The equipment must be available to the employer's employees generally. Also, it must be used mainly for the aforementioned journeys.

1.28 There is no taxable benefit in respect of workplace parking for bicycles or motorcycles.

Scholarship and apprenticeship schemes

1.29 If an employer allows an employee to go on a full-time course lasting at least a year, with average full-time attendance of at least 20 weeks a year, then the employer may pay the employee up to £7,000 a year tax free. However, if the £7,000 limit is exceeded, the whole amount paid is taxable income of the employee.

Work related training and Individual Learning Accounts

1.30   No taxable benefit arises in respect of work related training or any related cost.

1.31   Work related training is training that is likely to be useful to an employee performing his duties and training that better qualifies the employee for the employment or for any charitable or voluntary activity associated with the employment.

1.32   Similarly, no taxable benefit arises on:

(a)   contributions paid directly to an individual learning account (ILA). The ILA must be eligible for a grant or discount and contributions must be available to all employees on similar terms.

(b)   any related costs whether paid directly or reimbursed to the employee.

1.33   For these purposes, related costs include incidental costs incurred wholly and exclusively as a result of the employee undertaking the training (eg the cost of additional child-care), assessment or examination fees and the costs of any qualification, registration or award arising as a result of the training. Related costs also include travel and subsistence costs to the extent that such costs incurred by the employee would have been deductible if he had undertaken the training in the performance of his duties (see below).

1.34   No taxable benefit normally arises in respect of training material, or any asset either made during training or incorporated into something so made.

Air miles and car fuel coupons

1.35   If an employee flies on business, uses a company credit card or buys fuel for business travel, and thereby earns air miles or car fuel coupons which he uses for private purposes, there is no taxable benefit.

Travel

1.36   There is no taxable benefit in respect of:

(a)   work buses;
(b)   subsidies to public bus services provided employees pay the same fare as the public.

The bus must have a seating capacity of 12 or more and be available generally to employees of the employer concerned. The bus must mainly be used by employees for journeys to and from work and for journeys between workplaces.

1.37   The following amounts paid by an employer are exempt benefits.

(a)   Transport/overnight costs where public transport is disrupted by industrial action.

(b)   Late night taxis.

(c)   Travel costs exceptionally incurred where car sharing arrangements unavoidably breakdown.

2 BENEFITS IN KIND: EMPLOYEES EARNING £8,500 OR MORE A YEAR AND DIRECTORS

2.1 **The benefit in kind rules discussed in this section apply to an employee whose 'emoluments' are at the rate of £8,500 a year or more ('P11D employees'). 'Emoluments' for this purpose include salary, commissions, fees, reimbursed expenses and also benefits in kind taxable on such employees.** In other words, one must assume that an employee falls into this category in order to determine whether or not he really does. In seeing whether he does, we ignore any deductible expenses.

2.2 Where a car is provided but the employee could have chosen an alternative benefit, the benefit to use for the £8,500 test is the sum of:

(a) the higher of the car benefit plus any fuel benefit and the value of the alternative;

(b) any expense payments in relation to the car or benefits relating to it obtained by non-cash vouchers or credit tokens.

2.3 **A 'director' is taxed on benefits in kind in the same way as an employee earning £8,500 or more a year. The term 'director' refers to any person who acts as a director or any person in accordance with whose instructions the directors are accustomed to act** (other than a professional adviser). An individual is not, however, subject to the special benefit in kind rules solely because he is a director, if he has no material interest in the company ('material' means more than 5%) and either:

(a) he is a full time working director; or
(b) the company is either non-profit making or is established for charitable purposes.

But such a person will be subject to the special rules if he earns £8,500 or more a year.

2.4 A benefit is taxable if it arises 'by reason of the employment' and is provided either to the employee or to a member of his family or household. There is no need for the employer to provide it directly.

General business expenses

2.5 **If business expenses on such items as travel or hotel stays, are reimbursed by an employer, the reimbursed amount is a taxable benefit.** To avoid being taxed on this amount, **an employee must then make a claim to deduct it as an expense** under the rules set out in the previous chapter. **In practice, however, many such expense payments are not reported to the Inland Revenue and can be ignored because it is agreed in advance that a claim to deduct them would be possible (a P11D dispensation).**

2.6 When an individual has to spend one or more nights away from home, his employer may reimburse expenses on items incidental to his absence (for example meals and private telephone calls). Such incidental expenses are not taxable if:

(a) The expenses of travelling to each place where the individual stays overnight, throughout the trip, are incurred necessarily in the performance of the duties of the employment (or would have been, if there had been any expenses).

(b) The total (for the whole trip) of incidental expenses not deductible under the usual rules is no more than £5 for each night spent wholly in the UK and £10 for each other night. If this limit is exceeded, all of the expenses are taxable, not just the excess. The expenses include any VAT.

2.7 This incidental expenses exemption applies to expenses reimbursed, and to benefits obtained using credit tokens and non-cash vouchers.

Expenses connected with living accommodation

2.8 In addition to the benefit of living accommodation itself, which is taxable on all employees, **employees earning £8,500 or more a year and directors are taxed on related expenses paid by the employer,** such as:

(a) **heating, lighting or cleaning the premises;**
(b) **repairing, maintaining or decorating the premises;**
(c) **the provision of furniture** (the annual value is 20% of the cost).

2.9 Unless the accommodation qualifies as 'job related' (as defined above) **the full cost of ancillary services** (excluding structural repairs) **is taxable. If the accommodation is 'job related',** however, **taxable ancillary services are restricted to a maximum of 10% of the employee's 'net emoluments'.** For this purpose, net emoluments are all amounts taxable under Schedule E (excluding the ancillary benefits (a) - (c) above) less any allowable expenses, contributions to approved pension schemes and personal pension plans, and capital allowances. If there are ancillary benefits other than those falling within (a) - (c) above (such as a telephone) they are taxable in full.

Question: Expenses connected with living accommodation

Mr Quinton has a gross salary in 2000/01 of £28,850. He normally lives and works in London, but he is required to live in a company house in Scotland which cost £70,000 three years ago, so that he can carry out a two year review of his company's operations in Scotland. The annual value of the house is £650. In 2000/01 the company pays an electricity bill of £550, a gas bill of £400, a gardener's bill of £750 and redecoration costs of £1,800. Mr Quinton makes a monthly contribution of £50 for his accommodation. He also pays £1,450 superannuation contributions.

Calculate the Schedule E income for 2000/01.

Answer

	£	£
Salary		28,850
Less superannuation contributions		(1,450)
Net emoluments		27,400
Accommodation benefits		
Annual value: exempt (job related)		
Ancillary services		
Electricity	550	
Gas	400	
Gardener	750	
Redecorations	1,800	
	3,500	
Restricted to 10% of £27,400	2,740	
Less employee's contribution	(600)	
		2,140
Schedule E income		29,540

Cars

2.10 **For employees earning £8,500 or more a year and directors, a car provided by reason of the employment gives rise to a taxable benefit.**

(a) A tax charge arises whether the car is provided by the employer or by some other person. The benefit is computed as shown below, even if the car is taken as an alternative to another benefit of a different value.

(b) **The benefit chargeable to tax each year is found as follows.**

(Price of car – capital contributions) × % × age factor

(c) The price of the car is the sum of the following items.

(i) The list price of the car for a single retail sale at the time of first registration, including charges for delivery and standard accessories. The manufacturer's, importer's or distributor's list price must be used, even if the retailer offered a discount. A notional list price is estimated if no list price was published.

(ii) The price (including fitting) of all optional accessories provided when the car was first provided to the employee, excluding mobile telephones and equipment needed by a disabled employee. The extra cost of adapting or manufacturing a car to run on road fuel gases is not included.

(iii) The price (including fitting) of all optional accessories fitted later and costing at least £100 each, excluding mobile telephones and equipment needed by a disabled employee. Such accessories affect the taxable benefit from and including the tax year in which they are fitted. However, accessories which are merely replacing existing accessories and are not superior to the ones replaced are ignored. Replacement accessories which *are* superior are taken into account, but the cost of the old accessory is then ignored.

(d) There is a special rule for classic cars. If the car is at least 15 years old (from the time of first registration) at the end of the tax year, and its market value at the end of the year (or, if earlier, when it ceased to be available to the employee) is over £15,000 and greater than the price found under (c), that market value is used instead of the price. The market value takes account of all accessories (except mobile telephones and equipment needed by a disabled employee).

(e) If the price or value found under (c) or (d) exceeds £80,000, then £80,000 is used instead of the price or value.

(f) Capital contributions are payments by the employee in respect of the price of the car or accessories. In any tax year, we take account of capital contributions made in that year and previous years (for the same car). The maximum deductible capital contributions is £5,000: contributions beyond that total are ignored.

(g) If the car is at least four years old (from the date of first registration) at the end of the tax year, then the age factor is ¾. Otherwise it is 1.

(h) The 'percentage' for 2000/01 depends on the **business** mileage in the tax year:

Business mileage	First car	Other cars
Less than 2,500	35%	35%
At least 2,500, less than 18,000	25%	35%
At least 18,000	15%	25%

The 'other cars' percentages apply when two or more cars are provided simultaneously. The car with the greatest business mileage is the first car, and the 'first car' percentages are used for that car only.

(i) In *Henwood (HMIT) v Clarke 1997* a car was made available to the taxpayer for private and business use throughout the year but the first car was replaced by another car during the year. The taxpayer's total business mileage exceeded 2,500 miles in the tax year but the proportion of business miles travelled in each car differed. It was held that the mileage threshold applied to each car separately rather than to the driver.

(j)   The benefit is reduced on a time basis where a car is first made available or ceases to be made available during the tax year or is incapable of being used for a continuous period of not less than 30 days (for example because it is being repaired). The mileage factor limits of 2,500 and 18,000 miles are also reduced on a time basis in such cases. If a car is unavailable for less than 30 days and a replacement car of similar quality is provided, the replacement car is ignored and business mileage in it counts as business mileage in the usual car.

(k)   The benefit is reduced by any payment the user must make for the private use of the car (as distinct from a capital contribution to the cost of the car). Payments for insuring the car do not count *(IRC v Quigley 1995)*. The benefit cannot become negative to create a deduction from the employee's income.

(l)   Pool cars are exempt. A car is a pool car if **all** the following conditions are satisfied.

- It is used by more than one director or employee and is not ordinarily used by any one of them to the exclusion of the others.

- Any private use is merely incidental to business use.

- It is not normally kept overnight at or near the residence of a director or employee.

2.11   Employers must make quarterly returns in respect of changes to cars provided to employees on form P46 (car). These returns must be made within 28 days of the end of each income tax quarter (quarters end on 5 July, 5 October, 5 January and 5 April).

Fuel for cars

2.12   **Where fuel is provided there is a further benefit on a set scale in addition to the car benefit.** The fuel benefits are given in the Rates and Allowances Tables in this text.

No taxable benefit arises where either

(a)   all the fuel provided was made available only for business travel; or

(b)   the employee is required to make good, and has made good, the whole of the cost of any fuel provided for his private use.

Unlike most benefits, a reimbursement of only part of the cost of the fuel available for private use does not reduce the scale charge.

The benefit is reduced in the same way as the car benefit if the car is not available for 30 days or more, but it is not adjusted for business mileage.

2.13   There are many ancillary benefits associated with the provision of cars, such as insurance, repairs, vehicle licences and a parking space at or near work. No extra taxable benefit arises as a result of these, with the exception of the cost of providing a driver.

Question: Car and Fuel benefit

An employee was provided with a new car (2,500 cc) costing £15,000. During 2000/01 the employer spent £900 on insurance, repairs and a vehicle licence. The employee did 20,000 miles of which 15,000 were on business. The firm paid for all petrol, costing £1,500, without reimbursement. The employee paid the firm £270 for the private use of the car. Calculate the taxable benefit.

Answer

	£
Car benefit £15,000 × 25%	3,750
Fuel benefit	3,200
	6,950
Less contribution towards use of car	(270)
	6,680

If the contribution of £270 had been towards the petrol the benefit would have been £6,950.

Vans and heavier commercial vehicles

2.14 **If a van** (of normal maximum laden weight up to 3,500 kg) **is made available for an employee's private use, there is an annual scale charge of £500, or £350 if the van is at least four years old at the end of the tax year.** The scale charge covers ancillary benefits such as insurance and servicing (but not van telephones). Paragraphs 2.10 (a), (i), (j) and (k) above apply to vans as they do to cars, but there is no adjustment for mileage.

2.15 If a commercial vehicle of normal maximum laden weight over 3,500 kg is made available for an employee's private use, but the employee's use of the vehicle is not wholly or mainly private, no taxable benefit arises except in respect of the provision of a driver.

Mobile telephones

2.16 **No taxable benefit arises in respect of a mobile telephone** made available to an employee or a member of his family (**the employer retaining ownership of the telephone**).

Other assets made available for private use

2.17 **Assets made available to employees earning £8,500 or more a year and directors are taxable on an annual value of 20% of the market value when first provided as a benefit to any employee, or on the rent paid by the employer if higher.** The 20% charge is time-apportioned when the asset is provided for only part of the year. The charge after any time apportionment is reduced by any contribution made by the employee.

2.18 If an asset made available is subsequently acquired by the employee, **the taxable benefit on the acquisition is the** *greater* **of:**

- the **current market value minus the price paid by the employee;**

- the **market value when first provided minus any amounts already taxed (ignoring contributions by the employee) minus the price paid by the employee.**

This rule prevents tax free benefits arising on rapidly depreciating items through the employee purchasing them at their low secondhand value.

2.19 EXAMPLE: ASSETS MADE AVAILABLE FOR PRIVATE USE

A suit costing £400 is purchased by an employer for use by an employee on 6 April 1999. On 6 April 2000 the suit is purchased by the employee for £30, its market value then being £50.

The benefit in 1999/00 is £400 × 20%   £80

The benefit in 2000/01 is £290, being the *greater* of:

		£
(a)	Market value at acquisition by employee	50
	Less price paid	(30)
		20

		£
(b)	Original market value	400
	Less taxed in respect of use	(80)
		320
	Less price paid	(30)
		290

Computer equipment

2.20 **The first £500 of any benefit which arises under the above rules in respect of computer equipment** made available for the private use of an employee or a member of his family/household is **exempt**. If the benefit exceeds £500, the excess is taxable.

Assets sold to employers

2.21 If an employee sells an asset to his employer (for example his house when he is being relocated), **there is a taxable benefit of the amount paid minus the market value of the asset.** If the employer pays his own transaction costs (for example solicitors' fees), they do not count as a taxable benefit. However, if the employer pays the employee's transaction costs, there is a taxable benefit unless a specific exemption (for example the removal expenses exemption) applies.

Scholarships

2.22 If scholarships are given to members of a director's or employee's family, the director or **employee is taxable on the cost** unless the scholarship fund's or scheme's payments by reason of people's employments are not more than 25% of its total payments.

PAYE tax liabilities

2.23 **If a company pays any tax** which should have been deducted from a director's (not an employee's) remuneration under PAYE but was not so deducted, **any amount not made good by the director is a taxable benefit.** Directors with no material interest in the company (that is, not more than 5%) who are full time working directors or who work for non profit making or charitable companies are excluded from this rule.

2.24 An employer is required to deduct tax under PAYE from notional payments. These are non-cash payments. If, in such a case, the tax cannot be deducted because there is not enough cash pay, the employer must account for the tax. If the director or employee does not reimburse the employer for the tax within 30 days of receiving the taxable payment from the employer, the tax is treated as Schedule E income of the director or employee.

Beneficial loans

2.25 **Loans to employees, directors and their families give rise to a benefit equal to:**

(a) **any amounts written off** (unless the employee has died); and

(b) **the excess of the interest based on an official rate prescribed by the Treasury, over any interest actually charged**. Interest payable during the tax year but paid after the end of the tax year is taken into account, but if the benefit is determined before such interest is paid a claim must be made to take it into account.

2.26 The following loans are normally ignored altogether for the purposes of computing taxable income because of low interest (but not for the purposes of the charge on loans written off).

(a) A loan on normal commercial terms made in the ordinary course of the employer's money-lending business.

(b) A loan made by an individual in the ordinary course of the lender's domestic, family or personal arrangements.

Calculating the interest benefit

2.27 There are two alternative methods of calculating the taxable benefit. The simpler '**average**' **method** automatically applies unless the taxpayer or the Revenue elect for the alternative '**strict**' **method**. (The Revenue normally only make the election where it appears that the 'average' method is being deliberately exploited.) In both methods, the benefit is the interest at the official rate minus the interest payable.

2.28 The 'average' method averages the balances at the beginning and end of the tax year (or the dates on which the loan was made and discharged if it was not in existence throughout the tax year) and applies the official rate of interest to this average. If the loan was not in existence throughout the tax year only the number of complete tax months (from the 6th of the month) for which it existed are taken into account.

2.29 The 'strict' method is to compute interest at the official rate on the actual amount outstanding on a daily basis.

Question: Loan benefit

At 6 April 2000 a low interest loan of £30,000 was outstanding to an employee earning £12,000 a year, who repaid £20,000 on 7 December 2000. The remaining balance of £10,000 was outstanding at 5 April 2001. Interest paid during the year was £250. What was the benefit under both methods for 2000/01, assuming that the official rate of interest was 10%?

Answer

Average method

	£
$10\% \times \dfrac{30,000 + 10,000}{2}$	2,000
Less interest paid	(250)
Benefit	1,750

Alternative method (strict method)

	£
$\pounds30,000 \times \dfrac{245}{365}$ (6 April – 6 December) $\times$ 10%	2,014
$\pounds10,000 \times \dfrac{120}{365}$ (7 December - 5 April) $\times$ 10%	(329)
	2,343
Less interest paid	(250)
Benefit	2,093

The Revenue might opt for the alternative method.

The de minimis test

2.30 **The benefit is not taxable if:**

(a) The **total of all loans to the employee did not exceed £5,000** at any time in the tax year, or

(b) **The loan is not a qualifying loan and the total of all non-qualifying loans to the employee did not exceed £5,000** at any time in the tax year.

2.31 **A qualifying loan is one on which any interest would qualify as a charge.**

2.32 In applying the £5,000 test, ignore any loans which are to be ignored under the rules above.

2.33 When the £5,000 threshold is exceeded, a benefit arises on interest on the whole loan, not just on the excess of the loan over £5,000.

2.34 When a loan is written off and a benefit arises, there is no £5,000 threshold: writing off a loan of £1 gives rise to a £1 benefit.

Qualifying loans

2.35 When an employee is treated as receiving emoluments because the actual rate of interest is below the official rate, he is also treated as paying interest equal to the emoluments. If the loan is used in a business for some other qualifying purpose, this **deemed interest paid may qualify as a business expense or as a charge in addition to any interest actually paid.**

Employers are not required to report a beneficial loan on form P11D, where interest on the loan qualifies for tax relief in full. Such loans are not subject to Class 1A NICs (see next chapter).

Question: Beneficial loans

Anna, who is single, has an annual salary of £30,000, and two loans from her employer.

(a) A season ticket loan of £2,300 at no interest
(b) A loan to buy shares in her employee-controlled company of £54,000 at 3% interest

The official rate of interest is to be taken as 10%.

What is Anna's tax liability for 2000/01?

Answer

	£
Salary	30,000
Season ticket loan: not over £5,000	0
Loan to buy shares £54,000 × (10 - 3 = 7%)	3,780
Schedule E	33,780
Less: charge on income (£54,000 × 10%)	(5,400)
	28,380
Less personal allowance	(4,385)
Taxable income	23,995

Income tax	
£1,520 × 10%	152
£22,475 × 22%	4,945
Tax liability	5,097

Note: The loan to buy the shares is a qualifying loan. This means that Anna's employer is not required to report the loan on Form P11D and no Class 1A NICs (see below) are due in respect of the loan.

Medical services and insurance

2.36 The cost of medical diagnosis and treatment provided by an employer is a taxable benefit, except for the cost of routine check-ups. **Private medical insurance premiums are also taxable benefits**, except for premiums or extra premiums to cover treatment when the employee is outside the UK in the performance of his duties.

Staff parties

2.37 The **cost of staff parties is taxable, except** when the parties are open to staff generally and the **cost per staff member per year (including VAT) is £75 or less**. The £75 limit may be split between several parties. If it is exceeded, the full amount is taxable, not just the excess over £75.

Uniforms

2.38 If employees must wear uniforms as part of their duties, there is no taxable benefit when employers provide those uniforms for them.

Chapter roundup

- Certain benefits are assessable on all employees.
- P11D employees are taxable on nearly all benefits received by reason of their employment.
- There are specific rules dealing with certain benefits for example cars, fuel and computers.

Quick quiz

1 What accommodation does not give rise to a taxable benefit? (see para 1.12)

2 What is the fixed profit car scheme? (1.22)

3 In what circumstances will there be no taxable fuel benefit where fuel is provided for private use? (2.12)

4 To what extent will an employee suffer a taxable benefit in respect of computer equipment lent to him by his employer? (2.20)

5 What is the de minimis test for no taxable benefit to arise on beneficial loans? (2.30)

Now try the question below from the Exam Question Bank

Number	Level	Marks	Time
28	Exam	14	25 mins

Chapter 21

OCCUPATIONAL PENSION SCHEMES. NICs FOR EMPLOYEES

Topic list		Syllabus reference
1	Occupational pension schemes	3b
2	NICs for employees	3c

Introduction

We finish our consideration of employees with two topics.

First we consider the provision of pensions for employees under an occupational pension scheme. Remember that employees may also make pension provisions through personal pensions, already considered.

Lastly we look at the national insurance contributions payable under Classes 1 and 1A in respect of employment.

Study guide

Occupational pension schemes and NIC

- State the main features of an occupational pension scheme

- Explain the significance of an occupational pension scheme being approved by the Inland Revenue.

- Calculate Class 1 NIC

- Calculate Class 1A NIC

Exam guide

Although sections 3b and 3c are not key topics, the examiner has indicated that they may form part of Question 2 in Section A for a maximum of 10 marks.

1 OCCUPATIONAL PENSION SCHEMES

> ### KEY TERM
>
> Employers may set up an **occupational pension scheme**. Such schemes may either require contributions from employees or be non-contributory. The employer may use the services of an insurance company (an insured scheme) or may set up a totally self administered pension fund. The members of a scheme must be entitled to select at least 1/3 of the scheme's trustees.

1.1   Schemes can be of two kinds: Revenue approved and unapproved. **Approved schemes have significant tax advantages** that have made them very popular.

1.2   The Revenue may withdraw approval of a scheme if approval is no longer warranted, or if the scheme is changed in a way which has not been approved, either specifically or through being on the list of changes which do not require individual approval.

1.3   **If a scheme is Revenue approved:**

- **contributions made by the employee are deductible from his Schedule E income** (up to a limit of 15% of gross emoluments, with gross emoluments limited to the earnings cap (see below));

- **the employer's contributions actually paid** (not merely provided for) **are deductible in calculating profits** subject to tax (although deductions for large contributions above the normal level may be spread over several years);

- **the employer's contributions are not regarded as benefits in kind for the employee** and are not earnings for NICs purposes;

- **the fund of contributions, and the income and gains arising from their investment, are not, in general, liable to tax**. It is this long-term tax-free accumulation of funds that makes approved schemes so beneficial;

- provision can be made for a **lump sum** to be **paid on the employee's death in service**. Provided that it does not exceed four times his final remuneration, it is **tax-free**;

- **a tax-free lump sum may be paid to the employee on retirement.**

1.4   The following limits apply to an approved occupational pension scheme.

- The maximum pension is normally two thirds of the individual's final remuneration, being calculated as one sixtieth for each year of service, with a maximum of 40 years.

- A scheme may provide for part of the pension to be taken as a lump sum. The maximum lump sum is 1.5 times final remuneration, being calculated as 3/80 for each year of service, with a maximum of 40 years.

1.5   The Revenue have discretion to approve schemes which do not comply with these limits. In particular, many schemes provide for a pension of two thirds of final salary after less than 40 years service.

1.6   The parties to a divorce can share pension rights without affecting the tax approved status of the pension scheme.

1.7   There is a surplus in an occupational pension scheme if the amount held in the scheme exceeds the amount needed to meet the scheme's pension liabilities plus 5%. This surplus may, subject to certain conditions, be repaid to the employer.

The earnings cap

1.8   An earnings cap applies to tax-approved occupational pension schemes. The cap is £91,800 for 2000/01.

1.9   The earnings cap has two consequences.

- The maximum pension payable from an approved scheme is the cap $\times$ 2/3.
- The maximum tax-free lump sum is the cap $\times$ 1.5.

BPP PUBLISHING

Additional voluntary contributions

1.10 **An employee who feels that his employer's scheme is inadequate may make additional voluntary contributions (AVCs), either to the employer's scheme or to a separate scheme** operated by an insurance company (freestanding AVCs). **AVCs are deductible from the employee's taxable pay,** but only to the extent that they, plus any contributions by the employee to the employer's scheme, do not exceed 15% of gross emoluments (limited to the earnings cap). The limits on pensions and lump sums which may be taken must be applied to the total sums derived from the employer's scheme and the AVCs.

Freestanding AVCs are paid net of basic rate tax.

1.11 Employers can establish unapproved schemes to operate alongside approved schemes. Employer contributions to unapproved schemes are taxable as earnings of the employee. Employee contributions are not tax-deductible.

Small self-administered schemes

1.12 All employees, including owner-directors of small companies, may join approved schemes. The creation of a self-administered pension scheme is an important part of tax planning for the smaller company. However, regulations restrict the extent to which pension schemes can invest in the companies setting them up (a common practice with smaller companies).

1.13 In addition, there is a special tax charge when a scheme with fewer than 12 members, or one with a controlling director (a director holding at least 20% of the ordinary shares) as a member, loses its Revenue approval. Tax of 40% of the value of the scheme's assets at that time must be paid. Thus such schemes must be careful not to lose their approval.

2 NICs FOR EMPLOYEES

2.1 Both employees and employers pay Class 1 NICs related to the employee's earnings. NICs are not deductible from an employee's gross salary for income tax purposes. However, employers' contributions are deductible Schedule D Case I expenses.

2.2 'Earnings' broadly comprise gross pay, excluding benefits in kind which cannot be turned into cash by surrender (eg holidays). No deduction is made for superannuation contributions or contributions under the payroll giving scheme.

2.3 An employer's contribution to an employee's approved personal pension or an approved occupational pension scheme is excluded from the definition of 'earnings'. However, NICs are due on employer contributions to funded unapproved retirement benefit schemes.

2.4 In general income tax and NIC exemptions mirror one another. For example, payment of personal incidental expenses covered by the £5/£10 a night income tax de minimis exemption and professional indemnity insurance payments exempted from income tax are excluded from NIC earnings. Relocation expenses of a type exempt from income tax are also excluded from NIC earnings but without the income tax £8,000 upper limit (although expenses exceeding £8,000 are subject to Class 1A NICs as described below). Similarly, the income tax rules for travel expenses are exactly mirrored for NIC treatment.

2.5 An expense with a business purpose is not treated as earnings. For example, if an employee is reimbursed for business travel or for staying in a hotel on the employer's business this is not normally 'earnings'. However, if an employee is reimbursed for his own home telephone charges the reimbursed cost of private calls (and all reimbursed rental) is earnings.

2.6   Where an employer reimburses an employee using his own car for business mileage, the earnings element is the excess of the mileage rate paid over the Inland Revenue 'up to 4,000 business miles' Fixed Profit Car Scheme rate appropriate to the engine size. This applies even where business mileage exceeds 4,000 pa.

2.7   In general, non cash vouchers are subject to NICs. However, the following are exempt.

- Childcare vouchers for children up to 16 years old
- Vouchers for the use of sports and recreational facilities (where tax exempt)
- Vouchers for meals on the employer's premises
- Other luncheon vouchers to a maximum of 15p per day
- Transport vouchers where the employee earns less than £8,500 a year.

2.8   The rates of contribution for 2000/01, and the income bands to which they apply, are set out in the Rates and Allowances Tables in this text.

Non-contracted out employees pay contributions of 10% of earnings between the primary threshold of £3,952 and the upper earnings limit of £27,820.

Employers pay contributions of 12.2% on earnings above the earnings threshold of £4,385.

2.9   If an employee is in a contracted out occupational pension scheme, reduced contributions are payable. Employee contributions are 8.4% of earnings between the primary threshold and the upper earnings limit. There is also a rebate of 1.6% on earnings between the lower earnings limit and the primary threshold.

Employer rates are cut for earnings between the secondary threshold of £4,385 and the upper limit. Rebates are given on earnings between the primary and secondary thresholds (the reduced rate and rebate depends on the type of scheme).

If an employee contracts out of the state earnings related pension scheme through a personal pension, full contributions are payable but the Department of Social Security pays a proportion of these contributions to the insurance company running the personal pension scheme.

2.10   **Employers must pay Class 1A NIC in respect of most taxable benefits for example, private medical insurance. However, benefits are exempt if they are:**

- within class 1; or
- covered by a PAYE dispensation; or
- provided for employees earning at a rate of less than £8,500 a year; or
- included in a PAYE settlement agreement; or
- otherwise not required to be reported on P11Ds

In addition, all kinds of childcare provision in kind, for example, where the employer contracts for places in commercial nurseries, are exempt from Class 1A NICs. However, if an employer provides cash to meet or reimburse childcare expenses the cash is 'earnings' for employer and employee Class 1 NIC purposes. There is also exemption for certain other minor benefits already noted in the text (eg small private use of employer's assets).

2.11   **Employee contributions are not charged on benefits in kind.**

2.12   Class 1A contributions are collected annually in arrears, and are due by 19 July following the tax year.

2.13   The provision by an employer of fuel for use in an employee's own car does not lead to a Class 1A charge. However, mileage allowances in excess of the fixed profit car scheme rates lead to Class 1 (primary and secondary) contributions on the excess (subject to the usual upper limit for primary contributions).

2.14 If Class 1 contributions for a year are not paid to the Revenue by 19 April following the year, or Class 1A contributions due in a year are not paid over by 19 April following the year, interest is charged from the relevant 19 April onwards. Interest is paid to employers on excessive payments refunded to them, but only from the end of the year of payment and never from earlier than 12 months after the end of the year for which the contributions were paid.

Chapter roundup

- Employers may set up occupational pension schemes for their employees; approved schemes have tax advantages
- Contributions by both employer and employee to an occupational pension scheme are deductible for tax purposes
- There are limits on the benefits that may be provided under an occupational pension scheme
- Class 1 NICs are payable by employees and employers on earnings
- Class 1A NICs are payable by employers on benefits in kind provided for employees

Quick quiz

1   What are the tax effects of an occupational pension scheme having Inland Revenue approval? (see para 1.3)

2   What are AVCs? (1.10)

3   What National Insurance contributions are payable by employers and employees?(2.1, 2.10)

Now try the question below from the Exam Question Bank

Number	Level	Marks	Time
29	Exam	25	45 mins

Part D
Tax planning

Chapter 22

TAX PLANNING

Topic list		Syllabus reference
1	Employment and self-employment	4a
2	Remuneration packages	4b
3	The choice of a business medium	4c
4	The incorporation of a business	4d
5	Disposal of a business	4e
6	Directors and shareholders	4f

Introduction

In this final chapter, we will bring together several different topics by considering some typical tax planning problems.

Study guide

Tax planning

- Compare the tax implications of employment as compared to self-employment

- Compare alternative remuneration packages

- Compare the tax position of a director/shareholder with that of a sole trader

- Explain the factors that must be considered when incorporating a business

- Explain the tax implications arising on the disposal of a business

- Compute whether remuneration or a dividend is the most tax efficient way to extract profit from a company.

Exam guide

Question 6 (15 marks) will be on one of the six listed planning topics.

1 EMPLOYMENT AND SELF-EMPLOYMENT

1.1 **A taxpayer who has a choice between being employed and being self-employed, on similar gross incomes, should consider the following points.**

(a) An employee must pay **income tax and NICs as salary is received, under the PAYE** system and on a current year basis. A self-employed person pays **Class 2 NICs during the year, but income tax and Class 4 NICs are at least partly payable after all of the profits concerned have been earned.** There is thus a cash flow advantage in self-employment.

(b) **An employee is likely to suffer significantly higher NICs in total than a self-employed person**, although the employee's entitlement to state benefits will also be higher.

(c) An **employee may receive benefits in kind as well as salary.** Taxable values of benefits may be less than their actual value to the employee and benefits do not attract employee NICs (this is however only relevant if salary does not exceed the upper NIC limit). Most benefits attract Employer's Class 1A NIC.

(d) The **rules on the deductibility of expenses are much stricter for employees** (incurred wholly, exclusively and necessarily in the performance of duties) than for the self-employed (normally incurred wholly and exclusively for the purposes of the trade).

2   REMUNERATION PACKAGES

2.1 **An employee will usually be rewarded largely by salary, but several other elements can be included in a remuneration package. Some of them bring tax benefits to the employee only, and some will also benefit the employer.** Consider the following:

(a) Bonuses are treated like salary, except that if a bonus is accrued in the employer's accounts but is paid more than nine months after the end of the period of account, its deductibility for Schedule D Case I purposes will be delayed.

(b) Benefits in kind do not generally attract employee Class 1 NIC (but see paragraph 1.1 above). However, most benefits attract employer's Class 1A NIC.

(c) Benefits in kind do give rise to income tax charges on the employee, which may make the benefits unattractive. The cost of providing benefits is generally deductible for the employer, but if a car costing over £12,000 is provided, the employer's capital allowances (or deductions for lease payments) are restricted.

(d) A pension scheme could be provided, or an existing one improved. This is tax-efficient, and should give employees long-term security, especially if pensions are index linked. The option to take a tax-free lump sum on retirement could be useful to employees.

Question: Comparison of two remuneration packages

Employee A receives a salary of £20,000.

Employee B receives a salary of £15,000, the use of a video camera which cost £800 and the use of a car which cost £17,732 on 1.1.00. The Schedule E benefit for this car is £4,433. No fuel is supplied. Employee B is also in a pension scheme (not contracted out) to which he contributes 5% of his gross salary (excluding benefits) and his employer company contributes 10% of his gross salary (excluding benefits).

A and B are both single and have no other income.

Show the tax and the NIC effects of the two remuneration packages on both the employees and their employers. Assume that any asset attracting capital allowances has already had one year's writing down allowance. Use 2000/01 tax rates and allowances and assume that the employer prepares accounts to 31 March each year.

Answer

A's income tax and NIC computations are as follows.

	£
Schedule E	20,000
Less personal allowance	(4,385)
Taxable income	15,615

Income tax	£
£1,520 × 10%	152
£14,095 × 22%	3,101
	3,253

NICs

£(20,000 − 3,952) × 10%	£1,605

A's employer must pay NICs of £20,000 − £4,385 × 12.2% = £1,905, and can deduct £(20,000 + 1,905) = £21,905 in computing trading profits.

B's income tax and NIC computations are as follows.

	£
Salary	15,000
Use of video camera £800 × 20%	160
Car	4,433
	19,593
Less pension contribution £15,000 × 5%	(750)
Schedule E	18,843
Less personal allowance	(4,385)
Taxable income	14,458

Income tax	£
£1,520 × 10%	152
£12,938 × 22%	2,846
	2,998

NICs

£(15,000 − 3,952) × 10%	1,105

B's employer must pay NICs as follows

Class 1 NICs	
£15,000 − £4,385 × 12.2%	1,295

Class 1A NICs	
£(4,433 + 160) × 12.2%	560
	1,855

B's employer will have the following deductions in computing profits.

	£	£
Salary		15,000
Pension contribution £15,000 × 10%		1,500
NICs		1,855
Capital allowances		
Car (WDV b/f £14,732)	3,000	
Video camera £800 × 75% × 25%	150	
		3,150
		21,505

NIC planning for employment situations

2.2 NIC is payable on 'earnings' which is defined as 'any remuneration or profit derived from employment'. Remuneration packages structured to include the following items which are not 'earnings' would reduce the NIC burden;

(a) **Dividends** - director/shareholders could take remuneration in the form of dividends. Dividend waivers and adjustments to bonuses would probably be required. There are CT implications as salary and NIC costs are allowable business expenses whereas dividends are not.

Provided the starting rate or small companies rate of CT applies dividends are an efficient way of avoiding NICs. However dividend income is not earnings for pension purposes. There is also a cash flow impact since PAYE would no longer apply to such remuneration.

(b) **Rents** - a director owning a property used by a company could be paid rent instead of remuneration. Again the rental expense is a deductible business expense for the company and the income is not earnings for pension contribution purposes for the individual.

2.3 Employers must pay Class 1A NIC on benefits in kind. This means that, in general, the substitution of benefits for salary is not an NIC - efficient planning point unless the benefit is specifically NIC - free eg certain childcare provision for employees.

3 THE CHOICE OF A BUSINESS MEDIUM

3.1 When starting in business the first decision must be whether to trade as a company (with the entrepreneur as a director taxable under Schedule E) or as an unincorporated business, either as a sole trader or a partnership. Certain professions may not be practised through a limited company (although unlimited companies are often allowed), while other associations of more than 20 people are legally required to incorporate.

3.2 **The attraction of incorporation lies in the fact that a sole trader or a partner is liable for business debts to the full extent of his personal assets. A limited company's shareholder's liability is limited to the amount, if any, unpaid on his shares.** However, limited liability is often reduced by the demands of bankers or landlords for personal guarantees from company directors. In addition, compliance with the statutory obligations (eg annual returns, audit or compliance report, maintenance of registers, need to hold meetings etc) that apply to a company can be costly.

3.3 A company often finds raising finance easier than an unincorporated business. This is partly because of the misguided view that a company has greater reliability and permanence. A company can obtain equity finance through venture capital institutions and can borrow by giving a floating charge over its assets as security whereas a sole trader or partnership cannot do this.

A business may be seen as more reputable or creditworthy if conducted through the medium of a company.

Companies, however, have to comply with disclosure requirements and this may be unattractive to proprietors who wish to keep information from employees, potential competitors etc. This could be avoided by using an unlimited company but in that case any advantage of limited status is lost. The disclosure requirements could be reduced by filing abbreviated accounts.

The effect of marginal tax rates and national insurance

3.4 **A trader's profits whether retained or withdrawn are taxed at a marginal rate of 40% on taxable income in excess of £28,400. In addition Class 2 and Class 4 national insurance contributions are payable.** The maximum total contributions for 2000/01 are £104 (Class 2) + £1,641 (Class 4) = £1,745.

3.5 **A controlling director/shareholder can decide whether profits are to be paid out as remuneration or dividends, or retained in the company.**

3.6 If profits are retained, the consequent growth in asset values will increase the potential capital gain when shares are sold (although taper relief may reduce the amount of the taxable gain). Where remuneration is paid the total national insurance liability is greater than for the proprietor of an unincorporated business.

3.7 Where a spouse is employed his or her salary must be justifiable as 'wholly and exclusively for the purposes of the trade': the Revenue may seek to disallow excessive salary cost. On the other hand, a spouse as active partner can take any share in profits, provided that he or she is personally active in the business and there is evidence of a bona fide partnership. Thus the spouse's personal allowance and starting and basic rate bands can be used.

3.8 In choosing a business medium, we should also remember that a sole trader will be denied the enhanced state benefits, that are available to an employee who pays Class 1 national insurance contributions.

Question: Net income from a business

Alan, who is single, expects to make annual profits of £30,000 before tax and national insurance. Consider the fiscal effects of his choosing to trade as a sole trader or, alternatively, through a company, paying him a salary of £15,000 and then the largest possible dividend not giving rise to a loss of capital. Assume that accounting profits equal Schedule D Case I profits. Use 2000/01 tax rates.

Answer

As a sole trader	£
Profits	30,000
Less personal allowance	4,385
Taxable income	25,615

	£
Tax thereon at 10%/22%	5,453
National Insurance Classes 2 (52 × £2.00) and 4 (£(27,820 – 4,385) × 7%)	1,744
	7,197
Net income £(30,000 – 7,197)	£22,803

Through a company

	£	£
Profits		30,000
Less: salary		(15,000)
employer's NI 12.2% (£15,000 – £4,385)		(1,295)
Taxable profits		13,705
20% × £13,705	2,741	
Less starting rate marginal relief £ (50,000 – 13,705) × 1/40	(907)	
Less: corporation tax		(1,834)
Net profits		11,871

A dividend of £11,871 can be paid without loss of capital.

	Non-savings £	Dividends £	Total £
Schedule E	15,000		
Dividends £11,871 × 100/90		13,190	
STI	15,000	13,190	28,190
Less personal allowance	(4,385)		
Taxable income	10,615	13,190	23,805

Non-savings income	
£1,520 × 10%	152
£9,095 × 22%	2,001
Dividend income	
£13,190 × 10%	1,319
	3,472
Less tax suffered £13,190 × 10%	(1,319)
Income tax payable	2,153

Net income	£	£
Salary		15,000
Dividends		11,871
		26,871
Less: income tax	2,153	
Employee's NIC (£15,000 – £3, 952) × 10%	1,105	
		(3,258)
		23,613

Trading as a sole trader would give annual net income of £(22,803 – 23,613) = £810 less than trading through a company.

Benefits and expenses

3.9 **The restrictions on deducting Schedule E expenses may make self-employment rather more attractive than employment as a company director.** Although the same expense deduction rules apply to a company and a sole trader, the company's deductible business expenses may give rise to Schedule E taxable benefits for directors.

3.10 **On the other hand, the provision of fringe benefits can be an advantage of incorporation,** the major attraction perhaps being the company car (with the possibility of a second car for a director's spouse). Other benefits can be used to maximise directors' net spendable income, although care is required because not all benefits are tax-efficient.

Opening Years

3.11 Companies have no equivalent to the opening year rules that apply for income tax purposes. For a sole trader or partnership, profits earned when basis periods overlap are taxed twice. Relief is available for such overlap profits but that may not take place for many years, by which time inflation may have reduced the value of the relief for overlap profits.

3.12 **If a partnership is envisaged it may be worthwhile to commence trading with the prospective partner as a salaried employee for a year or so, thereby obtaining tax relief twice on his salary during the overlap period.**

Losses

3.13 **Losses in the first four years of an unincorporated business can be used to obtain tax repayments** (using s 381 claims) **and payments of interest on overpaid tax**. In these and later years a s 380 claim permits **relief for trading losses against other income** (and capital gains) of either or both of two tax years.

3.14 With corporation tax, although there is considerable flexibility for the company itself, **a company's losses are not available to reduce shareholders' taxable incomes**.

Capital gains tax

3.15 One difference between companies and individuals is that **companies do not benefit from an exemption from tax on the first £7,200 of total gains** (for 2000/01).

3.16 Chargeable gains of an individual are charged to capital gains tax at 10%, 20% or 40%. By contrast, companies' gains are charged at normal corporation tax rates (30% full rate, 20% small companies rate, 32.5% effective marginal rate or 10% starting rate with an effective marginal rate of 22.5%).

3.17 **The principal disadvantage of incorporation is the double charge to tax which arises when a company sells a chargeable asset. Firstly, the company may pay corporation tax on the chargeable gain. Secondly, the shareholders may be taxed when they attempt to realise those proceeds, either in the form of dividends or when the shares are sold, incurring a further charge on capital gains.**

3.18 If there are no tax advantages in the company owning an asset, the asset should be held outside the company, perhaps being leased to the company.

What if things go wrong?

3.19 Sound tax planning should always take account of possible changes in circumstances. A successful business may fail or a struggling concern may eventually become profitable.

3.20 Running down an unincorporated business does not normally give rise to serious problems. The proprietor may be able to cover any balancing charges with loss relief.

3.21 Taking a business out of a company (disincorporation), or winding up a corporate trade altogether is more complex and involves both tax and legal issues. Consider the following:

- No subsequent relief is available for a company's unused losses once the trade ceases.
- A double charge on capital gains may arise.

Tax cashflows

3.22 **Under self assessment a sole trader/partner is assessable to income tax and NIC (Class 4) on a current year basis but will use a prior year basis to calculate two payments on account** due on 31 January in and 31 July directly following the tax year. The balance of tax is due on 31 January following the tax year. Thus tax on profits earned in the year to 30 April 2000 (assessable 2000/01) will not be payable in full until 31 January 2002 and will be used to calculate payments on account due 31 January 2002 and 31 July 2002. **Where profits are rising this lag gives a considerable benefit**. In fact, where profits are falling reduced payments on account can be requested. A sole trader's/partner's drawings do not of themselves attract or accelerate a tax charge. Class 2 NIC is usually paid by direct debit monthly or billed quarterly in arrears but is fairly insignificant. The state benefits secured under Class 2 NIC are lower than under Class 1.

3.23 **A company pays CT nine months after the end of its accounts period.** Companies paying tax at the full rate are required to make **quarterly payments on account** based on the current year's estimated liability. As an employer it will have to account for **PAYE and NIC 14 days after the end of each tax month** in which the pay date falls.

3.24 **Generally therefore a business held by a company will bear tax earlier than a business held by a sole trader or partnership.**

4 THE INCORPORATION OF A BUSINESS

Why incorporate a business?

4.1 Advantages

(a) Retained profits subject only to corporation tax not income tax or NIC

(b) Easier to dispose of shares in a company than interest in a business - thus advantage for raising equity and selling to outside investors

(c) More generous pension provision can be made by employer (the company) for employees (eg: directors) than under the personal pensions scheme rules

(d) Benefits for employees can be more tax efficient

(e) Loan finance easier to arrange as lender can take out charge on company assets

(f) Limited liability for shareholders

(g) A company arguably has a more respectable image than a sole trader or partnership

(h) Incorporation is a means of converting the value of a business into shares which could be brought to the AIM or even achieve a full stock market quote. This provides for succession of ownership and can make the original proprietors very wealthy

4.2 Disadvantages

(a) Potential double capital gains charge on assets (see above)

(b) Trading losses restricted to set-off against corporate profits

(c) No carry back of trading losses in opening years (ie no s 381 equivalent)

(d) Partner's share of profit not openly challenged by Revenue provided the recipient is a genuine partner. Conversely excessive remuneration to employee/director can be challenged

(e) NIC for employer company and employee will generally exceed the contributions required of a self-employed person

(f) Paydays for tax on a company and its' employees (MCT, PAYE, NIC) are generally well in advance of paydays for self-employed.

(g) There may be statutory requirement of audit, keeping books, filing accounts etc

(h) Disclosure requirements of published accounts may give information to employees/ competitors that business owners would not have willingly disclosed.

Income tax

The choice of a date

4.3 When an unincorporated trade is transferred to a company the **trade is treated as discontinued for tax purposes and the cessation rules apply**. Careful consideration of the level of profit and date of transfer is required to avoid large taxable profits in one year from a basis period of more than 12 months. For example a trader with a 30 June year end will be assessed on 21 months of profit in his final year if he incorporates on 31 March whereas only 10 months of profit will be taxed in that final year if he delays incorporation to 30 April.

Capital allowances

4.4 On the transfer of a trade to a company **a balancing charge will usually arise as plant and machinery are treated as being sold at market value**. However, where the company is controlled by the transferor, **the two are connected and an election may be made so** as not to treat the transfer as a permanent discontinuance for capital allowances purposes. **Fixed assets are then transferred at their tax written down values**.

Trading losses

4.5 **Unrelieved trading losses** cannot be carried forward to a company as such, but **may be set against any income derived from the company** by way of dividends, remuneration and so on, provided the business is exchanged for shares and those shares are still held at the time the loss is set off. Terminal loss relief may also be available for the loss of the last twelve months of trading.

Capital gains tax

4.6 When the transfer takes place the **chargeable assets are deemed to be disposed of to the company at their open market values**. Capital gains tax liabilities are likely to arise, particularly on land and buildings and on goodwill. The gains will be reduced by business assets taper relief.

4.7 **If the whole business** (or the whole business other than cash) **is transferred to the company as a going concern in exchange for shares in the company, any chargeable gains (before taper relief) are rolled over,** reducing the base cost of the shares on a subsequent disposal. As no capital gains tax arises on death, the tax liability may never arise.

4.8 It may not be desirable for all the assets comprised in the business to be transferred to the company. **As an alternative,** an individual can **use gift relief** to transfer chargeable business assets to a company and **defer any gains by deducting them from the base costs of the assets** to the company.

Value added tax

4.9 **The transfer of assets will not be treated as a supply for VAT purposes** (called the Transfer of Going Concern (TOGC) relief) if all of the following conditions are satisfied.

(a) The assets are to be used by the company in the same kind of business (whether or not as part of an existing business) as that carried on by the transferor, the business being transferred as a going concern.

(b) If only part of the business is transferred, that part is capable of separate operation.

(c) If the transferor is a taxable person, the company is a taxable person when the transfer takes place or immediately becomes one as a result of the transfer.

4.10 An application may be made for the company to take over the existing VAT registration number. In this case the company will take over all the debts and liabilities of the business but it will be able to claim VAT bad debt relief in respect of supplies made before the transfer.

4.11 If the above conditions cannot be satisfied VAT will be charged on the transfer, but this will only represent a cash flow problem in most cases.

4.12 Customs should be notified of the incorporation within 30 days.

5 DISPOSAL OF A BUSINESS

5.1 A purchaser could acquire the business of a '**target**' company by either acquiring the 'target' company's assets or by acquiring the 'target' company's shares. The advantages/ disadvantages of each method of acquiring a business are listed below. If an unincorporated business is bought/sold, this must be done by a sale of assets.

5.2 **Advantages of buying assets**

(a) The purchaser can **choose which assets to acquire** rather than take the entire business

(b) The expenditure on plant and certain buildings will attract **capital allowances**

(c) The **capital gains base cost of the assets is the price paid** on acquisition. If shares are acquired the assets retain their original base cost

(d) There is some latitude to apportion the consideration over the assets acquired to best tax effect. For example plant attracts WDA at 25% but industrial buildings only 4% WDA

(e) For the purchaser who is already trading it might be possible to **argue that it is not a separate trade which is acquired but an extension of the existing trade**. This is **important where losses are being carried forward**

(f) **By acquiring assets, the liabilities** (including tax liabilities) whether known or unknown are **left behind** in the vendor company thus minimising the need for tax warranties and indemnities

5.3 **Advantages of buying shares**

(a) The **business continues uninterrupted**

(b) The 'target' company does not have to provide for tax on the profit from asset sales

(c) **Unused tax reliefs** of the 'target' company **are potentially available** for the 'target' company

(d) The **sale consideration is paid to the vendor shareholders** and not, as in the case of an asset sale, to the target company. The need to extract proceeds through a dividend or liquidation is thereby avoided

(e) **If the purchaser is a company**, a share purchase opens up the **group** tax advantages although it also increases the number of associated companies in the group by one.

(f) The vendors would be able to **defer capital gains tax if the deal was paper-for-paper**

5.4 The choice of the best method of sale is partly determined by:

(a) The **vendor might be prepared to accept a sale of assets by the target company if it can shelter the resulting gains and balancing charges with capital losses and trading losses** brought forward respectively. Alternatively can the gains be sheltered by group-wide roll-over or group capital losses?

(b) **If the purchaser cannot recover (or fully recover) VAT paid on acquiring the assets this may be unattractive.** VAT may not actually apply provided the business is transferred as a going concern and the assets are used by the transferee in the same kind of business as before. If only some of the assets are transferred the 'going concern' point may be uncertain and will result in problems between the parties.

Reorganisation prior to sale

5.5 **The target company may pay a dividend out of distributable profits** prior to sale. Individual vendors normally bear less tax if their consideration is in the form of dividends (25% of the net dividend) rather than capital (40% of the gain). A corporate shareholder pays no tax on a dividend but may pay up to 32.5% on a gain. Of course a gain may be reduced by indexation.

Consideration for the disposal

5.6 The **date of disposal is normally the date of exchange of contract,** except that, where there is a condition in the contract, it is the date the contract becomes unconditional.

Any shares element in the consideration will result in deferral of the gain if:

(a) The vendor is selling shares

(b) The purchaser is a company who issues shares or debentures to the vendor

(c) The purchaser owns or will own over 25% of ordinary share capital in the 'target' company, or there is a general offer to all shareholders in the 'target' company

(d) The exchange is for bona fide commercial reasons and not with the object of tax avoidance

In this case the vendor's base cost of the 'new' paper is cost of the original shares with indexation running as though the new shares has been acquired when the original shares were acquired.

Losses and other reliefs

5.7 **If the 'target' company has trading losses or capital losses it is important where possible not to waste them.**

5.8 The trading losses of the 'target' company can only be carried forward if the trade in which they arose continues. This carry forward is however denied if:

(a) Within a three year period there is both a change in ownership of the company and a major change in the nature of conduct of the company's trade

(b) There is a change in ownership of the company after the scale of activities has become small or negligible before it revives

Capital losses of the target can be carried forward even if there is a change in ownership of the company.

5.9 The trading losses of the 'target' company are not automatically transferred with the trade.

Capital allowances will be available on plant at 25% WDA on consideration. Industrial buildings allowances may be available on industrial buildings acquired.

Tax warranties and indemnities

5.10 Tax warranties and indemnities are only really necessary on a purchase of shares. **Warranties** are express undertakings that the company and in certain circumstances the vendor have fulfilled or will fulfil specific conditions. **Indemnities** are covenants by the vendor indemnifying the purchaser against depletion of the net assets, in consequence of specific claims against the company

6 DIRECTORS AND SHAREHOLDERS

The decision whether to pay dividends or remuneration

6.1 Payments of dividends or remuneration will reduce a company's retained profits which means a reduction in net asset value and hence the value of the shares, ultimately reducing any chargeable gain on the disposal of those shares. However, the immediate tax cost of paying dividends or remuneration must be weighed against this advantage.

6.2 **Remuneration and the cost of benefits will be allowed as deductions in computing the company's profits chargeable to corporation tax.** The decision whether or not to make such payments could affect the rate of corporation tax by reducing the level of profits. However, **the national insurance cost must also be borne in mind.** A combination of dividends and remuneration may give the best result.

Question: Dividends and remuneration

A Ltd makes a profit before remuneration of £15,000 in the year to 31 March 2001. The shareholder/director is entitled to only the personal allowance. Consider the director's disposable income available by paying out the profit entirely as salary (of £13,846) or by paying it out as a mixture of salary (at £5,000, so that a low amount of national insurance contributions are payable to thus entitle the director to benefits) and dividends.

Answer

		Salary only £	Salary and dividend £
(a)	**The company's tax position**		
	Profits	15,000	15,000
	Less: salary	(13,846)	(5,000)
	employer's national insurance	(1,154)	(75)
	Taxable profits	0	9,925
	Corporation tax at 10%		£993
	Cash dividend £(9,925 – 993)		£8,932

(b) **The director's tax position**

	Non-savings £	Dividend £	Total £
Salary only			
Schedule E	13,846		
Less personal allowance	(4,385)		
Taxable income	9,461		9,461
Salary and dividends			
Schedule E	5,000		
Dividends (× 100/90)		9,924	
Less personal allowance	(4,385)		
	615	9,924	10,539

	Salary only £	Salary and dividend £
Non-savings income		
£1,520/£615 × 10%	152	62
£7,941 × 22%	1,747	-
Dividend income £9,924 × 10%		992
Less tax credit on dividend		(992)
Tax payable	1,899	62
Disposable income	£	£
Salary	13,846	5,000
Less employee's national insurance	(989)	(105)
Dividend		8,932
Tax (payable)	(1,899)	(62)
	10,958	13,765

The overall saving through paying a dividend is £(13,765 – 10,958) = £2,807.

6.3 Remuneration and benefits give rise to an entitlement to pay personal pension premiums, whereas dividends do not.

The timing of dividend payments

6.4 If dividends are paid, timing can be important.

(a) The tax year in which a dividend is paid affects the due date for any additional tax, and if a shareholder's other income fluctuates it may determine whether or not there is any additional tax to pay.

(b) The tax credit attaching to dividends is 10%. However the different rates of tax to apply to dividend income for individual shareholders will ensure such people will not pay more tax on such income compared with other forms of savings income. However, the tax credit attaching to dividends cannot be repaid. Thus taxpayers with no or low income will not have the tax credit refunded to them from dividend income.

BPP PUBLISHING

Chapter roundup

- As a general rule, self-employment leads to lower overall tax and NIC burdens than employment. If someone is to be an employee, the tax effects of the remuneration package should be taken into account.

- An entrepreneur must choose between trading as a sole trader and trading through a company. The choice, and if a company is chosen, the choice between dividends and remuneration, can significantly affect the overall tax and NIC burden. Cashflow is also an important consideration.

- The incorporation of a business should be carefully planned, taking account of consequent tax liabilities. There are both advantages and disadvantages to incorporating a business. A disposal of shares can also have several tax consequences.

- Structuring the sale/purchase of a business correctly can have major tax saving opportunities.

- For director/shareholders the decision whether to pay dividends or remuneration is a major planning consideration.

Quick quiz

1   What are the main differences between the tax positions of employees and the self employed? (see para 1.1)

2   What is a major attraction of incorporation? (3.2)

3   Why might a trader employ a prospective partner at first, before forming a partnership? (3.12)

4   What are the advantages of an unincorporated business where opening year losses are anticipated? (3.13, 3.14)

5   How may a double tax charge on capital gains arise with an incorporated business? (3.17)

6   What are the positive and negative consequences of incorporation? (4.1 - 4.2)

7   What are the advantages of buying the assets of a target business? (5.2)

8   What impact does the choice of dividend versus bonus payments to directors have on a company's profits? (6.1, 6.2)

Now try the question below from the Exam Question Bank

Number	Level	Marks	Time
30	Exam	15	27 mins

Exam question and answer bank

1   TREE LTD   *36 mins*

(a)   Tree Ltd, a company with no associated companies, had the following results for the eighteen months to 31 December 2000:

	£
Trading profits	180,000
Chargeable gain - realised 1.6.00	172,000
Gift aid donation - paid 30.9.00	5,000
Gift aid donation - paid 30.9.99	22,000
Schedule D Case III	36,000
Dividend received 30.3.00	27,000

The Schedule D Case III income accrued evenly over the period

Required

Compute the corporation tax liability in respect of the profits arising in the eighteen months to 31 December 2000.   (14 marks)

(b)   Dealers plc had profits chargeable to corporation tax of £420,000 for its year ended 31 December 2000.

Required

Compute Dealers plc's mainstream corporation tax liability for the year.   (3 marks)

(c)   Springer had profits chargeable to corporation tax of £6,200 in the year to 31 December 2000.

Required

Calculate Springer Ltd's mainstream corporation tax liability for the year.   (3 marks)

(Total 20 marks)

2   TRADERS LTD   *22 mins*

Traders Ltd's profit and loss account for the year to 31 March 2001 was as follows.

	£		£
General expenses	73,611	Gross trading profit	246,250
Repairs and renewals	15,000	Bad debts recovered	
Legal and accountancy charges	1,200	(previously written off)	373
Subscriptions and donations	2,000	Commissions	800
Bad debts written off	500	Profit on sale of investment	5,265
Directors' remuneration	20,000	Interest on gilts (net, received 1	
Salaries and wages	18,000	December)	80
Patent royalties (gross)	5,000	Loan interest (gross)	1,000
Depreciation	15,000		
Rent and rates	1,500		
Net profit	101,957		
	253,768		253,768

Notes

(i)   *General expenses include the following.*

	£
Travelling expenses of staff, including directors	1,000
Entertaining suppliers	600

(ii)   *Repairs and renewals include the following.*

	£
Redecorating existing premises	300
Renovations to new premises to remedy wear and tear of previous owner (the premises were usable before these renovations)	500

(iii) *Legal and accountancy charges are made up as follows.*

	£
Debt collection service	200
Staff service agreements	50
Tax consultant's fees for special advice	30
45 year lease on new premises	100
Audit and accountancy	820
	1,200

(iv) *Subscriptions and donations include the following.*

	£
Donations under the gift aid scheme	200
Donation to a political party	500
Sports facilities for staff	500
Contribution to a local enterprise agency	200

(v) The commissions received were not incidental to the trade.

(vi) The chargeable gain arising on the sale of investments was £770.

(vii) All interest received was on investments made for non-trading purposes. The amounts received were the same as the amounts accrued in the year.

Required

Compute Traders Ltd's profits chargeable to corporation tax for the accounting period to 31 March 2001, and the corporation tax liability thereon. **(12 marks)**

3 HARDY LTD

20 mins

Hardy Ltd, makes accounts to 30 June. Despite substantial investment in new equipment, business has been indifferent and the company will cease trading on 31 December 2000. Its last accounts will be prepared for the six months to 31 December 2000.

The tax written down value of fixed assets at 1 July 1996 was as follows.

Pool	£
General	23,400
Cars	6,300

Fixed asset additions and disposals have been as follows.

		£
20.9.96	Plant cost	2,300
25.9.96	Computer cost	4,400
15.7.98	Car for managing director's use cost	13,400
14.7.99	Plant sold for	340
10.5.00	Computer sold for	2,000

An election to depool the computer was made when it was acquired in 1996. Private use of the managing director's car was agreed at 20% for all years.

At the end of 2000, the plant would be worth £20,000, the managing director's car £10,600 and the other cars £4,000.

Required

Calculate the capital allowances for the periods from 1 July 1996 to 31 December 2000. **(10 marks)**

4 CUCKOLD LTD

29 mins

(a) Cuckold Ltd makes up accounts to 31 March each year. It is considering the purchase of an additional, secondhand factory on 1 April 2001. It has decided to spend £150,000 and the following details refer to four possible factories which could each be acquired for that sum. All are equally suitable for Cuckold Ltd's purposes and all have been used for qualifying industrial purposes throughout their lives.

	Original cost to first owner £	Date of first use
(i)	100,000	31 March 1977
(ii)	80,000	31 March 1976
(iii)	160,000	31 March 1999
(iv)	120,000	31 March 1993

Required

Advise Cuckold Ltd of the amount of industrial buildings allowances which would be available as a result of purchasing each of the above factories, indicating the periods for which the allowances would be available. Which building would you advise it to purchase? (10 marks)

(b) Having acquired a factory Cuckold Ltd intends to incur further capital expenditure on the following items.

(i) Installation of display lighting in a showroom where customers will view his products
(ii) Thermal insulation of the factory
(iii) Construction of a canteen, within the factory premises, for the use of the workforce

Required

Advise Cuckold Ltd of the extent to which capital allowances would be available in respect of the above items of expenditure. Cuckold Ltd is a small or medium sized enterprise for FYA purposes. (6 marks)

(Total 16 marks)

5 **SCHEDULE A** *20 mins*

P Ltd starts to let out property on 1 July 2000. The company has the following transactions.

(a) On 1 July 2000, it lets an office block which it has owned for several years. The tenant is required to pay an initial premium of £20,000 for a 30 year lease, and then to pay annual rent of £4,000, quarterly in advance. The office is let unfurnished.

(b) On 1 October 2000 it buys a badly dilapidated office block for £37,000. During October, it spends £8,000 on making the office habitable. It lets it furnished for £600 a month from 1 November 2000, but the tenant leaves on 31 January 2001. A new tenant moves in on 1 March 2001, paying £2,100 a quarter in arrears. Water rates are £390 a year, payable by P Ltd. P Ltd also pays buildings insurance of £440 for the period from 1 October 2000 to 31 August 2001. P Ltd financed the purchase (but not the repairs) with a bank loan at 15% interest. P Ltd decides to claim the renewals basis. It replaces some furniture on 1 May 2001, at a cost of £350. The tenant is responsible for all repair costs and council tax.

Required

Compute P Ltd's Schedule A income for the year to 31.3.01. **(11 marks)**

6 **GAINS AND LOSSES** *9 mins*

E Ltd disposed of assets as follows.

(a) On 1 January 2000 it sold a car which had been used by a company director at a loss of £10,700.

(b) On 28 February 2000 it sold some shares at a loss of £16,400.

(c) On 1 May 2000 it sold some shares and realised a gain of £7,200.

(d) On 1 October 2000 it sold some shares at a loss of £2,000.

(e) On 1 December 2000 it sold a picture to a collector for £50,000, making a gain of £3,000.

Required

What loss, if any, is available to be carried forward at the end of its year ended 31 March 2001. **(5 marks)**

7 HARDUP LTD

27 mins

Hardup Ltd made the following disposals in the year ended 31 March 2001. All disposals were to unconnected persons except where otherwise stated.

(a) On 12 May 2000 it sold an office block for £120,000. The company had bought the offices for £65,000 on 1 July 1988.

(b) On 18 June 2000 it sold a plot of land for £69,000. It had bought it for £20,000 on 1 April 1982 and had spent £4,000 on defending its title to the land in July 1985.

(c) On 25 June 2000 the company exchanged contracts for the sale of a workshop for £173,000. Completion took place on 24 July 2000. It had bought the workshop for £65,000 on 16 October 1983.

Required

Compute Hardup Ltd's capital gains for the year end 31.3.01. **(15 marks)**

8 FERRARO LTD

18 mins

Ferraro Ltd has the following results.

	y/e 31.12.96 £	y/e 31.12.97 £	9m to 30.9.98 £	y/e 30.9.99 £	y/e 30.9.00 £
Trading profit (loss)	10,000	34,480	6,200	4,320	(100,000)
Bank deposit interest accrued	100	200	80	240	260
Rents receivable	3,000	1,200	1,420	1,440	1,600
Capital gain				12,680	
Allowable capital loss		5,000			9,423
Patent royalties (gross)	1,000	1,000	0	1,000	1,500

Required

Compute all profits chargeable to corporation tax, claiming loss reliefs as early as possible. State any amounts carried forward as at 30 September 2000. **(10 marks)**

9 H, S AND N

36 mins

H Ltd has owned 60% of the issued ordinary share capital of S Ltd since its incorporation, the remaining 40% being held by Mr S. Both companies have always prepared accounts to 30 June, their most recent accounts showing the following.

	H Ltd Year ended 30.6.99 £	H Ltd Year ended 30.6.00 £	S Ltd Year ended 30.6.99 £	S Ltd Year ended 30.6.00 £
Adjusted trading profit	2,000		30,000	100,000
Adjusted trading loss		(48,000)		
Charges paid (gross)			12,000	12,000

On 1 January 1999, H Ltd acquired 80% of the issued ordinary share capital of N Ltd, a company which had always prepared accounts to 31 December.

N Ltd's accounts for the period of 1 January 1999 to 30 June 2000 show the following.

	£
Adjusted trading profit, before capital allowances	65,250
Chargeable gain, after indexation allowance on land bought in 1981 and sold in February 2000	20,000

N Ltd had a written down value on plant at 1 January 1999 of £5,000 and had incurred expenditure as follows.

		£
3 February 1999:	new car to be used by the managing director of N Ltd 80% for business, 20% for private use	16,000
4 January 2000:	new plant	31,000
20 March 2000:	secondhand plant bought on hire purchase, the cash price being £8,000, a deposit of £2,000 being paid on the above date followed by 24 monthly instalments of £300, commencing 20 May 2000.	

No dividends were paid or received.

Required

Compute the mainstream corporation tax payable by H Ltd, S Ltd and N Ltd for the above periods of account, assuming all available claims and surrenders are made to minimise the mainstream corporation tax payable by the group. **(20 marks)**

10 **APPLE LTD (PILOT PAPER)** *27 mins*

Apple Ltd owns 100% of the ordinary share capital of Banana Ltd and Cherry Ltd. The results of each company for the year ended 31 March 2001 are as follows:

	Apple Ltd	*Banana Ltd*	*Cherry Ltd*
	£	£	£
Tax adjusted Schedule DI profit/(loss)	(125,000)	650,000	130,000
Capital gain/(loss)	180,000	(8,000)	-

Apple Ltd's capital gain arose from the sale of a freehold warehouse on 15 April 2000 for £410,000. Cherry Ltd purchased a freehold office building for £290,000 on 10 January 2001.

Required

(a) Explain the group relationship that must exist in order that group relief can be claimed. (3 marks)

(b) Explain how group relief should be allocated between the respective claimant companies in order to maximise the potential benefit obtained from the relief. (4 marks)

(c) Assuming that reliefs are claimed in the most favourable manner, calculate the corporation tax liabilities of Apple Ltd, Banana Ltd and Cherry Ltd for the year ended 31 March 2001.

You should ignore the election that allows companies in a capital gains group to choose which company is treated as making a disposal. (8 marks)

(Total 15 marks)

11 **M LTD** *29 mins*

M Ltd is a UK resident company which owns controlling interests in two other UK resident companies and in two non-resident companies.

It also has the following interests in three non-resident companies:

Company	Shareholding	Rate of Withholding tax	Profits post tax y/e 31.03.01	Foreign tax paid
	%	%	£	£
A Inc	6	15	400,000	80,000
B P G	8	25	900,000	300,000
C S A	12	20	800,000	200,000

M Ltd had experienced a prolonged period of poor trading and, as a result of losses brought forward from earlier years, its chargeable Schedule DI income for the year ended 31 March 2001 is only £20,000.

During the year, patent royalties of £75,000 (gross) had been paid and these had been added back in arriving at the adjusted Schedule DI income.

The only other income received by M Ltd during the year consisted of dividends from the above three companies, each of which had substantial undistributed profits. The figures (net of withholding tax) were:

	£	Date received
A Inc	170,000	1.6.00
B P G	150,000	10.9.00
C S A	120,000	31.12.00

Required

Compute the MCT payable by M Ltd in respect of the year ended 31 March 2001. Your answer should show clearly your treatment of the patent royalties payment and of the foreign taxes suffered. You should explain why you are dealing with items in a particular way and you should use a columnar layout. **(16 marks)**

12   HOGG LTD AND BARNETT LTD   *35 mins*

(a)   Hogg Ltd prepares accounts for the year to 31 December 2000. In June 2000 it estimates that its corporation tax liability for the year will be £500,000. In January 2001 it revises its estimate to £520,000. In July 2001 it submits its return and self-assessment, showing a total liability of £525,000. The company has always paid corporation tax at the full rate.

Required

State the amounts and due dates for the payment of corporation tax by Hogg Ltd in respect of the year to 31 December 2000. (7 marks)

(b)   In 2005 Hogg Ltd changes its accounting date to 31 October 2005. Assume that the liability for the ten months to 31 October 2005 is expected to be £600,000.

Required

state the due dates for and the amount of instalments of corporation tax that Hog Ltd will be required to pay in respect of this period. (6 marks)

(c)   Barnett Ltd, a UK trading company, was formed in 1992 with the following capital structure which has remained unchanged since that date.

	£
£1 ordinary shares issued at par	256,000
50 pence 10% preference shares	80,000
12% debentures 2001/05	100,000

During the year to 31 March 2001, the following transactions occurred. The amounts stated are the actual cash amounts paid or received.

Payments
15 April	Six months' debentures interest to 31 March 2000
16 October	Six months' debenture interest to 30 September 2000
31 March	£425 patent royalty

Receipts
20 May	£1,000 bank deposit interest
15 June	£3,404 patent royalties
16 February	£11,062 patent royalties

Required

Schedule the details to be included on form CT 61 (quarterly returns) for all relevant periods, stating the due dates of payment where applicable and how any balances outstanding at 31 March 2001 would be dealt with. (8 marks)

(Total 21 marks)

13   INDUSTRIAL LTD (PILOT PAPER)   *54 mins*

Industrial Ltd is a UK resident company that manufactures furniture. The company's results for the year ended 31 March 2001 are summarised as follows:

	£
Trading profit (as adjusted for taxation but before taking account of capital allowances)	1,689,710
Income from property (note 1)	110,400
Bank interest received (note 2)	12,500
Loan interest received (note 3)	36,000
Profit on disposal of shares (note 4)	87,200
Patent royalties payable (note 5)	(12,000)
Donation to charity (note 6)	(2,000)

Note 1 – Income from property

Since 1 January 2001 Industrial Ltd has leased an office building that is surplus to requirements. On that date the company received a premium of £80,000 for the grant of a ten-year lease, and the annual rent of £30,400 which is payable in advance.

Note 2 – Bank interest received

The bank interest was received on 31 March 2001. The bank deposits are held for non-trading purposes.

Note 3 – Loan interest received

The loan interest was received on 31 March 2001. The figure of £36,000 is gross, and income tax has been deducted at source. The loan was made for non-trading purposes.

Note 4 – Profit on disposal of shares

The profit on disposal of shares is in respect of a shareholding that was sold on 15 January 2001 for £223,000. The shareholding was purchased on 1 April 1994 for £135,800. The indexation allowance from April 1994 to April 1998 is £17,300, and from April 1994 to January 2001 it is £24,200.

At 1 April 2000 Industrial Ltd had unused capital losses brought forward of £6,800.

Note 5 – Patent royalties payable

The figure for patent royalties payable is calculated as follows:

	£
Payments made	11,500
Accrued at 31 March 2001	2,000
	13,500
Accrued at 1 April 2000	1,500
	12,000

The above figures are all gross. Income tax has been deducted from the payments.

Note 6 – Donation to charity

The donation to charity was made under the Gift Aid Scheme.

Note 7 – Industrial building

Industrial Ltd has a new factory constructed at a cost of £400,000 that was brought into use on 30 September 2000.

	£
Land	80,000
Levelling the land	9,200
Architects fees	24,300
Heating system	12,800
Fire alarm system	7,200
Strengthened concrete floor to support machinery	16,500
General offices	62,500
Factory	187,500
	400,000

Note 8 – Plant and machinery

On 1 April 2000 the tax written down values of plant and machinery were as follows:

	£
General pool	84,600
Expensive motor car	15,400

The expensive motor car was sold on 31 August 2000 for £19,600.

In addition to any items of plant and machinery included in the cost of the industrial building (see note 7), the following assets were purchased during the year ended 31 March 2001.

		£
15 June 2000	Computer	3,400
15 August 2000	Motor car	17,200
12 October 2000	Lorry	32,000

Industrial Ltd is a medium-sized company as defined by the Companies Acts.

Note 9 – Other information

Industrial Ltd has no associated companies. For the year ended 31 March 2000 Industrial Ltd has profits chargeable to corporation tax of £1,650,000.

Required

(a) Calculate the corporation tax payable by Industrial Ltd for the year ended 31 March 2001.

(25 marks)

(b) (i) Explain why Industrial Ltd is required to make quarterly instalment payments in respect of its corporation tax liability for the year ended 31 March 2001. (2 marks)

 (ii) State the relevant due dates for payment of the corporation tax liability. (3 marks)

(Total 30 marks)

---

14 **INVOICES, THE TAX POINT AND RETURNS** *22 mins*

Write brief notes on:

(a) VAT invoices; (4 marks)
(b) the tax point; (4 marks)
(c) VAT returns. (4 marks)

---

15 **JUSTIN** *18 mins*

Justin has the following transactions in the quarter ended 30 June 2000. All amounts exclude any VAT.

	£
Purchases	
Furniture for resale	275,000
Computer for use in the business	2,400
Restaurant bills: entertaining customers	1,900
Petrol for cars owned by Justin and used only by his employees	2,800
Sales	
Furniture	490,000
Books on interior design	2,400

Only one employee's car has petrol for private motoring provided by Justin. That car's cylinder capacity is 2,400 cc.

Required

Calculate the amount of VAT which Justin must pay to HM Customs & Excise for the quarter.

(10 marks)

16 NEWCOMER LTD, ONGOING LTD AND AU REVOIR LTD (PILOT PAPER)   *27 mins*

(a) Newcomer Ltd commenced trading on 1 October 2000. Its forecast sales are as follows.

		£
2000	October	9,500
	November	14,200
	December	21,400
2001	January	12,300
	February	14,700
	March	15,200

The company's sales are all standard rated, and the above figures are exclusive of VAT.

Required

Explain when Newcomer Ltd will be required to compulsorily register for VAT.   (4 marks)

(b) Ongoing Ltd is registered for VAT, and its sales are all standard rated. The following information relates to the company's VAT return for the quarter ended 30 September 2000:

(1) Standard rated sales amounted to £120,000. Ongoing Ltd offers its customers a 5% discount for prompt payment, and this discount is taken by half of the customers.

(2) Standard rated purchases and expenses amounted to £35,640. This figure includes £480 for entertaining customers.

(3) On 15 September 2000 the company wrote off bad debts of £2,000 and £840 in respect of invoices due for payment on 10 February and 5 May 2000 respectively.

(4) On 30 September 2000 the company purchased a motor car at a cost of £16,450 for the use of a salesperson, and machinery at a cost of £21,150. Both these figures are inclusive of VAT. The motor car is used for both business and private mileage.

Unless stated otherwise, all of the above figures are exclusive of VAT. Ongoing Ltd does not operate the cash accounting scheme.

Required

Calculate the amount of VAT payable by Ongoing Ltd for the quarter ended 30 September 2000.
(8 marks)

(c) Au Revoir Ltd has been registered for VAT since 1990, and its sales are all standard rated. The company has recently seen a downturn in its business activities, and sales for the years ended 31 October 2000 and 2001 are forecast to be £55,000 and £47,500 respectively. Both of these figures are exclusive of VAT.

Required

Explain why Au Revoir Ltd will be permitted to voluntarily deregister for VAT, and from what date registration will be effective.   (3 marks)
(Total 15 marks)

17 INCOME TAX   *13 mins*

Mary, a single 24 year old, has business profits of £14,000. She also receives building society interest of £6,400 net, dividends of £1,800 (net), and pays a charge of £2,500 (gross) each year. How much cash will she have available to spend in 2000/01? Ignore national insurance.

(7 marks)

18 MR AND MRS LOWRIE   *18 mins*

John Lowrie and Helen Lowrie who are both in their thirties are a married couple. Mr and Mrs Lowrie received the following income in 2000/01.

	Mr Lowrie £	Mrs Lowrie £
Salary (gross)	36,000	20,000
PAYE tax deducted	6,000	2,611
Dividends (amount received)	1,090	2,538
Bank deposit interest (amount received)	200	76
Building society interest (amount received)	143	420

BPP PUBLISHING

Required

Compute the net tax payable by Mr Lowrie and by Mrs Lowrie for 2000/01. **(10 marks)**

19 MR COBBLER

27 mins

Mr Cobbler starts a business as a sole trader on 1 January 2000.

His business plan shows that his monthly profits are likely to be as follows.

January 2000 to June 2000 (inclusive)	£800	a month
July 2000 to December 2000 (inclusive)	£1,200	a month
Thereafter	£2,000	a month

Mr Cobbler is considering two alternative accounting dates, 31 March and 30 April, in each case commencing with a period ending in 2000.

Required

Show the Schedule D Case I profits which will arise for each of the first four tax years under each of the two alternative accounting dates, and recommend an accounting date. **(15 marks)**

20 MISS FARRINGTON

22 mins

Miss Farrington started to trade as a baker on 1 January 1998 and made up her first accounts to 30 April 1999. Adjusted profits before capital allowances are as follows.

	£
Period to 30 April 1999	16,000
Year to 30 April 2000	13,400

Miss Farrington incurred the following expenditure on plant and machinery.

Date	Item	£
4.1.98	General plant	5,475
1.3.98	Secondhand oven acquired from	
	Miss Farrington's father	1,200
25.3.98	Delivery van	1,800
15.4.98	Typewriter	425
15.5.98	Car for Miss Farrington	2,600
1.1.00	General plant	1,000
30.4.00	Computer	778

In addition Miss Farrington brought into the business on 1 January 1998 a desk and other office furniture. The agreed value was £940.

The agreed private use of the car is 35%.

Required

Calculate the taxable profits for the first four tax years and the overlap profits carried forward.

(12 marks)

21 MORGAN

27 mins

Morgan started to trade on 6 April 1997. His business has the following results.

Year ending 5 April		£
1998	Profit	12,000
1999	Profit	16,000
2000	Profit	18,000
2001 (projected)	Profit	15,000
2002 (projected)	Loss	(32,000)

It is expected that the business will show healthy profits thereafter. In addition to his business Morgan has gross investment income of £8,000 a year.

Required

(a) Outline the ways in which Morgan could obtain relief for his loss. (5 marks)

(b) Prepare a statement showing how the loss would be relieved assuming that relief were to be claimed as soon as possible. Comment on whether this is likely to be the best relief (5 marks)

(c) Describe briefly how the situation would alter if Morgan were to cease trading on 5 April 2002.

(5 marks)

(Total 15 marks)

22 ADAM, BERT AND CHARLIE

22 mins

Adam, Bert and Charlie started in partnership as secondhand car dealers on 6 April 1997, sharing profits in the ratio 2:2:1, after charging annual salaries of £1,500, £1,200 and £1,000 respectively.

On 5 July 1998 Adam retired and Bert and Charlie continued, taking the same salaries as before, but dividing the balance of the profits in the ratio 3:2.

On 6 May 2000 Dick was admitted as a partner on the terms that he received a salary of £1,800 a year, that the salaries of Bert and Charlie should be increased to £1,800 a year each and that of the balance of the profits, Dick should take one tenth and Bert and Charlie should divide the remainder in the ratio 3:2.

The profits of the partnership as adjusted for tax purposes were as follows.

Year ending 5 April	Profits
	£
1998	10,200
1999	20,800
2000	12,600
2001	18,000

Required

Show the taxable profits for each partner for 1997/98 to 2000/2001 inclusive. **(12 marks)**

23 PARTNERSHIPS (PILOT PAPER)

27 mins

(a) *Required*

Briefly explain the basis by which partners are assessed in respect of their share of a partnership's Schedule DI or DII profit. (3 marks)

(b) Anne and Betty have been in partnership since 1 January 1995 sharing profits equally. On 30 June 2000 Betty resigned as a partner, and was replaced on 1 July 2000 by Chloe. Profit continued to be shared equally. The partnership's Schedule DI profits are as follows:

	£
Year ended 31 December 2000	60,000
Year ended 31 December 2001	72,000

As at 6 April 2000 Anne and Betty each have unrelieved overlap profits of £3,000.

Required

Calculate the Schedule DI assessments of Anne, Betty and Chloe for 2000/01. (6 marks)

(c) Daniel and Edward have been in partnership since 6 April 1995, making up accounts to 5 April. On 31 December 2000 Edward resigned as a partner, and was replaced on 1 January 2001 by Frank. For 2000/01 the partnership made a Schedule DII loss of £40,000, and this has been allocated between the partners as follows.

	£
Daniel	20,000
Edward	15,000
Frank	5,000

Each of the partners has investment income. None of them have any capital gains.

Required

State the possible ways in which Daniel, Edward and Frank can relieve their Schedule DII trading losses for 2000/01. (6 marks)

(Total 15 Marks)

24 DENISE

Denise started in business on 6 April 1999 as a designer dress maker, having been a housewife for many years. Her Schedule D Case I profits have been:

| 1999/00 | £25,000 |
| 2000/01 | £100,000 |

She was born on 27 March 1964 and has made no pension provision.

Required:

(a) Calculate the maximum personal pension contribution that Denise can make in respect of the years 1999/00 and 2000/01, showing all your workings. (4 marks)

(b) Show the Class 2 and Class 4 contributions payable by Denise in 1999/00 and 2000/01. Use the rates for 2000/01 throughout. (3 marks)

(Total 7 marks)

25 SUSAN WHITE (PILOT PAPER) *27 mins*

Susan White disposed of the following assets during 2000/01.

1 On 15 July 2000 Susan sold 20,000 £1 ordinary shares in Red Ltd for £55,000. Susan bought 25,000 shares in the company on 2 June 1999 for £37,500. She bought a further 5,000 shares on 18 July 2000 for £15,000.

2 On 25 August 2000 Susan sold 50,000 £1 ordinary shares in Blue Ltd to her son for £70,000. The market value of the shares on this date was £200,000. The shareholding was purchased on 15 April 1985 for £18,000, and the indexation allowance from April 1985 to April 1998 is £12,800. Susan and her son are to elect to hold over the gain as a gift of a business asset.

Red Ltd and Blue Ltd are unquoted trading companies. Susan's shareholding in each company qualifies as a business asset for the purposes of CGT taper relief.

Required

(a) Describe the types of shareholding that qualify as a business asset for the purposes of CGT taper relief. (4 marks)

(b) Calculate the capital gains arising from Susan's disposal during 2000/01. You should ignore the annual exemption. (11 marks)

(Total 15 marks)

26 TIM *15 mins*

Tim is a medical consultant. His total tax liability for 1999/00 was £16,800. Of this £7,200 was paid under the PAYE system, £800 was withheld at source from bank interest and £200 was suffered on dividends received during the year.

Tim's total tax liability for 2000/01 was £22,000. £7,100 of this was paid under PAYE system, £900 was withheld at source from bank interest and there was a £250 tax credit on dividends.

Tim did not make any claim in respect of his payments on account for 2000/01. The Revenue issued a 2000/01 tax return to Tim on 5 May 2001.

Required

State what payments Tim was required to make in respect of his 2000/01 tax liability and the due dates for the payment of these amounts. **(8 marks)**

27 EMPLOYMENT AND SELF-EMPLOYMENT *20 mins*

Required

Discuss the factors to be taken into consideration when deciding whether a person is employed or self employed for the purposes of income tax. **(11 marks)**

28   CARS AND LOANS   *25 mins*

The following items have been provided by a UK company to employees earning more than £8,500 a year.

(a)   A loan of £16,000 at 5% a year to Mr Andrews on 6 October 2000 which has been used to improve his private residence.

(b)   A £1,000 interest free loan to Mrs Preece on 6 April 2000 which was used to finance her daughter's wedding.

(c)   The loan of a TV and video system to Mr Charles from 6 June 2000, the asset having cost the company £800 in 1997 and having had a market value of £500 in June 2000.

(d)   A long service award in December 2000 to Mrs Davies, the company secretary, comprising a gold wrist watch costing £400. Mrs Davies has been employed by the company since December 1975.

(e)   The loan of a 2,500 cc petrol engined BMW motor car to Mr Edgar from 6 April 2000. The company had acquired the car new on 1 August 1997 at a cost of £23,000 and its market value in April 2000 was estimated to be £15,000. Mr Edgar's total mileage for 2000/01 was 30,000 miles of which 30% related to private motoring. The company pays all running costs, including fuel.

(f)   The exclusive private use of a company flat in central London, by Mr Ford, the managing director. The company acquired the flat in February 1998 for £100,000 and Mr Ford has used it since that date. The flat is fully furnished at a cost of £5,000 and the council tax paid by the company amounted to £500. The rateable value is £900. The running costs of the flat amounting to £1,200 for 2000/01 were paid directly by Mr Ford.

Required

State in detail how each of the above items would be treated for the purpose of Schedule E for 2000/01, computing the amount of any taxable benefit.   **(14 marks)**

Assume an official rate of interest of 10%.

29   LAI CHAN (PILOT PAPER)   *45 mins*

Until 31 December 2000 Lai Chan was employed by Put-it-Right plc as a management consultant. The following information relates to the period of employment from 6 April to 31 December 2000.

(1)   Lai was paid a gross salary of £3,250 per month.

(2)   She contributed 6% of her gross salary into Put-it-right plc's Inland Revenue approved occupational pension scheme. The company contributed a further 6%.

(3)   Put-it-Right plc provided Lai with a 2600 cc motor car with a list price of £26,400. The motor car was first registered on 1 January 1995. During 2000/01 Lai drove 19,000 miles, of which 2,100 were for business purposes. Lai paid Put-it-Right plc £130 per month for the use of the motor car.

       Put-it-Right plc paid for the petrol in respect of all the mileage done by Lai during 2000/01. She paid the company £30 per month towards the cost of her private petrol.

       The motor car was returned to Put-it-Right plc on 31 December 2000.

(4)   Put-it-Right plc provided Lai with an interest free loan of £30,000 on 1 January 1997. She repaid £20,000 of the loan on 30 June 2000 with the balance of £10,000 being repaid on 31 December 2000. The loan was not used for a qualifying purposes.

On 1 January 2001 Lai commenced in self-employment running a music recording studio. The following information relates to the period of self-employment from 1 January to 5 April 2001.

(1)   The Schedule DII profit for the period 1 January to 5 April 2001 is £21,400. This figure is *before* taking account of capital allowances.

(2)   Lai purchased the following assets:

1 January 2001	Recording equipment	£9,300
15 January 2001	Motor car	£14,800
20 February 2001	Motor car	£10,400
4 March 2001	Recording equipment	£2,600

The motor car purchased on 15 January 2001 for £14,800 is used by Lai, and 40% of the mileage is for private purposes. The motor car purchased on 20 February 2001 for £10,400 is used by an employee, and 10% of the mileage is for private purposes.

The recording equipment purchased on 4 March 2001 for £2,600 is to be treated as a short-life asset.

(3)   Since becoming self-employed Lai has contributed £500 per month into a personal pension scheme.

Required

(a)   Calculate Lai's income tax liability for 2000/01.   (20 marks)

(b)   Briefly explain how Lai's income tax liability for 2000/01 will be paid to the Inland Revenue.

(5 marks)

(Total 25 marks)

---

30   SASHA SHAH (PILOT PAPER)   *27 mins*

Sasha Shah is a computer programmer. Until 5 April 2000 she was employed by Net Computers plc, but since then has worked independently from home. Sasha's income for the year ended 5 April 2001 is £60,000. All of this relates to work done for Net Computers plc. Her expenditure for the year ended 5 April 2001 is as follows:

(1)   The business proportion of light, heat and telephone for Sasha's home is £600.

(2)   Computer equipment was purchased on 6 April 2000 for £8,000.

(3)   A motor car was purchased on 6 April 2000 for £10,000. Motor expenses for the year ended 6 April 2001 amount to £3,500, of which 40% relate to journeys between home and the premises of Net Computers plc. The other 60% relate to private mileage.

Required

(a)   List eight factors that will indicate that a worker should be treated as an employee rather than as self-employed.   (4 marks)

(b)   (i)   Calculate Sasha's liability to Class 2 and Class 4 NIC if she is treated as self-employed during 2000/01.

(ii)   Calculate Sasha's liability to Class 1 NIC if she is treated as an employee during 2000/01.

(4 marks)

(c)   (i)   Calculate the amount of income assessable under Schedule DII if Sasha is treated as self-employed during 2000/01.

(ii)   Calculate the amount of income assessable under Schedule E if Sasha is treated as an employee during 2000/01.   (7 marks)

(Total 15 marks)

1   TREE LTD

(a)   Tree Ltd

	Year to 30.6.00 £	Six months to 31.12.00 £
Trading profits (12/18: 6/18)	120,000	60,000
Chargeable gain	172,000	
Schedule D Case III (12/18: 6/18)	24,000	12,000
Less: charge on income	(22,000)	(5,000)
Profits chargeable to corporation tax	294,000	67,000

Year to 30.6.00
Corporation tax (W1)
FY99

£220,500 × 30%		66,150
Less 1/40 (1,125,000 – 243,000) × $\dfrac{220,500}{243,000}$		(20,008)
FY2000		
£73,500 × 30%		22,050
Less 1/40 (375,000 – 81,000) × $\dfrac{73,500}{81,000}$		(6,669)
		61,523

Six months to 31.12.00 (W2)

£67,000 × 20%	£13,400

(b)   Dealers plc's profits for small companies rate purposes are £420,000 so tax is payable at the marginal rate in both FY 99 and FY 00.

	FY 1999 and FY 2000 £
Profits chargeable to corporation tax	420,000
'Profits'	420,000
Upper limit	1,500,000
Lower limit	300,000
Corporation tax	
FY 1999 and 2000	
£420,000 × 30%	126,000
Less small companies marginal relief	
£(1,500,000 – 420,000) × 1/40	(27,000)
Mainstream corporation tax	99,000

(c)   Springer Ltd's 'profits' are £6,200. This means they qualify for the lower rate in FY 2000 and the small companies rate in FY 1999:

	£
FY 1999	
£6,200 × 3/12 × 20%	310
FY 2000	
£6,200 × 9/12 × 10%	465
	775

Workings

1   Tax rate: year to 30.6.00

The year to 30.6.00 falls into FY99 and FY2000

	FY99 (9/12) £	FY2000 (3/12) £
PCTCT	220,500	73,500
'Profits' (£294,000 + £27,000 × 100/90)	243,000	81,000
Small companies lower limit	225,000	75,000
Small companies upper limit	1,125,000	375,000

As 'profits' are between the small companies' upper and lower limits in both financial years, small companies marginal relief applies in both financial years.

2   The six month period to 31.12.00 falls in the financial year 2000. As profits of £67,000 are above the starting rate upper limit of £25,000 and below the small companies rate lower limit of £150,000 for this period, the small companies rate applies.

2   TRADERS LTD

CORPORATION TAX COMPUTATION

	£	£
Net profit per accounts		101,957
Add: entertaining	600	
tax consultancy	30	
lease on new premises	100	
gift aid donation	200	
political donation	500	
patent royalties payable	5,000	
depreciation	15,000	
		21,430
		123,387
Less: commissions (chargeable under Schedule D Case VI)	800	
profit on sale of investment	5,265	
loan interest	1,000	
interest on gilts	80	
		(7,145)
Schedule D Case I		116,242
Schedule D Case III £1,000 + £80 × 100/80		1,100
Schedule D Case VI		800
Chargeable gain		770
		118,912
Less charges paid (patent royalties and gift aid)		(5,200)
Profits chargeable to corporation tax		113,712

The profits for small companies rate purposes are below the lower limit, so the small companies rate applies.

The corporation tax liability is £113,712 × 20% = £22,742

Note: gift aid donations are paid gross.

3 HARDY LTD

	Pool £	Car pool £	Expensive car £	Short life asset £	Allowances £
1.7.96-30.6.97					
Brought forward	23,400	6,300			
Acquisitions	2,300			4,400	
	25,700				
WDA	(6,425)	(1,575)		(1,100)	9,100
	19,275	4,725		3,300	
1.7.97 - 30.6.98					
WDA	(4,819)	(1,181)		(825)	6,825
	14,456	3,544		2,475	
1.7.98 - 30.6.99					
Acquisition			13,400		
WDA	(3,614)	(886)	(3,000)	(619)	8,119
	10,842	2,658	10,400	1,856	
1.7.99 - 30.6.00					
Transfer	2,658	(2,658)			
Disposals	(340)			(2,000)	
	13,160			(144)	(144)
WDA	(3,290)		(2,600)		5,890
	9,870		7,800		5,746
1.7.00 - 31.12.00					
Disposals	(24,000)		(10,600)		
Balancing charge	(14,130)		(2,800)		(16,930)

4 CUCKOLD LTD

(a) Cuckold Ltd chould acquire factory (i), as shown in the working below.

Factory (ii) is clearly unattractive since, with its tax life expired, industrial buildings allowances cannot be claimed. Factories (iii) and (iv) have greater total allowances available than factory (i) but the annual allowance is much smaller.

Working: industrial buildings allowances on alternative factories

	Factory (i)	Factory (ii)	Factory (iii)	Factory (iv)
Residue after sale*	£100,000	£80,000	£150,000	£120,000
Remaining tax life**	1 yr	0	23 yrs	17 yrs
Allowances available	£100,000	0	£150,000	£120,000
in y/e 31.3.2002	1 yr		23 yrs	17 yrs
	= £100,000		= £6,522	= £7,059

*   The residue after sale is the lower of the price paid by the new purchaser and the original cost.

**   The tax life of an industrial building begins when it is first brought into use and ends 25 years later (except for expenditure incurred before 6 November 1962, when the relevant period is 50 years rather than 25 years).

(b) (i) *Showroom display lighting*

Expenditure on display lighting will be eligible for plant and machinery capital allowances. The most important general test in determining whether expenditure is eligible is the 'functional test'. This asks whether the item concerned fulfils a *function* in the carrying on of the trade or merely forms part of the setting *in* which the trade is carried on.

This test was used with regard to lighting in *Cole Bros Ltd v Phillips 1982*, where lighting equipment which produced higher levels of lighting than normal and which was specialised in order to display goods to customers was held to be plant.

BPP PUBLISHING

Expenditure on plant and machinery is eligible for a first year allowance of 40%. The balance of the expenditure is then eligible for a 25% writing down allowance in subsequent years on a reducing balance basis.

(ii)   *Thermal insulation*

Expenditure on thermal insulation for a qualifying industrial building is specifically allowed as expenditure on plant and machinery: thus a first year allowance followed by writing down allowances will be available as described above. When the building is eventually sold, the disposal value of the thermal insulation is taken to be zero, so no balancing charge can arise in respect of it.

(iii)   *A factory canteen*

Expenditure on a factory canteen will qualify for industrial buildings allowances. The definition of an industrial building includes any building or structure provided by the person carrying on a qualifying trade (that is, one using a building that qualifies for industrial buildings allowances) for the welfare of workers employed in the trade.

5   SCHEDULE A

P LTD: SCHEDULE A INCOME

	£	£	£
First house			
Premium £20,000 × [1 − 0.02 (30 − 1)]			8,400
Rent £4,000 × 9/12			3,000
			11,400
Second house			
Rent £600 × 3		1,800	
Rent £2,100 × 1/3		700	
		2,500	
Less: water rates £390 × 6/12	195		
insurance £440 × 6/11	240		
repairs: capital	0		
furniture: in year to 31.3.02	0		
		(435)	
			2,065
Schedule A income			13,465

The interest on the loan is dealt with under the loan relationship rules. It is not a Schedule A expense.

6   GAINS AND LOSSES

Motor cars are exempt assets, so the loss brought forward from the year ended 31 March 2000 is £16,400.

The position for the year ended 31 March 2001 is as follows.

	£
Gains	
Shares	7,200
Picture	3,000
	10,200
Less loss on shares	(2,000)
	8,200
Less loss brought forward	(8,200)
Chargeable gains	Nil

The racehorse is a chattel and is an exempt asset.

The loss carried forward at 31 March 2001 is £(16,400 − 8,200) = £8,200.

7   HARDUP LTD

CAPITAL GAINS COMPUTATION

	£
Office block (W1)	16,715
Plot of land (W2)	19,876
Workshop (W3)	45,080
Taxable gains	81,671

Workings

1   *The office block*

	£
Proceeds	120,000
Less cost	(65,000)
	55,000
Less indexation allowance $\dfrac{169.5 - 106.7}{106.7}$ (0.589) × £65,000	(38,285)
Chargeable gain	16,715

2   *The plot of land*

	£
Proceeds	69,000
Less: cost	(20,000)
expenditure in July 1985	(4,000)
	45,000
Less indexation allowance	
$\dfrac{170.0 - 81.0}{81.0}$ (1.099) × £20,000	(21,980)
$\dfrac{170.0 - 95.2}{95.2}$ (0.786) × £4,000	(3,144)
	19,876

3   *The workshop*

	£
Proceeds	173,000
Less cost	(65,000)
	108,000
Less indexation allowance $\dfrac{170.0 - 86.4}{86.4}$ (0.968) × £65,000	(62,920)
	45,080

The date of disposal for chargeable gains purposes is the date that the disposal becomes unconditional. In this case the date of exchange, not the date of completion.

8   FERRARO LTD

	Accounting periods				
	12m to	*12m to*	*9m to*	*12m to*	*12m to*
	31.12.96	*31.12.97*	*30.9.98*	*30.9.99*	*30.9.00*
	£	£	£	£	£
Schedule D Case I	10,000	34,480	6,200	4,320	0
Schedule D Case III	100	200	80	240	260
Schedule A	3,000	1,200	1,420	1,440	1,600
Chargeable gain (12,680 – 5,000)	0	0	0	7,680	0
	13,100	35,880	7,700	13,680	1,860
Less s 393A - current	0	0	0	0	(1,860)
	13,100	35,880	7,700	13,680	0
Less charges	1,000	1,000	0	1,000	0
	12,100	34,880	7,700	12,680	0
Less s 393A - c/b				(12,680)	(0)
PCTCT	12,100	34,880	7,700	0	0

The loss carried forward against future profits of the same trade is £100,000 − £ (12,680 + 1,860) + £1,500 trade charges = £86,960.

The allowable capital loss of £9,423 during the year ended 30 September 2000 is carried forward against future chargeable gains.

9 H, S AND N

H Ltd: corporation tax computations for the accounting periods of 12 months to	30.6.99	30.6.00
	£	£
Schedule D Case I	2,000	
Less loss of y/e 30.6.00, s 393A(1) ICTA 1988	(2,000)	
Chargeable profits	0	0
MCT payable	£0	£0

S Ltd: corporation tax computations for the accounting periods of 12 months to	30.6.99	30.6.00
	£	£
Schedule D Case I	30,000	100,000
Less charges	(12,000)	(12,000)
Chargeable profits	18,000	88,000

S Ltd: corporation tax computations for the accounting periods of 12 months to	30.6.99	30.6.00
	£	£
Corporation tax		
£18,000 × 21% × 9/12	2,835	
£18,000 × 20% × 3/12	900	
£88,000 x 20%		17,600
MCT payable	3,735	17,600

N Ltd: corporation tax computations for the accounting periods of 12 months and 6 months to	31.12.99	30.6.00
	£	£
Adjusted profit split 12:6	43,500	21,750
Less capital allowances (W2)	(4,250)	(17,569)
Schedule D Case I	39,250	4,181
Chargeable gain	0	20,000
	39,250	24,181
Less group relief surrendered by H Ltd (W1)	(19,625)	(24,000)
Chargeable profits	19,625	181

Corporation tax	£	£
(£19,625 × 21% x 3/12) + (£19,625 x 20% x 9/12)	3,974	
£181 × (3/6 × 20% + 3/6 x 10%)		27
MCT	3,974	27

Workings

1 *Group relief*

		£
Loss of H Ltd y/e 30.6.00 available for group relief		48,000
Surrendered to N Ltd		
6 months to 31.12.99 restricted to 6/12 × £39,250		(19,625)
6 months to 30.6.00 restricted to 6/12 × £48,000		(24,000)
		4,375
Less s 393A(1) claim by H Ltd		(2,000)
Loss of H Ltd carried forward		2,375

Group relief is not available for S Ltd because it is only a 60% subsidiary.

2 *Capital allowances*

	£	Pool £	Expensive car £	Allowances £
12 months to 31.12.99				
WDV brought forward		5,000		
Addition: car			16,000	
WDA 25%/£3,000		(1,250)	(3,000)	4,250
		3,750	13,000	
6 months to 30.6.00				
WDA 25% × 6/12		(469)	(1,500)	1,969
Additions: plant	31,000			
plant on HP	8,000			
	39,000			
FYA 40%	(15,600)			15,600
		23,400		17,569
WDV carried forward		26,681	11,500	

10   APPLE LTD

(a) Group relief is available within a 75% group. This is one where one company is a 75% subsidiary of another company or both are 75% subsidiaries of a third company. The holding company must have at least 75% of the ordinary share capital of the subsidiary; a right to at least 75% of the distributable income of the subsidiary; and the right to at least 75% of the net assets of the subsidiary were it to be wound up.

Two companies are in a group only if there is a 75% effective interest eg if Company A holds 90% of Company B which holds 90% of Company C, all three companies are in a group because 90% × 90% = 81%.

(b) Group relief should be allocated to the company with the highest marginal rate of tax. This is Cherry Ltd to the extent of profits between £130,000 and £100,000 since the small companies rate lower limit is £300,000 ÷ 3 = £100,000. Such profits are taxed at 32.5%. Then, the remainder of the loss should be set against the profits of Banana Ltd which bears tax at 30%. The capital loss cannot be group relieved.

(c) Rollover relief for part of Apple Ltd's gain can be claimed in respect of the investment by Cherry Ltd. The excess of amount of proceeds over the amount invested remains in charge ie £(410,000 – 290,000) = £120,000.

Apple Ltd should then make a current year loss relief claim to bring its profits down to £100,000.

	Apple Ltd £	Banana Ltd £	Cherry Ltd £
Schedule DI	-	650,000	130,000
Capital gain	120,000		
	120,000	650,000	130,000
Less: s 393A(1)	(20,000)		
group relief		(75,000)	(30,000)
PCTCT	100,000	575,000	100,000
Tax @ 20%	20,000		20,000
Tax @ 30%		172,500	

Note that the SCR upper limit is £1,500,000 ÷ 3 = £500,000.

11   M LTD

Year ended 31 March 2001

	Total £	UK £	A Inc £	B PG £	C SA £
Schedule D Case I	20,000	20,000			
Schedule D Case V (W1)	587,500	-	200,000	200,000	187,500
	607,500	20,000	200,000	200,000	187,500
Less: Charge on income	(75,000)	(20,000)	(55,000)	-	-
Profits chargeable to corporation tax	532,500	-	145,000	200,000	187,500
CT @ 30%	159,750	-	43,500	60,000	56,250
Less: DTR (W2)	(136,250)	-	(30,000)	(50,000)	(56,250)
Mainstream corporation tax	23,500	-	13,500	10,000	-

In order to maximise the set off of double tax relief, charges are allocated firstly to UK profits and then to overseas sources of income that have suffered the lowest rate of overseas tax. There are five associated companies so the full rate of corporation tax applies.

Workings

1   *Dividend from C SA*

Since M Ltd's shareholding in C SA is at least 10%, relief for underlying tax is available:

	£
Dividend from C SA	120,000
Withholding tax (× 20/80)	30,000
	150,000
Underlying tax	
£150,000 × $\dfrac{200,000}{800,000}$	37,500
Gross dividend	187,500

2   *Overseas dividends*

	Net £	Tax credit £	Gross £
A Inc (15%)	170,000	30,000	200,000
B PG (25%)	150,000	50,000	200,000
C SA (20%)	120,000	67,500	187,500

3   *Double tax relief*

	A Inc £	B pg £	C Sa £
Lower of			
(i) UK tax	43,500	60,000	56,250
(ii) Overseas tax	30,000	50,000	*67,500
	£30,000	£50,000	£56,250

* Underlying tax + withholding tax.

288

Note: The main point in this question is to ensure that any deductible charges are first deducted from UK income with the balance of charges being deducted from that part of foreign income bearing the LOWEST rate of foreign tax. This allows a maximisation of the foreign tax credits.

12 HOGG LTD AND BARNETT LTD

(a) The due dates for the payment of corporation tax by Hogg Ltd in respect of the year to 31.12.00 are:

	£	£
14 July 2000 1/4 × (72% × £500,000)		90,000
14 October 2000 1/4 × (72% × £500,000)		90,000
14 January 2001 1/4 × (72% × £520,000)	93,600	
plus underpaid 2 × £(93,600 – 90,000)	7,200	
		100,800
14 April 2001 1/4 × (72% × £520,000)		93,600
1 October 2001 balance of instalments 72% × £525,000		
– £90,000 – £90,000 – £100,800 – £93,600		3,600
Balance of tax 28% × £525,000		147,000
Total		525,000

(b) The due dates for the payment of corporation tax instalments by Hogg Ltd in respect of the ten months to 31 October 2005 are:

14 July 2005	£180,000
14 October 2005	£180,000
14 January 2006	£180,000
14 February 2006 (4th month of next accounting period)	£60,000 (balance)

Tutorial note: The amount of the instalments is $^3/n \times CT = {}^3/10 \times £600,000 = £180,000$.

(c) *Income tax*

Return period	Tax on payments £	Tax on income £	Income tax Due £	Income tax Repayable £	Due date
1.4.00 - 30.6.00	1,200	960	240	0	14.7.00
1.7.00 - 30.9.00 No return	0	0	0	0	
1.10.00 - 31.12.00	1,200	0	1,200	0	14.1.01
1.1.01 - 31.3.01	120	3,120	0	1,440	14.4.01*

* This is the due date for the return. There is no due date for the Inland Revenue to make a repayment.

The net income tax suffered over the year (£1,560) will be deducted from the company's corporation tax liability for the year. No amount is carried forward.

13 INDUSTRIAL LTD

(a) *Corporation tax payable y/e 31.3.01.*

	£	£
Trading profit	1,689,710	
Less: Capital allowances		
- on Factory (W1)	(12,000)	
- on Plant and machinery (W2)	(42,110)	
Schedule D Case I		1,635,600
Schedule D Case III - BI received	12,500	
- Loan interest received	36,000	48,500
Schedule A (W3)		73,200
Capital gains (W4)		56,200
Total profits		1,813,500
Less: charges on income		
- patent royalties paid	11,500	
- Gift Aid	2,000	(13,500)
PCTCT		1,800,000

Tax

	£
£1,800,000 × 30%	540,000
Less: income tax repayable (W5)	(4,670)
Corporation tax payable	535,330

Workings

1 IBA

Expenditure eligible for IBAs

	£
Levelling the land	9,200
Architects fees	24,300
Concrete floor	16,500
Factory	187,500
General offices (less than 25% of total)	62,500
	300,000
IBA @ 4% (building in use on 31.3.01)	£12,000

2 Plant and machinery

	FYAs £	General pool £	Expensive car (1) £	Expensive car (2) £	Allowances given £
TWDV b/f		84,600	15,400		
Addition not qualifying				17,200	
Disposal			(19,600)		
Balancing charge			4,200		(4,200)
WDA @ 25%		(21,150)		(max) (3,000)	24,150
		63,450		14,200	
Additions qualifying for FYA					
Heating system	12,800				
Fire alarm system	7,200				
Computer (N)	3,400				
Lorry	32,000				
	55,400				
Less: FYA @ 40%	(22,160)	33,240			22,160
TDWC c/f		96,690	–	14,200	
Allowances given					£42,110

Note. The computer equipment does note qualify for 100% FYA as Industrial Ltd is not a 'small' enterprise.

3   *Schedule A*

	£	£
Premium		
Amount received	80,000	
Less: 2% × (10 − 1) × 80,000	(14,400)	
Assessable under Schedule A		65,600
Rental (3/12 × £30,400)		7,600
Schedule A profit		73,200

4   *Capital gain on sale of shares*

	£
Proceeds	223,000
Less: cost	(135,800)
Unindexed gain	87,200
Less: indexation allowance (4.94 − 1.01)	(24,200)
Indexed gain	63,000
Less: loss b/f	(6,800)
Net gains	56,200

5   *Income tax repayable*

	£
Income tax paid on patent royalties £11,500 × 22%	2,530
Less: income tax withheld on loan interest £36,000 × 20%	(7,200)
Net income tax repayable	4,670

(b) (i)   Industrial Ltd is a 'large' company as it pays corporation tax at the full rate and did so in the previous year. Therefore it is required to make quarterly payments on account of corporation tax.

(ii)   Since this is Year 2 of the quarterly instalment regime, Industrial Ltd must pay 72% of its liability in four instalments of 18%. These are due on 14th October 2000; 14 January 2001; 14th April 2001 and 14th July 2001. The balancing payment (28%) is due on 1 January 2002.

14   INVOICES, THE TAX POINT AND RETURNS

(a)   A VAT invoice is necessary to reclaim input tax suffered. The issue of such an invoice usually sets the tax point for a supply. A VAT invoice must show an identifying number, the supplier's name and address and VAT number, the date, the type of supply made, the amount payable excluding VAT, a description of the goods and services supplied and the VAT chargeable.

(b)   The tax point determines the period in respect of which value added tax is payable or reclaimable. These periods are usually three months in length, but may be one month especially if a trader makes zero rated supplies and thus receives regular repayments of VAT. The tax point is often the invoice date; it may however be when goods are removed or when services are performed. The tax point also dictates the rate of VAT which applies: it is the rate in force on the day of the tax point.

(c)   A VAT return is sent to HM Customs & Excise within one month of the end of each VAT period. It shows the VAT payable or repayable and total outputs and inputs for the period. Any VAT payable is sent with the return.

15 JUSTIN

	£	£
Output VAT		
Furniture: £490,000 × 17.5%		85,750
Books: £2,400 × 0%		0
Petrol: £478 (VAT inclusive scale charge) × 7/47		71
		85,821
Input VAT		
Furniture: £275,000 × 17.5%	48,125	
Computer: £2,400 × 17.5%	420	
Entertaining: irrecoverable	0	
Petrol: £2,800 × 17.5%	490	
		(49,035)
VAT to account for		36,786

16 NEWCOMER LTD, ONGOING LTD AND AU REVOIR LTD

(a) The registration threshold is £52,000 (from 1.4.00) during any 12 month consecutive period.

This is exceeded in January 2001:

		£
2000	October	9,500
	November	14,200
	December	21,400
2001	January	12,300
		57,400

Therefore, Newcomer Ltd must register within 30 days of the end of the period ie by 2 March 2001.

Newcomer Ltd will be registered from 1 March 2001 or an earlier date agreed between the company and Customs & Excise.

(b)

	£	£
Output tax		
£120,000 × 95% = 114,000 × 17.5% (note 1)		19,950
Input tax		
£(35,640 − 480) = 35,160 × 17.5% (note 2)	6,153	
£2,000 × 17.5% (note 3)	350	
£21,150 × 7/47 (note 4)	3,150	(9,653)
VAT payable		10,297

Notes

1 Where a discount is offered for prompt payment, VAT is chargeable on the net amount, regardless of whether the discount is taken up.

2 VAT on business entertaining is not recoverable where the cost of the entertaining is not a deductible Schedule D Case I expense.

3 Bad debt relief is only available for debts over six months old (measured from when the payment is due).

4 VAT incurred on the purchase of a car not used wholly for business purposes is not recoverable.

(c) A person is eligible for voluntary deregistration if Customs and Excise are satisfied that the rate of his taxable supplies (net of VAT) in the following one year period will not exceed £50,000 (from 1.4.00). However, voluntary deregistration will not be allowed if the reasons for the expected fall in value of taxable supplies is the cessation of taxable supplies or the suspension of taxable supplies for a period of 30 days or more in that following year. HM Customs & Excise will cancel a person's registration from the date the request is made or an agreed later date.

17 INCOME TAX

	Non-savings	Savings (excl.dividend)	Dividend	Total
	£	£	£	£
Business profits	14,000			
Building society interest × 100/80		8,000		
Dividends × 100/90			2,000	
	14,000	8,000	2,000	
Less charge	(2,500)	0	0	
Statutory total income	11,500	8,000	2,000	21,500
Less personal allowance	(4,385)	0	0	
Taxable income	7,115	8,000	2,000	17,115

	£
Non-savings income	
Starting rate band £1,520 × 10%	152
Basic rate band £5,595 × 22%	1,231
Savings (excl dividend) income	
£8,000 × 20%	1,600
Dividend income	
£2,000 × 10%	200
	3,183
Less: tax suffered on building society interest	(1,600)
tax credit on dividend income	(200)
Balance of tax still to pay	1,383

	£	£
Profits received		14,000
Building society interest received		6,400
Dividend received		1,800
		22,200
Less: charge paid	2,500	
income tax to pay	1,383	
		(3,883)
Available to spend		18,317

18 MR AND MRS LOWRIE

	Non-savings	Savings (excl. dividends)	Dividends	Total
Mr Lowrie	£	£	£	£
Schedule E	36,000			
Dividends × 100/90			1,211	
Bank deposit interest × 100/80		250		
Building society interest × 100/80		179		
STI	36,000	429	1,211	37,640
Less personal allowance	(4,385)			
Taxable income	31,615	429	1,211	33,255

	£	£
Non savings income		
£1,520 × 10%		152
£26,880 × 22%		5,914
£ 3,215 × 40%		1,286
31,615		7,352
Savings (excluding dividend) income		
£429 × 40%		172
Dividend income		
£1,211 × 32.5%		394
		7,918
Less: tax credit on dividend	121	
tax suffered on savings income	86	
PAYE	6,000	
		(6,207)
Tax payable		1,711

	Non-savings	Savings (excl. dividends)	Dividends	Total
	£	£	£	£
Mrs Lowrie				
Schedule E	20,000			
Dividends × 100/90			2,820	
Bank deposit interest × 100/80		95		
Building society interest × 100/80	-	525		
STI	20,000	620	2,820	23,440
Less personal allowance	(4,385)			
Taxable income	15,615	620	2,820	19,055

	£	£
Non-savings income		
£1,520 × 10%		152
£14,095 × 22%		3,101
15,615		3,253
Savings (excluding dividend) income		
£620 × 20%		124
Dividend income		
£2,820 × 10%		282
Tax liability		3,659
Less: tax credit on dividends	282	
tax suffered on savings income	124	
PAYE	2,611	
		(3,017)
Tax payable		642

19   MR COBBLER

THE TAXABLE PROFITS FOR THE FOUR YEARS 1999/00 TO 2002/03

The accounts profits will be as follows.

Period ending in	Working	Accounting date 31 March	30 April
		£	£
2000	3 × £800	2,400	
	4 × £800		3,200
2001	3 × £800 + 6 × £1,200 + 3 × £2,000	15,600	
	2 × £800 + 6 × £1,200 + 4 × £2,000		16,800
2002	12 × £2,000	24,000	24,000
2003	12 × £2,000	24,000	24,000

The taxable profits will be as follows.

		Accounting date	
		31 March	30 April
		£	£
1999/00	Actual basis £2,400	2,400	
	£3,200 × 3/4		2,400
2000/01	Year to 31.3.01	15,600	
	First 12 months		
	£3,200 + £16,800 × 8/12		14,400
2001/02	Year to 31.3.02	24,000	
	Year to 30.4.01		16,800
2002/03	Year to 31.3.03	24,000	
	Year to 30.4.02		24,000
		66,000	57,600

30 April is the better choice of accounting date. Although the difference between the taxable profits will be compensated for on cessation, that may not be for many years, so choosing 30 April may give a considerable cash flow advantage.

20   MISS FARRINGTON

We must first work out the capital allowances.

	FYA	Pool	Car (65%)	Allowances
	£	£	£	£
1.1.98 - 30.4.99				
Car			2,600	
WDA @ 25% × 16/12			(867)	564
Desk and office furniture	940			
General plant	5,475			
Secondhand oven	1,200			
Delivery van	1,800			
Typewriter	425			
	9,840			
FYA @ 50%	(4,920)			4,920
		4,920	1,733	5,484
1.5.99 – 30.4.00				
WDA @ 25%		(1,230)	(433)	1,511
		3,690	1,300	
General plant	1,000			
FYA @ 40%	(400)			400
		600		
Computer	778			
FYA @ 100%	(778)			778
		4,290	1,300	2,689

Profits are as follows.

Period	Profit	Capital allowances	Adjusted profit
	£	£	£
1.1.98 - 30.4.99	16,000	5,484	10,516
1.5.99 - 30.4.00	13,400	2,689	10,711

The taxable profits are as follows.

Year	Basis period	Working	Taxable profit
			£
1997/98	1.1.98 - 5.4.98	£10,516 × 3/16	1,972
1998/99	6.4.98 - 5.4.99	£10,516 × 12/16	7,887
1999/00	1.5.98 - 30.4.99	£10,516 × 12/16	7,887
2000/01	1.5.99 - 30.4.00		10,711

The overlap profits are the profits from 1 May 1998 to 5 April 1999: £10,516 × 11/16 = £7,230.

21   MORGAN

(a)   Loss relief could be claimed:

    (i)   under s 380 ICTA 1988, against other income of the year of loss (2001/02), the investment income of £8,000;

        under s 380 ICTA 1988, against other income of the preceding year (2000/01). This would be Schedule D Case I income of £15,000 plus investment income of £8,000;

        under s 385 ICTA 1988, against the first available future profits of the same trade.

(b)   *The quickest claim*

The quickest way to obtain relief would be for Morgan to use s 380 ICTA 1988 in both years. The tax computations would then be as follows.

	2000/01 £	2001/02 £
Schedule D Case I	15,000	0
Investment income	8,000	8,000
	23,000	8,000
Less s 380 loss relief	23,000	8,000
Taxable income	0	0

The balance of the loss, £1,000, would be carried forward and relieved under s 385.

Although s 380 produces loss relief quickly, it has the disadvantage of wasting Morgan's personal allowance in both years. Morgan could, if he chose, delay his relief by carrying the loss forward under s 385 ICTA 1988. The loss would then be set off only against trading income, with the investment income using his personal allowance.

(c)   On a cessation, terminal loss relief under s 388 ICTA 1988 would be available. The loss would be set against profits taxable in the tax year of cessation and the three preceding tax years, later years first. This would probably be the best claim for Morgan. The effect would be as follows.

Year	Schedule D Case I		
	Original £	Loss relief £	Revised £
2001/02	0	0	0
2000/01	15,000	(15,000)	0
1999/00	18,000	(17,000)	1,000
1998/99	16,000	0	16,000

Because of Morgan's choice of accounting date, no overlap profits arose on commencement.

22   ADAM, BERT AND CHARLIE

	Total £	A £	B £	C £	D £
Year ending 5 April 1998					
Salaries	3,700	1,500	1,200	1,000	
Balance	6,500	2,600	2,600	1,300	
Total	10,200	4,100	3,800	2,300	
Year ending 5 April 1999					
6 April to 5 July					
Salaries	925	375	300	250	
Balance	4,275	1,710	1,710	855	
Total (3/12)	5,200	2,085	2,010	1,105	
6 July to 5 April					
Salaries	1,650		900	750	
Balance	13,950		8,370	5,580	
Total (9/12)	15,600		9,270	6,330	
Totals for the year	20,800	2,085	11,280	7,435	

	Total £	A £	B £	C £	D £
Year ending 5 April 2000					
Salaries	2,200		1,200	1,000	
Balance	10,400		6,240	4,160	
Total	12,600		7,440	5,160	
Year ending 5 April 2001					
6 April - 5 May					
Salaries	183		100	83	
Balance	1,317		790	527	
Total (1/12)	1,500		890	610	
6 May to 5 April					
Salaries	4,950		1,650	1,650	1,650
Balance	11,550		6,237	4,158	1,155
Total (11/12)	16,500		7,887	5,808	2,805
Totals for the year	18,000		8,777	6,418	2,805

Taxable profits are as follows.

		A £	B £	C £	D £
Year					
1997/98		4,100	3,800	2,300	
1998/99		2,085	11,280	7,435	
1999/00			7,440	5,160	
2000/01			8,777	6,418	2,805

23 PARTNERSHIPS

(a) Each partner is taxed like a sole trader who runs a business which starts when he joins the partnership; finishes when he leaves the partnership; has the same periods of account as the partnership; and makes profits or losses equal to the partner's share of the partnership profits or losses.

(b)

	Total £	Anne £	Betty £	Chloe £
1.1.00 – 31.12.00				
January to June	30,000	15,000	15,000	
July to December	30,000	15,000	-	15,000
Totals	60,000	30,000	15,000	15,000
1.1.01 – 31.12.01	72,000	36,000	-	36,000

Schedule DI assessments 2000/01

	Anne £	Betty £	Chloe £
Profits y/e 31.12.00	30,000		
Profits 1.1.00 – 30.6.00		15,000	
Profits 1.7.00 – 31.12.00			15,000
Profits 1.1.01 – 5.4.00			
3/12 × £36,000			9,000
	30,000	15,000	24,000
Less: overlap relief for Betty on cessation		(3,000)	
Profits assessable 2000/01	30,000	12,000	24,000

(c) (i) *Daniel*

Daniel can use his £20,000 loss:

- against total income of 2000/01 and /or of 1999/00 under s 380 ICTA 1988
- against future trading profits under s 385 ICTA 1988

    (ii)   *Edward*

        Edward can use his £15,000 loss:

- against total income of 2000/01 and/or of 1999/00 under s 380 ICTA 1988
- if there is a terminal loss in the last 12 months of trading, against Schedule D Case II income of the tax year of cessation and the three preceding years, later years first, under s 388 ICTA 1988

    (iii)   *Frank*

        Frank can use his loss of £5,000:

- against total income of 2000/01 and/or 1999/00 under s 380 ICTA 1988
- against total income of 1997/98, 1998/99 and 1999/00 under s 381 ICTA 1988
- against future trading profits under s 385 ICTA 1988

24 DENISE

(a) The maximum contributions are:

Year	Age at start of year	NRE £	% of NRE	Gross premium £
1999/00	35	25,000	17.5	4,375
2000/01	36	91,800 (capped)	20	18,360

(b) *Class 2 NICs (for both 1999/00 and 2000/01 using 2000/01 rates)*

    £2 × 52   **£104**

    Class 4 NICs 1999/00 (using 2000/01 rates)

    £(25,000 – 4,385) × 7%   **£1,443**

    Class 4 NICs 2000/01

    £(27,820 – 4,385) × 7%   **£1,640**

25 SUSAN WHITE

(a) The following shareholdings in trading companies qualify for CGT business asset taper relief.

    (i)   shares in unlisted companies;
    (ii)   shares in a company of which the shareholder is an officer or employee;
    (iii) shares in a company in which the shareholder can exercise at least 5% of voting rights.

(b) *Capital gains 2000/01*

    Red Ltd

                 £

    5,000 shares (acquired within next 30 days)

    Proceeds $\frac{5,000}{20,000} \times £55,000$ 13,750

    Less: cost   (15,000)

    Loss   (1,250)

                 £

    15,000 shares (acquired within next 30 days)

    Proceeds $\frac{15,000}{20,000} \times £55,000$ 41,250

    Less: cost $\frac{15,000}{25,000} \times 37,500$ (22,500)

    Gain before taper relief   18,750

    Taper relief period (2.6.99 – 1.7.00) = 1 year

Blue Ltd

	£
MV (sale between connected persons)	200,000
Less: cost	(18,000)
Unindexed gain	182,000
Less: indexation allowance to April 1998	(12,800)
Indexed gain	169,200

Gain not available for gift relief £(70,000 – 18,000)	£52,000

Taper relief period (6.4.98 – 5.4.00) = 2 years

Gift relief £(169,200 – 52,000)	£117,200

Summary

	1 year taper	2 year taper
	£	£
Gains	18,750	52,000
Less: loss (best use)	(1,250)	-
Net gains before taper relief	17,500	52,000
Gains after taper relief		
87.5% × £17,500	15,312	
75% × £52,000		39,000
Total gains £(15,312 + 39,000)		£54,312

26 TIM

Tim's Payments on Account for 2000/01 were based on the excess of his 1999/00 tax liability over amounts deducted under the PAYE system, amounts deducted at source and tax credits on dividends:

	£
1999/00 tax liability	16,800
Less: PAYE	(7,200)
Tax deducted at source	(800)
Tax credit on dividends	(200)
Total payments on account for 2000/01	8,600

Two equal payments on account of £4,300 (£8,600 / 2) were required. The due dates for these payments were 31 January 2001 and 31 July 2001 respectively.

The final payment in respect of Tim's 2000/01 tax liability was due on 31 January 2002 and was calculated as follows:

	£
2000/01 tax liability	22,000
Less: PAYE	(7,100)
Tax deducted at source	(900)
Tax credit on dividends	(250)
	13,750
Less: Payments on account	(8,600)
Final payment due 31.1.02	5,150

27 EMPLOYMENT AND SELF-EMPLOYMENT

The factors to consider in deciding whether someone is employed or self-employed for income tax purposes are as follows.

(a) How much control is exercised over the way work is done? The greater the control, the more likely it is that the worker is an employee.

(b) Does the worker provide his own equipment? That would indicate self-employment.

(c) If the worker hires his own helpers, that indicates self-employment.

(d) If the worker can profit by his own sound management, or lose money through errors, that indicates self-employment.

(e) If there is a continuing obligation to provide work for the workers, and an obligation on the worker to do whatever job is offered next, that indicates employment.

(f) If the worker accepts work from any independent sources, that indicates self-employment.

(g) If the worker can work whenever he chooses, that indicates self-employment.

These tests are summed up in the general rule that there is employment when there is a contract of service, and self-employment when is a contract for services.

28   CARS AND LOANS

(a) A taxable benefit must be computed for Mr Andrews. The benefit will equal the difference between the interest which would have arisen at the official rate and the actual interest paid. The benefit for 2000/01 is therefore £16,000 × (10 − 5)% × 6 months/12 months = £400.

(b) Because the loan to Mrs Preece does not exceed £5,000, the taxable benefit is zero.

(c) Mr Charles will have a taxable benefit of the annual value of the TV and video system, which will be computed as 20% of the value of the asset when first provided as a benefit to any employee. If the system had been lent to an employee when it was bought, the benefit for 2000/01 would be £800 × 20% = £160 × 10/12 = £133. If the system was first provided as a benefit in June 2000, the benefit would be £500 × 20% = £100 × 10/12 = £83.

(d) Long service awards of tangible property to employees with at least 20 years service are not taxed provided the cost to the employer does not exceed £20 for each year of service and no similar award has been made to the same person within the previous ten years. In Mrs Davies's case the limit on value would be £20 × 25 = £500, so there will be no taxable benefit.

(e) The car benefit and fuel scale benefit will apply to the car provided for Mr Edgar. The car benefit is calculated as price of car × % × age factor.

(i) Because the car was under four years old at the end of 2000/01 the age factor is 1.

(ii) Because business mileage for 2000/01, 30,000 × 70% = 21,000 miles, was at least 18,000 miles the percentage is 15%.

(iv) The fuel scale benefit will be at the highest rate, because of the car's high cylinder capacity.

(v) The charges will not be reduced on a time basis because the car was provided for the whole of 2000/01.

The taxable benefit will therefore be as follows.

	£
Car £23,000 × 15%	3,450
Fuel	3,200
	6,650

(f) Mr Ford will be taxed on the annual value of the flat and of the furniture. The company's payment of his council tax will also be a taxable benefit.

The following rules will apply.

(i) There will be a basic accommodation benefit equal to the rateable value.

(ii) There will be an additional accommodation benefit equal to the excess of the flat's cost over £75,000, multiplied by the official rate of interest at the start of the tax year.

(iii) There will be a benefit in respect of the use of the furniture, equal to 20% of its value when first provided as a benefit to any employee.

The taxable benefit will therefore be as follows.

		£
Flat:	rateable value	900
	extra charge £(100,000 - 75,000) × 10%	2,500
		3,400
Furniture £5,000 × 20%		1,000
Council tax		500
		4,900

29   LAI CHAN

(a)   *Income tax liability 2000/01*

	£	Non-savings income £
Gross salary 9 × £3,250	29,250	
Less: pension contribution (6%)	(1,755)	
	27,495	
Car benefit (W1)	2,542	
Fuel benefit (W2)	2,400	
Beneficial loan (W3)	1,250	
Schedule E		33,687
Trading profit	21,400	
Less: Capital allowances (W4)	(5,860)	
Schedule D Case II profit	15,540	
Less: personal pension £500 × 3	(1,500)	
		14,040
STI		47,727
Less: personal allowance		(4,385)
Taxable income		43,342

Tax

	£
£1,520 × 10%	152
£26,880 × 22%	5,914
£14,942 (43,342 − 28,400) × 40%	5,977
Tax liability	12,043

Workings

1   *Car benefit*

	£
25% × £26,400 × 9/12 (note)	4,950
Age factor 3/4 × £4,950	3,712
Less: contribution £130 × 9	(1,170)
Car benefit assessable	2,542

Note

Annualised business mileage is 2,100 × 12/9 = 2,800

2   *Fuel benefit*

£3,200 × 9/12   £2,400

No reduction for partial reimbursement of private fuel cost.

3   *Beneficial loan*

Average method

$$10\% \times \frac{30,000 + 10,000}{2} \times 9/12 = £1,500$$

Alternative method (strict method)

	£
£30,000 × 3/12 × 10% =	750
£10,000 × 6/12 × 10% =	500
	1,250

Elect for strict method

4

	FYA	General pool	Private car	Short life asset	Allowances
	£	£	£	£	£
Additions not qualifying for FYA					
- private car			14,800		
- employee car		10,400			
WDA @ 25% × 3/12		(650)			650
		9,750			
WDA @ 25% × 3/12 (restricted)			(750) × 60%		450
			14,050		
Additions qualifying for FYA					
- recording equipment	9,300				
- recording equipment				2,600	
Less: FYA @ 40%	(3,720)	5,580		(1,040)	4,760
TWDV c/f		15,330	14,050	1,560	
Allowances					5,860

Note that the WDA is restricted by the length of the basis period, but the FYA is not.

(b) Up to 31.12.00, PAYE will have been deducted from Lai Chan's salary. It is likely that her PAYE code was adjusted to take account of her benefits in kind. Further tax payable (or tax repayable) will be dealt with under the self-assessment system.

As Lai Chan was employed before starting in business on her own account, she is unlikely to have made any payments on account for 2000/01. Therefore, the tax on her net Schedule D Case II profit will be collected in full on 31 January 2002 under the self assessment system.

30   SASHA SHAH

(a) Factors that will indicate that a worker should be treated as an employee rather than as self employed are:

(i)   control by employer over employee's work;

(ii)   employee must accept further work if offered (and employer must offer work);

(iii)   employee does not provide own equipment;

(iv)   employee does not hire own helpers;

(v)   employee does not take substantial financial risk;

(vi)   employee does not have responsibility for investment and management of business and cannot benefit from sound management;

(vii)   employee cannot work when he chooses but when an employer tells him to work;

(viii) described as an employee in any agreement between parties.

(b) (i)   Class 2 and Class 4 NIC 2000/01

	£
Class 2 £2 × 52	104
Class 4 £(27,820 − 4,385) × 7%	1,640
Total	£1,744

(ii)   Class 1 NIC (Primary) 2000/01

£(27,820 − 3,952) × 10% = £2,387

Index

Note: **Key Terms** and their page references are given in **bold**.

BPP PUBLISHING

See overleaf for information on other
BPP products and how to order

ACCA Order – New Syllabus

To BPP Publishing Ltd, Aldine Place, London W12 8AA

Tel: 020 8740 2211. Fax: 020 8740 1184

Mr/Mrs/Ms (Full name)

Daytime delivery address

Postcode

Daytime Tel

Date of exam (month/year)

	2/01 Texts	9/01 Kits	9/01 Psscrds	MCQ cards	Tapes	Videos
PART 1						
1.1 Preparing Financial Statements	£19.95 ☐	£10.95 ☐	£5.95 ☐		£12.95 ☐	£25.00 ☐
1.2 Financial Information for Management	£19.95 ☐	£10.95 ☐	£5.95 ☐	£5.95 ☐	£12.95 ☐	£25.00 ☐
1.3 Managing People	£19.95 ☐	£10.95 ☐	£5.95 ☐	£5.95 ☐	£12.95 ☐	£25.00 ☐
PART 2						
2.1 Information Systems	£19.95 ☐	£10.95 ☐	£5.95 ☐		£12.95 ☐	£25.00 ☐
2.2 Corporate and Business Law (6/01)	£19.95 ☐	£10.95 ☐	£5.95 ☐		£12.95 ☐	£25.00 ☐
2.3 Business Taxation FA 2000 (for 12/01 exam)	£19.95 ☐	£10.95 ☐(4/01)	£5.95 ☐(4/01)		£12.95 ☐	£25.00 ☐
2.4 Financial Management and Control	£19.95 ☐	£10.95 ☐	£5.95 ☐		£12.95 ☐	£25.00 ☐
2.5 Financial Reporting (6/01)	£19.95 ☐	£10.95 ☐	£5.95 ☐		£12.95 ☐	£25.00 ☐
2.6 Audit and Internal Review (6/01)	£19.95 ☐	£10.95 ☐	£5.95 ☐		£12.95 ☐	£25.00 ☐
PART 3						
3.1 Audit and Assurance Services (6/01)	£20.95 ☐	£10.95 ☐	£5.95 ☐		£12.95 ☐	£25.00 ☐
3.2 Advanced Taxation FA 2000 (for 12/01 exam)	£20.95 ☐	£10.95 ☐(4/01)	£5.95 ☐(4/01)		£12.95 ☐	£25.00 ☐
3.3 Performance Management	£20.95 ☐	£10.95 ☐	£5.95 ☐		£12.95 ☐	£25.00 ☐
3.4 Business Information Management	£20.95 ☐	£10.95 ☐	£5.95 ☐		£12.95 ☐	£25.00 ☐
3.5 Strategic Business Planning and Development	£20.95 ☐	£10.95 ☐	£5.95 ☐		£12.95 ☐	£25.00 ☐
3.6 Advanced Corporate Reporting (6/01)	£20.95 ☐	£10.95 ☐	£5.95 ☐		£12.95 ☐	£25.00 ☐
3.7 Strategic Financial Management	£20.95 ☐	£10.95 ☐	£5.95 ☐		£12.95 ☐	£25.00 ☐
INTERNATIONAL STREAM						
1.1 Preparing Financial Statements	£19.95 ☐	£10.95 ☐				
2.5 Financial Reporting (6/01)	£19.95 ☐	£10.95 ☐				
2.6 Audit and Internval Review (6/01)	£19.95 ☐	£10.95 ☐				
3.1 Audit and Assurance services (6/01)	£20.95 ☐	£10.95 ☐				
3.6 Advanced Corporate Reporting (6/01)	£20.95 ☐	£10.95 ☐				
SUCCESS IN YOUR RESEARCH AND ANALYSIS PROJECT						
Tutorial Text (9/00)	£19.95 ☐					

SUBTOTAL £ ☐

POSTAGE & PACKING

Study Texts

	First	Each extra	
UK	£3.00	£2.00	£ ☐
Europe*	£5.00	£4.00	£ ☐
Rest of world	£20.00	£10.00	£ ☐

Kits/Passcards/Success Tapes/MCQ cards

	First	Each extra	
UK	£2.00	£1.00	£ ☐
Europe*	£2.50	£1.00	£ ☐
Rest of world	£15.00	£8.00	£ ☐

Breakthrough Videos

	First	Each extra	
UK	£2.00	£2.00	£ ☐
Europe*	£2.00	£2.00	£ ☐
Rest of world	£20.00	£10.00	£ ☐

Grand Total (Cheques to *BPP Publishing*) I enclose a cheque for (incl. Postage) £ ☐

Or charge to Access/Visa/Switch

Card Number ☐☐☐☐☐☐☐☐☐☐☐☐☐☐☐☐

Expiry date _____ Start Date _____

Issue Number (Switch Only)

Signature

We aim to deliver to all UK addresses inside 5 working days; a signature will be required. Orders to all EU addresses should be delivered within 6 working days. All other orders to overseas addresses should be delivered within 8 working days. * Europe includes the Republic of Ireland and the Channel Islands.

REVIEW FORM & FREE PRIZE DRAW

All original review forms from the entire BPP range, completed with genuine comments, will be entered into a draw on 31 January 2002 and 31 July 2002. The names on the first four forms picked out will be sent a cheque for £50.

Name: _____   Address: _____

_____

How have you used this Text?
(Tick one box only)

☐ Home study (book only)

☐ On a course: college _____

☐ With 'correspondence' package

☐ Other _____

Why did you decide to purchase this Text?
(Tick one box only)

☐ Have used complementary Study Text

☐ Have used BPP Texts in the past

☐ Recommendation by friend/colleague

☐ Recommendation by a lecturer at college

☐ Saw advertising

☐ Other _____

During the past six months do you recall seeing/receiving any of the following?
(Tick as many boxes as are relevant)

☐ Our advertisement in *ACCA Students' Newsletter*

☐ Our advertisement in *Pass*

☐ Our brochure with a letter through the post

Which (if any) aspects of our advertising do you find useful?
(Tick as many boxes as are relevant)

☐ Prices and publication dates of new editions

☐ Information on Text content

☐ Facility to order books off-the-page

☐ None of the above

Have you used the companion Kit/Passcard/Video/Tape * for this subject? ☐ Yes ☐ No
(* Please circle)

Your ratings, comments and suggestions would be appreciated on the following areas

	Very useful	Useful	Not useful
Introductory section (Key study steps, personal study)	☐	☐	☐
Chapter introductions	☐	☐	☐
Key terms	☐	☐	☐
Quality of explanations	☐	☐	☐
Questions and answers in each chapter	☐	☐	☐
Chapter roundups	☐	☐	☐
Quick quizzes	☐	☐	☐
Exam focus points	☐	☐	☐
Question bank	☐	☐	☐
Answer bank	☐	☐	☐
Index	☐	☐	☐
Icons	☐	☐	☐
Mind maps	☐	☐	☐

	Excellent	Good	Adequate	Poor
Overall opinion of this Text	☐	☐	☐	☐

Do you intend to continue using BPP Products? ☐ Yes ☐ No

Please note any further comments and suggestions/errors on the reverse of this page. The BPP author of this edition can be e-mailed at: suecann@bpp.com

Please return to: Katy Hibbert, ACCA Range Manager, BPP Publishing Ltd, FREEPOST, London, W12 8BR

REVIEW FORM & FREE PRIZE DRAW (continued)

Please note any further comments and suggestions/errors below

FREE PRIZE DRAW RULES

1   Closing date for 31 July 2002 draw is 30 June 2002. Closing date for 31 January 2002 draw is 31 December 2001.

2   No purchase necessary. Entry forms are available upon request from BPP Publishing. No more than one entry per title, per person. Draw restricted to persons aged 16 and over.

3   Winners will be notified by post and receive their cheques not later than 6 weeks after the draw date.

4   The decision of the promoter in all matters is final and binding. No correspondence will be entered into.